Revolutionary
Mexico on Film

ALSO BY BOB HERZBERG
AND FROM MCFARLAND

*Hang 'Em High: Law and Disorder in
Western Films and Literature* (2013)

*The Left Side of the Screen: Communist and Left-Wing
Ideology in Hollywood, 1929–2009* (2011)

*Savages and Saints: The Changing Image of
American Indians in Westerns* (2008)

*The FBI and the Movies: A History of the Bureau on
Screen and Behind the Scenes in Hollywood* (2007)

Shooting Scripts: From Pulp Western to Film (2005)

Revolutionary Mexico on Film

A Critical History,
1914–2014

Bob Herzberg

McFarland & Company, Inc., Publishers
Jefferson, North Carolina

LIBRARY OF CONGRESS CATALOGUING-IN-PUBLICATION DATA

Herzberg, Bob, 1956–
Revolutionary Mexico on film : a critical history,
1914–2014 / Bob Herzberg.
    p.   cm.
Includes bibliographical references and index.

ISBN 978-0-7864-7758-6 (softcover : acid free paper) ∞
ISBN 978-1-4766-1797-8 (ebook)

1. Mexico—History—Revolution, 1910–1920—Motion pictures and the revolution.
2. Mexico—In motion pictures.   3. Motion pictures and history.
4. Motion pictures—Political aspects.   I. Title.

F1234.H685 2015   302.23'430972—dc23   2014044974

BRITISH LIBRARY CATALOGUING DATA ARE AVAILABLE

© 2015 Bob Herzberg. All rights reserved

*No part of this book may be reproduced or transmitted in any form
or by any means, electronic or mechanical, including photocopying
or recording, or by any information storage and retrieval system,
without permission in writing from the publisher.*

On the cover: Jorge Martínez de Hoyos and
Pedro Armendáriz in *Café Colón* (1959)

Printed in the United States of America

*McFarland & Company, Inc., Publishers
Box 611, Jefferson, North Carolina 28640
www.mcfarlandpub.com*

To the grandparents I never knew,
taken away in cattle cars on their Final Journey.
With Love,
your grandson, Chaim

Acknowledgments

I'd like to thank those individuals and organizations that helped me immeasurably in my research for this book (and if I don't, they'll never speak to me again).

At the top of the list I must thank the Margaret Herrick Library of Beverly Hills who allowed me to go through their files, budget sheets, pressbooks and correspondence; everything from little-known films like *The Torch, Stronghold* and *The Fighter* to the A films *Vera Cruz, The Professionals* and *The Wild Bunch*. I am eternally thankful to the dedicated, hardworking folks at the Special Collections Desk, as well as administrators Barbara Hall, Jenny Romero and Linda Harris Mehr who helped me choose the proper files (which can now be done online!). I'd like to thank Sandra Day Lee and Jonathon Auxier, director and curator, respectively, at the Warner Brothers Archives at the School of Cinematic Arts at the University of Southern California for the correspondence and background on the filming of *Juarez*.

I'd also like to thank my lovely wife Colleen, who has now viewed more films about the Mexican Revolution, as well as the *Juaristas'* rebellion against the French, than any human being has a right to see. For her patience with my artistic pretensions, and certainly for our 28 wonderful years together, I am eternally thankful.

One of the rewards I've gotten in researching this book is the exposure, not only to Mexico and its great history, but to the works of *Época Dorada*, the golden age of Mexican film. I've been exposed to wonderful performers and craftsmen whose work I'll never forget, and for that alone I am grateful.

Now, what are you waiting for?

Este libro se lee con facilidad: This book reads easily.

Table of Contents

Acknowledgments vi

Introducción 1

   I—*Políticas*, 1914–1936: How Outsiders Influenced Depictions of the Revolution 7

   II—*Liberator*, 1937–1939: The Politics and Machinations Behind the Filming of *Juarez* 49

   III—*Declarar La Guerra*, 1940–1950: World War II and Época Dorada 75

   IV—*Revoluciónistas*, 1951–1959: The Cold War and the Mexican Revolution 100

   V—*Caos Internacional*, 1960–1969: Hollywood and Europe Film the Revolution 157

   VI—*Violencia*, 1970–1989: Censorship Disappears as Depictions of Revolutionary Mexico Get Even Bloodier 200

   VII—*Centenario*, 1990–2014: A Brief Look at the Films of Revolutionary Mexico as the Revolution Hits the 100-Year Mark 229

Chapter Notes 233

Bibliography 236

Index 239

Introducción

The Mexican Revolution is now a century old.

It began as the world at large was in relative peace, and continued as the European continent went up in flames; it started in the dawn of a new industrial age and climaxed at the so-called "age of prosperity." As much of North America had highways and telephones, automobiles, airplanes and cross-country trains, Mexico still existed in the nineteenth century, a long-dead past where the horse was still considered the primary mode of transportation. The reign of Porfirio Díaz and the Revolution that followed in its wake took thousands of Mexican lives and impoverished millions of Mexican citizens. The Revolution called for an end to the wealthy *hacendados,* but more times than not gave riches and power to a handful of men who merely *spoke* of reform. It sought to minimize the influence of foreign powers within Mexico, but at times found itself being cast as the excuse for foreign military intervention.

After the Mexican War (1845–1849), much of northern Mexico became part of the victorious United States. To the world at large, there was nothing new about America's expansionist aims; other nations had been gaining territory by right of conquest before the Mexican War and would continue to do so long after the middle of the 19th century. Yet even this traumatic loss of territory didn't keep the country down; its people elected the visionary leader Benito Juárez, whose groundbreaking reforms echoed into the next century and beyond. Even as Napoleon's army occupied Mexican soil from 1863 to 1867, most of the people enthusiastically backed their president and the rule of law, not anarchy.

For 35 years, from 1876 to 1911, Porfirio Díaz, one of Juárez's former generals, was president of Mexico and, as one can surmise from his many years in power, ran the country more or less as a dictatorship. Though the country seemed stable and economically sound, tensions boiled beneath the surface. His administration favored the rich *hacendados,* or wealthy landowners: the Dons, the merchants and especially the foreign capital that invested heavily in the nation's coal mining, oil and other natural resources—assets that enriched these investors far more than the average citizen. With little to stop it, the corruption spread to the military, with many high-ranking officers, including generals, getting their positions via family ties or their close alliances with local *jefes* (bosses). The *Federales,* the nation's military force, were both brutal and corrupt and many a poor peon cowered in hiding as they marched by.

By 1911, with the nation a tinderbox waiting to explode, its situation was watched closely by its giant neighbor to the north, the United States. To say that by the early twentieth century, the U.S. had a tendency to play policeman and insinuate its influence into the hemisphere's other nations would be an understatement. The U.S. fought Spain in 1898, and the U.S. victory brought independence to Cuba and possession of Guam, Puerto Rico and the

Philippines. Decades into the twentieth century, U.S. forces landed in Haiti, the Dominican Republic and other locales in the Caribbean for one reason or another. Outside of losing its territory in war, Mexico had dealt with other examples of American military intervention, particularly those of the U.S. cavalry pursuing hostile Apaches or other Native tribes who had raided ranches and murdered settlers north of the Rio Grande. These incursions were usually met with anger by those Mexican authorities who had failed to stop Indian raids launched from *their* side of the border.

The fact that Mexico seemed to have trouble keeping its own house in order caused grave concern in the administration of President Woodrow Wilson. His was a policy of "watchful waiting." However, watching and waiting meant little to those in corridors of power who sought to influence events in Mexico. The Díaz years had been good for American investors in Mexico. But with calls for a revolutionary overthrow of the Díaz dictatorship, industrialists with operations in Mexico and their backers in the U.S. government feared that what would follow would put an end to a very profitable status quo situation. Certainly, no one either in Mexico or the U.S. was fooled by Díaz's ability to *always* win elections after 35 years, despite the "elections" of three other presidents during the 1870s and '80s, all of whom happened to be controlled by Díaz.

However, with Díaz's overthrow and the fair and honest election of Francisco Madero, Jr. as president on November 6, 1911, the Wilson administration backed the new government, despite the fact that the new leader was, as it turned out, *not* very sincere in his desire for reform. Fifteen months after his election, the government was taken over by General Victoriano Huerta, who had both Madero and his vice-president, José María Pino Suárez, arrested. Shortly after this, both former leaders were taken from their cells and murdered by armed soldiers, allegedly on Huerta's orders.

With the death of the much-loved Madero (who seemed more beloved *after* his death than during his lifetime), the Revolution was re-ignited. It called for the return to the fight of former bandit leader Pancho Villa and his *División del Norte* (Division of the North; that is, Northern Mexico) and yet another charismatic revolutionary, this time from the southern state of Morelos, Emiliano Zapata. The Revolution's nominal leader, who saw himself as the nation's future president, was Venustiano Carranza, who immodestly called himself the First Chief. There were three people in the entire world that Venustiano Carranza truly loved. The first one was Venustiano Carranza; the second one was also named Venustiano Carranza; and the third one just happened to be, you guessed it. After the triumph of the Revolution came the presidencies of Álvaro Obregón and Plutarco Elías Calles, two men who, besides the First Chief, perpetuated the corruption of the Revolution that continued down through the decades.

Regardless of any perceived political chicanery, however, the dynamics of the Mexican Revolution seemed to have the elements for a good Hollywood success story. This was as close to openly siding with a revolutionary movement as the American film industry would ever get.

However, there were several roadblocks to filming Mexico's century-old difficulties with imperialism, revolution and system-wide corruption. Mexico itself was never very happy with American interpretations of the Revolution; and if a film company wanted authentic location shooting, permission from the Mexican government was imperative; this permission came with an insistence on a depiction of the Revolution as a flawless, nearly holy quest for Mexican independence, a moral battle against the forces of domestic oppression and a dominating foreign influence. Another impediment to filming the Revolution honestly and without restraint was Hollywood's Breen office. Buried in the thousands of dictates written into 1934's Production Code was the rule on "National Feelings." Under Article 10, this rule stipulated that "the history, institutions, prominent people and industry of all nations shall be represented fairly."

In the following years, this rather absurd rule would prevent American films from criticizing Nazi Germany, the Soviet Union or any other nation run by dictatorships. With the Holocaust on the horizon, the Breen office would openly insist that the film industry *not* show the oppression of Jews in films depicting Germany or Nazi-occupied countries. This heavily restrictive rule also effectively shot down any attempt by Hollywood to realistically deal with of the Mexican Revolution. In Hollywood, screenwriters would almost always retreat to the time-worn cliché of the "noble poor and oppressed" fighting against an oppressive aristocracy, sometimes military, sometimes civilian—and never *once* mentioning in what country these sterling battles were being waged. In another rather tiresome cliché, bandits and killers were suddenly revolutionary heroes, and acts of wanton plunder and mass murder suddenly became a fight for freedom.

This "Robin Hood" motif in Hollywood adventures that distorted reality to fit the cliché never seemed more appropriate than to the real-life tale of General Francisco "Pancho" Villa. A native of Durango, Villa came from poor origins to work his way up to becoming one of the country's greatest military leaders, but he was, and would always be known as, a bandit first and foremost. He was tall, imposing, charismatic, had a sense of humor and could be, at times, compassionate and forward-thinking. On the battlefield, he could be brilliant, and some of the nation's greatest battles against the dreaded armies of both Porfirio Díaz, Victoriano Huerta and Venustiano Carranza were won through his leadership. He inspired thousands to join him, and by the thousands they cheerfully flocked to his armies, eternally proud to call themselves *Villistas*.

But Villa had another side to him. Possessed of an explosive temper, giving no quarter to his enemies, he had thousands of soldiers, whether having surrendered or whether they were wounded, put to death in various ways. Sometimes they were hanged, sometimes they were shot to death by Villista firing squads. To save on bullets, the captured Federals were lined up four at a time and were all killed by firing just one bullet at them—as far as we know, a particularly sadistic Villa invention.

Villa was seen as a liberator to his people and a cruel thug to foreigners, and films portraying his life were few and far between pre–1934. In fact, outside of a handful of silent films and the ultimate Hollywood rewriting of his life, *Viva Villa!,* Pancho Villa rarely appeared in the close to 20-year reign of the Breen office either. Sensitive to Mexico's "national feelings," the Production Code office usually turned thumbs down on any attempt by Hollywood to honestly depict the Mexican Revolution; this, of course, included its sainted heroes like ol' "One-Bullet" Pancho Villa. By the same token, the Breen Office's "Dillinger Rule" pre-empted the film industry from depicting the actual exploits of any real-life gangster or other malefactor.

During the Breen years, Hollywood would rarely depict important figures of Mexican history; and when they did, as when Warners filmed *Juarez* in 1939, the Production Code office (and Warner screenwriters) made absolutely sure that the portrayal was intensely flattering. Certainly, Benito Juárez *was* a great man, and a forward-thinking, visionary leader, but Hollywood never entertained the idea of any serious critique to his rule. Even the portrayal of one of his generals, future dictator Porfirio Díaz, was a model of liberal idealism (even if he was played by the Bronx-accented John Garfield). The film *never* explored the fact that the two leaders never liked each other, and that Díaz would soon plot against his president.

However, it wasn't as if Hollywood totally ignored what the Revolution meant, if not to Mexicans, then to idealistic American movie fans. Without mentioning any actual figures of history (outside of *Juarez,* that is), Hollywood might give us a film depicting an oppressive Latino dictator, as well as the nobler-than-noble rebels who fought against his despotic reign. In this manner, Hollywood screenwriters were able to use the dynamics of the Mexican Revolution, and by extension, oppression in Latin America, without ever identifying the nation where the story was set or actually naming the real-life historical figures on whom the various characters were based. Many B westerns of the 1930s and '40s had Latino dictators or Villa-like bandits as their villains, oppressing their people until the usually Anglo good-guy appeared. Starting with *Under Strange Flags* with Tom Keene and continuing into the 1950s with Universal-International's *Border River* starring Joel McCrea and featuring Pedro Armendáriz as a Mexican dictator-general who was part Victoriano Huerta and part Porfiro Díaz, Hollywood sold us the idea that Mexican peons desperately needed white cowboy heroes to help free them.

Another subgenre within the Mexican Revolutionary film, which would only be prevalent in the post–Breen years of the 1950s and beyond, was that of the American mercenary who ventured south of the border to help aid the Revolution, or help support the French against the *Juaristas*—usually for a big windfall in cash—before becoming a convert to the Cause by the time of curtain. Rugged actors from Robert Mitchum (*Bandido*) to Rory Calhoun (*The Treasure of Pancho Villa*) to Gary Cooper and Burt Lancaster (*Vera Cruz*) all traveled Down Mexico Way to seek their fortunes in gold and plunder, only to realize that it was the People, not the Coin, that counted.

This book will not only deal with Hollywood's portrayal of Revolutionary Mexico, but will also compare certain American-made films with those of the Mexican film industry to see the difference in how the two countries depict a particular time in Mexican history.

In this book, I will concentrate on those Hollywood products that not only depict the Mexican Revolution of 1910, but earlier depictions of revolutionary conflict in post-independence Mexico, such as the French incursion into Mexico. This would include a discussion of the classic *Juarez* as well as Sam Peckinpah's, *Major Dundee,* whose major plot point deals with a Union major leading Confederate prisoners into Mexico only to end up fighting Maximilian's French troops. Both films were set in the 1860s.

The book will discuss in great detail the battles and politics of Revolutionary Mexico and compare them with Hollywood's mostly *un*informative take on these conflicts. I will discuss the major figures of Revolutionary Mexico whose influence has not dimmed with the passing of over a century: Benito Juárez, Porfirio Díaz, Pancho Villa, Emiliano Zapata, Venustiano Carranza, Álvaro Obregón, Victoriano Huerta, and Francisco Madero, Jr., as well as non–Latino leaders President Franklin D. Roosevelt, Emperor Maximilian, Empress Carlota, Brigadier General John J. "Blackjack" Pershing, and President Abraham Lincoln. As far as Hollywood is concerned, I'll discuss the actors, directors and source material for many of the films about Revolutionary Mexico, from John Steinbeck's take on the filming of *Viva Zapata!* to the background of the troubled production of *Viva Villa!;* from Peckinpah's controversial vision of Mexico in *The Wild Bunch, Villa Rides* and *Major Dundee* to an examination of the politics and chicanery behind the scenes in the filming of *Qué Viva México!;* from the vehicles of the stars of Mexico's Golden Age of Film to the lesser-known Hollywood Bs; from the silent *The Life of General Villa* to the Mexican-made *Cinco de Mayo* of 2013.

The Revolution itself, always portrayed as a fight to free the oppressed Mexican people from dictatorship, was exploited ruthlessly by many of the Revolution's participants, often, though not always, for their own self-serving ends. As with most internal conflicts around the world, idealism sometimes ended up a distant second to the ruthless power struggles within the dynamics of "the Movement." For instance, many of the major figures of the Mexican Revolution who fought against the nation's dictators would die violently—not in skirmishes on the battlefield, but through betrayal and greed. Pancho Villa, Álvaro Obregón, Venustiano Carranza, Emiliano Zapata and Francisco Madero, Jr., were among far too many figures who died through treachery; whereas the dictators they fought against, Porfirio Díaz and Victoriano Huerta, died shortly afterwards in exile, but of natural causes.

The real victims of both the oppressive policies of the dictators, as well as the cutthroat policies of their "liberators," were the Mexican people. Like the Russian people under Stalin, their triumph was in endurance and survival, and their dream of a stable Mexico would not come until decades after the various conflicts ended. Unlike the Russian Revolution, the Mexican Revolution was not built on political theories concocted in parlor rooms by pompous Bolsheviks, but "boots-on-the-ground" realities fought in its cities, valleys and mountains. It was a war of *hacendadas* against peons; foreign influence against domestic initiatives; land reform against aristocratic acquisition; free elections against dictatorship; and the rights of Mexico's indigenous peoples against the nation's pervasive racism.

Hollywood took in all of these elements of the Revolution, using what they could in their stories, and discarding what they felt was controversial. The Mexican film industry also chose which information to use to show their own struggles for freedom, from glorifying the Revolution's major players without criticism, to using the conflict as background for vehicles for its stars.

Here is Mexico and its revolutions on film as written by a *yanqui desde Brooklyn, Nueva York*. I hope you like it.

I
Políticas, 1914–1936
How Outsiders Influenced Depictions of the Revolution

Though the Mexican Revolution has captured the world's attention, there weren't too many stories of the conflict dramatized for theater and film while it was happening in the 1910s—though there were exceptions.

In 1913, Jack London published the short story "The Mexican" which, though set in the United States, had a strong plot element dealing with the Mexican Revolution. In Hollywood, most of the few silent films dealing with the Revolution were undistinguished; however, in 1914, the Mutual Film Corporation endeavored to make a groundbreaking move and actually put history on film as it was happening, not as a newsreel, but as a feature-length drama. For years, bandit-turned-revolutionary Pancho Villa had been trying to get Hollywood to film his battles—in exchange for gold to finance the Revolution. No one in Hollywood bit at the chance to see *Villistas* and Federals go at it; they weren't too thrilled to part with their money anyway, and certainly not to go into the pockets of the mercurial Villa, who might just take the *pesos* and run.

Many believe that this idea originated with D.W. Griffith, with the aim being for the helmsman to eventually direct the project. This is quite possible. However, some credit Mutual producer Frank Thayer, who would have major input into negotiations with the guerrilla chief. Either way, the idea was for a Mutual crew to film one of Villa's battles, in this case, his attack on the federal outpost at Ojinaga. In preparations for this undertaking, a crew from Mutual was allowed a bird's-eye view of *Villista* tactics when they fought the federals in Ciudad Juárez in Chihuahua (Pancho Villa's traditional home base), just over the border from El Paso. Apparently the Mutual scouts liked what they saw and concerted efforts were made to contact the guerrilla chief. Finally, in early 1914, Thayer crossed the border into Juárez to negotiate terms. Though the producer was certainly instrumental in these contacts, coming along for the ride was a handsome young man who was on the rise as an actor and director at Mutual: Raoul Walsh.

A stage actor and rider (that's right, a stage *rider;* he had performed on a horse in the stage version of Thomas Dixon's novel *The Clansman*), Walsh traveled to New York where he eventually got dual jobs as both stuntman and rider for Pathe and Biograph films shot in Fort Lee, New Jersey (the Hollywood of its day). It was at Pathe where Walsh, becoming proficient at riding and rope tricks, was complimented by one of the studio's busiest directors, a young former Annapolis man named William "Christy" Cabanne. Liking the way Walsh was sitting his horse, the helmsman insisted that he not renew his contract with Pathé, and to instead join him and his boss, D.W. Griffith, at Biograph. After just a couple years at the studio, under Griffith's tutelage, Walsh became a director and soon took to the job as if it were second nature to him. When Mutual opened a studio in Los Angeles called Fine Art Studios in 1913, Griffith went west, taking with him his now-growing stock company, including Mary Pickford, Donald Crisp, Henry B. Walthall and Griffith cameraman Billy Bitzer, as well as Cabanne and Walsh. Also on the trip was another former Biograph performer named Miriam Cooper, a beautiful young actress who eventually became Mrs. Raoul Walsh (that is, until she divorced him ten years later over his cheating on her with his soon-to-be-*second* wife Lorraine Walker, who was twenty years younger than Walsh[1]).

Returning to L.A., Thayer had a deal with Villa to make *The Life of General Francisco Villa,* which would have *many* alternate titles, including the one it's always been known as: *The Life of General Villa.* Griffith sent Walsh to Mexico to turn over $500 in gold to Villa as a kind of "signing bonus," and convince the rebel icon that Fine Arts had a story to film that would be worthy of cooperation from the *"centaur del norte"* (centaur of the north). If Walsh was known to fabricate and, let's face it, out-and-out lie in his own autobiography, one can easily envision the extremely contrived story the young man improvised for the skeptical guerrilla chief. The tale was full of every cliché both literature and Hollywood films would promote through the subsequent decades; full of the young hero's growing up in the shadow of *hacendado* oppression, and how his own mother and baby sister were murdered and his home burned to the ground by federal troops. Not only does the young man named Villa vow eternal vengeance on the federals (the "heavies," as Walsh called them), but the tormented hero decides to dedicate his life to fighting for the poor and the oppressed. Ironically, this was the same scenario, with many variations (which changed countless times in the retellings), that Villa himself would tell journalists down through the years. (His oft-repeated claim that his sister had been raped by a *hacendado* would also appear in the Mutual film.) In fact, by the time MGM was ready to film *Viva Villa!* in 1933, the studio practically pirated Walsh's worshipful improvisation and aimed to depict a Villa who was a hero for the oppressed, while totally ignoring his bandit past. This is not to fault Walsh, if indeed he was the one to create this scenario; outliving many of his collaborators, of course he put *himself* center-stage in the Villa negotiations. However, even if Mutual had opted to do an honest version of his life, it's obvious that Villa himself would never have approved of a photoplay that depicted him as anything but a flawless hero.

As it turned out, Griffith was too busy to direct it himself. He was preparing to direct a far more important and controversial project: the film version of Thomas Dixon's *The Clansman,* now called *The Birth of a Nation.* Christy Cabanne was assigned to direct *The Life of General Villa,* with Walsh as his assistant director shooting backgrounds as well as playing Villa as a young man. However, despite Villa's cooperation, there were the realities of early twentieth century filmmaking to consider; for instance, battles would have to be fought in broad daylight so the cameras could record them. Of course, to ask a general to stage his attacks only in the daylight hours was an unrealistic request; military attacks at night had been a staple in the history of armies since the dawn of time, mostly for their elements of surprise. Also to be considered was the request for Villa to hold off his executions till sunrise. According to Walsh:

> He used to have [executions] at four or five in the morning, when there was no light. I got them to put them off until seven or eight. I'd line the cameramen up, and they'd put these fellows against the wall and then they'd shoot them. Fellows on this side with rocks in their

hands would run in, open the guys' mouths, and knock the gold teeth out. The fellows on the other side would run in and take the shoes and boots off them. Later on, they made the picture, but D.W. Griffith didn't direct it—he was busy on something else....

Of all the people I've seen executed—not one of them ever wanted to be blindfolded, not one of them gave a damn. Some of them stood there and cursed, you know, but no cowards—no falling down or anything like that.[2]

Of course, the "something else" Griffith was going to direct was the pro–KKK film, a production Walsh himself shied away from mentioning since, as he had in the stage version, he played a Klan rider (as did future director John Ford).

Ironically, for *The Life of General Villa,* the actual battles, including the attack on Ojinaga, didn't have enough dramatic flair to please Griffith, Thayer and the other moguls at Mutual. Therefore, Cabanne and Walsh, without Villa and his men, recreated the battles in the San Fernando Valley (where Griffith had staged many an Indian attack for his silent westerns at Biograph).

According to the film, after the Revolution was won and the federals were defeated, Pancho Villa is elected president of Mexico. For those who knew of Villa's temperament as well as his lack of ambition (he never wanted to be president), the ending is totally fantastic.

The film was well-received by Walsh's elated bosses at Mutual (who would soon be fielding charges of racism for financing Griffith's *The Birth of a Nation*—a film that *also* made the studio a fortune). Walsh remembered that the film played for a long time in many Mexican-American neighborhoods in Los Angeles; the same venues, in fact, that provided an American audience during *Época Dorada,* Mexico's Golden Age of Film (the 1940s). Soon, however, Mutual executives took some of Christy's footage from another project called *The Battle of Torreón* and inserted it into both his and Walsh's footage for the Villa film. In fact, *The Life of General Villa,* as one can tell from its many subsequent title changes, would be chopped up, re-edited, re-circulated and, sadly, finally disappear. Certainly, after Villa's attack on Columbus, New Mexico, on March 9, 1916, any filmic depiction of Villa as a hero would become *verboten* to American audiences. To this day, only bits and pieces of the film exist in other works, basically documentaries on the Revolution that are themselves hard to find, as well as a few production stills.

Griffith would go on to more filmmaking greatness, but his racist portrayals of African-Americans in the inflammatory *Birth of a Nation* ultimately had a disastrous effect on his career. With the failure of *Intolerance* and other works, he became unemployable in Hollywood, with his decline into alcoholism sealing his fate. Cabanne would go on to an undistinguished, but apparently very busy filmmaking career, making mostly B flicks, including Monogram westerns and Universal's *The Mummy's Hand,* surviving a good 33 years more in the business. Walsh became one of Warner Brothers' greatest house directors, with a career that lasted until 1964.

The story of Mutual's collaboration with Villa would inspire a young playwright named Eugene O'Neill to write a one-act comedy a year after the release of *The Life of General Villa. The Movie Man* deals with two young men, Henry (Hen) Rogers and Al Devlin, sent to Mexico by the "Earth Motion Picture Company" to shoot the battles of bandit-turned-revolutionary Pancho Gomez. Obviously, any resemblance to actual or living figures was clearly intentional. Needless to say, the characters speak in a stilted, stereotypical parody of what O'Neill thought was real speech. When Devlin, the photographer, plans to pick up a Mexican babe, Hen warns: "Have a care, little one, have a care! Some one of these Mexican dolls you're googooing at will carve her initials on your back with the bread knife one of these days!"[3]

The two men talk aimlessly for two-thirds of the play, with entrances by a randy *señorita* named Anita and later Pancho Gomez himself breaking up the pointless chatter. At one point, the two men try to get Gomez to hold off on the execution of Anita's father. Then, Gomez tries his "technique" on the *señorita:* (He walks over to ANITA, who shrinks back to the wall in terror.) "Have you fear of me, *Chiquita?* Of Gomez? But Pancho Gomez, he loav the ladies, that ees well known."[4]

O'Neill's play is full of stereotypical dialogue, complete with dialect spellings and a general feeling that both Americans and Mexicans were being caricatured (with the racist buzzwords "gringo" and "greaser" given equal play). By the end, when Devlin is apparently rejected by some Latina outside their shack, he raves: "Some nerve to that greaser chicken for giving a real white man the boot! (Scornfully.) I got a real slant at her this time. She isn't much to look at after all. Back in God's country, we'd use her photo for a before-taking ad."[5]

About ninety years later, movie and TV writer Larry Gelbart would give us his own take on Villa's flirtation with the movies, HBO's *And Pancho Villa Starring as Himself.* We assume Gelbart did *not* consult O'Neill's *The Movie Man* for research on the topic.

By the time the talkies arrived, one man wanted to film "the real Mexico," including a depiction of their decade-old Revolution. At the time, he was praised as one of the world's greatest filmmakers.

But even an *auteur* can screw up...

> Mexico is NOT a natural paradise where happy people live in peace and plenty!
> Mexico is NOT the idyllic picture of "beauty and charm" as it has been described by the sponsors of this film!
> Mexico is not merely the colorful land of the exotic magueys and majestic Mayan temples. In Mexico, the masses are oppressed, exploited and degraded by a military dictatorship whose record of cold-blooded murders and ruthless repression ranks with that of Machado, deposed Cuban tyrant.[6]

So began a flyer passed out in front of certain theaters by members of the American Communist Party showing a recently released film directed by a man hailed as one of the greatest filmmakers in the world. Said film was released in a truncated form in 1932; it was allegedly sliced and diced so extensively and was so far away from the director's vision that his many fans, instead of praising it, heaped scorn upon it as a bastardization of the original.

To an atheist nation like the Soviet Union, Sergei M. Eisenstein was a god. To the bureaucrats of Sovkino, the Soviet film agency which, on behalf of the government, financed his films, Eisenstein was a useful tool in its propaganda war with the West. There was no denying the genuine talent behind such works as *Strike, October, Old and New,* and, of course, *Battleship Potemkin.* For a nation under a new political system, Eisenstein seemed to be that rarity, a filmmaker who used striking images to offset the strident tone of the propaganda. His powerful visuals even affected audiences across vast political spectrums. Nazi propaganda minister Dr. Joseph Goebbels would praise the half–Jewish director's works as benchmarks in the making of propaganda films. Yet despite the Soviets' propaganda war against Capitalism and his cinematic works to aid that war, Eisenstein would claim in later years that he was fascinated by Mexico and always wanted to make a film about it.

In the early 1930s, before revelations of Stalin's genocidal atrocities on the Russian people were fully revealed, the Soviet Union was considered the Wave of the Future, with America's intellectuals in the forefront of praising the new government as a beacon of freedom, without actually having taken a close look at it. Hailed internationally as a cinematic genius, Eisenstein rode a wave of pro–Soviet love; unusually, a large part of that big love would come from that shining example of capitalism and the profit motive, Hollywood. No less a silent cinema icon than Douglas Fairbanks visited Moscow and suggested that the filmmaker come to Hollywood to make films. Like Fairbanks, Charles Chaplin was another performer who started the company called United Artists, and with little hesitation also called for Eisenstein to share his genius with America. Ironically, neither Fairbanks nor Chaplin put up any actual *money* for an Eisenstein project, but one of Hollywood's major studios, Paramount, did.

The filmmaker had a holier-than-thou view of America, and he bluntly referred to it as "the America of anti–Sovietism, of Prohibition; the imperialist America of Hoover."[7] Given a six-month contract with the studio, the helmsman was being spoken of as the man who would bring Theodore Dreiser's controversial *An American Tragedy* to the screen. When the studio realized that Eisenstein was going to use the film to bash the American legal system, Paramount pulled him off the project and replaced him with the talented, but apolitical, Josef von Sternberg. The Soviet filmmaker was also in talks to film *Sutter's Gold,* a project that the studio suddenly realized (especially in light of Eisenstein's blatantly anti–American remarks) was going to be turned into a Communist's version of *Money for Dummies*.[8] Certainly, some of the director's ideas for scenes were a bit on the bizarre side; one was totem poles sprouting out of the ground in the California desert for no discernible reason.

Cut loose from Paramount, and afraid to return to the Soviet Union after experiencing a free society, Eisenstein suddenly remembered his Great Dream to make a film about Mexico. It is said (especially by Communist author Marie Seton) that the director was inspired to make a film about America's neighbor to the south since he had seen a production of Jack London's *The Mexican* staged in the Soviet Union in 1920. In *Sergei Eisenstein and Upton Sinclair: The Making and Unmaking of Qué Viva México!,* edited by Harry M. Geduld and Ronald Gottesman, the writers emphasize the theory that the helmsman's dream was first crystalized with his experience on the production:

> The association of Cinema-Mexico-Opera-Childhood is probably fundamental to deeper understanding of the Mexican film. It throws some light upon the film's preoccupation with certain rituals, fiestas, costumes, headdresses, masks, children, etc., in terms of Eisenstein's own psychology. The Mexico of his imagination was an enchanted realm, and all that he was to find in the real Mexico increased the old enchantment and nostalgia. The Proletkult production of *The Mexican* was thus a focus and synthesis of childhood delight (the circus; clowns with whom he identified himself), a subject that was to become of immense future importance to him (Mexico), and the future director's first gropings towards his new medium.[9]

The pro–Eisenstein Seton couldn't have written it any clearer. However, there is something a bit off about this hypothesis. In London's original short story, written in 1913, the central character is a driven young Mexican who, as a child, saw his parents murdered by Díaz's troops. Devoting himself to the Revolution, he becomes a boxer and gives his winnings to revolutionaries who use his money to buy guns for the fighters. (London's story was made into a low-budget B in Hollywood in 1952.) Unfortunately, London, a socialist, saw the Mexican Revolution as a Marxist one, totally misreading the conflict in terms of a world revolutionary movement. Still, one wonders how Seton, as well as Guduld and Gottesman, were able to present a stage version of London's boxer story, produced just a few years after it was written, as a circus featuring clowns and acrobats. Eisenstein was also allegedly inspired by the silent Douglas Fairbanks swashbuckler *The Mark of Zorro,* something that called into question the director's insistent claims that he wanted to make a film depicting "the *real* Mexico" (and how many masked avengers were there fighting Díaz?).[10] However, in 1926, Eisenstein *did* meet Diego Rivera on the artist's visit to Moscow, and that meeting supposedly inspired the filmmaker to study Mexican art.

Yet the Legend was now told: Eisenstein *always* wanted to make a film about Mexico. However, if the Mexico of Eisenstein's imagination was indeed "an enchanted realm," it was plainly obvious that the director had absolutely no idea what the real Mexico was. Cut loose from Paramount in mid–1930 and still in Hollywood with his collaborators, assistant director Grisha Aleksandrov and cameraman Eduard Tisse, the director knew he was within miles of the Mexican border. And so, as if listening to a Siren calling him from Baja California, he cast about for a backer for his Great Mexican Film. However, according to author Mandy Merck in her excellent *Hollywood's American Tragedies: Dreiser, Eisenstein, Sternberg, Stevens,* the director might have had an ulterior motive for staying in North America besides his dream film:

> Four months of their contracted six had already passed and it was now September. The prospect of leaving Hollywood so soon must have weighed heavily on the Russians, who were escaping privation for the first time in thirteen years.[11]

With Soviet funds, the helmsman and his pals had already eaten at top restaurants, drank at the best bars and sampled the prostitutes of Western Europe on their way to America. During their time in the film capital, they were invited to the homes of movie stars, like the left-leaning Chaplin and the enthusiastic Fairbanks; they dove in humongous swimming pools, lounged in comfortable divans, ate sumptuous meals and again, as in Europe, sampled Hollywood's nightlife, including its women, and possibly its men (Eisenstein and Tisse were gay). Looking for a sucker—I mean, an *investor* for his Mexican project, Eisenstein took Chaplin's suggestion to hook up with socialist author Upton Sinclair, a man who not only admired the director, but was an enthusiastic supporter of the Soviet Union.

Born in Baltimore in 1878 to a liquor salesman who liked to sample his own wares and a mom who was a militant teetotaler, Sinclair learned to escape through books and started writing at a young age. Coming from a wealthy Southern aristocratic family who lost everything after the Civil War, the disillusioned author eventually became a socialist. An idealistic muckraker, for six months he disguised himself and worked (or rather slaved) in a Chicago meatpacking plant as research for a new novel. Written in 1904 and finally published by Doubleday in 1906, *The Jungle* horrified American readers as it depicted inhuman working conditions in the meatpacking industry.

Having made his fame with a novel attacking those who distributed meat, Sinclair eventually wrote dozens of books skewering America's sacred cows. He wrote books against organized religion, Wall Street, and capitalism in general. He did more than dabble in politics, and through the years, he ran for Congress several times. He would even attempt a run for governor of California in 1934.

However, Eisenstein and Sinclair didn't really have anything in common but their leftist politics. In 1949, Sinclair described his first meeting with the director in a letter to Marie Seton: "When E. first came to Hywd. I paid him a call. He was polite, but showed no special interest in me."[12] They met a second time at a huge celebration for theater critic Rene Fulöp-Miller where, again, Eisenstein made sure their meeting was brief. After Paramount cancelled the director's contract, Sinclair had actually written the director a consoling note, as well as a request to "drop me a note and tell me what you are planning to do." There is no record of any reply from Eisenstein. In their third meeting, however, Eisenstein deliberately sought out the author, a man he had previously "showed no interest in." In the fall of 1930, at a Hollywood get-together, Sergei Eisenstein sent Communist author Salka Viertel over to talk to Sinclair and ask if he wanted to meet him. Receiving a positive response from Viertel, the director chatted up Sinclair to finance his dream project.

Sinclair hadn't associated with the world of movies since he executive-produced and appeared on-screen briefly for the film version of his own hit novel *The Jungle* in 1914. However, he was excited by the prospect of returning to picture-making, and especially producing a film by the great Eisenstein. (Sinclair was an enthusiastic supporter of the Russian Revolution and constantly corresponded with the Soviets, who praised his anti–American books.) In record time, the business arrangements were handled by the author's second wife, Mary Craig Sinclair, who was able to raise $25,000 by November 24, 1930. That same day, the helmsman signed a contract with the Sinclairs' hastily formed company, the Mexican Film Trust.

However, in the next fourteen months, the word "trust" would be the *last* thing on anyone's mind...

The Sinclairs engaged Mary's brother, Hunter Kimbrough, to be the company's business manager. A fast worker, Kimbrough formed the company, prepared the contracts, got temporary extensions for American visas for Eisenstein and his friends, elicited the cooperation of the government of President Pascual Ortiz Rubio (of the National Revolutionary Party or PNR) and set to work raising funds for the independent production. It was Kimbrough who negotiated with Mexico's usually super-sensitive government censorship boards; he made travel arrangements, procured locations for filming, went through all the proper channels, purchased film stock and other supplies, hired translators, kept the books and faithfully reported on the production's progress to Sinclair. A businessman from way back, he had the Sinclairs' total faith. The former banker knew the value of a dollar, and was completely loyal to his sister and brother-in-law.

However, there were other things about the company's business manager that Eisenstein's many defenders love to mention: He was a drunk. He was also a conservative (usually seen as a kiss-of-death in artistic circles), and he was from Mississippi. It is alleged that he had made racist and anti–Semitic remarks, and that it was this prejudice, and *not* anything Eisenstein may have said or done, which triggered his eventually turning against the director. Though it's never been denied that Kimbrough, a man who *had* to schmooze with everyone from American bankers to Mexican police officials over some cocktails, might have liked a drink once in a while, there is a huge difference between enjoying a two-martini lunch and being blotto on a location shoot. Though Kimbrough was not fond of Bolshevism, from his many letters it's apparent that he was an early cheerleader for Eisenstein; this was not only done in letters to potential investors on the production, but in private correspondence to his brother-in-law as well. Apparently, he was professional enough to collaborate with a man whose political philosophy he found abhorrent (and his attackers seem to have forgotten that the conservative Kimbrough was the brother-in-law and friend of a rabid socialist writer).

Still, these widely disparate individuals also had to deal with the Mexican government, ten years after their hard-fought Revolution to free the people, an entity as touchy and as corrupt as existed in the year 1930. And so, a week after the party arrived in Mexico City and started to film the bullfight sequence, on December 21, 1930, they were unceremoniously arrested and held overnight in the local calaboose. Everyone's possessions, including Kimbrough's letters and correspondence, were confiscated. Eisenstein and the other Russians were permitted to return to the Regis Hotel after questioning; each man was detained in his room by a police officer, with Kimbrough noting, "Eisenstein's escort was as fat as he is, and they could only get a single bed."[13] The business manager had been warned days before by a friendly police official that they were going to be arrested for fear of spreading communism (an irony where Kimbrough was concerned). Eventually higher-ups in the administration (Kimbrough credits "General (Plutarco Elías) Calles' friend, the Minister of Education"[14]) secured the party's release. To this day, it is uncertain whether the Mexican government was pressured by anti–Communists in Washington or Hollywood, or whether the Mexicans themselves (who, despite their "revolutionary" leanings, were as rabidly xenophobic as the government they overthrew) was behind the arrest. Certainly, it gave the police time to ransack the party's luggage to find incriminating evidence. Apparently, all the Bolshevik material they found was a red book belonging to Eisenstein that had revolutionary songs. It is also suspected that the police moved in when they discovered Eisenstein's crew taking pictures of "the lower classes," an uncomfortable part of Mexican life that the government, revolutionary or not, had no intention of sharing with the rest of the world. Ironically, no one seems to have noticed (though perhaps Eisenstein and his cohorts did) that their arrest occurred on Stalin's 51st birthday.

New Year's Day 1931 ushered in one of the worst years of the Depression. Yet as millions around the world went jobless and starving, and as Stalin's genocide of the nation's farmers, or *kulaks* (which was known as "collectivization"), was going on, down in Mexico, the dictator's resident cinematic genius was trying to figure out just *what* he was going to film.

According to Geduld and Gottesman:

> After a month of Eisenstein's listening to the "heartbeat of Mexico," the lack of a "story" was more and more a matter of concern to the Sinclairs.... A brief news item in the *New York Sun* of January 7th quoted Eisenstein as saying: "We shall make a close study of Mexican manners and customs before starting work on the picture, and afterward shall take as our theme a typically Mexican subject."[15]

This admission alone seems to fly in the face of the constant assertion by the director's supporters that he *always* wanted to make a film about Mexico. Certainly, had that been the case, even an *idea* for a story should have taken shape long before the helmsman affixed his signature to one of Mary Craig's contracts.

The correspondence between Sinclair, Eisenstein, Kimbrough, various Soviet bureaucrats from Sovkino, and even telegrams from Josef Stalin, unfold like the gradual buildup of a chilling horror tale. Predictably, as the months passed and Eisenstein did nothing more than listen to the "heartbeat of Mexico," his investors were getting coronaries.

Despite his success as an author, Upton Sinclair and his wife were not wealthy. They had faith in Eisenstein to shoot a great film about Mexico and, despite the socialist author's frequent attacks on capitalism, hoped to make a lot of money on the project. On August 1931, reactionary studio head Louis B. Mayer took an option on the rights to Sinclair's bestseller *The Wet Parade*. Months later, still looking for investors for his Mexican film, Sinclair spoke to executives at MGM to see if they would be interested in financing the project. To a man, they all expressed shock that the studio was able to wrap up the filming of *The Wet Parade* while Eisenstein was still down in Mexico trying to figure out where to set up his cameras.

As the months dragged on, the party had to deal with the rainy season, which allegedly restricted the director's "hacienda" sequence to only a few hours a week. Then in an undated letter of May 1931, Eisenstein wrote to Sinclair, "$5,000 in the *release* expenses—which have nothing to do with *production* expenses, is by itself not so much...."[16] Perhaps not to Eisenstein since it wasn't his money, but to the Sinclairs it was *a lot*, especially since Mary was becoming ill and their money would soon be going for medical bills. As time went on, Eisenstein's charming requests for more money would turn into angry demands. As more and more money was poured into Eisenstein's project, the helmsman shot compiled thousands of feet of film, all to be sent up to Hollywood's Consolidated Labs for developing, with the upshot that most of it *wouldn't* be used. Then there was the Mexican government, whose bureaucracy held the production in its tight-fisted control. Permission for location shooting, as well as careful perusal of Eisenstein's script-in-progress (on those few times when the helmsman actually had a script), hung over the company like those constant storm clouds which allegedly slowed down the filming. Had Eisenstein paid less attention to the "heartbeat of Mexico" and more to its weather reports, perhaps the filming would have been more productive; however, with this particular director at the helm (he admitted that *Battleship Potemkin* took seven months to film), Mexico's rainy season probably wouldn't have made much of a difference in the film's slow progress. Yet the toll it was taking on the Sinclairs' bank account was deadly.

As Sinclair wrote to Kimbrough on June 17, 1931, a full six months after the party arrived in Mexico:

> [Mary] got money from relatives and fixed herself a home upon the promise that she would never mortgage it. But we broke that promise on account of the Eisenstein picture. We have borrowed on our home every dollar that we can, and we have also borrowed from friends.[17]

Two weeks later, on July 1, Eisenstein wrote to Sinclair to announce that

> an addition of only $5,000 dollar [sic]—*the picture cannot be completed*. Your friend who advises you about this probably has a very confused idea of what a motion picture is and that uncompleted parts do not stick together and do not for a *picture*. That is a product that can be shown and sold![18]

In another letter shortly after this one, the helmsman cavalierly announced that the film couldn't be completed for anything less than $15,000. As the months crept on, along with the equally creeping pace of Eisenstein's shooting, the tab went up. Clearly fans of the

Russian filmmaker, Geduld and Gottesman criticize "Sinclair's ignorance of Eisenstein's unique approach to film-making," a shocking assertion considering that after seven months spent in Mexico, the helmsman *still* couldn't finish his film.

On September 12, Mary, on top of her other ailments, was taken ill with ptomaine poisoning and remained in bed for three days. Before she could recover, Sinclair himself collapsed and was taken to the hospital. Stricken with nervous strain by the financial burdens of the Eisenstein picture (the accompanying kidney infection didn't help), the author stayed in the hospital until September 28. After his return home, Sinclair tried to convince the stubborn and pompous director to hurry things up:

> You can make the most wonderful picture in the world from the point of view of art, and you may get the most wonderful reception from the critics; but the trade conditions are such that if you arrive a month or two after the Mexican picture has been put on the market, the public will think you are imitating and the other fellow will get all the box office.[19]

Of course, mentioning the term "box office" to a Bolshevik filmmaker who had contempt for the trappings of Hollywood was probably not a tactful thing to do. However, Eisenstein's snail-like pace and desire for the absolutely perfect shot were already reaching the point of no return.

In a long letter to Sinclair, dated October 9, an obviously upset Kimbrough wrote:

> If I refuse (to give Eisenstein money) he simply says I am holding up production and he will stop the picture. I am going to wait a day or two before sending him this last hundred and let him rave and if necessary waste a day there. He has (already) wasted days when it is not necessary. He acts like a dictator. He demands money immediately, again and again and again. If I am hesitant about complying with his demands, he threatens to stop production.[20]

In a letter to Amkino (the Soviets' New York–based film purchasing agency) and its chief, L.I. Monosson, dated October 15, Sinclair described how stubborn Eisenstein could be when he wanted his own way: "(H)e goes right ahead and does what he pleases, and when Hunter tries to argue with him, he says that if he is not allowed to complete the picture as he wants, there will be no picture, and he will not allow us to use his name on it."[21]

It must be noted that this is not merely the supposedly prejudiced Kimbrough's opinion; in letters from Eisenstein later in the filming, the director himself had threatened that "there will be no picture" unless he's given all the money he demanded and makes it *his* way.

Eisenstein's Mexican Dream was fast becoming a nightmare for everyone else…

To accurately review the end product that became known as *Qué Viva México!*, or in its re-released form, *Thunder Over Mexico,* one might as well be criticizing a large pizza pie cut into six pieces with entirely different toppings on each piece.

Upton Sinclair was never crazy about Eisenstein's decision to shoot the film as separate sequences. This was almost certainly done to get as much Mexican culture on screen (as well as the fact that Eisenstein and his collaborators apparently couldn't come up with a complete script). In fact, as far we can ascertain, not only from Sinclair's subsequent correspondence but from the final accumulated footage of literally hundreds of thousands of feet of film shot by Eisenstein and his crew, the Soviet helmsman who had signed a contract with the Sinclairs to make only one feature-length film, actually wanted to stay in Mexico long enough to make *six*.

Shot from the fall of 1930, throughout 1931, and into early 1932, a time in cinema history when talkies were well established, *Qué Viva México!* has absolutely no dialogue. In fact, the film is very much a kind of silent movie with voiceover narration (of course, spoken in Russian to get that "*real* Mexico" feel). However, through the subtitles, we can get something of idea what's going on, if *anything*. Conceived by the director as six feature-length films (if one believes Sinclair and his supporters), what we have after a necessary severe editing job are six sequences in a film not exceeding 90 minutes. Of course, there also seems to be more than one version of the same film floating around at different running times, depending on who did the editing and where a particular version played.

The version released on DVD by Kino, in as complete a form as it will ever get, was called *Qué Viva México!* It's the version eventually released by the Soviet Union in 1979 and starts with a five-minute prologue featuring Eisenstein's assistant director Grigory Alexandrov. He introduces the film by explaining to us that Eisenstein was invited to Hollywood to make a film, "but didn't see eye to eye with the tycoons," using a typically Marxist slant which was disingenuous to say the least. He neglects to mention that Eisenstein turned down Paramount's script ideas, and when he offered his own ideas they made absolutely no sense and were not filmable. Alexandrov also fails to mention the famed director taking over a year to shoot what was sold to its producer, Upton Sinclair, as a project to be finished in four months and on a low budget, but that Eisenstein repeatedly violated his contract by his refusal to stop filming.

As it stands, the film opens with a shot of the great pyramids which are situated within the ancient Mayan ruins at Chichén Itzá on the Yucatán. Tisse's camera expertly photographs the faces of the stone figures of Mayan gods at the temple of the Native god Quetzalcoatl, and then cut to the faces of today's Indians as they stand around the pyramid, faces as proud and stoic as those of the stone gods above them. At one point in Eisenstein's framing, one stone face is actually juxtaposed with that of an Indian's standing before it. A master of montage, Eisenstein was always more successful at filming objects rather than people. However, the faces of these men and women are some of the most striking Eisenstein ever filmed. To top off this wonderful scene, we see a long shot of the pyramid in the foreground and, at the right side of the frame, a woman's face in profile looks like she's acknowledging the beauty of this ancient site. It is a stunning shot, and a harbinger of Eisenstein's shot of Ivan the Terrible from *Ivan the Terrible, Part I,* in which the 18th century Russian ruler's visage seems to watch over the people as they make their "exodus" into the desert.

Then we see a Mayan funeral ceremony. There is a body of a young man in a coffin, there are skulls, there are the pallbearers, their faces as immobile in their task as that of the corpse in his eternal sleep. Again, the shots are striking, the atmosphere real and even intoxicating. One can almost feel the oppressive heat of a day in the Yucatán as these people go through their ritual.

From there, we segue to "tropical Tehuantepec." In a sequence titled *The Sandunga,* Tisse's shots of the wildlife gradually fade into shots of people, with an eye-popping view of a braless Indian maiden brushing her hair, a shot that *definitely* would have been cut out had Joseph Breen viewed it just a few years later. In fact, several times we see female villagers going through the same task of brushing their hair, as if Eisenstein couldn't think of anything else for them to do. One of these hair-brushing beauties is Concepción, a gorgeous, *zaftig* maiden of the tropics who "has pride in her youthful beauty." To emphasize this, she even smiles right after the Russian narrator mentions this; in fact, throughout this rather amateurishly shot sequence, so different from the wonderful opening prologue at the Mayan temple, one can easily imagine the Russian director frantically prompting his non-actors to smile on cue. There is a *maguffin* about a necklace of gold coins that the maiden should have, and we are told that the culture is "Matriciarte, Rule by the Women." When this particular title comes up, in an unintentionally funny moment full of Freudian symbolism, an ugly old woman is slicing a large, round fruit with a machete. A young man named Abundio is "the object of Concepción's affections," and the director gives us some shots of the two lovers coyly smiling at each other. At another point, Concepción breaks into a very real laugh, as if she just couldn't take Eisenstein's directions seriously.

This scene segues into *Fiesta,* set during the Feast of the Holy Virgin of Guadalupe, "an annual reminder of Spain's conversion of Mexico into a colony of bloodshed and suffering." We are told of Cortés who came to Mexico in the 16th century; "The monks who came with him wiped out pagan cults with fire and sword." The sequence is, again, packed with Eisenstein's stunning visuals; we see celebrants in ancient costumes wearing large masks with outsized features. These ordinarily absurd-looking disguises are shot in such a way as to inspire fear rather than laughter. As the mask-wearing marchers of the procession hold up large crosses, we are not comforted by this display of Christian symbolism, but instead, as shot by a Communist director, we are disturbed by it; we see religion viewed not as piety and devotion, but as a ritual of the grotesque. Another shot has four monks (two on each side of the frame) standing in the background holding their wooden crosses and rosaries while three skulls sit in front of us in the foreground. After this, we see three young men climbing a long hill as they simulate Christ's bearing of the cross, and we are told that their arms have actually been pierced by cactus stems. Priests stand by genuflecting, a portrait of Mary is carried by the villagers, and one man prances about in a death costume. The conclusion to be drawn from Eisenstein's startling imagery, juxtaposed as it is between the priests presiding over this ritual, the grotesque masks, and the skulls is inescapable: Religion equals Death.

This segues into *Bullfight,* a sequence that was more appropriate to the talents of bullfighter-turned-director Budd Boetticher than Eisenstein. We see bullfighters getting into their outfits, preparing for the arena. We see them "call on their mother, to say goodbye for perhaps the last time." Here, Eisenstein seems to be taking a page out of Spanish author Vicente Blasco Ibáñez's *Blood and Sand* rather than his own research; one almost expects Rudolph Valentino to make an appearance. Though the director obviously filmed on location, we also see what could easily have been "stock footage," at times sped up like a silent movie of the '20s, as we view the crowd in the stands. We see the usual barbaric ritual of the bullfighters tormenting the poor animal, his hide already punctured by several lances, while the crowd roars its approval. After the bullfighters celebrate with their girlfriends out on some lake, the subtitles say: "Mexico. Tender and lyrical. And also cruel." When he wrote this, one wonders if Eisenstein was thinking of the government's censors who might not appreciate this observation.

To emphasize this cruelty, we cut to poor peons beneath the high walls of a hacienda, the film's most controversial sequence. It is the beginning of the twentieth century, and we are accommodatingly shown a portrait of "dictator Porfirio Díaz." Unfortunately, this portrait is shown to us several times throughout the sequence, as if the audience was too dumb to get the point. The sequence is called *Maguey,* named after the large cactus from which a refreshing liquid can be sucked out and turned into *pulque.* Sebastian, who works in the fields, is betrothed to the maiden Maria. Sebastian's brother is the happy-go-lucky Felicio. After the three young people display joy in being alive (or what passed for joy from a peon working on a hacienda), horror music comes on as Eisenstein cuts to that same portrait of Díaz; "the landlord and his friends" are toasting him. To emphasize their villainy, they are all drinking liquor, are all fat and swarthy and pig-like, and are all either belching or smiling wickedly for the benefit of the camera, as if they were members of someone's family purposely making faces and doing disgusting bits of business for a home movie.

Obviously, this is the first sequence in the whole film which actually has a story, with the actors, most of whom were amateurs, called upon to bring an actual script to life. The bride-to-be is supposed to be brought before the landlord for his approval; however, the looks the *hacendados* are giving her are not very respectful. Before you can say "Fate takes the form of a drunken guest," Fate takes the form of a drunken guest; the man grabs the innocent maiden and pulls her into a room for the Fate Worse than Death. When Sebastian tries to avenge her honor, the rich men throw him out and lock up Maria. Then the young man and four of his comrades, including Felicio, rebel.

Eisenstein's shots are a little obvious here; we see the *hacendados* drinking and laughing evilly, their booze dribbling off their chins in disgusting ways, we see the portrait of Díaz for the umpteenth time, and then we see a bunch of pigs gathering around and lapping up leftovers, with an obviously unsubtle comparison between the rich men and the hogs. Aiming to free Maria, the peons steal rifles and horses, but are pursued into the maguey fields by the hacienda's guards. Some of the combatants are wounded, and the landlord's cousin Sara, who joined in the pursuit, is killed. Ultimately, our rebel heroes are buried in the ground up to their heads and horses are ridden over them. With no one around, Maria is able to simply walk out of her cell (one wonders why she didn't do this before) and she finds her man's trampled body still in the ground.

At this point, Alexandrov appears to tell us of the *Soldadera* sequence which was never shot. This was a tribute to the soldiers of the revolution (we see the famous still shot of Pancho Villa and Emiliano Zapata sitting in the presidential palace in Mexico City). These revolutionaries unite, the still-communist A.D. proclaims, "to fight reaction." The epilogue features Mexico's Day of the Dead, a time when Mexicans gather together to laugh at Death. Almost repeating the earlier scenes, various individuals are dressed in skull masks and are roundly ridiculed. Then our Bolshevik helmsman gives us a scene (complete with stereotypical horror music stings) of skeletons dressed in the outfits of a millionaire (tuxedo and top hat), *hacendado* (with huge mustache and sombrero), and a policeman (in uniform). His narrator proclaims them "the corpses of a doomed class" and expresses the desire that some "*soldadera's* son" will be destined to forge "a truly free Mexico." The frame freezes on a little boy's smiling face, a definite sign that there was more to the scene that had nothing to do with propaganda. At the end, the titles announce that the film "was processed in the U.S.S.R." Released by the Soviets in 1979, long before the 1991 fall of Communism, the "optimistic" ending seems to have been tacked on by the Soviets to attack a still democratic Mexico. Alexandrov also doesn't mention Sinclair's accusation that the bureaucrats of Amkino, the Soviet government's New York–based film exchange, purposely stole pieces of the film once they received cans of it in Moscow.

Despite its obvious brilliance, Eisenstein's "Mexican Dream Film" becomes, more often than not, a glorified travelogue. And for the helmsman's enormous expenditure of time and money, one can hardly blame Upton and Mary Craig Sinclair, who gradually saw their life savings being sucked dry much as the peons in the film sucked dry a maguey plant. In far too many letters, Sinclair refers to the Soviet helmsman as "an intriguer," while Hunter Kimbrough more bluntly calls him "a liar." Kimbrough could have added "cold-blooded" to the character assessment. During the shooting of the *Maguey* sequence, the actor playing Felicio swiped cameraman Tisse's pistol (and what was the lensman doing with a loaded gun on a film set?) and accidentally shot his sister to death. The boy was actually chased by the same hacienda guard who chases him in the film. Eisenstein managed to get the boy released and put under police guard so that he could complete his shots in the picture before he was returned to prison.

Letter after letter leads us to the conclusion that Eisenstein and his crew were purposely stalling their return to the Soviet Union, and apparently had little regard for spending the Sinclairs' money in doing so. Treating business manager Hunter Kimbrough with respect for eight months, Eisenstein suddenly turned on the Southerner when Sinclair ordered a halt to the literally non-stop flow of money the helmsman was getting. In response to this, Eisenstein threatened that without more money, "there wouldn't be a film." As if this wasn't enough, behind Kimbrough's back, the Soviet director wrote to Sinclair and claimed that the business manager was an alcoholic who was squandering the Sinclairs' money on wild nights in cantinas. The accusation was angrily refuted by the author, who, after all, had known Kimbrough since they were youngsters. Even a total stranger, Horst Scharf, Tisse's assistant cameraman, vouched for Kimbrough.[22]

Then on November 21, 1931, Stalin wrote a telegram to Sinclair claiming that Eisenstein was seen as "a deserter who broke off with his own country STOP afraid the people here would have no interest in him."[23] The Soviet dictator, who was known to routinely *murder* his own people much less listen to their entreaties, was obviously speaking only for himself. He wanted no "escape attempts" by errant Communist filmmakers into freedom-loving capitalist nations, especially when said nations were the U.S. and Mexico. In early 1932, Sinclair called a halt to the production. Ironically, Kimbrough, thought to be Eisenstein's bitter enemy, tried to convince the author to allow the helmsman to continue so that he could film the *Soldadera* sequence.

After filming stopped, Communists in both America and Mexico, including film critic Stewart Stern and Mexican journalist Augustin Aragón Leiva, raked the Sinclairs over the ideological coals, calling them money-hungry capitalists, proto-fascists, and other infantile names. Doing his part in the slander, Eisenstein told his friends in the Mexican government, including his good pal the Minister of Education, that once his participation in the project ended, the film would be damaging to Mexico. This out-and-out lie delayed the film's shipment for development in Hollywood (which was being done by Consolidated Labs, owned by Herbert Yates of the soon-to-be-formed Republic Pictures). Forced to return from Mexico, Eisenstein and his crew decided to rub the Sinclairs' noses, and by extension "reactionary" America's noses, in the dirt. Eisenstein's trunks, supposedly containing stills for the film that were the property of Sinclair and his investors, were opened upon entry into the United States, as the director knew they would be. However, packed on top of the production stills, Texas border police found obscene sketches, drawn by Eisenstein himself, depicting Jesus Christ and two male disciples amidst plenty of homosexual imagery. In her excellent *Tramp: The Life of Charlie Chaplin,* author Joyce Milton wrote that while in Mexico, Eisenstein "pursued pubescent boys with a lack of discretion that terrified Hunter Kimbrough...."[24] With the company's time and money dependent on the Mexican government's total cooperation, one could hardly blame the business manager for being afraid of any scandal, if indeed these allegations were true, brought on by the director's lifestyle.

The footage was eventually bought up by future B producer Sol Lesser decades before the Soviet print of the film would be reconstructed in 1979. Stalin would punish the errant Eisenstein by blocking him from directing another film for six years until 1938, the year of *Alexander Nevsky*. Then, on February 11, 1948, after a meeting with Stalin and officials from Sovkino, Eisenstein died of a massive heart attack at the age of 50. Though it was considered a natural way to die in Stalin's Russia, for years the helmsman had been under enormous pressure from the dictator due to his *Ivan the Terrible, Part II*, a film which compared Ivan's brutal methods a *little too closely* to those of Uncle Joe.

Having learned much from the out-of-control Eisenstein, filmmakers in both America and Mexico would endeavor to film the Revolution as the era of the talkies opened up. In fact, in 1933, with news of Eisenstein's prima donna behavior still fresh in everyone's mind, MGM (the studio that filmed Upton Sinclair's *The Wet Parade*) decided to travel to Mexico to make a film on the life of an icon of the Revolution.

Again, the nation that confounded the driven Eisenstein, did the same to this fabled Hollywood film company—but for entirely different reasons...

It is an accepted fact that the Mexican Revolution's most famous figure was a man who started his controversial career as nothing more than a bandit. He was a cow thief, a robber, a killer, a user of women, a man who took the easy way out at a time in Mexican history when his countrymen were being ground into the dirt by the dictatorial Díaz regime. Prompted by a little man named Francisco Madero, Jr., he started to fight for an ideal, and in so doing, might have found his soul in a nation divided by those who oppressed and those who were oppressed. However, as his own legend spread, along with news of his many military victories, the man known as Pancho Villa also showed the world that the robber and killer that he was in the past, never really went away—even as he doubtlessly proved his sincerity to the Cause many times over.

He was both dreamer and pragmatist; emotionally sensitive, yet ruthlessly cold-blooded; decent to those who had been exploited and kicked around, yet cruel to his enemies; he loved women and treated them like queens, yet he also raped, abused and murdered them when they didn't cater to his whims; he sympathized with Mexico's Native population, whose blood flowed in his own veins, yet he had no problem murdering the country's Asians and other minorities whom he saw as aiding the Díaz regime. Pancho Villa had a mean streak, yet he also had an altruistic vision of helping those less fortunate, as his treatment of the nation's peons, especially in the state of Chihuahua, proved.

For much of his early career as a warrior, Villa was on friendly terms with the United States, but when the Woodrow Wilson administration eventually favored Venustiano Carranza over him, *every* American became his bitter enemy, something he proved when he had his men murder a train full of American oil company workers at Santa Isabel, and his attack on Columbus, New Mexico, on March 9, 1916. As a general, he was a brilliant improviser, taking advantage of the shifting winds of a particular battle, or adjusting his commands depending on a certain terrain. But once he held the winning cards, he could be clumsy and overconfident, quickly losing territory to the enemy due to stupid and impulsive commands.

He was born out of wedlock as Doreteo Arango on June 5, 1878 (some sources say 1879), in San Juan del Río in the state of Durango. His parents, Agustin Arango and Micaela Arambula, were peons working on the Rancho de la Coyotada, one of the state's largest haciendas. Agustin died young, and Doreteo and his four siblings were raised in the very *un*privileged ways of the peon on a hacienda during the Díaz regime. He would claim in later years that he left the hacienda, but after a short period of time he returned to avenge the rape of his sister by a *hacendado* named Agustin Lopez Negrete. He said he shot the rapist in the foot; to another interviewer he claimed to have killed him; to yet another he claimed to have stabbed him in the shoulder. There is also disagreement on *who* exactly raped his sister: Negrete, his son, a hacienda administrator, a sheriff, a *Federale*, or the local milkman. Any way you look at it, the story clearly stated that one should not mess with the man who would become Pancho Villa. In all probability, however, the girl might not have been raped at all. Years later, he joined the bandit gang of Ignacio Parra and Refugio Alvarez, earning far more as a robber in one day than he would as a peon in six years. He robbed mine owners, rustled cattle, and attacked trains and robbed the passengers, a course in life he always claimed he was "forced into." As Villa biographer Frank McLynn wrote:

> He claimed to have spent it all (his share of the loot) within a year, probably on high living, but, by the time he told the story of his early years, he was keen to portray himself as a "social bandit," so claimed he gave most of it away to his family or on charitable work. Keen to burnish his image as a latter-day Robin Hood, the myth-making Villa later claimed: "After eight or ten months I had returned to the poor the money the rich had taken from them."[25]

The name-change to Francisco "Pancho" Villa was done to throw off the law; his befriending of the forces of said law (judges, police chiefs, officers and *alcaldes* [mayors or town bosses]) was done for both intimidation and in order to bribe the official to grant him a light sentence. But the most important lesson he learned from Parra and Alvarez was, according to McLynn, "the importance of cultivating good relations with peasant support networks; if you paid your way with hard cash in the villagers, the peasants would always protect you against the authorities." Villa would claim that the murderous Díaz regime and the cruelty of the nation's *hacendados* drove him and many others into a life of crime but, as McLynn wrote, "why did he not settle down with the 50,000 pesos he received from the Parra raid instead of (allegedly) giving it to the poor?"[26]

There is little information on Villa's life for the first thirty years; and much of it has been oft-repeated stories from the Master himself, mostly unverified claims and thoroughly biased reports on his early life by either him or his men. Biographer Friedrich Katz probably went further than anyone else in investigating Villa's early life, and despite the author's painstaking research, this period *still* remains buried in the dust of time. What we do know is that he formed his own bandit gang, turned "legit" at periodic intervals with attempts to own his own butcher shop and run his own ranch, was "press-ganged" in the army only to escape, was arrested and escaped from jail many times, thus avoiding the Mexican lawman's traditional application of *ley fuga* (the Law of the Fugitive, or more realistically, "killed while trying to escape"), and loved and gleefully left dozens of women, many after actually marrying them. Also, it was said that Villa couldn't read, though some claimed that even *this* was exaggerated, and that he, in fact, *could* read, but that he never had the opportunity.

Communist journalist John Reed would continually romanticize the bandit leader as *always* being a noble revolutionary for whom the Cause was all-important. At the other end of the scale, author John Steinbeck called Villa "nothing but a bandit."[27]

Then came the magical day in 1910 when Abraham González, Chihuahua political agent for rebel leader Francisco Madero, Jr., sought out Villa to fight against Díaz. After contacts in Madero's Anti–Re-electionist Party set up a meeting between Villa and González in the latter's office in Chihuahua City, the rest, as they say, is history. However, the first time the two men met, one of them almost lost his life. One night, as González was approaching his office, Villa appeared out of the hallway darkness with fellow bandit Feliciano Dominguez. When González reached into his back pocket for the keys to his office, the two men mistook the gesture for a quick draw and pointed their revolvers at him. Seeing two cocked *pistolas* aimed at his head, the political agent calmly explained who he was and just what he was reaching into his back pocket for. The man's incredibly cool response completely won over Villa, a man who respected courage when he saw it ... sometimes ... depending on his mood.

Despite his exposure to González and Madero himself, Pancho Villa never became the revolutionary theorist that Emiliano Zapata was. His goals weren't necessarily land reform or destroying the haciendas or reforming the electorate or restraining the brutal *federales* or stopping Mexico's racist mistreatment of their Native population. He was a soldier, a warrior, his objective was to win battles, and his amazing victories helped overthrow Díaz. Later, after the assassination of Madero, he helped defeat General Victoriano Huerta as well. Disregard the fantasies of Marxist writers John Reed and Jack London; Villa's job was to win a revolution for Mexico, not world communism; he would fight for his nation, not the Soviet Union, nor the capitalists of the United States or England or the rest of Europe.

His personality makeup went to the mercurial; it was said that he could shed tears one moment, turn brutal the next; he could threaten murder one second, then burst into tears and embrace his would-be victim. With Villa, emotions dominated far more than intelligence. Though he didn't read, or rarely did anyway, Villa was emphatically *not* a stupid man. He had a hardscrabble education given to him by the many fights he had against his enemies, the love he received from his friends and followers, and the many, *many* trails he had ridden in a life more exciting than that of any ten men. He was a hero and a villain, a savior and an exploiter, an icon to his nation and a liar, cheat, robber, rapist and murderer.

None of us will ever see his like again, and there are those of us who might thank God for that.

But you'd be a fool to tell that to the people of Mexico...

Since Villa *was* a great man, it seemed appropriate that his first talkie film bio would be made, not only by a giant like David O. Selznick, but released by mighty MGM (Selznick was Louis Mayer's son-in-law). In early 1933, the future producer of *Gone with the Wind* optioned a book by Edgcumb Pinchon and O.B. Stade, *Viva Villa!: A Recovery of the Real Pancho Villa, Peon ... Bandit ... Soldier ... Patriot*. Besides this co-authored bio of Villa, Pinchon had also written a "biography" of Emiliano Zapata. The quotations marks are there due to the fact that, like Pinchon's Villa biography, both works are universally regarded as less than totally honest in their depictions; they're an untalented *yanqui* writer's stereotyped view of both the Revolution and Mexico itself. Elia Kazan had such contempt for Pinchon's work that he adamantly refused to give the author screen credit for the book that *Viva Zapata!* was obviously based on (the project had been knocking around MGM for 17 years before it was bought by Darryl F. Zanuck at Fox). Kazan gave sole credit to John Steinbeck, who gets a "Written by" designation right off the bat.

According to an item in a May 1933 issue of *The Hollywood Reporter*, the script for *Viva Villa!* was to be written by scenarist Oliver H.P. Garrett, who was already at MGM, and was credited for classic studio flicks like *Manhattan Melodrama* and *Night Flight* (and would later be hired by Selznick to contribute to *Gone with the Wind*). In 1935, Garrett would even provide a treatment of *Dracula's Daughter* when David O. Selznick briefly owned the property before selling it to Universal for a hefty profit. The *Hollywood Reporter* item also announced that talented MGM house director Jack Conway would direct the film. It turned out the item was wrong about his participation in the filming of *Viva Villa!*—that is, for *now*.

Selznick had Ben Hecht, Hollywood's busiest "rewrite man," former Chicago newspaperman and the film industry's highest paid scenarist, re-do the screenplay for the Garbo classic *Queen Christina* before he set him loose on *Viva Villa!*. Hecht would be paid $10,000 for the *Viva Villa!* script, with a $5,000 bonus if the scenarist would finish it within fifteen days. Juggling work on several screenplays for other studios at the same time, Hecht was also involved in writing a comedy called *Turn Back the Clock,* which would star a man whose larger-than-life presence had a lot to do with the many legends written about the filming of *Viva Villa!*: Lee Tracy.

According to Howard Hawks' biographer Todd McCarthy:

> Pancho Villa was, and remains, an equivocal historical figure, a man of the people who fought a corrupt dictatorship on behalf of the dispossessed, but was also a dissolute, unreliable drunkard who constantly cheated on his wife, could not solidify his gains, and led an ill-advised attack on the United States in 1915 (something not mentioned in the film).[28]

This was basically true except for the fact that the attack was in 19*16*, and the allegations about Villa being a drunkard. From all reports on Villa's life, the rebel icon did *not* drink or smoke. With his raw emotions always worn on his sizable sleeve, it was probably just as well; a man like Villa filled with alcohol would have been a far more explosive personality than he ordinarily was, if that was at all possible. However, McCarthy might have also questioned Villa's cheating on his wife; indeed, one might ask "Which one?" since the revolutionary icon married *every* woman who tickled his fancy.

As Frank McLynn archly writes in his *Villa and Zapata: A History of the Mexican Revolution:*

> There must be doubts about whether Villa was married in any full legal sense, and the marriage to Luz Corral (presumably Villa's "first" wife) had no more validity than Villa's earlier espousal to Petra Espinoza in Parral. Additionally, Villa had maybe a dozen women all over Mexico to whom he had either proposed marriage or with whom he had gone through some kind of ceremony. Villa took the pragmatic line that liaisons with women were all about the satisfaction of carnal appetites, and that if women were stupid enough to want a meaningless ceremony of wedlock, he would not disappoint them. However, Villa was aware that the law formally forbade polygamy so, although he "married" dozens of women in the presence of priests or civil officials, once the liaison was consummated, he would have his men destroy all relevant marriage records and copies. In Norse mythology, the goats slain in Valhalla by the warriors for their feasts were always alive again the next morning. In a similar way, Villa emerged from every honeymoon a bachelor.[29]

At this point, the film was to be directed by Howard Hawks and written by his pal and frequent collaborator (*Scarface* for one), Ben Hecht. These two men were known throughout Hollywood as serial cheaters who had betrayed their long-suffering wives with abandon, both of them vicariously living their fantasies through their cinematic incarnation of Villa, and ultimately seeing something of the lovable imp in the revolutionary icon's misogynistic and hurtful behavior.

Another source for information on the bandit-revolutionary was Hecht's frequent collaborator and close friend, Charles MacArthur. The playwright-screenwriter had been with General John J. Pershing's American Expeditionary Force on his so-called Punitive Expedition after Villa's men attacked Columbus, New Mexico, in 1916. Of course, Hecht quizzing MacArthur for info about Villa merely because he was a soldier on the Punitive Expedition was like asking World War I hero Alvin C. York what the Kaiser was like. Hecht also enlisted the help of Wallace Smith, a newspaperman who rode with Villa and covered his exploits for the Hearst papers. In fact, Smith might have participated in the film even *before* Hecht was hired to rewrite the script; in the *Hollywood Reporter* article, Smith was reported to be "returning from Mexico after receiving approval from the government there to proceed with the script for *Viva Villa!* written by Oliver H.P. Garrett."[30]

Both Hawks and Selznick wanted to film on location in Mexico—the Eisenstein fiasco be damned!—for their own personal reasons, though it does seem that both men deeply wanted to get far, *far* away from the maddeningly controlling head of MGM, Louis B. Mayer. An item in the October 27, 1933, issue of *Daily Variety* verified that scenes of the film were to be shot in "many towns in Mexico."

Selznick was about to find out what it was like to deal with that other maddeningly controlling entity he had to deal with in order to make his film Down Mexico Way: the government of Mexico. According to McCarthy in his Hawks bio:

> The problem was that there were at least three powerful politicians whose consent was critical: Plutarco Elías Calles, who had fought against Villa and was interested in a movie that showed the rebel as a spineless fool; President Abelardo Rodriguez, of course; and Army General and Michoacán state governor Lázaro Cárdenas, who looked as though he would unseat Rodriguez in the forthcoming election, which would take place while the film was in production.[31]

A little background on one of the men Hollywood had to deal with in order to film on-location in Mexico at the time:

Plutarco Elías Calles was indeed a general who had fought the *Villistas* for Venustiano Carranza's Constitutionalists. A pet of the self-appointed "First Chief" of the Revolution, Calles was at Carranza's side as many of his anti–Villa orders were given. After Villa's many defeats at the hands of the talented Álvaro Obregón, Calles' position rose among the Constitutionalists as he accepted an appointment as governor of Sonora. (Throughout the Revolution and for decades afterward, army officers, particularly generals with no previous political experience, were routinely appointed governors.) When Carranza, who despised any personality cult besides his own (his prime reason for hating Villa), turned against his successful new War Minister Obregón, Calles read the writing on the wall and switched his allegiance to the embattled but brilliant war minister in 1920. After the eternally selfish Carranza and his underlings attempted to loot the Mexican treasury (actually, they *did* loot it, commandeering a train to swipe millions of gold from the government) and even duck an assassination attempt by new presidential candidate Obregón, the now-disgraced First Chief was finally shot dead on May 21, 1920, while sleeping in a tent in Tlaxcalantongo in the Sierra Norte de Puebla Mountains.

After becoming president, Obregón rewarded Calles for his support and appointed him Interior Minister, a department within the Mexican government which encompassed educational material, cultural initiatives and, needless to say, entertainment media, including broadcast radio and the movies. Both the left-leaning Obregón and Calles, reflecting the anti-clerical stance of Venustiano Carranza, were violently anti–Catholic (both men were reportedly Freemasons), insisting on stern measures to restrict the power of the Church. This apparently included federal troops riding their horses into churches during services and destroying the Host, as well as the physical intimidation and mass arrest of parishioners. The oppression triggered the birth of a Catholic guerrilla group, the Cristeros. With Calles' own presidency set to end in 1928, his pal Obregón decided to go for the presidency again and, with Calles' political clout, he handily won. However, before Obregón could return to Mexico City to take the oath of office, a Cristero assassin shot the former hero of the Revolution in the face on July 17, 1928.

Again seeing the writing on the wall, and probably shivering in fear as he viewed his former mentor's corpse at his funeral, Calles refrained from running for office again. Holding several ministerial posts, he instead became the unofficial Power Behind the Mexican Throne. This was known as the years of the *Maximato* (the mid–1920s into the 1930s) when Plutarco Elías Calles declared himself *Jefe Máximo,* a new kind of First Chief, the supreme political boss of the Mexican government, no matter who was president. Violently anti–Catholic, Calles lost little time in acting on his hatred by committing atrocities against the Cristeros, murdering the Catholic guerrillas in front of their wives and children and even having 4,000 priests shot by federal troops. A peace treaty initiated by the United States (courtesy of Ambassador Dwight Morrow) had been signed between the Mexican government and the Cristeros in 1929. To this day, it's not known if Calles or his cronies personally benefited from any "peace money" given to him by the American government for his sudden change of heart.

Calles' political leanings were always to the left, and he had no problem opening the first Soviet embassy in Mexico in 1925, an act which shocked the U.S. government, but prompted the Soviet ambassador to say that "no two countries show more similarities than the Soviet Union and Mexico." Ironically, seven years later, flyers were given out by Communist Party members outside theaters showing Eisenstein's sliced-up *Qué Viva México!* criticizing the "Wall Street–controlled Calles-Rodriguez government of landowners." Certainly, Calles' obvious admiration for totalitarian movements made itself felt by the early 1930s, and there is strong evidence that the *Jefe Máximo* would have imposed on Mexico a social and political system that was clearly patterned after European fascism. He was a supporter of General Nicolás Rodriguez Carrasco's "Gold Shirts," a paramilitary fascist group which attacked Mexico's Natives, as well as Asians and Jews.

After Calles' presidency ended in 1928, the office was occupied by Emilio Portes Gil, Pascual Ortiz Rubio and Abelardo L. Rodriguez, all Calles puppets whose presidencies were of unusually short duration compared to the four-year runs of men like Obregón and Calles himself (Gil from December 1, 1928, to February 5, 1930; Rubio, from February 5, 1930, to September 2, 1932; and Rodriguez, the longest in office of the three, from September 2, 1932, to November 1934).

Next up at bat for the office of *presidente* was the left-leaning Lázaro Cárdenas. However, Cárdenas was no Communist; a true man of the people, he not only broke the back of the *Maximato* by having Calles and his gang deported to the United States on April 9, 1936 (in the U.S., the implacable enemy of the Cristeros tried to hook up with pro-fascist groups), he welcomed Republican refugees fighting against Franco's fascists (a charitable move thwarted by the Roosevelt administration). Proving himself anti–Stalinist, Cárdenas was also the only world leader to give refuge to hunted revolutionary icon Leon Trotsky. A reformist in fact as well as principle, Cárdenas cut his own salary in half, spoke for the poor and the working class and, unlike the Obregón-Calles combo, vastly improved relations with the Church and the country's Native population.

At the time of Cárdenas' elevation to president, however, Calles was still *Jefe Máximo*, the one man in charge of what the public was supposed to see. And it was Calles' viewpoint on Pancho Villa that would dominate the MGM film. There are those who harshly criticize Wallace Beery for his buffoonish depiction of Villa without taking into consideration these factors, especially those of the eddies and currents of that constantly changing, barely controllable force of nature, the Mexican government.

Further reinforcing this, Louis B. Mayer ordered studio executive Joe Schenck to reassure Mexico's most powerful government men about the sincerity of their film version of Villa's life. According to MGM screenwriter (and later producer) Samuel Marx, this coddling included telling "the country's most powerful politico, Plutarco Elías Calles, that the film would be a faithful picturization." "Schenck reported back that Calles, who has fought against Villa in the Revolution, wanted the movie to show the bandit-hero as an almost mindless peon, arrogant in victory, groveling in the dust before his captors."[32]

With this in mind, Selznick ordered Hecht to revise Garrett's script so that it was more along the lines of Calles' depiction of Villa. Mayer even sent MGM star Ramon Novarro's brother, Carlos Samaniegos, to get the government's support for the production. (Ramon had been born in Mexico; and he and his family, fleeing the Mexican Revolution, moved to Los Angeles, where Ramon started his career as a film extra.) After Hecht's new draft was read by Calles, both he and President Abelardo Rodriguez approved it. Or more likely, Calles approved it and Rodriguez, the erstwhile president, just went along with the decision. According to Marx, "Samaniegos reminded them that an election was drawing near and would occur while the picture was in production. 'What if President Rodriguez

Yanqui Bandido: White Midwesterner Wallace Beery in a publicity shot for *Viva Villa!*, a movie controversial to this day. Mexicans still hate its depiction of Villa as a buffoon, despite the fact that the Mexican government at the time wanted this portrayal.

was voted out of office?' he asked. Calles called army headquarters to send over Lieutenant Cárdenas. He signed, and Calles told Samaniegos, 'Now you have our next president's signature too!'"33

Marx's anecdote was revealing in many ways, particularly in the progressively more shady dealings of the Mexican government. Not only does this verify that Cárdenas was a cog in the Calles party machine early in his career, but it showed him to be a recipient of the *Jefe Máximo's* largesse; after all, not many army lieutenants make it from the barracks straight to the president's office. The above story also shows Calles clearly predicting the country's next president way before the election! (However, one does wonder why Marx refers to Cárdenas as a *lieutenant,* since he was most definitely a general and governor at the time.)

Marx's story is just one of many on the background of the making of *Viva Villa!,* a troubled production if there ever was one. Even if one doesn't consider Calles' enormous influence in the film's depiction of Villa as a total buffoon, MGM's idea of casting Wallace Beery in the lead role already demonstrated a certain racist contempt on the project from Selznick, Mayer *and* Hawks. Of course, Hollywood filmmakers had been making racist casting choices since the old Edison Trust days. Sure, they had Anna May Wong and Dolores del Río, but the Mexican actress had played Polynesians and other ethnicities besides Latinas; and as for Wong, the novelty of having an actual Asian actress playing an Asian woman would be offset by the traditionally racist casting of Caucasian co-stars like Warner Oland to play "insidious Chinamen." To the film industry, as long as you had dark hair (dark coloring or tanned skin was optional), you could play a Latino, Native-American, Asian or Pacific Islander with no problem. Just talk in a "funny" accent and you were fine.

However, Wallace Beery was something else. A big, blustery actor from Kansas City, Beery was already in his late 20s when the real Pancho Villa captured the strategic city of Torreōn in 1913. Conversely, a 49-year-old white actor from Missouri would now portray the Mexican icon, a warrior who fought the Revolution while he was still in his 30s. However, it was not as if the MGM star wasn't familiar with ethnic roles. A former vaudeville and circus performer, Beery had been in silent movies since before World War I, starting his film career somewhere around the time of President Madero's assassination in 1913. He had played Asians and Native-Americans (he played the evil Huron warrior Magua in 1920s *Last of the Mohicans*), Latinos and Polynesians, as well as Scotsmen, Austrians, Germans, Italians, Swedes and Irishmen. Fortunately, the beauty of silent film allowed us to use our imaginations to add to an actor's characterization, especially in the absence of vocal inflections; it also saved us from hearing an Anglo actor's attempt at a foreign accent. For a limited actor like Beery, his versatility in silent films was very much due to the fact that one couldn't hear a gravelly, whiskey-sodden Midwestern voice trying to play a wide variety of non-white humanity. It was also due to the silents' world of non-reality we can thank for Beery's casting as the intellectual Professor Challenger in 1925's *The Lost World.* However, in a lost ten-chapter Pathe serial of 1917 called *Patria,* co-starring opposite Irene Castle and Warner Oland, Beery had allegedly portrayed Pancho Villa, though strictly as a villain. One wonders if Mayer, Selznick or Hawks thought of this film when they made their decision to cast Beery as the revolutionary icon; certainly, it couldn't have been his recent performances that inspired that decision. Though Beery survived the transition to sound, once the actor opened his mouth for the new medium of talkies, *any* thought of him playing an ethnic character, much less a man of the world like Professor Challenger, went right out the window. Witness the actor's pathetic attempt at a Prussian accent in *Grand Hotel*.

However, Beery was MGM's dark and ugly alternative to handsome leads like Gable, Robert Montgomery and Robert Taylor. He was the big, dumb slob who went to the wall for kids like Jackie Cooper and Margaret O'Brien; he played gruff but sentimental softies opposite middle-aged contemporaries Marie Dressler and Marjorie Main; and portrayed lovable roughnecks who were ready to forgive-and-forget after a knockdown-dragout fistfight with the hero (see *Stand Up and Fight* opposite Robert Taylor for a good example). However, the off-screen Beery was a different animal altogether. The nicest thing Main could say about him was that he was "intolerable." Cooper and O'Brien vividly recalled his nastiness; directors and co-stars were repelled by his cheapness, his arrogance and his crude manners; he even stole props and furniture from MGM and demanded that the studio pay him to return them to the sets he stole them from. Yet somehow, the filmmakers of *Viva Villa!* translated the actor's real-life personality (or more likely, his thuggish but lovable on-screen persona) into that of Mexico's Centaur of the North. Beery had played comical badmen before (and would do so again, *ad nauseam*); therefore, Villa, the bandit who would fight for a cause, the cow thief who found his soul, seemed perfect for the man who routinely walked off with the studio's Ottomans, drapes, silverware and other bric-à-brac.

Howard Hawks had already started shooting on-location scenes in Mexico in September 1933, with Beery joining him soon after. However, the cantankerous Beery hated pretty much everything about Mexico as he presumably did many other things, places and people he'd been associated with. A boozer and allegedly a rapist and wife-beater (as his ex, Gloria Swanson, would later reveal), Beery's wild-man reputation was not helped by the fact that he fairly heaped contempt on his co-stars. If one is to believe the worst about him, in 1935 he was allegedly one of three men (not "college boys" as the L.A. newspapers claimed) who got into a drunken fight with a fellow MGM player, comic Ted Healy. (The other two "boys" were agent-mobster Pat DeCicco and his cousin, future James Bond producer Albert "Cubby" Broccoli.) The brutal beating reportedly contributed to the alcoholic comic's fatal heart attack. MGM sent Beery out of town rather quickly for a "vacation."[34] While on location for *Viva Villa!,* Beery, the man who was playing one of Mexico's great heroes, so hated the country that he flew his own plane back over the border to his hotel rooms in El Paso as soon as there was any pause in the filming. Other reports say he *chartered* the plane and had it on standby; however, Beery was too cheap to tip waitresses in the studio cafeteria, so paying for a chartered plane and having the pilot hired on a "stand-by" basis to fly him at a moment's notice, doesn't jibe with the man's Simon Legree–like persona.

"A mighty saga of amazing, romantic adventures ... with Beery as you love him ... blustering, ruthless but with a lovable heart of a boy ... swaggering through revolution and revelry ... galloping to the thrilling cry of VIVA VILLA!"[35] So went one of the usually over-the-top taglines for the film. Note the emphasis on fighting for the oppressed as some kind of romantic, thrilling adventure—as well as reminding audiences that, despite the fact that he was portraying a figure of history whose basic personality consisted of frightening mood swings, Beery would just be playing the same big, lovable slob MGM always had him playing.

In Mexico in the 1880s, its people are being crushed under the iron rule of Porfirio Díaz. We see a *hacendado* ordering peons off their land. One of them protests, claiming that he wants to leave his land to his son Pancho, a blatant error by either Garrett, Hecht or others who added scenes to the screenplay: At the time, the boy was known as Dorateo Arango; he would not call himself Francisco "Pancho" Villa until he became a bandit. One of the *hacendado's* men whips the father to death. That night, the boy comes along and stabs his dad's murderer to death, an incident which never happened. This seems to be a variation on Villa's old yarn that his sister was raped and he returned to avenge her; in Hecht's screenplay, sexual violence against Villa's sister is turned into the accidental murder of his father by the peons' oppressor. This is, of course, the kind of incident that galvanizes *all* B movie heroes to fight the Good Fight.

Meanwhile, title cards, a holdover from the silent days, provide a kind of passage of time, explaining in puffy prose that Villa "grew up in the shadows of Mexico. Injustice was his nurse, Oppression his tutor." In a small village, a kangaroo court, run by a snuff-taking judge, sentences six peons to hang for some unspecified minor infraction against an old *hacendado*. When Villa (that big lovable slob himself, Wallace Beery) arrives in town with his conquering Dorados, he is enraged by the sight of the hanged peons. His right-hand man Sierra (Leo Carrillo) starts shooting down the officers in the court, including the judge's "old friend, Don Miguel." The psychotic Sierra was obviously based on Villa's real-life psychotic right-hand man, Rodolfo Fierro, one of the most brutal men ever to be found in any revolution or at any time in world history. Indeed, in a later day, in other lands, one could see the psychotic Fierro doing his grisly work as an SS officer or an NKVD man. Stopping Sierra from murdering the judge, Villa allows his black sense of humor to take over, having his men seat the six hanged victims before the ruthless judge and claim that he heard them condemn him to death. This seems to be less Villa's sense of humor than *Hecht's*. Perhaps no scenarist of the pre–Code years took such blatant advantage of those free-wheeling days than did the former newsman from Chicago, as witness the black humor in *Scarface* and many of his other screenplays of the time. Impatiently, Sierra shoots down the now-whining judge and other officers of the court as Villa mildly reproaches him for it. Only with Hecht could humor go hand in hand with the mass killing of mass murderers.

When the Dorados attack a train, they run into newsman Johnny Sykes (Stuart Erwin). Claiming to be a bad choice for robbery victim, he whines, "I'm a journalist! All brains, no dough!" Obviously this is former newsman Hecht's wry comment on himself specifically, as well as his underpaid colleagues. Once in town, Villa surveys the women-flesh, inevitably picking the defiant spitfire Rosita Morales (Katherine DeMille, daughter of C.B.), a hot-blooded, kicking and scratching version of Villa's still-surviving first wife, Luz Corral. Johnny is writing a dispatch for his newspaper claiming that Villa and his "desert murderers" subjected the village to a "bestial orgy of destruction and rapine." When Villa grabs the dispatch, to Sykes' relief, he finds that the guerrilla chief cannot read, and instead the newsman improvises a phony dispatch praising Villa for his heroism. This is more tart commentary from former reporter Hecht, ridiculing the media for reporting events (with colorful, over-the-top verbiage) *before* they even happen.

Realizing that he needs an image-maker to make him look good to the *yanquis,* Villa kidnaps Johnny. As time goes on, the befuddled newsman becomes the bandit's friend, and even his collaborator, marrying him to Rosita in a comical scene as the federals close in. Soon, it is revealed that Villa marries *every* girl who strikes his fancy (an acknowledgment of Villa's real-life serial trips to the altar), with Hecht throwing in the barbed comment from the bandit that he marries all these women because "I'm very religious." Then the titles tell us of a little man who rose to help free Mexico (Hecht, or possibly Garrett, rather tactlessly call him a "Christ-fool"). Ready to take over the hacienda of a Spaniard named Don Felipe de Castillo (Donald Cook), Villa meets his guest, Francisco Madero (Henry B. Walthall), who persuades the bandit to fight for the Revolution. He also meets Don Felipe's gorgeous sister, Teresa. If the dark-haired Anglo actor Donald Cook is hard to believe as a Spanish Don, the audience is in for an even greater shock when they see that his sister is played by Fay Wray, the previously blonde-haired Ann Darrow of *King Kong* fame. A good actress, Wray at least tries for an accent, something most of the other cast members don't bother with.

Rejecting the involvement of Abraham Gonzalez by substituting Don Felipe as a reluctant go-between (assuming that Gonzalez never had a knockout sister that looked like Fay Wray), the meeting goes well and Villa is enlisted in the fight against Díaz, with the little man envisioning the bandit at the head of an "army of liberty." However, Villa's methods are still that of a bandit, and when he meets up with Madero again, the little man cold-shoulders him for his summary executions of federal prisoners. The rebel chief defends himself by claiming that in order to have a successful revolution, you *have* to hate the enemy. As history proved, even if Villa hadn't expressed this feeling, Madero's idealism was sorely misplaced when dealing with the mass murderers of the *Porfiriato*. After Madero triumphed

Guerrilla My Dreams: Wallace Beery is about to get hitched to fiery Katherine DeMille by correspondent Stuart Erwin in *Viva Villa!* Ben Hecht's script turned Villa's misogynist behavior and neurotic penchant for marrying the women he lusted after into broad comedy.

and Díaz voluntarily left for Spain, the little man quickly forgave the generals who had ordered the butchery of Mexico's citizens on a massive scale. Needless to say, these men rewarded Madero for his trust in them by plotting behind his back to seize power and return the country to the days of the *Porfiriato*. Principal among these psychopaths was a bald-headed drunkard who wore smoke-lensed, oddly shaped spectacles and went by the name of General Victoriano Huerta. In the film, the character is called General Pascal, and is played, with a full head of hair, by future Oscar-winner Joseph Schildkraut. The enmity between the two men as shown in the movie was quite real off-screen as well, as Villa and Huerta had an intense dislike for each other no less bitter than that between Villa and "First Chief" Venustiano Carranza.

When a drunken Johnny falsely wires news of a Villista victory at Santa Rosalia to an El Paso paper, the shame-faced newsman persuades the guerrilla chief to actually attack the town for real, despite its enormous fortifications. Again, Hecht pokes fun at his former colleagues, having one of them not only display a love of the sauce that causes him to print a false headline, but he has the newsman push Villa to enact the event in real life, and at great risk to the Dorados, just so he won't be proven a fraud. When Villa refuses to attack such a tough, well-garrisoned target, Johnny accuses him of ingratitude: "And I thought you were a pal!" Surprisingly, Villa and his men triumph and take Santa Rosalia, which pleases Madero but angers the jealous Pascal. Díaz resigns and Madero is the new president. In a strangely moving scene, with Madero not needing Villa's skills as a fighter any more, he parts with the former bandit, who modestly wants nothing for his efforts. Even more touching is the parting between Villa and Johnny, the newsman having gone from kidnap victim to close personal friend of the guerrilla chief.

In peacetime, however, old habits die hard, and when Villa goes to a bank to make a withdrawal after hours, the impatient Sierra knocks out the cashier with his pistol, killing him. The police come to Rosita's house as she's about to get married to Villa, but they are blocked by two children ("You can't come in. Our father and mother are about to be married!"). Thrown in jail, Villa is about to get shot by a firing squad commanded by his old enemy Pascal until a letter arrives from Madero sparing him. The situation forces Villa to cry and go to his knees in the dirt, something that amuses Pascal and his men. In reality, Villa was arrested by Huerta's men because the guerrilla chief (or his men) stole a horse. It's uncertain whether said animal belonged to one of Huerta's men or was merely a spoil of war stolen from someone during one of Villa's raids; nevertheless, the drunken and murderous Huerta used it as an excuse to incarcerate his bitter enemy. With little hesitation, Huerta had a firing squad in mind for Villa no matter what the trumped-up charge was. Villa would always claim that the tears he allegedly shed were to delay the firing squad, though with Villa's usually hair-trigger emotional makeup, it's quite possible the tears were real.

Madero also demands that Villa be exiled to America (Hecht's titles again using the racist epithet "gringos"). Again, this was not the way things happened. Though Villa was spared from the firing squad, he was ordered to serve out his sentence. Helped by a sympathetic young clerk who craved adventure, Villa (and the clerk) broke out of the prison and *then* the rebel chief crossed the border into America, where he spent much time in El Paso. Meanwhile, Pascal and his men burst into Madero's office and gun down the little man at his desk. In all the reenactments of the death of Francisco Madero in films made by the *yanquis*, this is the most far-fetched, despite Hecht's subtle handling of it. If anything, Elia

Kazan's staging of Madero's murder in *Viva Zapata!* (done at night in a dark courtyard illuminated by the headlights of the assassins' cars as the little man screams in fear) is the best one shot in an American film. And *this* scene wasn't the way it happened either! In real life, under the orders of General Huerta, his officers kicked, beat and cursed at the jailed ex-president and his vice-president, Jose Maria Piño Suarez, as they pulled them from a car into a courtyard and shot both of them in the head. Then they riddled the car with machine-gun bullets and threw their bodies back into the vehicle to make it look like unknown gunmen had murdered the two former leaders in a failed rescue attempt. Huerta's explanation was, literally, full of holes; for what gunmen would be stupid enough to machine-gun a car that contained the very men they were trying to rescue? Huerta was not around during the assassinations, though it is certain that his presence was felt in every brutal act his officers performed against the two unarmed victims.

Waking up a sleepy Villa in his hotel room, Johnny tells him of Madero's murder. That night, the now-activist newsman rides across the Rio Grande with Villa and Sierra. In montage, we see the call go out to men to join Villa's band, and by and large, they do (Hecht's titles call them "an army of vengeance"). Villa's summary executions of federal prisoners so despised by Madero are back with a ... well, *vengeance*. Even Sierra teaches his men the innovative method of saving ammunition by lining up three or four men at a time and shooting them with one bullet, an actual Villa invention. Certainly, Hecht's screenplay (or revisions by others, or perhaps a little input by Calles' people in the Mexican government) has Villa rather inexplicably going over to the Dark Side. We see this by his brutal handling of his prisoners (which was historically true), his hostility towards Felipe and Teresa, and especially the sudden disappearance of the Johnny Sykes character during all this madness. (Didn't Sykes ride across the Rio Grande with Villa and Sierra, an action that certainly implies that Johnny is now on Villa's team?)

Villa's journey over to the Dark Side is never more apparent than when he and his men storm into Don Felipe's house. The scenes shot there, especially Villa's manhandling of Teresa, were controversial, and even that depends on which version of the scene we're talking about. After Villa argues with the now-disillusioned Don Felipe, he and his men bully the Don, as well as his guests and servants, going wild, and drinking with abandon before Villa is set to take over Chihuahua where General Pascal is garrisoned. In the Don's study, Villa has a now-spiteful Teresa brought to him by Sierra. Alone with her, he tries to kiss her, but she struggles, finally pulling out the gun her brother gave her and wounding Villa in the arm. Her one brave statement before she fires, "I'd be glad to die if I could rid Mexico of you," certainly implied that either screenwriter Hecht, or his uncredited collaborators, or more likely *El Jefe* Calles, despite the earlier portrayal of Villa as a hero, now put the guerrilla chief on the same level as men like Díaz and Huerta. When he orders Teresa to use his neckerchief as a tourniquet, she pulls too hard, causing him to scream in pain, and then she laughs at him. Villa slaps her, or at least a slap is heard, since there is a sudden cut to Don Felipe bursting in. When he struggles with Villa, and Teresa tries to help her brother, Sierra bursts in and shoots her. Villa leaves "empty-handed" as he makes a wry comment about the rich and the poor being the same—yet coming out of the mouth of this would-be rapist, the statement doesn't say much for a man who sees himself as a champion of the poor. This scene, which revealed so much about Villa's reversion to barbarism, was severely cut once the film appeared before the newly reborn Hays office in 1934.

As the scene was originally shot, after Villa's wounding, Teresa hysterically laughs at him, so Villa grabs a whip and lashes the señorita several times. The whipping is shown via shadows cast on the wall. *Then,* Felipe enters, struggles with Villa, and Sierra enters and shoots Teresa. In the new version approved by Production Code enforcer Joseph I. Breen, the whipping is cut out in its entirety, as well as Teresa's hysterical laughter, and even the slap Villa gives her. It is this new cut that would forever be shown on TV and now exists in the video version. In fact, with the cuts, the scene is confusing, with audiences wondering (for a few seconds anyhow) whether Teresa's wound was indeed fatal.

All this is borne out by *New York Times* critic Mordaunt Hall, who saw the original scene as it played at Broadway's Criterion Theater. In his review of April 11, 1934, months before the Production Code dictates took effect, Hall wrote:

> [I]f there are disappointing moments in this fictionalized biography of the man who has been alluded to as the Mexican Robin Hood, Ben Hecht ... has done so well by most of it with his incisive style that it causes one to doubt that he had much to do with such a sequence as that wherein Villa strikes Teresa, played by Fay Wray—the blow sounding as though it must render her unconscious—and then lashes her with a heavy whip.[36]

In the finished film, there is no whip, heavy or otherwise, anywhere in sight. Hall certainly came up with a good point when he mentioned that Hecht's writing style is *not* evident in the scene where Villa beats Teresa, implying the work of other hands tampering with the script, hands that could have belonged to former president Calles and his underlings. The next scenes certainly verify the brutal direction the script had taken: Instead of shooting Pascal by firing squad, of which the general has no fear, Villa orders the traitorous officer staked to the ground, doused with honey and let the ants devour him—a grisly prospect that makes the general panic. Then the camera shows (as Pascal screams in terror off-screen) vultures also waiting to finish him off. Both this scene and the killing of Teresa are *not* examples of Hecht's breezy style, or even black humor. Instead, as purportedly written by others, they most definitely show Villa's cruelty.

Then come even more inaccuracies. With Pascal (the Huerta figure) now dead in a way the real one surely deserved, Pancho Villa and his men, without the mention of Zapata or any other guerrilla faction (even those commanded by Carranza, Obregón *or* Calles), ride into Mexico City to take control of the government. This was nonsense, for at no time did Villa *ever* run the Mexican government. He *was* the de facto head of Chihuahua, his usual home base. Unfortunately, the old phrase that pictures are worth a thousand words is very true here. Some filmmakers, and other folks ignorant of history, obviously saw the famous photograph of Villa seated in the president's chair, with Zapata right next to him in the vice-president's chair, and pretty much assumed that Villa ran Mexico. Certainly the two men had much to celebrate when they and their men stormed Mexico City after driving Huerta from power, but it was pretty much accepted that Carranza would be the president (and, unlike Villa and Zapata, without having to do a lick of fighting on the battlefield either). In a short period of time, both revolutionary icons would turn against him, but it was also obvious that both men, each a talented warrior in his own right, had no interest in being president. Zapata mistrusted all forms of established authority, especially politics; Villa honestly admitted that he wasn't educated enough to be president, pointing out that Mexico's president should at least be a man who was able to read and write.

Still, in a February 24, 1934, studio memo headlined RETAKES TO BE SHOT BY (second-unit man) DICK ROSSON IN MEXICO CITY, an unnamed MGM official orders, among other scenes, reshooting of the "entrance of Villa and his troops to the Capitol, to be shot with two cameramen taken from here and four cameramen to be picked up in Mexico City."[37] Special instructions advise Rosson that this parade "should be as thrilling and spectacular as possible, *inasmuch as the government is turning out troops for us* [my italics]." Here, Calles' "loan" of actual soldiers for the filming underlined the government's cooperation with the studio—at least for now. There are many notes in the memo on "transparency backgrounds," meaning back-projection. There was also to be a quick establishing shot of Felipe and his henchmen lying in wait." Three or four horsemen, "well-spaced, and riding just within the edge of the sidewalk as though to protect [Beery as Villa], in accordance with Mr. [Jack] Conway's suggestion; but I am afraid this may interfere with the shots we want of the flirting girls and of the vendor and it will be all right if Villa is riding alone without these protective horsemen."[38]

Also highlighted in the memo is the suggestion that Rosson "please try to get angles on the parade that will show the beauty of the city, gorgeous buildings, etc.," as well for the extras to cry out "'Villa,' 'Viva Villa!' and possibly break into a rendition of *La Cucaracha*."[39]

Emphasized here is how the filmmakers could enhance the big scene of Villa's triumphant ride into Mexico City, though trying to get the audience to accept gorgeous twenty-something babes openly flirting with big, slobbering Beery might be tough. Still, notice this unknown MGM exec using the name of contract director Jack Conway, a talented helmsmen who had directed every one of the studio's stars from Gable and Tracy to Garbo, Crawford, Shearer, and yes, even Wallace Beery. But why was *Jack Conway* even mentioned in the memo? Wasn't Howard Hawks directing this picture? More on that later.

Now officially the "president," Villa takes control of the nation—or, what *passes* for control of the nation. What Hecht actually does here is take Villa's control of Chihuahua and inflate it into a sequence in which the now-victorious rebel chief rules *all* of Mexico. In fact, though Villa abolished the abuses of the haciendas and cared for the poor in Chihuahua, his remedy to the lack of money in the treasury was to print up phony money—which, of course, was worthless. In the film, either Hecht or someone else accentuate Villa's buffoonery as he has the men who printed the counterfeit money (with his picture, of course) arrested because they wanted to be paid in *real* silver.

Finally, sick of dressing up in fancy uniforms, Villa abdicates as president (it isn't mentioned who will take his place) and goes back to the hills. Then, somewhere in Chihuahua, he is going to a butcher shop when he is gunned down by Felipe and his men, the former Don avenging the death of his sister. Coincidentally, Johnny shows up and gives the dying guerrilla a passionate rendition of what he'll write in his paper about his heroism. It's a silly scene, and it is helped, not by Beery's blustering, but by Erwin's sincere reading of his lines. At the end, the titles tell us that out of the battle "arose a new Mexico dedicated to justice and equality," but you'd be hard-pressed to sell that to its Native population.

First of all, when Villa was murdered, he wasn't alone. On December 1, 1920, Álvaro Obregón, the only man to consistently beat Villa on the battlefield, was elected president of Mexico. And though there are those who credit the former general and Carranza war minister with being the first president to provide post-revolutionary stability to Mexico, there are perhaps an equal number of folks who believe that the one-armed president merely continued the lunatic power struggle among the nation's leaders that was part and parcel of the Mexican Revolution. Indeed, with thousands of innocents killed in the crossfire between revolutionaries and federal soldiers as they fought each other for power, the legacy of the *Porfirios* may have been gone, but the Way of the *Pistolero* lived on.

Besides the mass murder of practicing Catholics during the Cristero War, perhaps the best example of this abuse of power was the assassination of Pancho Villa. On July 20, 1923, as he was driving a 1919 Dodge roadster with several of his bodyguards riding on the running boards, the guerrilla chief and all but one of his men were killed by seven men with rifles and pistols. Villa had driven from his ranch to Parral and took along some of his men (though *not* the core of his Dorado bodyguards, just a few men along for the ride). He had to run a few errands in town, such as withdrawing silver to pay his men, and after he was through, he was leaving town and driving past a schoolyard when a peanut vendor ran towards the car shouting, "Viva Villa!" This was a signal to the assassins. (The vendor was instructed to shout "Viva Villa!" if Villa was at the wheel, and just "Villa!" if he was in the back seat.) Some forty shots were pumped into Villa and his men. Reportedly, a quarter of this ammo hit Villa, with nine or ten bullets ripping apart his head and upper chest (the car's dashboard blocked the killers from riddling him even *more*). Supposedly, when Villa was found sprawled in his seat, his right arm was positioned reaching across his chest for the pistol in his shoulder holster. Some claim that the former revolutionary had said, "Don't let it end like this! Tell them I said something!" This may have sounded like the line Wallace Beery said to Stuart Erwin at the end of *Viva Villa!*, but it was just another old wives' tale. In reality, Villa died as soon as the bullets struck him. By 1921, tired of fighting, and still wanted by the United States for his attack on Columbus, New Mexico, Villa was receptive to Obregón's offer to pay him to retire. Consequently, thousands of pesos were paid to him and his men and their families and a huge ranch was built in Canutillo in Chihuahua to house all of them. It was a specially gated (and guarded) ex-guerrilla community, including schools for their children and medical facilities. As long as Villa and his men officially abandoned revolution, the Obregón government would protect him.

However, by 1923, Villa was making public statements about what he considered the corruption of the current rulers in Mexico City. Inevitably prodded by reporters, and the egotistical Villa needed little prodding, the ex-revolutionary started making increasingly loud noises about returning to the field of battle—with the implication that the target of his efforts would be the administration of the man who was paying him and his men to live free and easy for the rest of their lives. He also implied that he might actually run for office, apparently forgetting his own reluctance to do so previously due to his lack of reading and writing skills. For Álvaro Obregón, this was the last straw. He had had it with Villa's blustering, his arrogance, his stealing the spotlight from him, his administration's paying for his food while he ungratefully complained to the press about him, and especially the fact that he had lost an arm thanks to him (a Villista shell exploded near Obregón, the injury forcing doctors to amputate his mutilated arm). No one could actually prove that *El Presidente* had anything to do with it, but then again, Obregón wasn't supposed to have anything to do with Venustiano Carranza getting blown away in a pitch tent on some God-forsaken mountain either. Inevitably, the old one-armed general got the assassin's bullet himself in 1928.

But there was other chicanery afoot, including an incident that prompted the reshooting of much of the film.

The role of Johnny Sykes was reportedly based on Hearst correspondent John W.

Roberts, who followed Villa around Mexico and reported on his exploits. Hawks offered the role to Broadway actor and former Warner contract player Lee Tracy, now signed to a contract with MGM. Tracy initially turned down the role, but eventually changed his mind and accepted it in October. By early November, he was shooting scenes on location before Hawks' cameras. A note on the actor who figures so prominently in the many controversies about *Viva Villa!:* The talented Tracy liked the bottle; in fact, he liked *several* bottles. Unlike frequent imbibers and womanizers Hawks and Hecht, Tracy's drinking caused the actor to lose control more than once, with assaults and barroom brawls causing him to be frequently late to the set; on some days, he didn't show up at all. Warners lost no time in getting rid of him, despite the fact that Tracy's fast-talking newsman persona was ideally suited to the studio's own smarmy and smart-alecky pre–Code material. For MGM, Tracy excelled in classics like *Dinner at Eight,* where the actor more than held his own in his scenes with performers like John Barrymore. Perhaps seeing a man after his own wild heart (as well as Tracy being a perfect fit for Hecht's usual fast-talking, Depression-era newsman), Hawks hired him as Johnny Sykes.

Then an incident took place that blew the filming of *Viva Villa!* right out of the water. It isn't known whether Tracy had gone on a drunken spree in some Mexico City cantina the night of November 18, but the next morning it was quite possible that the actor was feeling no pain. Possibly he was sleeping it off in his hotel room when a parade of Mexican soldiers marched under the second-floor window of his hotel. Other reports say that the soldiers were merely cadets at the local academy and that the parade was to celebrate the Revolution, an irony if there ever was one. Tracy appeared on his balcony overlooking the parade; some say he was naked, some claim he was fully (if slovenly) clothed. Reportedly, a cadet, seeing the supposedly naked actor, made an insulting remark, and Tracy responded with some four-letter words which were duly understood by everyone on the street. In yet another version of the incident, the naked Tracy (or a fully-if-slovenly-clothed Tracy) merely urinated on the passing soldiers (or cadets). Whether the alleged pissing was provoked or not provoked by any remark from a soldier (or cadet) is uncertain. What was certain was that *something* outrageous had occurred and that *someone* was insulted.

Hawks, an inveterate liar, claimed that he had finished shooting in Mexico by that time and had left for Los Angeles, alleging that he was besieged by reporters about the incident he claimed he didn't know anything about. Not stopping there, the helmsman claimed that Tracy "peed on the Chapultepic Cadets during the Independence Day parade in Mexico and got put in the can." He also claimed that he had previously put Tracy in the hands of some Mexican major to keep him out of trouble, but that he got drunk anyway.

However, the film's cinematographer, Charles G. Clarke, disputes this story. He was on the street outside the hotel when Tracy appeared, and later said that a Mexican on the street made an obscene gesture at the actor who, being Lee Tracy, responded in kind. The next day, the Mexican newspapers reported that Tracy had insulted the Mexican people, the Mexican flag, and while he was at it, Mexico itself.

A memo sent to the State Department by the American ambassador to Mexico, Josephus Daniels, seems to back Clarke's version of the incident:

> Tracy appeared on a balcony of the Hotel Regis, unclad and using very profane and insulting language at the moment when the military cadets marching in the parade of November 19th were passing in front of the hotel. He was immediately arrested and ... was released at 1:00

o'clock in the morning of November 20th and left the capital by plane at 6:00 a.m. that day. His arrival in El Paso, Texas, was reported in press dispatches from there the following day, November 21st.[40]

As noted by Hawks' biographer Todd McCarthy, nowhere in Daniels' report to the State Department does he mention that the actor urinated on anyone. Nor is it mentioned in a more detailed report by the embassy's third secretary John Aguirre. Tracy himself had his own take on the incident, telling reporters in L.A. shortly after his arrival:

> After some strenuous weeks making *Viva Villa!,* I was just relaxing—feeling high. I had my pajamas and a bathrobe on. I was in my own hotel room—not on a balcony. Somebody yelled—I yelled back in the customary Tracy manner. There didn't seem to be anything vulgar nor offensive.
> Somebody shouted back at us (three unspecified members of the *Viva Villa!* company who were allegedly cheering the parade). Well, you know how those things are. We shouted back at 'em—"Go to —, ha hah!"—or something like that. Anyway, it was all a big joke with us.[41]

However, Louis B. Mayer wasn't laughing. In Tracy's version, the actor implies that he had been drinking ("just relaxing—feeling high"), and fought the interpretation of his being naked by claiming that he had been clad in pajamas and a bathrobe. No actual insults were being thrown about, just some good-natured heckling with the crowd. Mayer and Thalberg weren't buying it.

A much wilder actor than Tracy, Wallace Beery, reportedly offered to apologize to the Mexican government over the incident. Again, Beery would never have done such a thing on his own and the star's offer was probably insisted upon by Mayer.

Nevertheless, the studio was well aware that xenophobic Mexico could rear its ugly head at the drop of a hat—and it did. Newspapers were already complaining about the "gringos'" filming of Villa's life. The company basically returned to Hollywood, leaving only the second unit people behind to get background footage, but the country's newspapers insisted that the government expel the second unit as well. An item in the November 20 *Daily Variety* reported that two Mexican newspapers (including the *not* aptly named *El Imparcal*) were campaigning for the confiscation of *all* footage shot in Mexico and the cancellation of the company's permit to shoot there. They also claimed that the studio was guilty of bribery, as well as "malnutrition of (the Mexican) extras and degradation of Mexican characters,"[42] a charge these journalists failed to make *before* Tracy allegedly emptied his bladder. They also complained about the casting of the blustering Beery as Villa (a good point there) and the way Mexican history was being presented by Hollywood filmmakers—an interesting charge when one sees the Mexican film industry's own distortions on Villa when they endeavored to film the life of the revolutionary icon.

On the home front, Hawks claimed that Mayer insisted that the director tell the press that Tracy was "impossible to handle" and that was why he was fired. Hawks (the inveterate liar) claimed that he refused and actually took Mayer by the lapels of his expensive suit coat and pushed him up against the wall (something Hawks also ridiculously claimed he did with Humphrey Bogart on the set of *To Have and Have Not*). In reality, Mayer was no pushover; a former ironworker, the studio chief reportedly never shrank from a fight, and would have given Hawks a good battle if sufficiently provoked. Also, an altercation with the most powerful man in Hollywood would have resulted in Hawks' permanent blackballing from the film industry—which apparently didn't happen. Hawks would claim that his refusal to go along with Tracy's firing from the film (the actor was also kicked out of MGM altogether) was the reason he (Hawks) quit the production. However, a more realistic explanation comes from veteran MGM screenwriter John Lee Mahin, who says that Mayer fired Hawks because of his impossibly slow shooting pace. The film would now go through *many* personnel changes. Hawks was out, and Jack Conway was hired to replace him.

When a plane containing twenty thousand feet of negatives (most of Hawks' footage) flew from Mexico to El Paso, it crashed and burned, effectively destroying all the footage. No one knows exactly what caused the plane to go down, but the crash was highly suspicious. Hawks would later say that much of the released film was his, and wildly claimed that the studio (whose president he claimed to have physically assaulted) begged him to come back and finish filming. He also claimed that his replacement Conway would constantly call him up and ask him what to do. Of course, these dubious statements were made by Hawks long after Conway's death in 1952.

According to the February 22, 1934, issue of *Daily Variety*, MGM sent studio executive Joseph M. Schenk on a so-called "secret mission" to Mexico City to screen the film before President Abelardo Rodriguez (and for certain, his puppeteer, *El Jefe Máximo*) to get their approval, in the wake of the Tracy controversy, for the footage that had already been shot, presumably by Conway. In reply, the government insisted that when Villa triumphantly enters Mexico City, that he should be surrounded by more cheering soldiers, and promised to provide actual federals for background extras for the reshoot. This explains the previously quoted memo advising that second unit man Richard Rosson have more soldiers around Villa when he enters the city.

However, thanks to the Mexican government's heavy (and in many ways, heavy-*handed*) influence over the production, still another theory has arisen over that mysterious plane crash. Mayer and Schenck were forced to promise Calles that the film would be reshot with a new actor playing reporter Johnny Sykes. Though it was also obvious that Hawks' slow pace of shooting in Mexico doomed his remaining with the company, his portrayal of Villa might have also rubbed the government the wrong way. It might not be too far-reaching a theory to venture that, in order to keep the production company in *El Jefe Máximo's* good graces, a collusion was made between MGM and the Calles Combine whereby the airplane carrying the film's footage (footage featuring the now-tainted Tracy) the short flight between Mexico and El Paso might have been *compelled to* crash. Or did the alleged crash actually happen in the first place? Either way, the footage was reportedly destroyed. If indeed there *was* a plane crash, no one will know for sure.

There would be even more changes in the *Viva Villa!* company besides Tracy (replaced by Stuart Erwin) and Hawks (replaced by Jack Conway). Fay Wray's role of Teresa had reportedly been offered to Mexico's own Hollywood transplant, Dolores del Río. But the future icon of Mexico's *Época Dorada* was not interested, claiming, much as the Mexican press would, that the film would be damaging to Mexico. This apparently hadn't stopped her from playing a stereotypical hot-tempered spitfire in *Girl of the Rio* in 1932. Dark-haired B actress Mona Maris had originally played *La Doña* Teresa, though it's hard to gauge her performance since her footage was supposedly destroyed in that alleged plane crash. Enter the object of Kong's desire, the redoubtable Ms. Wray, a good actress, but no *señorita*. In fact, with the possible exception of Wallace Beery and Joseph Schildkraut, everyone in Hawks' original cast was replaced. Prominent among them was Donald Cook who replaced actor Donald Reed as Felipe, and Leo Carrillo (the only Latino in the cast), who replaced Irving Pichel as Sierra. Not until the eccentric Woody Allen replaced the entire cast of his pretentious soap opera *September* after he had already shot a first version, would a major production undergo such a cast change.

Selznick not only ordered Hecht to do another rewrite in February 1934, but he had studio screenwriters James K. McGuinness and Howard Emmett Rogers do versions of the script as well. And when Conway came down with the flu in December 1933, the hard-drinking director was replaced for one week by the even more hard-drinking William A. Wellman. Consequently, the usually obnoxious Beery demanded (and reportedly got) a new salary and a raise in pay for shooting the whole film over again. Selznick was forced by the film's various calamities to raise the budget to $1,017,400—a pittance for Hollywood today, a fortune back in 1934.

"HE HELD A NATION IN HIS POWER!" cried a tagline. "And he would have given it all for a kiss ... from the one woman he couldn't conquer!"[43] Of course, one can ask, which actress playing this particular role is the tagline talking about, and from which version of the released film?

In his review of April 11, 1934, Mordaunt Hall wrote:

> Riding high and wide, if not handsome, Pancho Villa, in the form of Wallace Beery, spills blood as bandit and patriot, taking an occasional day off for laughter and love.... The film is a mixture of sentiment, humor and melodrama, the major incidents having been suggested, but only suggested, by the Pinchon-Stade biography.
>
> It is for the most part a fast, furious and compelling tale, but there are a few episodes which might very well have been excluded. It is presumed that [MGM] had insufficient confidence in Villa as he was as big a drawing card at the box office and therefore they included examples of brutality that are by no means helpful to the production.[44]

After discussing the cut scene where Teresa is shot, Hall praised Leo Carrillo:

> Although there is no denying the effectiveness of Mr. Beery's portrayal, it is a pity that Leo Carrillo, who plays Sierra, Villa's chief lieutenant, is kept too much in the background; for whenever this smooth actor has an opportunity, he makes the most of it. If anything, this Sierra is more bloodthirsty than Villa, his fingers always itching to pull the triggers of his pistols. Yet with all the hearts he stops beating, Sierra wins a certain sympathy, sometimes even more than his slouching, ignorant but courageous and loyal chief.

It's obvious that Hall wasn't aware of the existence of Rodolfo Fierro, Villa's psychopathic right-hand man, on whom the Sierra was based. However, Hall is wrong in this respect: Carrillo does *not* win "a certain sympathy" in his playing of that lunatic.

Viva Villa! grossed $1,109,000 in the U.S. and $1,875,000 worldwide, barely enough to break even. It was nominated for Oscars, with the (we assume) harried John Waters winning for Best Assistant Director.

In a December 3, 1933, review of the unedited version, the unknown writer from *Variety* calls *Viva Villa!* "a corking western," adding:

> But Beery's characterization ... lets Pancho down too much. His Villa is a hybrid dialectician, neither Mex nor gringo, with a vacillating accent that suffers alongside of Leo Carrillo's charming dialect or the contra-renegade version as done by Joseph Schildkraut as Pascal. Both impart an unction and a style to their cruelties that makes Beery's boorish Villa show up too sadly.[45]

"Corking western" though it may have been, *Viva Villa!* remains a controversial movie to this day; a film hated by most Mexicans as a *gringo* distortion of their hero's life. And yet these same persistent detractors refuse to point fingers at their own countrymen in the government who basically called the shots to MGM on just how Villa was to be portrayed.

Like a restless ghost, Pancho Villa would return again and again to film, with America rejecting the darker side of Beery's portrayal as demanded by *El Jefe Máximo* and instead concentrating on his so-called "Mexican Robin Hood" persona. Of course, in Mexico, the depiction of Villa would be far more complicated; and though he would be more realistically portrayed as *sometimes* brutal, Mexican filmmakers would always find a *good reason* for his brutality. Ultimately, however, they would give us portrayals of the revolutionary icon as one-sided as those of the *yanquis* up north. To directors like Ismael Rodriguez, who would write and direct his own affectionate Pancho Villa trilogy 25 years after the Beery film, Villa would *never* be the abuser of women, bigot or hot-tempered murderer he had shown himself to be in real life.

Just three years after Wallace Beery first put on his sombrero before MGM's cameras, a film shot in Mexico by a major filmmaker, Fernando de Fuentes, presented a fascinating portrait of the *Centaur del Norte* that not only rejected Hollywood stereotypes, but the equally deceptive propaganda of his own countrymen...

On New Year's Eve of 1936, Mexican audiences saw the release of *Let's Go with Pancho Villa!* As directed by Fernando de Fuentes, the film played no games with its audience. Unlike previous (and especially *future*) Mexican productions dealing with Villa, this one painted a dark portrait of the Revolution as seen through the experiences of six naïve men who thought that glory could be attained without losing anything else.

The director, who also co-wrote the screenplay and adapted it from a novel by Rafael F. Muñoz, puts forward the ambivalence of the film's theme in its opening titles:

> This film is an homage to the loyalty and courage Francisco Villa infused in the warriors who followed him. The blame for the cruelty that occurred cannot be put on any group of people, for, remember this was an age which bathed in blood not only the hills of Mexico, but also a field called Flanders and the peaceful valleys of France.

It is 1914. In the little village of San Pablo, *someone* has been assassinating federal soldiers—fourteen so far. A vicious captain visits the home of Miguel Ángel del Toro (Ramón Vallorino) and, accusing the young man of selling his carbine to his friend Rodrigo (so he could fight for the rebels), the officer whips him with his riding prop. At the home of Don Tiburcio Maya (Antonio R. Frausto), the middle-aged husband and father is teaching his little son to shoot so he can fight for the Revolution. Assembling in the house with Tiburcio are the corpulent Melitón (Manuel Tamés), the carbine-carrying Rodrigo (Carlos López), Máximo (Raúl de Anda) and Martin (Rafael F. Muñoz, the author of the novel on which the film is based). The topic of conversation is the whipping of Miguel and his escape from the evil captain. Tiburcio insists that they all join the Revolution with the title phrase: "Let's go with Pancho Villa!" Tiburcio's wife looks on in worry, sensing that fighting for the Revolution will not change a thing; instead, it will only bring more tragedy. Soon Miguel appears and the die is literally cast as they will all join Pancho Villa.

Riding up to a train captured by *Villistas,* they are just in time to see the great man himself (played by Domingo Soler) flinging morsels of corn at hungry peons who adore the very ground the guerrilla chief walks. After telling the crowd to shut up, their hero makes a brief speech extolling his own virtues and, ironically, ends up sounding like some politician seeking election: "Look what Pancho Villa fights for. So you can all eat! Now I give you corn. When we have won, I give you land! Everyone will have a ranch. Nobody will be working as a peon."

The promise of every peon owning a ranch, a dubious proposal at best, ironically sounds like a revolutionary's version of an American politician's traditional promise of a chicken in every pot and two cars in every garage. In this scene, we clearly see the sincere love the peons have for the man they see as their liberator. However, there is something about *this* Villa that is different than previous and future incarnations of the rebel icon.

Soon, the *Liones de San Pablo* find themselves plunged into battle. Victorious against a federal garrison holed up in a village, the rebels pat themselves on the back for a job well done. When they present the gun and holster of a dead soldier to Villa, he magnanimously returns it, claiming (falsely) that he doesn't like taking loot. He *does,* however, show them that his own holster is "rigged" so that he can fire on an enemy without having to clear leather.

That night by the campfires, the Lions talk about their lives. Miguel optimistically maintains that "at this pace, we'll be home in six months." Tiburcio is more realistic, saying that "It's been five months and we see no end to this." In fact, he insists, "the fight is getting worse. Look at our fallen comrades." The discussion turns to mortality, and how all of them wish to die. Máximo wants to die fighting, claiming that nothing has been accomplished; that is, the Lions not proving their heroism in battle. "To die like a man, so everyone sings tribute to our courage!" cries Melitón, who is seen by the others as the *least* brave of all of them.

Soon they're on to the next battle. Fire from a federal machine-gun nest is devastating the *Villistas*. Cynically, not wanting to lose any more of *his* men, Villa orders the Lions to grab the machine-gun: "Let's see if you're lions and not pussycats!" The dare is taken up and Máximo lassos the machine-gun and returns, presenting it to Villa, but at the price of his own life, as he collapses over the captured weapon. Thanks to his sacrifice, Villa and his men move forward, though, it seems that this victory hasn't come cheap, as de Fuentes' camera pans from Máximo's body folded over the captured machine-gun and moves up the draw where we see the corpses of dead *Villistas* macabrely strewn about. That night, as the *Villistas* attack a fort, Martin crawls out to the fort's edge and lobs explosives at the federal breastworks, blowing open a pathway for the *Villistas;* however, he is shot dead during the attack, crying out "Long live Villa!" and collapsing on a Maguey plant. Thanks to Martin's sacrifice, Villa predicts a march on Torreón. Again, as with the death of the previous Lion, de Fuentes doesn't end the sequence on the *Villistas* and their cheers of victory, but on the corpse of the man who died for them.

Villa orders the Lions to present themselves to a federal general with a white flag as a delaying action. Not believing them, the officer locks up Tiburcio, Rodrigo and Melitón. In the cell, Tiburcio philosophically explains that the soldiers don't want to kill them, it's their *generals* who do; this is an unconsciously ironic statement since Villa, the man they're fighting for, is called "general" throughout the film. Officers take the three outside to hang them. When *Villistas* show up to rescue them, Rodrigo becomes a casualty of friendly fire.

Afterwards, Villa magnanimously promotes the surviving Lions to majors, puts them in his elite corps, the Dorados, and even presents them with military clusters for medals. Then he sends them off with a smile. After they leave, an officer tells Villa that General Urbina (the real-life Tomás Urbina) has insisted on the executions of captured musicians.

The following dialogue may seem like a light distraction, but it is pertinent to the film, especially in what it reveals about the supposedly benevolent Pancho Villa:

VILLA: Musicians? No, have them join us.
OFFICER: But every brigade already has a band.
VILLA: Is that so? Then go ahead and execute them.

That night in town, thirteen *Villistas,* including the remaining *Liones,* sit at the table of a cantina, a sign of sure bad luck. To emphasize this, several of them, prodded by the brutal Fierro (Alfonso Sánchez Telio), decide to play a grisly game, all to test their bravery. At midnight one of them will toss a loaded gun in the air and when it lands, it means one of them will die. Though he is against this nonsense, Tiburcio not only plays the game, but he is chosen to toss the gun. At midnight, he tosses the gun, the lights go off, and when they're turned back on, we see that the fat Melitón has been gut-shot. Writhing in pain, the formerly funny comic relief character demonstrates that he's no coward, pulls his own gun and shoots himself in the head.

Soon the call goes out to all the guerrillas to assemble for their victorious march to Zacatecas, a great Villa triumph before his march into Mexico City. However, Miguel is not only sick at heart over Melitón's wasteful death, but apparently sick in general. When told of the outbreak of smallpox and that Miguel has been infected as well, Villa callously orders that the sick be kicked off the train. When Fierro confronts Tiburcio and tells him that Miguel will have to be burned alive, the last Lion erupts: "Is this the payment of a revolutionary soldier? Is this an army of men or of dogs?"

Afterwards, Fierro orders his men to "burn down the car," meaning Tiburcio as well, if he and Miguel aren't out of there in five minutes. The veteran Lion trumps them and, instead of burning his young friend alive, shoots him and then burns his body. When Villa arrives, surrounded by his officers, he fearfully backs away from his last Lion. Coldly, he orders Tiburcio, one of his most loyal flag-wavers, to stay behind and then turns to go off with his lieutenants. The scene is a striking one, with Villa depicted as a cold-blooded, expedient bureaucrat surrounded by his hand-picked lackeys as his most loyal man cynically salutes his retreating back. "It's over," Tiburcio says, then he carries his rifle and gear back down the railroad tracks, we assume, towards his home and family. This is how the film ends in its released version. However, de Fuentes had more controversial aces up his sleeve *vis-à-vis* the ending.

Neatly sliced off the film was its *real* ending, a shocker in its time and still powerful today. This ending was found in a print that was discovered in 1973 in the Filmoteca at the Autonomous National University of Mexico, with audiences not seeing the sequence until it was inserted into the DVD release of the film in 2005. It is still not clear whether the sequence was removed by de Fuentes due to audience anger or by government censors.

Now back with his wife, son and daughter, Tiburcio has forgotten his bitterness against Villa and again sees his hero as a flawless god, something he again tries to impart to his weary loved ones (his wife refers to Villa as "just a bandit"). The now-fanatical Tiburcio orders his son to be quiet when he refers to his hero as "a bad guy" and insists that when, not if, but *when* Villa rides his way, that when he joins up with him, "it'll be forever."

Sure enough, Villa, Fierro and other *Villistas,* now reduced to a small band through constant defeats, ride up to Tiburcio's property. The meeting between them is odd, with Villa quickly forgetting that he kicked Tiburcio out and claiming that his Lion abandoned *him* when he needed him the most. Now claiming that he needs men for an important battle, Villa offers Tiburcio another chance to fight with him, but it is quickly explained that he can't go because of his wife and daughter. After riding up to the house, Villa meets the wife and nine-year-old girl and eats their food, claiming that they have nothing to fear from him. He says grace (while picking his teeth) and insists that he still needs Tiburcio, though he wouldn't want his wife and daughter to be cold and hungry. After sending Tiburcio outside to fetch Fierro, we hear a scream and two gunshots; Villa emerges from the house alone, having just murdered Tiburcio's wife and daughter. "Now you have no one to stay for," Villa tells him, "let's go." When the angry husband raises a rifle to kill Villa, Fierro shoots him dead. Villa becomes angry with his right-hand man, the only time we see *this* incarnation of Villa actually show any emotion. He then invites the sobbing, newly orphaned little boy to join his band and, as we can tell by the boy's smile, it looks like he will be accompanying the murderer of his family on his raids—with the implication that he will end up just like the other "Lions" who gave their lives for the glory of fighting for Pancho Villa.

Throughout *Let's Go with Pancho Villa!*, the *Centaur del Norte* seems to go out of his way to send his "Lions" on suicide missions, never once bothering to send his more experienced veterans. Before they even become Dorados, the Lions are blatantly coaxed, cajoled, ridiculed and bullied into battle by their supposedly fearless leader (who we never *once* actually see go into battle). Gung ho for their hero, they are ultimately victimized by him; proving themselves brave, they die in various ways as they wished, but their heroism has been callously used by their leader to ensure a victory for *him* as much as the Revolution. When we see Villa, he is always with his men, a strutting Mexican Caesar surrounded by his hand-picked senators. Certainly, throughout the narrative, there are signs that the Revolution was quickly becoming an endless struggle going nowhere, with the heavy implication that the only one getting any "glory" was their leader, Pancho Villa. In the campfire scene, the Lions themselves remark that, instead of victory, the fighting has gotten worse and that there was "no end" to it. While yearning to show their "bravery," the Lions instead become cannon fodder. While they're dying for Villa, the great man gives them his thanks in his own way, affectionately patting the corpse of a Lion once in a while and ceremoniously awarding "medals" and elevated rank to the survivors. But there is not one iota of acknowledgment from Villa that his Lions have given up their homes and families to fight for him.

As we see in the controversial ending cut from the film, Villa's status as a great general has been severely reduced. We see him with just a handful of men and it appears that he *still* needs men to ride for him, even desperately wanting Tiburcio, the man he snubbed, to come back into the fold. Indeed, Tiburcio's hair is whiter and Villa seems wearier; according to Wikipedia, the ending takes place ten years later; however, it *couldn't* have been ten years after 1914, since Villa was assassinated in 1923. Though claiming that Tiburcio's absence from the Battle of Zacatecas (a great victory for Villa) didn't make a difference, he needs the old farmer for a new battle. We can only assume that the sliced ending is set at the time of Carranza's rise; now with Díaz and Huerta gone, the Revolution would be a personal pissing match between Villa and Carranza, with land reform and freedom being permanently put on the ideological back burner. Certainly, Villa's cold-bloodedness was never more obvious than his cynical murder of Tiburcio's wife and daughter so that the farmer and his son can ride with him. When Tiburcio dies while trying to kill his former idol, Villa callously invites his son to ride with him, correctly figuring that his sterling image as a revolutionary hero would trump any protests from the boy about murdering his family.

Certainly, the material came from a man who knew the world he was writing about. Rafael F. Muñoz was born on May 1, 1899, in Chihuahua, Pancho Villa's future stomping grounds. As a 16-year-old cub reporter, he became acquainted with Villa, joining his army and getting invaluable experience in the modus operandi of the *Centaur del Norte*. He would later write dozens of stories with the Revolution as a backdrop. However, after Villa's many defeats, Muñoz became a supporter of Obregón, a no-no in the egomaniacal universe of new president Venustiano Carranza. Hunted by Carranza's thugs, the young journalist fled the country and settled in Southern California. In 1920, when the arrogant Carranza was given the typical "reward" for being a former Revolutionary (assassination), Muñoz returned to Mexico. After he wrote for various newspapers and magazines, he was appointed by the grateful Obregón as the head of his press office. Finally becoming a novelist, Muñoz published his controversial take on what it was like to ride with Pancho Villa (*Let's Go with Pancho Villa!*) eight years after the guerrilla chief's assassination in 1923 (which Muñoz also covered for *El Universal Gráfico*, a major Mexican news outlet). The novel (of which de Fuentes reportedly just filmed the *first third*) was published in Spain in 1931. Muñoz would remain a high official in the government's specially sanctioned press corps until his death in 1972.

Muñoz was a close observer of both Pancho Villa and his men, and it's quite possible that he didn't always like the excesses of the *Villistas* with whom he was acquainted. As a young man growing up during the Revolution, seeing it all unfold with a cold, journalistic eye, Muñoz saw not only the Dream, but he was front and center for the disillusioning End of the Dream as well. After he returned from exile, Villa's mortal enemy Obregón was now the president and Villa was put out to pasture. Through it all, Muñoz became a supporter of Obregón, with *El Presidente's* own prejudices against the Centaur of the North possibly rubbing off on the now powerful journalist. Certainly, we see the title of both Muñoz's novel and de Fuentes' film as darkly ironic, since both demonstrate good reasons *not* to go with Pancho Villa!

Though de Fuentes had been called "the Mexican John Ford" (obviously by *Americanos*), the film failed to attract an audience. Historian Ilene O'Malley wrote that it "did not give the public the Villa that had proven so popular in the literary versions of Muñoz's story."[46] In fact, the film goes against the popular image of Villa as Hero and also, as Zuzana M. Pick writes in *Constructing the Image of the Mexican Revolution*, "government efforts in the 1930s to recuperate Villa as an embodiment of macho ideals of the Revolution."[47]

In an interview in the February 13, 1936, issue of *Ilustrado*, Domingo Soler said: "In regards to the part I play, it is artistically the most risky because anybody who interprets on the screen or the stage such a renowned figure as Pancho Villa has to please those who imagine him in one way or another.... And not many men are imagined so diversely as Pancho Villa!"[48] Echoing this observation about the Mexican public's veneration of Villa, O'Malley observed: "They were enamored of Villa, the daring Robin Hood, the satyr and the monster, the unpredictable deviant, the grimy *guerrillero* and outlaw with an uncanny power over men."[49]

Instead, under de Fuentes' incisive direction, Soler gives an excellent performance, portraying Villa not as a daring hero, but as a cold-blooded, exploitative bureaucrat; or what Pick rightfully called "the most nuanced and authentic portrait of the revolutionary leader."[50]

In the end, the Lions die for nothing. Melitón is killed over a stupid macho "game"; Rodrigo is needlessly killed by Villa's own men; Miguel dies, not in glorious battle, but he succumbs to a disease and his idol orders that his body be burned while he's still alive; only Martin and Máximo die in battle, but their sacrifice is quickly forgotten. In the edited version, Tiburcio is thrown out by Villa and, it is inferred, leaves the Revolution as well; in the complete film, he and his loving family are cruelly murdered by the man he idolizes.

It is unknown whether western author Will Henry ever saw de Fuentes' film, but the whole plot structure of six young men (excepting, that is, Tiburcio) leaving their families and going off to war would be used in his cruelly cynical novel *Journey to Shiloh*. In this book, these youngsters go off towards the eastern theater of battle in the Civil War, dreaming of fighting for the Confederacy, with all the supposed glory they imagined would come with it. Instead, all the boys except one are killed off in various ways before they even get to the battlefield. It is possible that Henry used the Civil War as a powerful euphemism for American intervention overseas (the novel was written in 1960). Certainly its relevance increased during the Vietnam War, something which caused Universal to buy the rights to the novel in the mid–1960s (Universal's 1967 movie starred James Caan and Michael Sarrazin). As in de Fuentes' film, Henry's novel has the young men, all of whom romanticize heroism and are gung-ho to prove their courage, die needlessly.

In the 1960s, as almost a repudiation of Ismael Rodríguez's flattering film versions of Villa's life, as well as a new antiwar attitude fostered by America's then-current war in Vietnam, audiences and critics in Mexico found favor with *Let's Go with Pancho Villa*. Indeed, de Fuentes' film is powerful to this day. With excellent photography by a future genius of *Época Dorada,* Gabriel Figueroa, and acted by a wonderful cast (especially outstanding are Frausto and Soler), *Let's Go with Pancho Villa* was a firm rejection of the stereotypical *yanqui* interpretation of Villa *and* the pro–Revolution propaganda from Mexico's own government and press.

In the coming years, Hollywood returned to the subject of Revolutionary Mexico to make more films about that nation's heroes. One particular B film made three years after the MGM film and one year after de Fuentes' production again contained a depiction of Pancho Villa. However, unlike the Wallace Beery and Domingo Soler interpretations, *this* Pancho Villa was clearly on the side of the angels...

In 1937, a B cowboy movie outfit named Crescent Pictures released (on a double and perhaps triple-feature bill) a Tom Keene western called *Under Strange Flags*. A reliable cowboy star, formerly with Paramount (he starred in the film version of Zane Grey's *Drift Fence,* among others), Keene usually delivered the action goods while convincingly portraying the stalwart hero who defended the (a) ranch, (b) rancher's daughter, (c) rancher's land, and (d) rancher's cattle, heifers and horse stock from connivin' varmints.

Though a dependable and capable western actor, Keene never rose to the level of a Randolph Scott, another Paramount B western player who starred in several film versions of Zane Grey. Keene lacked Scott's versatility (he starred in more than westerns), presence, and Virginia accent which perfectly fit the genre. Born in Rochester, New York, Keene sounded too eastern to pretend to be from the west; yet he was able to survive in the genre, in both B movies and TV shows, because of his good looks and stalwart manner. Changing his name several times in his career (George Duryea, his birth name, Tom Keene, Tom Keen and finally Richard Powers) in hopes of getting better offers, the actor never broke out of the Bs or low-rank TV series guest shots, and his last film would be Ed Wood's *Plan 9 from Outer Space*.

However, in 1937, Keene appeared in *Under Strange Flags*, a B sagebrush flick virtually indistinguishable from the actor's other efforts for Crescent like *Old Louisiana*, which was written and directed by the same writing team that did *Under Strange Flags*, but co-starring an up-and-coming Rita Hayworth. The story of *Under Strange Flags* was written by future Republic producer-director John Auer and Mary Ireland, a little-known scenarist (and rare for a woman in a male-dominated genre) whose only other credit was the Keene-Hayworth effort from the same year. As directed by I.W. (Irwin) Willet, *Under Strange Flags* had its own interesting but simplistic B movie take on the Mexican Revolution, and in particular, one of its major figures, the redoubtable Pancho Villa. One wonders why the iconic name was not in the title to ensure more box office.

The plot is as simple as the film's depiction of Mexican politics. Stalwart miner and ranch foreman Tom Kenyon (Keene) and his friend Tequila (veteran sagebrush player Budd Buster) are transporting silver ore from Tom's La Paloma mine on the northern border of Mexico. They must protect the shipments from the forces of the villainous federal, General Barranca. In a quick scene with Barranca and his men, the general laughs and announces that Tom's silver will be split up for the benefit of himself and his obviously ruthless men. Meanwhile, back at the ranch, Tom's pretty boss is Dolores de Vargas (the tragic Luana Walters; convincing as the heroine, but not at all as a Latina). Dolores' brother is Denny (Paul Barrett, convincing as the heroine's brother, but *not* as a Latino). Unlike other characters in the film, Denny is loyal to General Barranca, and wants nothing better than to fight for the despotic federal and turn Dolores' silver over to him so that he can defeat the upstart Villa. He even dresses up in a federal uniform, an act which angers Tom and Dolores.

Denny is captured by Villa's men, jailed and slated for execution. Tom goes to Villa (Maurice Black) to get the boy out. However, the guerrilla chief is unaware of the duplicity of his senior officer General Morales (former silent actor Roy D'Arcy; a long way from the days of supporting Garbo and John Gilbert), who secretly works for Barranca. Morales quietly releases Denny and throws Tom into the cell in his place.

Villa believes Tom guilty and is ready to have the foreman executed. Hearing of Tom's predicament, his mom (former silent actress Jane Wolfe) pleads with Villa to spare her son. At first the guerrilla chief refuses; however, after she leaves, and much blustering and pacing about irritably, the revolutionary orders Morales to bring Kenyon to him. Reluctantly, the guerrilla finds himself liking the forthright *Americano*, and when the foreman promises on his word of honor to return, even for his execution, Villa is baffled by someone pledging "his word of honor." This is the Mexican Revolution, folks, where anyone's "word of honor" was considered a stalling tactic before the big double-cross. When Tom is reunited with his mom and Dolores, he finds out that Barranca has predictably betrayed Denny.

Keeping his word to Villa, Tom returns to his headquarters. Unfortunately, Villa and his right-hand man, Lopez (upcoming Latino supporting actor Chris Pin-Martin, who would portray Pancho to Cesar Romero's Cisco Kid for Fox's B series), are out riding with other Villistas. Morales orders Tom's execution, and the firing squad is about to pull the trigger when Villa rides up and halts the execution. Kenyon tells Villa of Morales' treachery and the guerrilla chief orders the general's execution instead (we hear the shots off-camera as Villa happily welcomes his new *Americano* friend back from the brink of death). Now with Villa and his men backing him, Tom rescues Denny and the wounded Tequilla and kills Barranca and his men. Happily Tom tells his new friend Villa just where the silver is, with the implication that there will be a hefty contribution to the revolutionary's war chest in his fight against the federals. Tom also tells the happy guerrilla chief that his mom thinks he's one of the greatest men ever.

The portrayal of Villa in this B is clearly along the lines of bedtime stories of Mexican revolutionaries that only *yanquis* ignorant of history tell their grandkids; it's akin to a politically correct version of Geronimo I've seen in children's bookstores where the Apache mass murderer is portrayed as a friend to white children and a lover of small animals and the environment. Maurice Black was a busy character actor who appeared in countless Bs, as well as a few As (like *Little Caesar*); the actor would be dead at age 47 by the end of the year. Though far less sloppy than Wallace Beery, and far more dignified (he actually has an office with a desk and a bell he uses to ring for his men), Black's version of Villa keeps the guerrilla chief's alleged claim to being a principled man, but also makes him ignorant in other ways. When confronted with someone's mom calling for him to spare the life of her son, he is at first adamant that the execution take place; then after she leaves, he blusters and paces about in frustrated anger, as if the *real* Villa had never been asked to spare a loved one's life. He is frankly confused by Tom's pledge to return to his execution "on his word of honor," honor being presumably the *last* thing anyone had in mind while fighting the Mexican Revolution.

At least, unlike Wallace Beery, Black has Villa's big moustache and is far less obnoxious than the MGM star. Still, the propaganda is plain for all to see; instead of indicting an actual Mexican head of state (like a Díaz or a Huerta), the film portrays a fictional general and his ruthless men as the bad guys, almost a microcosm of the cruel *federales* who oppressed Mexico for so long. Unfortunately, *Under Strange Flags* also depicts Pancho Villa as a fair man, one who thinks sensibly and comes to the right conclusions; that he needed the *yanqui* hero to help him understand the full meaning of "honor" is beside the point. *This* Pancho Villa has no frightening mood swings, only kills those who deserve it and, even more amazingly, has not *one* female to chase after in the entire film (the aging Mrs. Kenyon is the only woman he has a scene with—and a relationship with her was *out*). All the complications involved in the Revolution, and especially what it was *really* like to fight for the guerrilla chief that was in *Let's Go with Pancho Villa* are never addressed here. Of course, this is a *yanqui* B western released by Crescent Pictures, not a startlingly original work by Fernando de Fuentes.

Meanwhile, essentially washing its collective hands of the Mexican Revolution of the 1910s, or at least as long as the Breen Office was around, Hollywood decided to focus instead, not on a bandit-turned-revolutionary, but on Mexico's most heroic president...

II

Liberator, 1937–1939

The Politics and Machinations Behind the Filming of Juarez

The late 1930s were *not* good days for democracy.

As fascist and communist rule solidified its gains in both Europe and Asia, the North American hemisphere looked across its oceans with dread, not knowing if the disease of totalitarianism would be heading our way. In reality, these systems of oppression were already making themselves felt on the continent in the form of pro-isolationist and native fascist and communist movements in both the United States and Mexico. (Canada had them too, but the Canadians were also eternally loyal to the British Empire and France, which were directly in the path of Nazi aggression.)

With few exceptions, the Hollywood studios, backed by the isolationist Breen Office, avoided making waves by showing the evil of rising dictatorships across the globe. One studio was a glaring exception to this rule: Warner Brothers. The home of many leftist screenwriters, directors and performers, the fabled Burbank studio was not allowed to directly attack fascism, due to the Breen Office's dictates on "National Feelings" which barred the film industry from slamming sovereign nations, including, apparently, Nazi Germany, fascist Spain, Imperial Japan and the Soviet Union. As far as the latter nation was concerned, since Hollywood, particularly liberal Warner Brothers, had many Communist screenwriters, the Soviets were *never* going to be attacked. However, Party members or not, many of these left-wing artists should be applauded for at least attempting to show us the evils of fascism despite the pressure from the Breen Office and the Catholic Legion of Decency to block these portrayals.

Certainly by the time Warner Brothers decided to make a film on President Benito Juárez's fight against Mexico's French invaders of 1862, the world at large had changed considerably, and it should not be taken for granted how behind-the-scenes machinations and big power politics influenced the making of *Juarez*.

In 1937, fascist nations Germany, Italy and Japan signed an Anti-Comintern Pact (which Nazi Germany would break two years later by signing the Nazi-Soviet Pact with the U.S.S.R.). These fascist strongholds would put out feelers to Latin American countries whose own governments were brutal dictatorships. These south-of-the-border countries were heavily Catholic (though the Church, for the most part, seems to have had no problem with this kind of government), places where their religious doctrines held all forms of Marxism in contempt, something they had in common with European and Asian fascists. President Franklin D. Roosevelt and his advisors were well aware of this and, while turning a blind eye to this oppression in our own backyard, emphatically did *not* want Nazi doctrines penetrating our hemisphere.

Roosevelt's people put out feelers of their own to Latino nations south of the border; unfortunately, these initiatives were at first met with contempt, with various dictators seeing *yanqui* imperialist designs behind these overtures. Seeking to trade with Central and South American nations, Roosevelt supported a declaration of non-interference in Latin American affairs at the Inter-American Conference in Montevideo, Uruguay, in 1933. Three years later, he called for a conference (which he attended in Buenos Aires in December) calling for mutual cooperation between the United States and its Latin American neighbors which included a united defense against fascist penetration in the hemisphere. Though the president didn't get the agreement he wanted, at least the various delegates (more used to *yanqui* "gunboat diplomacy" than negotiations) praised his efforts and agreed to consult one another in case of any breach of their sovereignty by European fascists.

In 1938, Roosevelt made a stirring speech (in Canada, not a Latin American country) warning Nazi Germany that an attack on North America would find the continent united against them—a baseless assertion that was more wishful thinking on the part of the president than boots-on-the-ground reality. When he made another speech, this time at the Inter-American conference in Lima, Peru, later that year, he was roundly praised by the delegates, but once again, none of them wanted to sign a pact pledging mutual cooperation. Instead, they just repeated their old mantra to "consult" one another in the event of trouble. Despite this foot-dragging response, there was certainly an urgency among delegates of these various conferences concerning outside influence in their affairs which was not necessarily born of American interference. In the mid–1930s, a paramilitary fascist organization calling itself the Integralists tried to overthrow the Brazilian government; and though the group failed, it never took much to push the authoritarian governments of Latin America into embracing the fascist brand of oppression, especially if they felt it suited their needs (which was, again, to resist American influence in their affairs).

Paramount to Roosevelt's Good Neighbor Policy was Mexico, whose lucrative business dealings in oil hit a snag with the world's *yanquis* when liberal president Lázaro Cárdenas nationalized the oil industry in 1938. The move did little to please Britain, France *or* the United States, but then Cárdenas knew full well that *they* didn't elect him; the Mexican people did. Due to restrictions in profit for *yanqui* nations doing business with Mexico, the policy would boomerang and Mexico would find itself in an economic crisis by the end of the decade. This would pave the way for the election of the pro-business conservative Manuel Ávila Camacho as president on December 1, 1940.

In the midst of all this international *sturm* and *drang,* Nazi agents certainly took advantage of Mexico's xenophobia by emphasizing a kinship with America's neighbor to the south in its supposed rejection of foreign influences and its veneration of its ancient peoples (for the Nazis, it emphasized the sterling qualities of Germany's ancestors {or Aryan "*volk*"). It was even said that Himmler himself admired the Aztec warriors of Mexico's past. Something they also shared with Mexico was its sometimes tumultuous anti-immigration stance, a pernicious bigotry even shared with revolutionary liberators whose own governments followed the *Porfiriato,* with attacks on Jews, Asians and other minorities frequent during times of economic chaos; in other words, the Nazi playbook, Latino-style. Yet this so-called Mexican-German connection, like the so-called Mexican-German connection during World War I, may have been cordial at first, but in the long run Mexicans had no stomach for the totalitarian way. Despite former president Calles' admiration for fascist doctrines (an admiration that also fed *Época Dorada* filmmaker Emilio Fernández), the Mexican people themselves had had enough of strongmen leaders on the level of Díaz, Huerta, and the triumphant revolutionaries who tried to start their own cult-of-personality dictatorships (like Carranza, Obregón and Calles). In the long run, a bullet usually solved the problem of would-be dictators in Mexico when the voting booth didn't do the trick.

To Hollywood, its leaders wholeheartedly agreed with FDR's Good Neighbor Policy. Nazi and Soviet aggression had choked off the film industry's European markets. Now, thanks to the Good Neighbor Policy, the industry *had* to respect Latin American nations whose peoples the moguls had previously ridiculed in their films as lazy and stupid. Thanks to the need for the dollars from these nations, and at the insistence of high-level players in the Roosevelt administration, the Mayers and Warners of Hollywood would now find a need for racial tolerance—at least as far as giving us positive images of Latinos living *outside* the United States anyway.

Of course, not every film that was set in Latin American nations was liked, much less praised, by the very people who were allegedly being portrayed. The wartime south-of-the-border–set musicals from Twentieth Century–Fox gave us wonderful production values and talented performers, but the stereotypes, including Latinos speaking in pidgin English (and sometimes played by Anglo performers), remained as strong as ever. Portuguese singer, actress and comedienne Carmen Miranda was a good example of this harsh criticism from her South American countrymen, despite her immense talent and likability.

But Benito Juárez was another matter. He was a hero to all Mexicans (except perhaps those in the Catholic Church), so Warners had to go gently here; their depiction *had* to be reverential, FDR was counting on that. The story of this great man was certainly one of inspiration and triumph in a tormented land seeing little of either in its tumultuous history.

Benito Juárez (or Benito Pablo Juárez García) was a full-blooded Zapotec Indian born in the village of San Pablo Guelatao in Oaxaca on March 21, 1806. His parents, he said later, were "Indians of the primitive race of the country." Like his parents, he toiled in the corn fields and worked as a shepherd before walking, at the age of 12, to Oaxaca de Juárez to attend school. (There are stories of Abraham Lincoln, a man whom Juárez would be linked more than once, *also* hiking many miles to school when he was a boy.) At first, he only spoke Zapotec, but the young Indian learned Spanish quickly. In the city, his sister worked as a cook, and through her, Benito attained a position as a domestic servant for a friendly man named Antonio Maza. Impressed by the young Zapotec's constant desire to learn, a wealthy patron named Antonio Salanueva pulled strings to get Benito placed in a seminary. The Catholic Church's power in those days was absolute in post-independence Mexico; *all* establishments of learning were run by priests, and consequently, readin,' writin' and 'rithmatic would go hand-in-hand with learning church doctrine. Benito was well aware of this; a youth with little tolerance for what he considered tiresome religious dogma coupled with intolerance for other points of view, the young Zapotec essentially played the game, using the prestige of a religious education to forge ahead in Mexican society, fully aware that he would abandon these teachings when it suited him. In fact, Salanueva was extremely hurt when Benito ultimately left the seminary.

Juárez became a lawyer in 1834, and attained a judgeship seven years later. The ambitious young Zapotec was then elected governor of his home state of Oaxaca, serving from 1847 to 1852. The next year, his outspoken criticisms of then-dictator Antonio López de Santa Anna (the general who had massacred Texas defenders at the Alamo and Goliad) forced the liberal governor into exile in New Orleans. After Santa Anna's resignation in 1855, Juárez returned to Mexico and helped his liberal party draft a new constitution in a period known as *La Reforma*. These Reform laws were controversial in their day, curtailing the power of the Catholic Church, big landowners (*hacendados*) and a persistently growing military bureaucracy (a problem that would remain in Mexico for over a century and a half). However, Benito Juárez was no closet Marxist; he wanted Mexico to advance as both a capitalist economy and an enlightened democracy more along the lines of the United States, a nation he had always admired. Now a powerful legislator under president (and former general) Juan Álvarez, in 1855 Juárez successfully supported the *Ley Juárez* (Juárez Law) which officially declared all Mexican citizens equal before the law, a dictum which severely curtailed the power of the Catholic Church and the *hacendados*. Appointed to the Mexican Supreme Court of Justice by moderate president Ignacio Comonfort, Juárez helped push through the Constitution of 1857, another landmark document that established the rights of ordinary Mexicans and put the nails into the coffin of the Church oligarchy.

Predictably, the country's forces of reaction were not pleased. The Reform Wars of the late 1850s in Mexico (*Guerra de Reforma*) demonstrated to the whole world that the government of Mexico was, without a doubt, one of the most dysfunctional political bodies ever to reign anywhere on this earth at any time in the history of Man. President Comonfort tried to compromise with the right-wing bureaucrats, led by General Félix María Zuloagua. Unfortunately, as Francisco Madero, Jr. would tragically learn 57 years later, there would be no compromise with the *caudillo* culture of the Mexican government. The rebels took over from the weak Comonfort and Juárez and his allies were arrested, with Zuloagua taking over as president. However, surprising the governing junta, Comonfort suddenly freed all the prisoners who stood against the *caudillo,* including Juárez. Under the new Constitution, the president of the Supreme Court of Justice was next in line for succession to the office of *presidente;* and so, confident of their righteousness, the Liberals declared Juárez to be the new president. This oddball situation now gave Mexico *two* presidents, Zuloagua and Juárez, the latter losing little time in ordering the confiscation of church property in 1859. However, since Zuloagua had full control of the military and police apparatus, guess who eventually had to flee for his life? Yet Juárez had the support of many of the country's state governments, the governors swinging the support of *their* militias to help the *Juáristas*; Juárez even had the full support of President James Buchanan but the president couldn't convince Congress to send aid to the *Juáristas*.

Defeating the reactionaries, including his spirited defense of Veracruz earlier in the year and his retaking Mexico City on New Year's Day 1861, Benito Juárez would finally be elected president in March. However, *Guerra de Reforma* and the despotic rule of various crooked administrations had bankrupted the government. With debts owed to Britain, Spain and France, the frugal Juárez immediately cancelled repayments on all foreign loans until the country was back on its feet. Enraged over Juárez's edict, the three debtor nations sent a huge expeditionary force to Mexico and in record time took over the customs house in Veracruz in December of 1861. (Over 50 years later, the United States military would seize the customs house in Veracruz to stop Victoriano Huerta from receiving weapons from Imperial Germany.) However, Britain and Spain abandoned their plans and withdrew from Veracruz when they realized that the French, under Napoleon III, wanted to overthrow Juárez and, with the backing of the reactionary Mexicans who fought him during the Reform War, take over the government. Juárez was forced to flee (yet *again*). However, his inspiring leadership, even in hiding, was powerful. Soldiers loyal to him, such as those led by General Ignacio Zaragoza, defeated the mighty French army at Puebla on May 5, 1862 (*Cinco de Mayo*), delaying Napoleon's eventual takeover of the country later in the year and buying more time for the Union to defeat the Confederacy by the spring of 1865.

Now with American arms showing up on the Mexican border earmarked for *Juárista* guerrillas, the days of ruling Mexico for Emperor Maximilian and Empress Carlota were numbered. With Prussian armies threatening France, Napoleon was forced to abandon Mexico to the *Juáristas,* who were doing a good job attacking French forces, as well as Mexican Quislings, as they reestablished *Ley Juárez* all over the country. However, refusing to leave his loyal Mexican generals, Maximilian was arrested in 1867. Many around the world begged Juárez to spare the former emperor from the firing squad, but the liberal president stubbornly refused. Now with Maximilian dead and Empress Carlota (now in Europe) declared insane, most threats to Juárez's rule were gone. He served as president of Mexico five times. Two of those times, he was reelected after the French departure by his grateful people. Undoubtedly, the formerly poor Zapotec boy from Oaxaca elevated his country further than any past Mexican leader. By the time of his death on July 10, 1872, he was one of the world's greatest men, an idealist and reformer who broke his country away from the feudalism and despotism of previous governments and showed his people a better way to live than to accept the ignorance of the past. The fact that the despots of the *Porfiriato* would take control for decades after his death would not diminish his sizable legacy (much of this future dictatorship controlled by one of Juárez's former generals, Porfirio Díaz).

His words continue to echo down through history and are as relevant in the 21st century as they were in the mid–19th century: "Among individuals, as among nations, respect for the rights of others *is* peace."

Unfortunately, in the years after Juárez's death, very few people would take these words to heart...

In 1937, Warner Brothers purchased the rights to a little-known 1934 novel, *The Phantom Crown, the Story of Maximilian and Carlota of Mexico* by Bertita Harding; and indeed, it looked like the title of their project would be shortened to *The Phantom Crown*. When this didn't sound right (anything with "phantom" sounded like a horror film), the title was instead changed to *Maximilian and Carlota,* with the idea that Bette Davis would play Carlota. However, when the actress was going through another one of her many suspensions from the studio, the focus of the script was changed. Since it was virtually impossible to do a story on Maximilian without the strong presence of Carlota (and considering President Roosevelt's insistence on depicting Latin heroes onscreen for his Good Neighbor Policy), Hal B. Wallis ordered the scenarists to instead have their screenplay focus on the man who was their implacable enemy: Benito Juárez. Warners would now make their screenplay another vehicle for King of the Film Biographies, Paul Muni.

Studio attorney Roy Obringer apprised Wallis of the existence of yet *another* vehicle, a Broadway play which depicted the lives of Maximilian and Carlota. *Juarez and Maximilian* was written by Franz Werfel, author of the bestselling novel *The Song of Bernadette* and, later, the Broadway comedy *Me and the Colonel*. His original production of *Juarez and Maximilian* in the mid–1920s, directed by the great Max Reinhardt, was performed all over Europe, with cheering crowds and curtain calls greeting the play in top culture venues like Vienna and Berlin. Crossing the Atlantic and debuting at Manhattan's Hudson Guild Theater on October 11, 1926, the play barely lasted a month, despite the fact that it starred Broadway giant Alfred Lunt as Maximilian. The play's supporting cast was a potpourri of future film character actors and, in a couple cases, play producers, with some of these actors later forming the nucleus of Broadway's left-leaning Group Theater: Morris Carnovsky, Dudley Digges, Edward Van Sloan, future acting teacher Sanford Meisner, play producer-directors Cheryl Crawford and Harold Clurman; and, in the pivotal role of Porfirio Díaz, a young (and presumably thinner) Edward G. Robinson.

To understand the dynamics involved in this production, from the personalities who would become far more famous in the years ahead, to the politics underpinning the play, we must examine Werfel's text. It was staged on Broadway in the fall of 1926, just six years after the Mexican Revolution ended and while the Mexican government was under the tight-fisted control of Álvaro Obregón and *El Jefe Máximo,* Plutarco Elías Calles. At the time, Harold Clurman was just an actor with the Theater Guild, but he aspired to run his own company, an entity that performed plays far more radical and controversial than *Juarez and Maximilian;* and Cheryl Crawford was an actress–assistant director–stage manager, and even did the sound effects—and from all reports took her various jobs seriously and did them all well. (She even conducted a small orchestra backstage whenever the play called for background music.) Clurman would distinguish himself by his violently adversarial relations with the board of the Theater Guild, including Philip Moeller, the director of *Juarez and Maximilian.*

Certainly, *Juarez and Maximilian* is far less radical than any play to come out of the Group Theater of the Depression years, yet we can certainly see little hints of the subversive, particularly in its controversial portrayal of the Church, as personified by the character of Archbishop Labastida (Digges). Unlike the usual portrayal of priests and ministers in films and on stage as kindly and principled men, Werfel's version of Labastida shows us an ugly and selfish soul. In his first meeting with Maximilian, the archbishop heaps contempt on the new emperor's reforms:

> His majesty has its Indian problems among other problems, but the Indian problem is a question of schools. Where shall we find teachers? Not only a Catholic prince, even a heretic would have to answer "from the monastery, the lay clergy," since there are no seminaries outside the church. But his Catholic Majesty himself confirmed the Reform Law of the Archtraitor Juárez, confiscating church land, abolishing the monasteries, and beggaring the clergy. The starving priest stands apart, weeping. What help could he give?

The Archbishop also seems to have the demeanor of a scoundrel; at one point, Maximilian's friend from childhood, Herzfeld, calls the cleric just that. Later in the play, when it looks like the people are flocking to Juárez's side, Labastida reluctantly attempts to open negotiations with Porfirio Díaz to show some leniency to the Church. Their meeting, with both characters hiding their mutual contempt beneath acidic observations, is probably the best scene in the play out of its so-called "Thirteen Pictures" (scenes). With a future Hollywood star like Robinson portraying Díaz and talented character actor Digges, one can only imagine the power of this scene when it was played before New York audiences. When the archbishop claims that, as far as the fighting is concerned, "the Church is neutral," Díaz snidely asks whether this is the same bishop who "was the leader of the royalist agitation two years ago." Smugly calling the French intervention "Providence," Labastida also concedes that Maximilian was "as they say in the theater, badly caste (sic)."

However, the following exchange pulls few punches in showing the character of Juárez's enemies:

> LABASTIDA: (*With the patient forbearance of a good teacher.*) I repeat, dear sir, that I represent a foreign power which chooses its allies whenever it thinks best.
> DÍAZ: Yes, you feel very much deserted. When Maximilian made the incomprehensible mistake of confirming Juárez's Church Law, he confirmed Juárez's greatness. And of course, your income was cut down considerably.

This scene not only illustrates the perfidy of the 19th century Church in Mexico's woes by the self-righteous character of the archbishop, it emphasized the clergy's easy ability to betray those to whom it previously gave support (Labastida is all too willing to sell Maximilian down the river and negotiate with Díaz for some kind of special treatment for the Church). Unfortunately, Werfel's depiction of Porfirio Díaz as an idealistic hero revealed an incredible ignorance of Mexican history on the part of the Austrian playwright-novelist. Díaz's following speech is not only a rebuttal to Labastida, but a total fantasy on the part of the playwright concerning the future dictator's alleged heroism:

> Very well, Archbishop of Mexico. You offer Maximilian's person and cause. I have two answers to give you. First: We despise and reject your offer. We will never soil our triumph. I wouldn't conduct any war that was not a moral crusade. That is the only excuse on earth for violence. I am not fighting Maximilian, who is a martyr to his birth and your rascality. I am fighting the whole tribe of grafters and jingoists, slave-drivers and ghouls, who have raised his throne as a screen for their crimes. I'll wreck and uproot every last one of them. I'll have no mercy for them. And the second answer, Citizen Archbishop, Pelagio de Labastida, would be a pair of handcuffs.

Outside of the sometimes florid and overwrought dialogue spouted by Maximilian in his many, *many* moments of self-pity, the romance between the two monarchs is well-handled, but Carlota exits midway through the play's "thirteen pictures," allowing Maximilian to carry the ball towards its predictable climax. The empress was played by Clare Eames, a dependable actress who also happened to be on the Board of Directors of the Theater Guild.

Werfel's stage description of one of his characters, Dr. Samuel Basch, is certainly revealing:

> (*The EMPEROR feels slightly constrained with him, hiding it beneath a great friendliness. Respect for the man, pleasure in having a European about him fight with an unconscious inherited antisemitism* [sic].)

The play also has the loaded left-wing buzzwords and phrases of the later Group Theater. When Díaz meets with Maximilian, he indicts him for being "the tool of Napoleon and those captains of industry who gladly shed blood to float more stock." Besides repeated phrases referring to the oppressed as "red *Juáristas*," the play also uses the French abandonment of Mexico as a harbinger of the post–World War I overthrow of Europe's monarchists.

Towards the end of the play, as he faces death, Maximilian declaims to the sympathetic Dr. Basch: "The age of royalty is over. In the shipwreck of the privileged classes, poor little kings who are not kings must perish. The hour of the dictator has come. Juárez."

"Woe to the victorious masses," Basch dryly replies.

Was Werfel (and by extension, the future members of the Group Theater) comparing the heroic Juárez to some left-wing dictator? Certainly, the real-life career of Porfirio Díaz points in that direction rather than the liberator Juárez. Indeed, it is one of the play's ironies that its main spokesman for freedom should, in real life, become one of Mexico's greatest oppressors.

European audiences appreciated Werfel's rather naïve yet sympathetic depiction of a Habsburg. However, in the United States, which had helped end the reign of the Hapsburgs for all time during World War I, the show ran for just 48 performances on Broadway. Yet the very existence of the play might prove an impediment to Warners' desire to control the material lock, stock and barrel. Advising the studio that Werfel and his backers who had produced the decade-old show would cite copyright infringement once *Juarez* was released, Roy Obringer insisted that the studio buy the rights to the play as well.

However, there is a long, tortured history to even *this* aspect of *Juarez*'s production, a tale that reveals uncomfortable dealings between a Jewish-run studio making a film that euphemistically attacked fascism and a European fascist who sought to profit off the work of a Jewish playwright. Incisively contradicting producer Hal Wallis' self-serving autobiography *Starmaker*, film historian Bernard F. Dick writes in his excellent biography, *Hal Wallis: Producer to the Stars:*

> Although Wallis discusses some of [*Juarez's*] problems in *Starmaker*, he neglects to mention that the $6,000 the studio paid for the 1926 play *Juarez and Maximilian* (which Wallis calls *Maximilian and Carlotta*) required an additional $1,200 to the Nazi-controlled publisher, Paul Szolany Verlag, who owned the copyright. Since the Jewish Werfel ... would not give Warners the right if Szolany received any money, Wallis worked out an arrangement with Szolany, giving the publisher 20 percent of the amount Warners paid for the rights—in other words, $1,200.[1]

Apparently, the deal was worked out secretly. Though a self-hating Jew, Werfel was also a dedicated anti-fascist and would have fought this under-the-table arrangement had he known about it. (In 1936, despite initial enthusiasm from Irving Thalberg, MGM was forced to abandon their production of Werfel's *The 40 Days of Musa Dagh,* the novelist-playwright's searing indictment of the Armenian genocide, after protests by the Turkish and French governments.) Seeing no choice in the matter, Wallis authorized the sale, though this would by no means end the problem of dueling Maximilian and Carlota vehicles in the years ahead.

Paul Muni was nothing if not a thorough actor, insisting to the studio that he take a few weeks off to travel to Mexico in September 1938 to study everything about the heroic president. He ultimately took along not only his wife Bella, but producers Wallis and Henry Blanke, as well as director William Dieterle. Muni spoke with elderly people who had known or met Juárez; he prodded them with hundreds of questions about the man; what did he sound like?, did he laugh often?, was he quiet a lot?, etc. Muni was also invited to meet with President Lázaro Cárdenas, who seemed enthusiastic about the production and, unlike the bureaucrats of the *Jefe Máximo,* readily offered help to the studio in any way. (Cárdenas also invited the actor as a way of international fence-mending; his policy of nationalizing the oil industry still rankled American businessmen.) Jack Warner was no fool in this sense; he had no intention of repeating the mistakes of MGM or Upton Sinclair and constantly show-

Savior: Paul Muni as President Benito Juárez in a publicity shot for *Juarez*. The film tried to compare Emperor Maximilian and Napoleon III's occupation of Mexico to growing Nazi aggression in Europe.

ing new drafts of the script to the usual nationalists in the Mexican government, even one run by a tolerant, open-minded man like Cárdenas. He did not want his liberal writers, Aeneas Mackenzie, Wolfgang Reinhardt (son of the play's original European director) and future director John Huston, to have to submit their work to Mexican censorship boards, and have a virtual repeat of the *Viva Villa!* fiasco, where Hollywood filmmakers took the full blame for a buffoonish portrayal of Pancho Villa, and Calles and his cronies evaded responsibility. (Afterwards, they even had the nerve to slam the "gringos" for the one-sided portrayal of Villa that *they* insisted upon.) Warner also probably wanted to avoid any more Lee Tracy incidents. Thus, the entire filming of *Juarez* would be done, not Down Mexico Way, but in their Burbank studios and their Calabasas ranch (which substituted for Mexico City) over a period of eleven weeks.

However, original screenwriter Mackenzie would have his own take on the dynamic between Maximilian, Carlota and their implacable Zapotec foe, a depiction that unfortunately bordered on racist condensation. In memos from September 1937, Mackenzie wrote, "Indians do not look about them and Indians do not talk to each other as they go along the road to their destination."[2] Continuing with this scrambled logic, he claimed that Juárez

> had to contend with the dazzling figure of the Hapsburg emperor whose great golden beard suggested the reincarnation of the Fair God Quetzalcoatl. And besides Maximilian stood the beauteous Empress of the Shining Eyes, before which a hating, subject race had already bowed down in adoration. Against such glamorous figures, how could a poor, ape-like Indian hope to survive in the hearts of people which scorned his humble and downtrodden breed?[3]

Someone should have told the liberal screenwriter (whose later screenplays for *They Died with Their Boots On* and *Buffalo Bill* were emphatically *pro*–Indian) that Quetzalcoatl was not a Nordic god, but a Toltec Indian.

With work on the script beginning in 1937, the company gave itself plenty of time to develop the material (hence, Muni's working "vacation" in Mexico). Allegedly, Muni and the screenwriters were given 272 books and other materials to pore over to get under Juárez's skin, and get a thoroughly accurate picture of the French occupation and the supposedly benign rule of Emperor Maximilian and Empress Carlota. The budget was set at $1.75 million, the highest yet for a Warner film. But even the money allotted to the production (including huge sets and literally hundreds of painstakingly accurate period costumes), director William Dieterle never let the pageantry get in the way of the film's contemporary political slant, as he clearly stated in a memo to Wolfgang Reinhardt from February 15, 1938:

> The dialogue, as far as it is political and ideological, must consist of phrases from today's newspapers; every child must be able to recognize that Napoleon in his Mexican intervention, is none other than Mussolini plus Hitler in their Spanish adventure.[4]

It was interesting that the French intervention in Mexico was being compared to the Spanish Civil War, especially when you consider that Spain was not on another continent, but in the backyard of the fascist nations of Europe. Nevertheless, it was awfully hard *not* to see the French incursion as a euphemism for the road to World War II. Filming began in mid–November 1938. By then, the Nazis had already committed the pogrom known as *Kristallnacht,* a fact not lost on the company's liberal filmmakers, especially its Jewish leading man Muni. As filming progressed, Juárez and his people would now be seen as fighting not only against French imperialism of the 1860s, but fascist imperialism and the beginning of racial extermination of the 1930s. This is brought home to us by the supporting characters' barbed comments on the ethnicities of both Juárez and Maximilian's Native general Tomás Mejía; here, the filmmakers euphemistically compare Mexican bigotry against their Natives to Germany's racism against its Jews. Underlining this approach, Warners' coming attraction trailer of *Juarez* has the announcer proclaiming that "for then (1863) as now (1939), power-mad dictators were imposing their will upon helpless minorities!"

By the time filming began, Bette Davis was off suspension, with the tempestuous star actively seeking the role of Carlota, even though she knew it was not the focus of the film and it would be a reduction of her star status. As far as Muni was concerned, he wholeheartedly agreed to Davis' casting as Carlota.

Still, to portray Juárez, the actor insisted on accurate makeup; and his attempts to both look and act like the former president bordered on obsession. He practically instructed Warners makeup maven Perc Westmore to make him as unrecognizable as possible. Thanks to Muni's dedication and Westmore's artistry, the actor has an uncanny resemblance to what we've seen of the Mexican president through ancient portraits and drawings. However, the end result did not thrill Jack Warner, who made the barbed comment that he was paying Muni all this money and no one could recognize him. Underplaying to the max, Muni didn't see Juárez as a hero who went out of his way to achieve greatness, but as a simple man whose quiet wisdom, innate modesty and stubborn dedication to freedom molded him as the man who saved his nation. In this sense, Muni's Juárez dispenses wise platitudes throughout the film without the slightest change in facial expression. This was, of course, partly due to Westmore's thick makeup, but the downplayed persona was also Muni's adherence to historical accuracy and perhaps a nod to Juárez's Zapotec origins (the image of the Indian as *not* showing emotion, or being demonstrative).

One peculiarity about Werfel's *Juarez and Maximilian* is that Juárez, one of the char-

New York Revolutionaries: Broadway veterans John Garfield (left) as General Porfirio Díaz and Paul Muni as President Benito Juárez in *Juarez*. The film ignored Díaz's growing lust for power and, just like Franz Werfel's play *Juarez and Maximilian*, turned him into a spokesman for democracy.

acters in the title, does not appear *at all* in the play; it really focuses on the Austrian-Hungarian emperor and empress. However, if Warners was to compare Maximilian and Napoleon to worldwide fascism, the screenwriters *had* to show the fighter for freedom, meaning Juárez, as well. Muni not only insisted on Davis' casting as the Empress Carlota, but also the casting of his old friend from his Broadway days, John Garfield, now an emerging Warner star, as General Porfirio Díaz—and wanted *his* part expanded as well. This last request was not hard for Warners to do since Garfield had become a major star shortly after the release of *Four Daughters* in 1938. Díaz was originally written as a small part; now with Garfield in it, the role of the one man who would be considered the antithesis to Juárez's democratic principles shortly after the president's death, was expanded. This became another dilemma for the screenwriters: How were they to reconcile the general who had been a *Juárista* liberator with the tyrant who rose to power years later? Perhaps wisely, Mackenzie, Reinhardt and Huston avoided this question. There *are* certainly implications of Díaz's later attraction to despotism when he almost falls for Maximilian's line about a monarchy being better for the people than a democracy.

In 1863 France, Napoleon III (Claude Rains) is holding court in his enormous dining room with his wife Empress Eugenie (Gale Sondergard) and various sycophants. His pompous speech to his guests could easily be seen as an arrogant self-justification of the Nazis' declared intention to rule over everyone they deem inferior:

> I, Louis Napoleon, emperor of France, pledge our wealth and the might of our army, not in a spirit of selfish conquest, but in a crusade to restore to our race and the rest of the civilized world our ancient force and prestige! Let the world know that our conquest of Mexico is only the beginning of the fulfillment of our holy mission!

Cut from the post–1952 version of the film is the Prologue (Scenes 1–29) which shows the births of both Maximilian and Juárez; the former born of wealth and privilege, and the latter born in poverty. This was done to show the striking contrast between the two future leaders and opponents. Now, in the versions currently on VHS and DVD, the film begins with Napoleon's speech, the filmmakers losing no time in establishing the comparison between Emperor Napoleon's global ambitions and those of Europe's then-current dictators (note Napoleon's emphasis on race superiority).

Thanks to Rains' decidedly over-the-top performance in this opening scene, we see the filmmakers' sly wink at the international situation. Bedecked in a black wig and wearing a black moustache, sometimes rolling his eyes and pacing back and forth like a spoiled child when he learns that the Union has emerged victorious at Gettysburg (which will allow them to enforce the Monroe Doctrine once the South is defeated), Rains uses Napoleon's petulance as a familiar reminder of Hitlerian tantrums.

Meanwhile, in Mexico, a mostly illiterate populace is tricked into voting by plebiscite that they actually *want* Maximilian to rule over them. When a peasant spits defiance and runs away from a soldier to proclaim "Viva Juárez!" he is shot dead. This scene would be reenacted years later when an anti-fascist is shot dead by pursuing Vichy police at the beginning of *Casablanca*.

In the next scene we see a man at his desk, though we only see the back of his head, an introduction only worthy of truly great men on screen. (Warners would use this kind of scene to introduce Abraham Lincoln and the pro–Warner Brothers president FDR as well.) After General Porfirio Díaz (Garfield; not as camp as later critics would claim) reads the man's proclamation on Mexicans fighting foreign oppression, it is signed and at last we see President Benito Juárez (Muni). From this first shot of him in Westmore's makeup, we see in the first few seconds how Muni will play the role; there will be none of his trademark overplaying. Muni took the role very seriously, and despite his stone face and refusal to even raise his voice, it's obvious that the actor deeply respected the heroic man he was playing.

Emperor Maximilian (Brian Aherne) and Empress Carlota (a totally miscast Bette Davis) arrive and are welcomed by French troops and Mexican quislings, like French general Marechal Bazaine (Scotsman Donald Crisp, stretching it as a Frenchman), Colonel Miguel López (an outstanding Gilbert Roland) and Jose de Montares (British actor Montagu Love). Roland is the *only* Mexican actor in any significant role in the entire film.

As Erich Wolfgang Korngold's pageant music thunders on the soundtrack, we actually hear some notes that remind one of the German national anthem, though the arrival of the Austrian royals is hardly a Nuremberg rally. And if that isn't enough of a clue as to who these people should be compared to, a vulture oversees the welcome of the royals, and are informed by de Montares that there are vultures all over Mexico. (Get it, get it??) However, despite the comparisons with contemporary fascist dictators, the script also emphasizes the innocence of the two foreign monarchs, with Maximilian asking why there are no people on the street to welcome them (López explains that it's because of a "black plague"). In their coach, the two monarchs find a letter from Juárez demanding that they leave Mexico and return home. Though it was obviously left by the *Juárista* coachman, this mysterious letter routine where the sender issues a warning to a would-be oppressor puts Juárez on the level of Zorro, another mysterious figure revered by the people.

The machinations behind Maximilian and Carlota's arrival in Mexico were certainly more complicated. In 1859, Mexican monarchists, that is, those reactionaries who couldn't stand Juárez's reforms, approached the Hapsburgs (who had already ruled New Spain years before Mexican independence) about having a Hapsburg royal rule Mexico. Napoleon III might have also come up with this idea, or merely approved it after he heard of it; either way, there were long discussions in the Court of Hapsburg between the emissaries of the French dictator and Emperor Franz Joseph. The emperor knew that his own son would be next in line for the throne, effectively shutting out his younger brother, Ferdinand Maximilian, a fact that probably pleased him. Yet there were also those who probably would have approved of the rule of the more open-minded Maximilian rather than the cutthroat Franz Joseph, a little fact not lost on the Austrian ruler. What better way to kill two birds with one stone; that is, shipping his charismatic younger sibling off to a foreign land and giving him something to do that wouldn't interfere with the rule of Franz Joseph, yet *still* allow the Austrian emperor to curry favor with the power-hungry Frenchman who wanted only to rule the world?

Informed that a plebiscite was taken of Mexican voters that resulted in a high approval rating for Maximilian as their king, the young man swallowed this lie hook, line and sinker (he was only told of the lie shortly before he embarked on his voyage). Accepting this mission, Maximilian also forfeited whatever rights he had as an Austrian noble, another little victory for his jealous elder brother, the emperor. And so, accompanied by his loving wife, the equally charismatic Archduchess Charlotte of Belgium (who would henceforth become the Empress Carlota), he set sail for Mexico in the spring of 1864. On his way there, they received the blessings of Pope Pius IX and Queen Victoria, two little details that emphatically do *not* end up in the Warners film. Arriving at the port of Veracruz on May 21, 1864, the royal couple was also met by wildly applauding crowds of ordinary Mexicans. This is but another little detail that Warners' liberal screenwriters neglected to show us, having us think instead that all Mexicans purposely cold-shouldered the royals on their arrival.

Another discrepancy occurs in an early scene when Juárez is meeting with his top officials and Juárez's allegedly power-hungry vice-president Alejandro Uradi (played by the always villainous Joseph Calleia). Smiling wickedly, the veep takes note of the fair-skinned emperor's resemblance to Quetzalcoatl "the blonde god of the Aztec Indians," Mackenzie again ignoring the fact that Quetzacoatl was not blonde at all but a Toltec Indian. Throughout this exchange, Garfield stands out, as he almost always does in anything he attempts, by sheer force of personality. Despite the Bronx-accented Latino cadences, his Díaz, reflecting the actor's usual fiery and rebellious screen persona, literally wipes out everyone else in the room—with the exception of Muni.

Indeed, the star is so far into his role that, despite critics' later complaints about the stiffness of his features under "all that makeup," his is a deeply felt performance of great skill and personal integrity. The actor's restraint prompts the viewer to try to see the wheels working in the character's mind; his reactions are not necessarily in his face or body, but Muni does fascinating things with his eyes, letting them reflect how he feels without resorting to any facial exaggerations. While addressing his officers on how to approach a battle, or when defying Uradi's attempts to usurp him, his eyes reflect amusement while his voice drips cutting sarcasm without the usual smirk or mocking curl of the lip other actors would employ. When he faces Pepe after the boy takes a French bullet for tearing down the emperor's poster calling for the execution of guerrillas, one can almost see the coming tears behind the president's mask of solitude. The actor's subtlety, as he holds back both his rage and his compassion at the boy's death, causes *us* to be angry at the French as well. In many ways, Benito Juárez is one of Muni's finest performances.

Meanwhile, in the emperor's chambers, upon hearing of Republican attempts to oust the French, Maximilian declares that he "didn't come here to conquer, but to rule peacefully." However, when he insists on opening negotiations with the *Juáristas,* the suggestion is condemned by Bazaine, who declares that "the whip, the bullet and the bayonet" are the only language the guerrillas understand. Afterwards, we see a montage of battles showing the guerrillas suffering under Bazaine's iron fist. Forced to move once more, Juárez and his men go to another town where the president insists to a lackey that the portrait of Abraham Lincoln must come with them. Actually, despite the fact that the two great leaders never met, they reportedly *did* admire each other from afar. But Juárez emphatically did *not* take Lincoln's portrait everywhere he went.

Still, this "Lincoln connection" is emphasized not by the screenwriters, but due to the input of the man playing Juárez himself. "Try to get in the connection between Lincoln and Juárez," Muni reportedly told the screenwriters, "not only that he (Juárez) has a picture of him (Lincoln) in the room, but that they correspond with each other. Not that Juárez was an admirer from afar, but that they had actual contact."[5] Capping this "Lincoln Connection," whenever Muni's Juárez is outdoors, he always wears an all-too-familiar stovepipe hat.

According to Warner's pressbook for the film, Muni affirmed that Juárez was "much like Lincoln, a man born in abject poverty, absolutely self-educated, who rose by the brilliant powers of his own mind to save the nation who had born him. Juárez not only rekindled the great flame of democracy in Mexico, but he kept it alive during the time the powers of Europe established a dictator monarch, Maximilian, on its throne."[6]

One can't fault the actor's passion and commitment to his role, yet exaggerating the so-called Juárez-Lincoln connection into something it plainly wasn't, did service to neither of them. Still, in one scene on a mountain range with his followers, Juárez is told of Lincoln's assassination; quietly he walks away from his friends and, presumably facing north, solemnly removes his stovepipe hat in homage to his ideological American brother. Despite the misplaced attempts to make Juárez's connection to the sixteenth president stronger than it was, thanks to Muni's performance, it's a very moving scene.

Meanwhile, in the emperor's court, Maximilian appoints General Miguel Miramón (Warner contract player Henry O'Neill, usually cast as district attorneys and other Anglo authority figures) as his minister of war. Then the emperor turns to his Indian general Tomás Mejía (Native-American actor Billy Wilkerson) and appoints him to head the entire Imperial Mexican army, an announcement that gets a chilly reaction from the obviously racist members of the emperor's Mexican court. There is further rage still, when the forward-thinking monarch refuses to overturn Juárez's edict confiscating the land from 85 *hacendados* and returning it to the people.

Here the studio, despite its claim of authenticity, clearly omits a major part of Mexican history as they depict this tumultuous period. Anyone who has read of Benito Juárez knew full well that one of the president's major enemies was the Catholic Church. They held an

Extras on the March: Paul Muni (center, in top hat) leads hundreds of pro-democracy demonstrators in *Juarez*. Thanks to the liberal star, the script draws comparisons between Juárez and President Abraham Lincoln.

iron-fisted, dictatorial control over everything from education to newspapers, and made its influence felt in every aspect of Mexican life. It was they who fought tooth and nail to destroy Juárez's landmark Constitution of 1857 which granted ordinary Mexican citizens full and equal rights under the law (known as *Ley Juárez*). When the president confiscated church lands to redistribute among the peons (the church owned more lands than even the *hacendados*), he became their implacable enemy. When the French took control and imposed their approved monarch on the country, the Catholic Church backed this foreign intervention heart and soul, hoping that the new dictators would restore their power (the Pope himself blessed this blatant imperialism just before Maximilian took over Mexico). Despite all this historical evidence blatantly showing the Church's collusion with foreign oppressors, Warners couldn't point a finger in their direction. They knew that the Breen Office would literally shut the film down and the production would alienate the nation's Catholics if *Juarez* even *once* indicted the Church for much of Mexico's troubles. Therefore, the screenwriters had characters like Jose de Montares (played by Englishman Montagu Love) pointedly apprise Maximilian of the backing of "the conservative party, the party that put you on the throne," without any mention of wealthy landowning priests who controlled much of the country.

At court, Maximilian constantly refuses Bazaine's entreaties to sign a decree calling for the execution of guerrillas, even if they are caught with guns *before* they attack. Under Maximilian's benign rule, Porfirio Díaz is captured rather than killed. The emperor visits the imprisoned rebel general in a meeting that never happened. We first see Díaz munching on a Mexican corn cob. As the emperor enters, Dieterle's camera catches a shot, not of Porfirio Díaz, but actor John Garfield, whose screen persona usually spat defiance to those he's fighting against, as he does in this scene. Very little in this film compares with Garfield looking up from his food and gazing at his royal jailer with a mixture of aloofness and contempt.

However, even the fiery Garfield persona can't resist Maximilian's charisma and impressive charm as the ruler convincingly persuades the general that only a word stands between the rule of Juárez and his own, that word being "democracy." Yet when the newly released Díaz goes to Juárez (had Bazaine been in charge, he would have put a tail on him), the wise president refutes Maximilian's words. "When a monarch misrules, he changes the people; when a *presidente* misrules, the people change *him*." As Juárez is giving a little speech about democracy raising even the most oppressed people up to tolerance and human dignity, Dieterle and Muni make sure that Lincoln's picture is hung obtrusively in the background. The shot not only makes the connection between Juárez and Lincoln yet again, but it also conjures up images of the very people Lincoln helped to free, African-Americans whose descendants were still victims of segregation in 1939.

The scene elicited barely concealed sarcasm from Latino film historian Carl J. Mora, who wrote in his fascinating *Mexican Cinema: Reflections of a Society, 1896–1980*:

> Perhaps one of the most incongruous scenes in all film history (and there are many) is the sight of Díaz (Garfield) kneeling at Juárez's feet (Muni) and asking the deliberately Lincolnesque president to explain democracy to him. The movie never went on to reassure its viewers as to how well Juárez's definition of this elusive political art had been absorbed by his eager protégé.[7]

From the viewpoint of any Mexican familiar with the bloody and despotic rule of Porfirio Díaz, the scene is indeed ludicrous, and one can easily chastise the liberal filmmakers for ignoring history and whitewashing the future dictator. However, contrary to Mora's claim, Garfield's Díaz is *not* kneeling at Juárez's feet.

Maximilian and Carlota (who can't have any children) decide to adopt a boy named Augustín to inherit the throne. In reality, they adopted *two* boys, Augustín and Salvador Iturbide, grandsons of Mexico's first emperor in the 1820s, Augustín de Iturbide (ultimately, he was shot by firing squad on the orders of the *next* rebel government). In real life, it was rumored that their mother wasn't happy about the adoptions, and that her children were seized by the emperor's soldiers. In the film, right after Augustín's coronation as the prince and the family's gathering on the palace balcony, *Juáristas* blow up the nearby arsenal and fire shots within range of the little boy. This attack causes Maximilian to change course from his desire never to sign the execution decree. Now with the damning paper in his possession, Bazaine lets loose his men on the populace, executing suspected guerrillas at will. Dieterle's imagery is nothing if not obvious, as Maximilian pours hot wax on the document before affixing his royal stamp, the obviously red ink (even on black and white film stock) suggests a small pool of blood.

The American ambassador visits Napoleon and informs him that the United States, now having won the Civil War, will not tolerate French troops in Mexico and hints rather strongly that American soldiers will kick out the French by force. The emperor backs down. By letter, the French emperor orders a full withdrawal of all troops from Mexico. With their protective army now called back to France, Maximilian and Carlota seem to have no recourse but to abandon Mexico, something the Austrian emperor refuses to do (though his mind will change back and forth a couple times during this final third of the film). When Carlota sails to France and indicts Napoleon for double-crossing her husband, Bette Davis' penchant for overacting is on full display, down to the bulging eyeballs and the raised, shouting, hysterical voice. Of course, this is supposedly when Carlota goes insane, though it's highly doubtful she did it right in front of Napoleon and Empress Eugenie in such a theatrical manner. Instead, it was quite possible that, having endured the dictator's stubborn refusal to reconsider abandoning Maximilian, she probably went crazy sometime *after* her meeting. Still, Dieterle gives us a wonderful shot of Carlota fleeing from the emperor's study into a space of absolute darkness, a scary metaphor for the decades-long escape from reality the poor woman would suffer to the end of her days.

Refusing to leave his loyal Mexican generals to the vengeance of the *Juáristas*, Maximilian remains behind despite entreaties from the ruthless Bazaine, who now grudgingly respects the monarch for his courage. Finally captured by *Juáristas*, the principled ruler refuses to let his men go to their doom without him even after General López has made a deal for them to let him escape. With the now ex-emperor facing death, a priest sent to comfort Maximilian is comforted by him instead. Here, even the militant Díaz calls for Juárez to spare him, but to no avail. Given a chance to live, Miramón and Mejía instead opt to die with their ruler; and so, put before the firing squad, the three men die with honor and dignity. Right after the shots have been fired, Dieterle cuts away from the men and we see a white dove taking off. Is this an implication of a coming peace or future turmoil? Unfortunately, after Juárez's rule came to an end, the latter was exactly what happened.

At the church with Maximilian's body, Juárez, now restored as president, gazes down at the corpse of the principled man he never met and says, "Forgive me...." Then, as Korngold's music thunders on the soundtrack, Juárez walks solemnly towards the camera, and we assume, on to greatness.

Unfortunately, this curtain line infuriated bureaucrats in the Mexican government when they saw the film. Why should one of Mexico's great leaders ask forgiveness from a man they consider nothing more than a *gringo* invader? The decision was made at Warners to cut the offending line only on prints of the film that were shipped to Mexico. In this version, Muni bends over the coffin and his lips move, but Mexican audiences never hear the offensive words.

From first to last, *Juarez* is a liberal *yanqui's* version of a great Mexican's life. Yet it also features an unusually compassionate portrayal of a would-be foreign dictator as well. In World War II–era propaganda films, no one would dare show a Nazi's loving relationship with his wife or girlfriend, yet this film, made for the express purpose of comparing Maximilian and Carlota to Nazi imperialists, boomeranged on the liberal filmmakers in the worst way. Apparently, the screenwriters, despite their obvious intention of making a statement about foreign intervention and trash the oppressor, researched their subject matter *too* well. And they soon found that the man they were supposed to be attacking was *not* the oppressive ogre meant to suggest Nazi brutality. Indeed, shocked by the conditions in Mexico's slums, Maximilian and Carlota reportedly held parties for the rich to raise money to alleviate the misery of the poor. The emperor also cut down Mexico's long working hours, ended corporal punishment, abolished child labor, and sought to end debt peonage. Also omitted by the screenwriters was the fact that Maximilian only signed the infamous decree ordering the execution of *Juáristas* as a *response* to the guerrillas' summary execution of captured soldiers. Added to all these historical details is the very real love the emperor and empress had for each other more or less accurately shown in the finished film, and suddenly the man who was supposed to seen as an 1860s version of Hitler is shown not to be such a bad guy after all.

Part of this confusion was that Dieterle shot two separate films; one was the film featuring Maximilian and Carlota, the other featuring Juárez. Muni had already been attacked by Brian Aherne in his autobiography for insisting that the film focus on Juárez and not Maximilian and Carlota (Aherne doesn't bother to speculate on how Mexican admirers of the president might have felt about the focus being on Mexico's foreign rulers instead of their hero). In fact, it was a foregone conclusion that John Huston, blowing his own horn as usual, would have his own take on former collaborators he didn't like. In his autobiography *An Open Book* and later in *Conversations with John Huston,* the director slammed Muni for his ego and claimed that the screenplay was rewritten by "his brother-in-law" so that the focus would be more on Juárez.[8] The very claim that an actor's brother-in-law can rewrite a role in the actor's favor was a malicious misinterpretation (and, unfortunately, typical of Huston). For all through his recollections of the production, Huston neglects to mention that Muni's brother-in-law was Abem Finkel, a contract scenarist for Warners. Not only does Huston never once mention Finkel's name in his autobiography or *Conversations with John Huston,* but he also seems to have intentionally forgotten that Finkel rewrote his screenplay for *Jezebel* (released in 1938, a year before *Juarez*). Huston would also immodestly claim (without giving credit to Mackenzie and Reinhardt) that Hal Wallis told him that his screenplay for *Juarez* was the best he'd ever seen.[9] However, if Wallis had actually said this (the producer doesn't mention it in his own autobiography), then why did Finkel have to rewrite it?

This accusation of nepotism is more than a little hypocritical coming from Huston, a man who more than once fell back on using his father Walter to bail him out of one of his own less-than-perfect screenplays.

Muni was certainly a hands-on actor, the kind of personality a megalomaniac like Huston couldn't stand. After shooting the Maximilian and Carlota sequences, Muni reportedly saw the rushes, took notes and made suggestions. These notes were found in Warner Brothers' files on the film; however, despite the accusations of egomania aimed at Muni from both Brian Aherne and John Huston, they reveal the actor as far more honest and self-effacing about his own performance than they cared to admit. In one memo to Wallis and Dieterle from March 1939:

> My first speech to the crowd at Matamores shocked me—it was so bad. I don't know whether it was printed, but I tied in this same speech in a few takes with Uradi in another angle. I'm sure there was a better quality there. I'd advise checking up on it.[10]

Commenting on both sections of the film, Muni also had some sound advice which had nothing to do with giving himself more footage:

> Mexico and its people are missing in the picture. Juárez would become a greater figure if the audience would have a few visual glimpses and know that Juárez is not simply building up a cause, but that there *is* a cause; a cause which would make every right-thinking person feel that he would like to do what Juárez is doing. At present, Mexico is hazy and the people foreigners, and as such it will be very difficult to win sympathy. Actors can only do so much with dialogue. What a vivid flash can do, no actor can do.
>
> The awesomeness and grandeur of the country; its gigantic trees that are thousands of years old; the mysterious Aztecs—something of that must be seen—we can't only take Maximilian's and Carlota's word for it.[11]

The actor obviously knew what he was talking about, having been to Mexico to research—something neither Aherne, Davis or, at the time, Huston had done. To Muni, Mexico was a vast, beautiful land, and the actor deeply respected both the people and their culture. To macho directors like Huston (and later Sam Peckinpah), despite giving lip service to the beauty of Mexico, the country was one giant cantina.

There are certainly other schools of thought on the man who was installed as Mexico's foreign emperor and, despite the thousands of volumes of research material that the screenwriters allegedly had at their disposal, the film is considered a crock by most history buffs. Indeed, unlike the wilting flower that she's portrayed as in the film (at least until Davis' horribly overacted mad scene), it seems that Carlota wore the pants in the family. An outcast in her own family, Carlota would insist on her hubby being strong, and when Maximilian expressed doubts about the Mexican people ever accepting him as their emperor, Carlota pushed and prodded him to accept the mission. Another glaring omission in the film is Maximilian's serial cheating on his wife, and it is said that he had numerous affairs in both Europe and other continents. To this day, it is uncertain whether she couldn't have any children because she was infertile, he was infertile or she was rejecting him because of her anger over his affairs. (Note that in the film, it is heavily implied that *she* was the reason that they couldn't have any children, the Breen Office apparently refusing to even recognize that a *man's infertility* could be the reason.) However, the two royals *did* love each other, and other members of the royal court readily acknowledged Carlota's sharp intelligence, with the archduke quickly designating her as his regent when she visited other lands on diplomatic missions, a rare position for a woman while a male member of a royal family was still in power.

Maximilian, though not hostile towards his Mexican subjects in any way, didn't want to go too far out of his way to help them either. He was not the cold-blooded and ignorant tyrant as depicted in the Mexican production *Furia Rosa* or its English-language version *Stronghold* (1951). Yet the emperor was still the archduke of the Hapsburg Empire, preoccupied with pomp and royal surroundings, and therefore spent much time building a castle that he thought would impress the Mexican people. Instead, it only reinforced their image of him as a European snob who cared nothing about the poor, despite the parties the royal couple sometimes hosted in order to help them. Carlota tried in vain to get him to focus on his job of improving Mexico's practically bankrupt economy (the supposed excuse why the Europeans came to Mexico to collect their debts in the first place), but his obsession with matters of replicating the Hapsburg court on Mexican soil sapped the treasury even more.

The film seems to blame Maximilian's controversial decision to sign the infamous execution decree on pressure from both Napoleon from outside Mexico and Juárez from within it, as well as depicting the order as the brainchild of Marshal Bazaine. But it seems that no one should be blamed for its creation but the emperor himself. Maximilian conceived of the decree in meetings with his cabinet, and ultimately signed it on October 3, 1865, with the importance of the decree seen as merely putting an official stamp on what had been standard policy anyway. After all, French troops and Mexican soldiers were executing guerrillas way before the decree was ever conceived. Conversely, *Juáristas* (many, though not all, were bandit gang members pretending to fight for "the cause") were executing soldiers just as barbarously as their French occupiers all through the conflict, something never shown once in the Warner film.

Another discrepancy occurs when one realizes that the picture never shows Benito Juárez with a wife and children. Margarita Maza was the young daughter of Antonio Maza (the man who took in Juárez), who happened to be their cook Josefa's younger brother. Juárez was indeed present when the Mazas welcomed into their lives a beautiful baby girl whom they would name Margarita. In 1843, with Juárez now a Mexican Supreme Court judge, he married the former baby girl of the Maza household; he was 37, she was 17. The union worked better than anyone would realize. Despite his many exiles from the country by his various enemies and ducking capture from Mexican troops during the Reform War and escaping French soldiers during Maximilian's reign, the hunted politician sired a dozen children with Margarita—one wonders when he had the time. Sadly, she would precede him to the grave by several years, dying on January 2, 1871. Yet the filmmakers, despite the studio's extravagant and much-repeated claims of meticulous research, make sure that neither Margarita nor their many children make an appearance. Apparently, for the sake of not deviating from the film's many political points, the screenwriters decided to make the Zapotec leader a bachelor. (Even the villainous Napoleon is allowed to have a wife!)

Juarez premiered in New York City on April 24, 1939, and opened wide on June 10. Then, as Warners held its collective breath, the film premiered in Mexico two weeks later. The film had already been shown privately to President Cárdenas in May. Having met and immediately liked the personable Muni in 1938 and wisely seeing the film as a patriotic ode to Mexico as well as an attack on European imperialism in the late 1930s, *El Presidente* ordered that the film open at the Palace of Fine Arts in Mexico City, the first time any movie had ever been so honored. Though the audience liked the film, Mexico's journalists, xenophobic as usual, once again ridiculed the sight of "gringos" playing their heroes, a not altogether unjustified critique. *La Prensa* angrily denounced the film as "an historical caricature commercially adopted to deceive boobs and persons lacking in genuine affection for Mexico"[12]; apparently they didn't know about the visit to the country by Muni, Dieterle and Blanke. *Excelsior* called it a pretext to divert the viewer from "ideals and doctrines of Yankee absorption."[13] And, in a stunning display of ignorance on the subject of totalitarian behavior on other continents, the paper proclaimed that "the real imperialists lay to the north." In Veracruz, far from the government's palatial offices, Mexicans hated the portrayal of Maximilian as a hero. Indeed, though many Latinos in official government positions throughout South and Central America politely praised the film's intentions (which might have been their way of currying favor with FDR rather than Warners), for the most part, Mexicans on the street reacted angrily to the film, though perhaps not as vindictively as they did when Wallace Beery played Pancho Villa. However, Mexican reaction was nothing when compared to lingering French resentment over the portrayal of their government as imperialist villains. With the coming Nazi conquest and occupation of their nation on the horizon, French audiences would not see *Juarez* until it was released there on September 2, 1971. (Similarly, Warners' *Devil's Island,* starring Boris Karloff, was frowned upon by the French government, who wanted it withdrawn; Warners did just that. However, after France's subjugation by the invading Nazis, and without having to deal with any complaints about the film from Paris, Jack Warner cynically re-released the film in 1940, *and* it made a profit.)

Juarez did not make back its investment and was considered an interesting failure for Warners. Yet the story would not quite end there, a new threat appeared on the horizon, one that the studio imagined would jeopardize *Juarez*'s chances at the box office. And the danger came, not from our shores, but from Down Mexico Way, a rival film dealing with the same topic as the Muni version.

And it focused, not on the great Mexican leader, but on the Hapsburgs' most tragic royals…

In 1934, Mexican filmmaker Miguel Contreras Torres shot a picture called *Juárez y Maximiliano*. It top-billed the lovely Liechtenstein-born actress Medea de Novara as Carlota, Enrique Herrera as Maximilian, Alfredo del Diestro as Bazaine, Antonio Frausto as Porfirio Díaz and Froylan Tenes as Benito Juárez. Co-directed by Raphael J. Sevilla, the film boasted wonderful locations in Cuernavaca and Veracruz. Novara was Torres' wife, and though she was certainly a physically stunning Carlota, the actress was apparently so good in the role that she would play the iconic royal in three more films after *Juárez y Maximiliano* (and Novara would make only a dozen films in a fifteen-year film career from 1931 to 1946). *Juárez y Maximiliano* was released in Mexico City on June 28, 1934, and in the United States on February 15 the following year, with its American distribution financed by Columbia Pictures. The film was reportedly made with the full cooperation of *El Jefe Máximo* himself, Plutarco Elías Calles, which enabled Torres' crew to use actual Mexican cavalry troops in battle scenes shot on location in Mexico City. With a little more persuasion (and probably some cash), he was also able to convince *El Jefe Máximo* to order the removal of hundreds of telephone poles along the route to the National Palace just to show Maximilian's arrival in Mexico City.

However, Torres wasn't quite through with the subject: He directed and produced another version of the Maximilian and Carlota story, *La Paloma* (meaning "the pigeon" or "dove"), released in Mexico on August 20, 1937, and in the U.S. on February 15, 1938. Novara and Herrera again portrayed Carlota and Maximilian, respectively, and del Diestro repeated as Bazaine, but the cast also included the up-and-coming Arturo de Córdova as a Mexican general. Little is known of this film and one wonders whether this is actually a reedited version of *Maximiliano y Carlota* with added scenes featuring de Córdova and others not in the original cast (*La Paloma* is only seven minutes longer than the 1934 film).

Torres returned to the topic of his favorite foreign royals *yet again* in early 1938, this time calling the film *The Mad Empress* (that is, when not called *Carlotta, the Mad Empress,* throwing in the added "t" in her name that most English-speaking writers use) and showcasing his wife. Independently produced by Torres, the film inevitably ran out of funds, and production was shut down in February, putting the filmmaker some $18,000 in debt. According to Wallis' autobiography *Starmaker,* he had never heard of Torres and denied the existence of any recent film covering the same subject matter as *Juarez,* a claim exposed as a lie by Wallis biographer Bernard F. Dick:

> Wallis confused the 1934 film (*Juárez y Maximiliano*) with *The Mad Empress,* which Torres made as a showcase for de Novara, now his wife, focusing mainly on Carlota's descent into madness. Wallis never mentions *The Mad Empress,* alluding instead to lawsuits, including one threatened by Jean Bart, who Wallis would have us believe contributed to the script of the 1934 film. Bart had nothing to do with *Juárez y Maximiliano;* however, she had a great deal to do with *The Mad Empress.*
>
> Torres used the failure of *Juárez y Maximiliano* to try to pressure Warner Brothers into releasing *The Mad Empress,* which had been made before *Juarez.* Quite possibly, the *Juarez* screenwriters might have seen *Juárez y Maximiliano* during its American release; any writer working on a history-based screenplay in the late 1930s would have been foolish to ignore a potential source, especially since a few strategically placed calls to Columbia could have led either to a print or a script. The issue then, was not *Juárez y Maximiliano,* which was passé, but *The Mad Empress,* which needed a distributor.[14]

The "pressure" Dick was talking about was a one million dollar plagiarism lawsuit against Warners which also included a charge of loss of distribution rights. Even before the studio got word of the suit, it's also possible that the studio's research department, in their quest to find out everything they could about Juárez and Maximilian, stumbled across the 1934 Columbia release and, in learning about Torres' work, also discovered his recent production on Maximilian and Carlota. Still, despite Warners' claim that they owned the rights to the Franz Werfel play and the Berdita Harding novel, Torres knew that no one had a claim on any story depicting an actual historical event in the entertainment medium; and so, confident of his position, he took his film to Harry Cohn's Columbia Pictures. Warners realized that the quick-shooting B directors at Columbia could get *their* Maximilian and Carlota picture into theaters before they could finish *Juarez,* so they had little choice but to buy the rights to Torres' film *on condition that they distribute it as well.* This enabled the studio to withhold its release until well after *Juarez* cleaned up at the box office (or at least, that's what they hoped).

Several scenes were cut and English-speaking actors replaced Spanish actors from the earlier film versions. We plainly see these Hollywood actors doing their lines on sets built at Talisman Studios in Hollywood, yet (in the movie) they're gazing out at locations shot in Mexico from earlier Torres productions. It's also quite possible that there were more scenes originally featuring Juárez but, due to the Warner film set to be released in the U.S. on June 10, 1939, in Torres' film the Zapotec president is now reduced in stature to a few quick walk-ons. When Warners purchased the production, they not only recut the film, but redubbed it as well; therefore, when guns or cannons are fired, they are the familiar Warner sound effects we would hear in their films for many decades (they're *very* prominent during battle scenes in *Juarez*).

Even more blatant is the intrusion of familiar Erich Wolfgang Korngold music from *Juarez* playing at certain moments in the film. B film editor Carl Pierson (at Monogram he edited several East Side Kids pictures) had his hands full blending English-speaking actors with Mexican location footage and then overdubbing everything with Warner sound effects and Korngold's opulent score. The resulting film is an odd-looking patchwork; a low-budget co-production between a Mexican and an American studio featuring better-budgeted battle scenes opposite static talky scenes set in palace chambers where Hollywood veterans mix uncertainly with bi-lingual performers still speaking in their native accents.

Bernard Dick was wrong on this score: *The Mad Empress* did *not* concentrate solely on "Carlota's descent into madness." If anything, the film was about Maximilian and Carlota's fateful stay in Mexico as its rulers; the Empress' so-called "madness" comes much later. In fact, it would be surprising if Mackenzie, Huston and Reinhardt did *not* see this film; so alike are its Maximilian and Carlota sequences to their script for *Juarez,* that Torres and his co-writers had a damn good case for a plagiarism lawsuit—which is exactly what playwright-screenwriter Jean Bart tried also. Bart (real name Marie Sarlobous) was a French-born playwright whose most famous play was the antiwar *The Man Who Reclaimed His Head,* which was made into a film in 1934 with Claude Rains, Joan Bennett and Lionel Atwill. Joseph Chodorov was a far more successful playwright (author of the long-running *My Sister Eileen*) and a member of the Communist Party who would be blacklisted during the McCarthy era. Though it would seem to take on a leftist taint, the film that was released has a remarkably sympathetic portrait of the royal couple that might have been inspired by Werfel's play. *The Mad Empress* originally ran a full 95 minutes, yet the standard version of this film available today runs 72 minutes. Torres had always filmed the Maximilian and Carlota story in Spanish, but in early 1938, he endeavored to shoot with an English-speaking cast at Talisman Studios on Sunset Boulevard in Hollywood, indicating that scenes previously done in Spanish were eventually removed.

The new Hollywood version starred Torres' wife, de Novara repeating her role as Carlota (known here as Carlotta); Englishman Lionel Atwill (who had appeared in the film version of Bart's play *The Man Who Reclaimed His Head*) played French officer Bazaine; Enrique Herrera could not speak English, and so was replaced as Maximilian by Conrad Nagel; Guy Bates Post played Napoleon III; Evelyn Brent played Empress Eugenie; and Jason Robards appeared in brief scenes as Benito Juárez. Despite her thick accent, de Novara *could* speak English, though it is a little unsettling to hear her sound like someone from Eastern Europe, while her husband, played by Hollywood veteran Nagel, sounds like he grew up in the Midwest (which is where he was from).

As with the Warner film, it opens in Napoleon's chambers. Gone is Claude Rains' elaborately evil French emperor, replaced by Guy Bates Post's depiction of Napoleon as less of a fascist dictator than a wealthy aristocrat seeking to extend his influence into another sphere. Post may look Mephistophelean with his black spade beard and mustache, but unlike Rains, he's dressed in formal attire, not a military uniform, implying less of a warlike attitude. Also gone are Rains' allusions to racial superiority and colonial entitlement; *this* Napoleon seems far more reasonable. Opposite him is B queen Evelyn Brent, usually playing villainesses and fallen women, unusually attired in the gown of a princess and never looking more beautiful on screen. She lacks the presence of a Gale Sondergaard, yet she's far more restrained. She has a gentle nature rather than an overbearing one (as when Sondergard's Eugenie enthusiastically endorses her husband's imperialist plans for Mexico).

Lionel Atwill is also too English to play the French general Bazaine, but he's far less stiff and formal than Donald Crisp. Atwill was an actor who knew how to play with a line, pausing or emphasizing for maximum effect; his Bazaine is far more fun and the performance perfectly fits the kinder, gentler tone of Torres' film. The actor also throws in bits of business; for instance, when Bazaine quickly grabs a pinch of snuff and then sneezes in the middle of a speech to his generals, it looks suspiciously like an Atwill ad-lib (after the sneeze, two of Bazaine's aides glance knowingly at each other while suppressing their smiles). During the speech, Bazaine wryly notes that the archduke is "a man of high ideals, *democratic ideals*," then proclaims that he will secure Maximilian's election as emperor "even if I have to use force!"

We are introduced to Maximilian and Carlota, not as they arrive in Mexico but at the Hapsburg palace in Miramar. Medea de Novara is, without a doubt, the most beautiful Carlota on screen until María Teresa Piana's empress in *Stronghold* in 1951. She's much easier on the eyes than Bette Davis' over-aged, miscast royal in the Warner film; and she also convincingly exhibits Carlota's aggressiveness as she pushes her husband into accepting the throne of Mexico. (During the archduke's acceptance of the Crown, we hear the familiar Korngold music from *Juarez*.)

The reporter character from the Werfel play (though not using the same name) tries to see the always busy Juárez, a scene not in the Warner film. Unfortunately, even when filmed from behind, American Jason Robards doesn't even *attempt* to sound like he's from Mexico. There is another comparison between Lincoln and Juárez; this time the characters call them both "self-made men" from "humble" surroundings. When the royal couple arrives in Mexico, in a glaring difference from the Warner film, there are multiple shots (filmed years before in Mexico City) showing the people welcoming them with open arms. In this film, General López doesn't have to explain to Maximilian why the people aren't out to greet them. The Warner film *doesn't* show us these real Mexican faces, nor can they match in sets the actual road leading to the National Palace and the addition of real Mexican troops, courtesy of *El Jefe Máximo*.

Again, Maximilian heaps contempt (though in a quiet way) on Bazaine's decree calling for execution of all men carrying firearms. Soon, Juárez is told of the capture of Díaz (by Apache actor and grandson of Geronimo, Charles Stevens, playing one of literally dozens of Latinos through the years). In fact, within seconds after this news, one of Juárez's men sneaks in a knife to Díaz and two seconds later he is over the wall as French guards open fire on him, giving us without a doubt the quickest plot-moving sequence on record. As released by Warners, the film also forgoes any jailhouse meeting between Maximilian and Díaz, or any controversial discussions of the word "democracy." In the next scene, we actually see Bazaine amused by the attentions of his young Mexican bride, a comment on the real general's penchant for *extremely* young women not mentioned in the Warner film (we can hardly see the stiff-necked Donald Crisp with a young bride or even one his own age). Also featured is Rudolph Anders as the royals' Austrian-Jewish friend Herzfeld, a role from the Werfel play emphatically *not* in the Warner film. We learn from him more blatantly what the Warner film infers, that the court in Mexico has hidden the truth from them on how unpopular they are. Unlike *Juarez,* we actually see a Lincoln clone rejecting Maximilian's rule and endorsing the Mexican president. Also, after a brief argument with Bazaine, Maximilian signs the infamous execution with little fuss; there are no melodramatic scenes where little Augustin is in danger of gunfire from *Juáristas* to prompt him to make his decision.

Finally after a mere 37 minutes of film, Napoleon decides to abandon Maximilian. Carlota goes to Europe to convince him to remain. Unlike Bette Davis' hamming, de Novara's "mad" scene is a model of restraint. After accusing the French emperor of cowardice and telling Eugenie not to touch her, she quietly leaves, and it is only after visiting the Pope that she goes insane.

Maximilian is trapped with his men at Queretaro. After his capture, he's sentenced to death, and is shot with his two main generals. However, unlike the Warner film, he is allowed to say "Carlota" in a choked voice before the bullets strike. Also, unlike *Juarez,* in a scene back in France, Bazaine is allowed to be sarcastic to Napoleon without any arrogant rebuttal from the emperor who, instead of displaying Rains' megalomania, is actually humble and even a little ashamed about the way things turned out.

At the end, confined by her relatives in her palace, we see Carlota, not aware of the death of her husband, now living the rest of her life in a dream world. It is a heartbreaking ending that shows great sympathy for the royals that the Warner film would never have explored. Despite an altogether positive portrayal of them, *Juarez* still had to show them as imperial interlopers who, it is implied, deserved their fates.

Nagel is far less mannered than Aherne and lacks the affected higher-pitched voice that the latter uses to forcefully defend his compassion towards the Mexican people. In many ways, Nagel's is the simpler, no-frills, cut-to-the chase emperor without a hint of the pomposity that infuses Aherne's portrayal. Besides de Novara's far more attractive portrayal of Carlota, the other actors are merely adequate, with the exception of Atwill, who gives Bazaine eccentric flourishes and wry humor sorely lacking in Crisp's performance.

However, the biggest omission in *The Mad Empress* is the liberal political slant comparing Napoleon and Maximilian to foreign dictators. In Torres' film, it seems that not only Maximilian and Carlota, but Napoleon as well, are victims of fate.

Released in the United States on December 16, 1939, long after *Juarez* failed at the box office, *The Mad Empress* was finally seen by Bosley Crowther. In his *New York Times* review of February 15, 1940, the esteemed critic wrote:

> Comparisons being inevitable between two pictures of such perfect parallel, it is necessary to state that the Mexican and prior-made product is not in the same league as *Juarez*—except in the matter of scenic backgrounds, which in *The Mad Empress* are generally superior. Whereas the film of the Warners was essentially the story of a relentless conflict between democracy and monarchism, with the stolid champion of the former very much to the fore and with contemporary parallels unmistakably implied, *The Mad Empress* is simply the sad, romantic account of Maximilian's and Carlota's ill-starred adventure in a foreign land.[15]

Though praising Medea de Novara (whom he calls "Medea Novara") as "beautiful and impressively regal as Carlota," he still preferred Davis' performance. However, he did justifiably praise Lionel Atwill.

After its release, and like the bigger-budgeted production that overshadowed it, *The Mad Empress* also failed to make any profits at the box office and quietly disappeared into obscurity.

As the new decade opened and the world plunged into war, plotlines dealing with the Mexican Revolution disappeared as condemnations of international fascism and (until Hitler attacked the Soviet Union) communism filled the American screen. However, in Mexico itself, huge changes were taking place in politics, the economy, and especially the arts.

A new dawn would come to the Mexican film industry in the 1940s. As we would see, those years would be the greatest decade they ever had…

III

Declarar La Guerra, 1940–1950
World War II and Época Dorada

"I've had a particularly fascinating life.
Would you like to hear about it?"

So said the character of Kerim Bey in *From Russia with Love*. But the actor who portrayed him could have been speaking of his own life. Pedro Armendáriz, a character actor in Hollywood, was a star in his native Mexico.

Pedro Gregario Armendáriz Hastings was born in Mexico City to a Mexican father and Irish-American mother, during the reign of Francisco Madero, on May 9, 1912. His parents' nationalities gave the boy an appreciation for both cultures, and instilled in him a bilingual ability at an early age. It was said that when he performed in films made in Hollywood and (usually) cast as Latino characters, he had to exaggerate the Mexican cadences in his speech to sound more south-of-the-border. Armendáriz had grown up in both Churubusco, a suburb of Mexico City, and Laredo, Texas; eventually he earned an engineering degree from the California Polytechnic State University at San Luis Obispo. After his graduation in 1931, he traveled to Mexico and landed a variety of jobs, which included railroad worker, insurance salesman and journalist; his knowledge of both English and Spanish helped immensely in the latter job writing for the bilingual magazine *Mexico Real*.

His employment as a Mexico City tour guide really put him on the road to success. Legend has it that the young man, who had become friendly with one of the people on the tour, told him of wanting to be an actor. The tourist asked him to recite something and Armendáriz delivered the "To Be or Not to Be" speech from *Hamlet* for the tourist as they both sat in some cafeteria. This monologue was witnessed by, of all people, Mexican film director Miguel Zacarías. Indeed, watching the Pedro Armendáriz we know from his later, better-known films, one can easily understand the veteran filmmaker being impressed; ruggedly handsome at 22 when Zacarías first saw him, Armendáriz also had a strong onscreen presence that would remain with him to the end of his days. In 1935, Zacarías cast his young discovery as the romantic lead in his next film, *Rosario*. Zacarías was impressed yet again when the film came out and audiences responded favorably to Armendáriz' charisma. The director had also started the careers of several of Mexico's future stars, including Esther Fernández, Marga López and a woman who would become a frequent co-star of Armendáriz', as well an icon of the Mexican film industry: a tall, striking brunette named María Félix.

In the next few years, Armendáriz acted in dozens of films, sometimes in a supporting part, but gradually rising to starring roles. Receiving both critical and popular acclaim for his dynamic performances, he would also get a title that would always remain with him; using a Hollywood superstar as a yardstick, he would be referred to as "the Clark Gable of Mexico." Predictably, the Mexican film industry would make films dealing with its great Revolution, and Armendáriz would be frequently cast as a revolutionary. One of his more memorable works in this period is *El Indio,* shot in early 1939 and released in Mexico on April 12 of that year. Directed by Armando Vargas de la Maza and based on the novel by Gregorio Lopez y Fuentes, *El Indio* featured Armendáriz as Felipe, an Indian peon in love with Maria (Consuelo Frank), the daughter of a *hacendado.* Gonzalo (Eduardo Vivas), a jealous rival and another *hacendado* who is persecuting the Indians workers, hates Felipe and plots to have him killed. The beginning of the film depicting the Revolution (in battle stock footage) establishes the time in which the film is set. After the first few minutes, this emphasis on the Revolution disappears and the rest of the plot concerns itself with clichéd romantic melodrama dealing with the young Gonzalo's attempts to rid himself of Felipe and his need to get into Consuelo's pants. After the villainous young man is shot dead, the two lovers are reunited, but the fight for justice comes first; and so, the film goes back to showing footage depicting the Revolution, with a strong implication of its triumph in the end.

A star by the early 1940s, Armendáriz even played Zorro in the 68-minute *El Zorro de Jalisco.* Somewhere down the cast list was an actor-director who would have an enormous impact on Armendáriz's career: Emilio Fernández. This interesting Zorro clone was so obviously influenced by the Hollywood B westerns then made by Monogram and PRC that it left no sagebrush cliché untouched. With Armendáriz starring as the Clark Kent–like lawyer and his alter ego Zorro and Fernández co-starring as the evil villain out to grab land, the film could have been directed by Hopalong Cassidy helmsman Lesley Selander. It even had a saloon singer breaking up the action with a song or two (though the lady *is* a bit on the *zaftig* side compared with our own B starlets). In fact, after this diverting and lively B Mexi-western, Armedáriz and Fernández would collaborate on certainly one of the oddest films to come out of *any* country during those tumultuous times: *Soy Puro Mexicano!* (*I'm a Real Mexican!*).

Emilio Fernandez had already worked opposite Armendáriz as an actor, but Fernández had first directed him in 1941 in his debut film as a helmsman, *La Isla de la Pasión* (*The Island of Passion*). *Soy Puro Mexicano!* would be the future auteur's second film as a director. By any standards, the picture is a ludicrous addition to the canon of a man whose works would be so much a part of *Época Dorada.* Try thinking of it as a Mexican version of *All Through the Night* (where Humphrey Bogart and his fellow gangsters are pitted against Nazi saboteurs in Manhattan), though *Soy Puro Mexicano!* isn't even an *eighth* as good as the Bogie film, and you get the idea. With Mexico's neighbors to the north now at war with the fascist nations of Europe and Asia (that is, excepting the neutral Spain of Generalissimo Francisco Franco), its film industry produced an unusual tribute, not only to *yanqui* resolve, but to Mexico's outlaws, who just might reveal a hidden streak of patriotism when it counts the most. However, in *Soy Puro Mexicano!,* even this cliché takes a backseat to the film's confused setting. As co-written by Fernández, the film was a goof and the future auteur knew it; therefore, the plot borders on delirium, with *nothing* making any sense.

Armendáriz plays Lupe, variously described on several Mexican film websites, as well as the DVD box, as both a "Mexican revolutionary," meaning, basically, a guerrilla fighting against the *Porfiriato,* or possibly an anarchist fighting against present-day Mexico. Another

DVD box will describe him as a "bandito"; however, Lupe is clearly dressed as if he stepped out of the early twentieth century, with wide sombrero, boots, holstered pistols, and instead of traveling by car, just like the revolutionaries of an earlier time, he rides around on a saddled horse.

The movie begins with Lupe about to be executed for murder; he even has a wife who's been trying to get him a last-minute reprieve. Interestingly, she and other characters are dressed like it's 1941, yet Lupe still looks like he's ready to ride for Pancho Villa. His two comic assistants outside the prison walls are trying to figure out a way to free their boss. (Being a macho revolutionary, especially one created by Fernández, Lupe has no fear at all with execution only hours away.) The two dolts, seated by a cannon, suddenly realize that the means to free Lupe is right there: They fire the cannon at the wall and blow a hole in it large enough for the bandito to escape through. (Armendáriz is very funny as he beats the two idiots with his large sombrero since they almost killed him in the process.) Forget the fact that a cannon placed in front of any public structure in the twentieth century would *not* be able to fire ammo of any kind, much less a cannonball capable of blowing apart a prison wall, but this lack of logic informs Fernandez's script from beginning to end, and emphasizes the fact that he really didn't care how nonsensical it looked; he would have bigger fish to fry in the coming years.

Meanwhile, three fascist agents are arriving by train and plan an invasion of Mexico. They are a German (who, of course, screams frequently in a high-pitched voice), an Italian and a Japanese man, all played by Mexican actors. There is also an American reporter played by David Silva (who starred that same year for Fernandez in *La Isla de la Pasión*) and a gorgeous brunette who happens to be an American agent. Somehow, these two end up at the mansion which doubles as the headquarters of the Axis spies. Then, in another example of pure delirium (and an uncaring Fernández), Lupe and his men *also* show up at this mansion and, not realizing how dangerous their hosts are, take over the place and hold everyone hostage. When the Japanese spy almost has Lupe poisoned, the American female agent warns him, putting the bandito in her corner. (Here we see the very real charm Armendáriz has always been able to put across onscreen with the opposite sex.) Though the woman is ultimately killed by the fascists, the spies fail in their mission thanks to Lupe and his men. Confronting the three fascists in the mansion's basement, the bandito accuses them of not being men, and when they attack him (fighting dirty of course), he guns them all down with his ubiquitous revolver. Now Lupe reunites with his wife and, apparently forgetting the fact that he's slated for execution, the film allows him to live a happy life on the run.

Soy Puro Mexicano! is a work by an up-and-coming Mexican filmmaker who would graduate to creating classic works almost immediately after this; in purely American terms, imagine John Ford giving us a piece of schlock made for PRC and then making *How Green Was My Valley* and *My Darling Clementine*. The film was made merely for patriotic home consumption, as well as American audiences (both *La Isla de la Pasión* and *Soy Puro Mexicano!* would be imported to the United States and shown in the spring of 1943, with bookings especially prevalent in the Latin American neighborhoods of Los Angeles). For Fernandez, the film was made for hire and clearly *not* what he was interested in doing. Indeed, the irony of the enterprise had him condemning fascist aggression when he himself had been known to be sympathetic to Nazism. Ultimately, this was not a major impediment in his career, especially in a Latin America, particularly Mexico, that still harbored anti–Semitic sentiments. In fact, a decade later, Fernández would make bitter comments condemning the "influence" of Hollywood's Jews.[1]

However, one of the pluses in this film was an actor way down the cast list who, nevertheless, made his presence felt while playing one of Lupe's more trustworthy men: Alfonso Bedoya.

If anything, the one who walked off with the film's laurels, if indeed anyone did, would be Pedro Armendáriz. There was no doubt about it, the actor looked great in a big sombrero, boots, vaquero outfit and wearing holstered guns; he could also ride like an experienced horseman (remember, he was raised in both Mexico *and* Texas). Exuding *machismo,* charming with the ladies, laughing easily, and convincingly reliable as he battled the fascist spies on his own terms, Armendáriz almost made this horrible B film worth watching; in the immediate future, the actor would return to the world of the Mexican Revolution for his native country. Indeed, to Mexican audiences, despite seeing every actor in their country play a revolutionary, Pedro Armendáriz was the definitive cinematic incarnation of the Revolutionary hero. In the years ahead, he would crown his contribution to Mexican history on screen with his dynamic portrayal of Pancho Villa.

However, his frequent director was another matter. Though starting as an actor, Emilio Fernández's real talent was behind the camera, and the next four films he would write and direct after *Soy Puro Mexicano!* were classics of the Mexican cinema: *Flor Silvestre, Maria Candelaria, Las Abandonadas* and *Bugamilia*. Most of them had the Revolution as their background, and all of them would be shot by his most frequent cameraman, the great Gabriel Figueroa. Certainly, Fernández's origins would not only explain why the Revolution was his frequent choice of story material, but why it would also be portrayed more or less positively.

Fernández (El Indio) was born on March 26, 1903 (some sources say 1904), during the final years of the *Porfiata,* in Hondo, in the state of Coahuila. If anything can be said for his early life, it is that, like his hero Pancho Villa, it is incredibly hard to verify; and again, like Pancho Villa, Fernandez was known to make his life sound a lot more thrilling and adventurous than it may have been in reality. The auteur seems to have constantly given (*again,* like Pancho Villa) conflicting versions of his life. His father was an army captain (at other times, he was a major). However, two things are for certain: His father was indeed an army officer and his mother was a Kickapoo Indian (in Spanish, it is spelled Kikapu); hence the auteur's future moniker, "El Indio." Being a child of the Revolution, Fernández couldn't help but become part of it—or at least that's what Fernández would have us believe. In reality, he was ten years old when Madero was assassinated and fourteen when Carranza took control of the country and Villa was losing battles against Álvaro Obregón. Again according to Fernández, he was nine when he caught his mother in bed with another man. He allegedly killed the man, or killed both the man as well as his mom, or killed neither but wounded the man with a knife—or was it a gun? Any way you look at it, this was a hell of an accomplishment for a nine-year-old. He then allegedly left home with his father, or escaped a possible jail sentence for allegedly murdering his mom's lover. According to him, he and his dad fought the Revolution for Villa; at another time he claimed to have fought for Carranza, something that would have allowed the youngster to literally fight for both sides since Villa and Carranza became mortal enemies after Huerta's overthrow. He claimed to have fought with the *Villistas* at Torreón, one of Villa's greatest triumphs and a veritable charnel-house; thousands of men lost their lives. Villa had captured Torreón twice: The first time on October 1, 1913, and the second time in the final week of March 1914. If indeed Fernández was at Torreón, as he claimed, this would have made him either nine or ten years old—an incredible experience for someone so young, but then again, after supposedly killing his mom and her lover while he was nine, maybe he took it all in stride.

Fernández allegedly entered a military college when he was thirteen (it's not known which one, or which one would actually accept a thirteen-year-old) and supposedly went on a tour of duty which included Argentina and Puerto Rico. By 1923, with Villa dead, he joined former Minister of the Interior Adolfo de la Huerta's guerrillas and fought against President Obregón, something that was, needless to say, *not* appreciated by President Obregón. (Hoping to attain the presidency himself, Huerta was infuriated to find that Obregón had *Plutarco Elías Calles* in mind to succeed him, *not* Huerta—hence, a new Revolution.) *El Presidente's* loyal army was able to defeat Huerta and he was banished to the United States, where the former government minister-turned-guerrilla leader taught music. Fernández didn't have it that easy; he was sentenced to twenty years in prison. Yet El Indio couldn't just be released for good behavior; that wouldn't be very exciting, and so, according to him, he escaped prison with Obregón's army hot on his trail and fled to the United States.

However, even *this* was too mundane for El Indio. He also traveled around the United States, where he ended up in Chicago. Once there, he met Rudolph Valentino, who complimented the future architect of *Época Dorada* on his ability to dance the tango. In the Windy City, he also quickly got on good terms with some the country's most notorious gangsters; he claims to have broken bread with Al Capone, made a bitter enemy of Baby Face Nelson, and played poker opposite some of the most powerful made men of the Mafia. Fleeing Chicago and the wrath of Baby Face Nelson, he made his way west. Once in Southern California where his mentor, de la Huerta, was teaching music, Fernández wandered into the movie industry where he played bit parts in silent films. Legend had it that he was the model for the Oscar, though there are others who claimed that Fernández was just *one* of the men who modeled for the little statuette. Picking up experience as a bit player, he was in a position to watch Hollywood directors at work. Homesick, and with Obregón long dead, Fernández returned to his country where he figured he could help the growing Mexican film industry, first as an actor and scenarist, later as a director.

Inspired by Hollywood's own Golden Age of filmmaking in the 1930s, Fernández would become *the* major filmmaker of *Época Dorada* in the following decade. With the conservative government of President Manuel Ávila Camacho promoting Mexican pride and identity through its films, the mayhem and backstabbing that was part and parcel of the Mexican Revolution would be swept aside in favor of a portrayal that only accentuated the positive aspects of the struggle. Now the Revolution was a movement that successfully fought for freedom and equality, replaced systematic corruption with reform, and overthrew the powerful so that that Mexico's future generations could be free. Despite all the uncertainty about Fernández's early life, one thing was for sure: He *was* marked by the Revolution, and when he did make films depicting it and the people who fought it, they were portrayed as heroes and nothing but. Pedro Armendáriz was his muse, the personification of both the Revolution's bravery and its righteous rage.

However, to Fernández, *Época Dorada* would be boring had just one talented male actor dominated this new interpretation of the Revolution on screen. And so, El Indio also helped guide the careers of two women, both dynamic performers. One of them was a hot-tempered, defiant actress who loved Mexico and hated everything about Hollywood, the other had already been a star in Hollywood and was now returning to her native land to become an even greater star...

> She was the most exciting woman I've ever known.[2]

So said no less a filmmaking genius and prolific Hollywood lover than the great Orson Welles. And his praise was justified, since it was going to a woman whom the most beautiful women in Hollywood would refer to as the most beautiful woman in Hollywood. As audiences around the world would discover, there were screen beauties and sex goddesses, but there was only *one* Dolores del Río.

As an actress, del Río was undeniably gifted; as a screen beauty, she attracted international audiences and had countless lovers; and as a Latina in racist Hollywood, she had to break through barriers other icons of screen glamour never had to face. She was a pioneer, an iconic performer, and an authentic enchanting presence in a town where enchanting presences were routinely manufactured on a massive scale by the front office and packaged for mass consumption. But there was nothing manufactured about Dolores del Río, who arrived in Hollywood as beautiful as the day she left it for her native Mexico in 1942. However, being a Latina in a Hollywood dominated by Anglo performers, she held her own whereas others would have given up. Certainly, the world she came from had a lot to do with forming her incredible resolve to overcome adversity.

For she was also a child of the Mexican Revolution.

She was born in Durango, Mexico, on August 3, 1904 (some sources say 1905), and Christened Lolita Maria de los Dolores Asùnsolo Lòpez-Negrete. Her parents were Jesus Leonardo Asunsolo Jacques and Natonia López-Negrete. She was also a cousin to future Mexican film stars Ramon Novarro and Andrea Palma. Jesus was a director of the Bank of Durango, a position which made him and his family cherished members of Mexico's ruling class at the height of the *Porfiriato*. A child of privilege, young Lolita grew up in relative wealth and comfort as rage grew against the dictatorial control of the *hacendados*. By the time of her seventh birthday, riots hit the state of Durango. Soon, with all his assets gone, Jesus moved his family to Mexico City, where they all lived under the protection of the victorious new president Francisco Madero (who happened to be a cousin of Lolita's mother).

Lolita Maria de los Dolores was a strikingly beautiful little girl. Being a daughter of privilege, she was a gorgeous presence at her family's many social gatherings, and she quickly learned how to navigate among the country's men of power. Her poise and charisma were sharpened when the young beauty attended the prestigious Liceo Franco Mexicano School in Mexico City and also studied dance, expressing a special admiration for the great Russian ballerina Anna Pavlova.

On April 11, 1921, she married the aristocratic Jaime Martinez del Río y Viñent; he was 34, she was 16. Legend has it that Lolita, still interested in dancing before audiences, did a tango at a dinner party in Mexico City that hit Hollywood film director Edwin Carewe like the proverbial ton of bricks. As so many men had (and would do so down through the years), Carewe fell in love with Lolita Maria de los Dolores and cajoled the couple into taking the trip to Hollywood where the 21-year-old beauty would star in films. Lolita told herself that it was also an opportunity for Jaime to get his feet wet with professional writing credits in silent films; but it would be ridiculous to assume that Lolita wasn't thinking of herself as well. Dazzled by Carewe's offer (with Lolita probably realizing the director's interest in her was not entirely altruistic), the two moved to Hollywood, fully aware of the danger of their venture, not only from decadent Hollywood, but from their own social set back in Mexico City. As Lolita said years later: "I was mad to do it. My family and friends would have ostracized me if I'd been a failure."³

She was quickly put under contract to Carewe, who decided to act not only as producer and director of her vehicles, but also as her agent and manager. He paid her $250 a week to start, not exactly the kind of money a former princess of the aristocracy was used to. He then put her in front of his camera and shot hours of footage, minutely editing it down to something viewable for the heads of the major studios. Her older *yanqui* Svengali also hired veteran Hollywood mover and shaker Henry Willson to handle her P.R., with the publicity emphasizing her aristocratic bearing, her Catholic background and her obvious talents as a dancer. He also shortened her name to Dolores del Río. In record time, the amorous director sent Jamie off to the studios to study every aspect of filmmaking while making sure that he (Carewe) was in close proximity to Dolores. Every day, she was reportedly taught swimming, gymnastics, singing, acting, took lessons in diction, horseback riding, learned new styles of American dancing and, most important of all, expanded her English.

Latin Beauty: One of the most beautiful women in the world was Dolores del Río. She was the first Latina star in Hollywood, but had to fight both racism and ageist sentiment, then returned to Mexico to "become an actress again." Ultimately, she would become a major star of Mexico's *Época Dorada*.

With Carewe behind the camera, she made her film debut in a melodrama called *Joanna* as a Latina vamp. Though she was mistakenly billed as *Dorothy* del Río, Carewe assured her that her appearance was a success; he then had Willson give her a buildup as a "female Rudolph Valentino," continuing the then-popular stereotype of the Latin lover—though with a twist. Dolores was to be the first *female* Latin lover, or rather Latina lover, a sexy, hot-blooded vamp; a woman of everything *but* virtue. In an industry in which most gorgeous starlets were white and blonde, and opposite dark-haired white vamps like Theda Bara and Pola Negri, Dolores was a revelation to film audiences. With stereotypes still ruling the day in silent Hollywood, Dolores' image as a Latina allowed her screen characters to travel into sexual territory white actresses, even the ones used to playing villainesses, couldn't go. Subsequently, the Latina actress was cast in other ethnic roles as well, and even started to appear in productions *not* directed by Carewe. With each new film, her popularity increased; indeed, as time went on, it was awful hard *not* to be charmed by Dolores no matter what part she played. When talkies arrived, Dolores literally shocked radio audiences by singing the title tune of her recent hit *Ramona*. (She had already made the song a hit on radio, despite the fact that it couldn't be played over the titles of the still-silent film it came from.)

Those years were hectic for the young film star. Already jealous of Carewe and overshadowed by his famous young wife, Jaime divorced Dolores and fled to Europe where he died of a mysterious blood poisoning. (Ridiculously, Jaime's parents would blame Dolores for his unhappy last years, as well as his early death.) Soon, with UA backing her, Dolores dumped Carewe as her "manager" and gave him a substantial settlement. In 1932, she hit box office gold as a Polynesian woman opposite Joel McCrea in RKO's *Bird of Paradise*, especially in the film's heartbreaking finale. After appearing opposite Astaire and Rogers in *Flying Down to Rio,* she was then cast her as a fiery señorita opposite Leo Carrillo's Villa-like bandit in *Girl of the Rio*. Rejecting the bandito, she instead falls in love with *Americano* Norman Foster. Predictably, a furious Mexican government, parroted by a tightly controlled press, condemned her appearance in the film; *this* time, however, the arrogant bureaucrats of *El Maximata* were right. The film repeated, ad nauseam, Hollywood stereotypes of Latins as lazy and not-too-bright, with Dolores herself (playing Dolores, and of the Rio yet; get it?) talking in a particularly insulting rendition of pidgin English. After this atrocity was released in Mexico, the government-sanctioned newspaper *La Opinión* shrilly announced, "We have lost del Río!" Apparently, they seemed to have forgotten that they had *already* lost del Río. Frightened by the reaction of her countrymen, when MGM offered her the role of *Doña* Teresa in the troubled production of *Viva Villa!* in 1933, she angrily rejected it, declaring that it stereotyped Mexicans.

In the early 1930s, she had signed non-exclusive contracts with both MGM and Warner Brothers, but neither studio really advanced her talent, outside of just keeping her working. In 1937, she starred as the scheming wife in *The Devil's Playground,* in a performance which *The Hollywood Reporter* described as "uncomfortably real."[4] Soon, however, despite her talent, the writing was writ large on Hollywood's wall—and it would all be in *English*. Under the usually bigoted ways of the Breen Office, displays of ethnicity would be severely restricted, unless of course, the example of said ethnicity spoke in a comic way and did dumb things that usually slandered an entire people. Del Río's films suffered, with the nation's theater exhibitors declaring that she, along with other icons of feminism like Marlene Dietrich, Katharine Hepburn and Mae West, were box office poison. However, in the early 1940s, both her personal and professional lives would radically change forever.

Although she was married to MGM art director Cedric Gibbons, she carried on an affair with the also-married Orson Welles which scandalized a usually scandal-ridden Hollywood. Welles had already fallen madly in love with the older del Río as a youngster while watching her swimming nude (or what was *supposed* to be swimming nude) in a silent film. The crush bloomed into full-throttle lust by the time the two met at a party given by Jack Warner. Through his lackey, Louella Parsons, William Randolph Hearst was ready to publicly reveal the affair as a way of getting back at Welles for the alleged portrayal of him in *Citizen*

Kane, apparently forgetting that *he* could be scandalized for cheating on his wife with Marion Davies.

Certainly, there is much to make of that old cliché that behind every successful man, there's a woman who helped him get there. While he was completely energized and creatively inspired, Welles directed and starred in undoubtedly his greatest work while making love with his former childhood crush. For it was not Garbo or Dietrich or even his own wife, but *Dolores del Río* the great Welles was involved with while he was making *Citizen Kane,* a union that most likely sparked his creative juices. This point was brought home by Welles biographer Barbara Leaming:

> It was evident that his sustained relationship with Dolores had been highly beneficial to his work on *Kane* and [*The Magnificent*] *Ambersons,* since it allowed him to concentrate more fully on his filmmaking than if he had been unattached. Outside a steady relationship like this, women were likely to be less understanding of his peculiar work habits and more demanding of his time and attention. Dolores was there when he needed her, at whatever hours.[5]

In February of 1941, Welles finished a script for a project he titled *Mexican Melodrama,* and he traveled to Mexico to scout for locations. Based on Arthur Calder-Marshall's novel *The Way to Santiago* (which was in *Chile,* not Mexico), the film was to star del Río and be directed by Welles. However, its plotline which dealt with Nazi spies in Mexico did not exactly thrill the Mexican government, and they emphatically denied Welles' permission to shoot on location. When Dolores tried to intercede with the Camacho administration on Welles' behalf, they predictably stalled her. Certainly, any student familiar with the Mexican government's xenophobic aims, especially vis-à-vis *Época Dorada,* would not have been surprised at their thumbs-down of the project. This was certainly the case with a script that might have implied, even for a moment, that Mexican authorities were less than vigilant about Nazi activities in their country.

In 1942, Welles cast Dolores as a Frenchwoman in the film version of Eric Ambler's *Journey into Fear* (where we first see her performing in a nightclub wearing cat's ears—or was it leopard's?). Needless to say, the affair with Welles spelled the finish for her dozen-year marriage to Cedric Gibbons. Though Dolores and Welles would continue to retain both love and undying respect for each other through the years, they spilt at some point in 1942. However, the scandal affected Dolores' film work. Combined with the Breen Office's reluctance to view Latin Americans as anything more than either pidgin–English caricatures or flag-waving props for the war effort, and as a Latin *woman* in traditionally sexist and ageist Hollywood, Dolores' career now reached an impasse. She was 37 and a Latina in a racist town where a gang of American sailors and Marines would soon go on a rampage through downtown Los Angeles and attack young Chicanos merely because they were wearing Zoot suits. It was time for the woman known as Lolita Maria de los Dolores to make a change—*a big one...*

To Hollywood in those days, icons of feminism on screen were the likes of Bette Davis, Katharine Hepburn, Barbara Stanwyck, etc. Yet Mexico was Latin America's main procurer of *macho* in North America; their men swaggered on-screen and in other male-dominated fields of popular culture. Much of this so-called manly behavior would be encouraged, both on-screen and off, by *Época Dorada*'s major *auteur* Emilio Fernández (whose brutal treatment of women off-screen was just one symptom of a chillingly violent personality).

Yet one actress came along in 1941 who would become a major star of Mexico's Golden Age of Film, someone whose brazen personality both on- and off-screen effectively blew away her countrymen's conception of *macho* and effectively empowered the image of Latinas for all time. Tall, dark and handsome, with a glare that could stop a clock, much less the approach of randy men, she was both beautiful and powerful, a striking presence and a talented performer. A proud Mexican, she had nothing but contempt for Hollywood and its racist and sexist treatment of Latinas, and vowed *never* to work there. She was as good as her word, remaining in Mexico for the bulk of her long career (that is, when she didn't work in Europe). There were many talented actresses who made their own mark during *Época Dorada,* and even fought the Good Fight against Mexico's traditional sexism, but there was only *one* María Félix.

She was born María de los Angeles Félix Güereña in Alamos in the state of Sonora, five weeks after Francisco Madero's assassination, on April 8, 1914. Her father Bernardo was of Yaqui descent, and her mom Josefina was of Spanish ancestry. Her penchant for being unconventional started at an early age. The ninth of *twelve* children, she reportedly preferred playing with her six brothers rather than her five sisters, something that didn't sit well with the girls. In her teens, the unconventional turned into the obscene; and if one believes sources like Wikipedia, she had an incestuous relationship with her brother Pablo. After the alleged affair, the tormented young man was committed to a hospital in Mexico City and died mysteriously shortly after admission.

In 1931, the tall, dark-haired 16-year old beauty married salesman Enrique Álvarez Alatorre (who sold Max Factor products). They had a son, Enrique, but in 1938 the couple divorced, with the custody of their child going back and forth between mother and father. Legend has it that María was discovered walking down the street by businessman Fernando Palacios. Through Palacios, Maria met Mexican filmmakers, the Calderón brothers, and through them, she had a meeting in Hollywood with Cecil B. DeMille. She reportedly turned down C.B.'s offer to work in Hollywood, declaring her resolve to make films in Mexico. Another story claims that, typically, when Palacios asked her whether she wanted to act in movies, Maria couldn't take him seriously; one wonders if she also projected this attitude towards the pompous DeMille—that is, if she did indeed ever meet him. Years later, Maria would claim that the only work DeMille had in mind for her was to play small Native-American roles.

La Doña: Dolores del Río's major rival during *Época Dorada* was the one and only María Félix. She always portrayed powerful women who made life hell for sexist males, including Mexico's revolutionaries. A feminist off-screen as well as on, she rejected all offers from Hollywood and only worked in Mexico and Europe.

However, back in her native land, fortune smiled on Maria soon enough. She was a leading lady right away in *El Peñón de las Ánimas* (*The Rock of Souls*), co-starring with her future husband, the tragic singer-actor Jorge Negrete, and in the title role in *María Eugenia*. Her third starring role had such an impact on international audiences that it marked her entire film career. *La Doña Bárbara* (*The Lady Barbara*) was released in Mexico on September 16, 1943 (her third film that year), and in Mexican areas of Los Angeles on April 10, 1944. She played aggressive women in her first two films, but even these ladies paled in comparison to Doña Bárbara, the female owner of a ranch who ruled both her property and the men who worked for her with iron-fisted cruelty.

Based on the 1929 novel by Venezuelan author Romulo Gallegos (who would become president of that country in 1948), the film centered on the character of Barbara, who is raped by four men early in the film and also witnesses the death of the man she loves. Becoming a cattle trader, she builds a vast empire in the desert by sheer force of will, letting *nothing*, especially men, stand in her way. In America, this kind of role would be played in westerns by Joan Crawford (in *Johnny Guitar*) and Barbara Stanwyck (in *Forty Guns*), but that was over a decade away; Felix would be whipping and subjugating men on her own terms at a time when many of them were fighting on the battlefields of Europe and Asia. Co-directed by Fernando de Fuentes (the helmsman who caused controversy with 1936's *Let's Go with Pancho Villa*), *La Doña Bárbara* cast the mold for Félix for the rest of her life. Fiery and defiant off-camera as well as on, María became the larger-than-life female icon of *Época Dorada* who not only stood up to sexist men, but made them crawl. With this powerful female persona, María also fit snugly into the world of the Mexican Revolution where she gave as good as she got opposite the various *macho* antics of violent revolutionaries who mistreated *soldaderas* as they fought against the *Porfiriata*. In the future, she would be nominated as Best Actress for the Silver Ariel Award (Mexico's Oscars) and would win the coveted award in 1947 for *Enamorada* (*Beloved*), 1949 for *Río Escondido* (*Hidden River*) and 1951 for *La Doña Diabia* (*The Lady Devil*), and win the Golden Ariel in 1986 for Lifetime Achievement.

Armendáriz, del Río, Félix and Fernández were the core and spark of the Mexican Revolutionary film during *Época Dorada,* as well as the decades beyond. But there was one more artist who played a part in depicting the world of the Mexican Revolution for a mass audience. An iconic and versatile performer, his range expanded to genres that had nothing to do with plotlines about the Revolution, but when he *did* appear in such a film, he put his usual stamp on the sub-genre.

In 1943, as Félix and her contemporaries consolidated their fame, singer-actor Pedro Infante starred in one of the year's most rousing flag-wavers, a patriotic ode to a Mexico that stood up to foreign colonialists of the nineteenth century just as other democracies of the time stood up to fascist aggression...

El Día de la Batalla de Puebla.
This pretty-sounding phrase which lyrically rolls off the tongue of those who can pronounce it well, might not mean very much to those who know little of Mexican history. But to those who lived in North America, its impact is felt to this day, especially to those Mexicans and their American neighbors who cherish freedom.

The Day of the Battle of Puebla was May 5, 1862, *Cinco de Mayo.* It was a day when a would-be victim became a surprise victor. As *Time* magazine once put it, the day "came to symbolize unity and pride for what seemed like a Mexican David defeating a French Goliath." The story of this sudden and unpredictable burst of national pride started over a century and a half ago.

A full 37 years after their own independence from Colonialist Spain and a full decade after losing much of their territory in the Mexican-American War, Mexico was going through its own Civil War in 1858, and their "Reform War" in 1860. With the country having lost much of their land and undergoing a fierce class struggle between the aristocracy and the *peons,* the government also owed a staggering debt to the nations it had borrowed from, England, Spain and France.

Napoleon III was well aware of Mexico's difficulties. To his advisors he made it plain that he sought a French foothold in North America, and what better excuse to attack and overpower "helpless little Mexico" than to say that they were doing so *only* to recover what they were owed? The French dictator certainly had no qualms about letting loose his elite troops upon a supposedly divided nation; and after the Mexican spoils were safely within France's iron grip, the next step was to move its forces north. With Lincoln's Union at war with Jefferson Davis' Confederacy, it seemed an all-too-predictable scenario that France was hoping for an alliance with the South. And so, backed by French guns and artillery, the Confederacy would overpower the North, spreading slavery up to the Canadian border, destroying the Constitution and the Bill of Rights and establishing a French-backed dictatorship over the United States.

On July 17, 1861, with the Mexican treasury practically bankrupt, President Benito Juárez issued a moratorium on all payments of foreign debt. *El Presidente* did not do this for spite, or in arrogance (unlike Adolf Hitler, who nullified all of Germany's debt to the allied victors of World War I); he did it to buy his nation time to economically heal and, when financially sound, pay the debt back (the moratorium extended a mere two years). However, *this* was just the excuse Napoleon III was waiting for.

The plan was for the ships of Spain, England and France to storm the port city of Veracruz (a city that would be "stormed" more than once in its long, tempestuous history). However, when agents from England and Spain reported to their leaders that France had no intention of leaving Mexico even if the debt had been paid, the two nations uncharacteristically backed off and refused to have their navies join French ships when they docked at Veracruz.

This was exactly what Napoleon III wanted, not caring to share the spoils with his fellow colonialists. Veracruz was the closest port to Mexico City, and once the French army polished off the locals, they were to march some 600 miles to the capital. Once there, they would install Austrian Archduke Maximilian as emperor of Mexico. Late in 1861, the French ships landed, and the imperialists were promptly met with stiff Mexican resistance by local defenders who emphatically did *not* roll out the welcome mat.

Joined by Mexican Quislings under the command of General Charles Ferdinand Latrille Compte de Lorencez (a reactionary career officer who detested both Juárez *and* the Mexican army), the French continued their march on to the capital. However, they would find, to their frustration, that they were effectively blocked on the outskirts of Puebla by Forts Loreto and Guadalupe. These outposts were populated by a poorly armed militia of some 4,500 men commanded by General Ignacio Zaragoza Seguin; added to this defensive position was the hill overlooking the terrain, Cerro de Guadalupe, where Mexican riflemen could easily draw a bead on any attacking force hoping to storm the fort. Seeing an easy victory within his grasp, on May 5, 1862, Lorencez and his French helpers sent their infantries to charge the center of the Mexican line. However, to their horror, they soon found that *these* soldiers weren't going to fold up and run away as some lesser men might have. The defenders not only withstood the attack, but struck back. Opposite a numerically superior force (some say the combined French and turncoat–Mexican armies totaled 6,500; other sources put the figure as high as 8,000), the Mexican garrison eventually paid the attackers back with a brutal body count of over a thousand dead. Seeing their "easy victory" turned into a hopeless nightmare, the French and their allies turned tail and ran.

This would give Napoleon III an excuse to send 30,000 *more* troops to invade Mexico, forcing the government of President Benito Juárez to flee. However, "Mexico's Lincoln" was hardly one to run out of fear (unlike, say, the French army); there would hardly be a time-gap between his escape and his quickly organizing a potent guerrilla force to take back the country in the years ahead.

Under the dictatorship of Mexico's new emperor and empress, Maximilian and Carlota, backed by French guns, Mexico became in effect a French satellite. However, the victory over the French on May 5, 1862, was not only an enormous morale booster to a Mexico that had been kicked around and abused by all outsiders, as well as themselves, for far too long; it effectively bought time for Lincoln and his Union forces fighting their own war. Backing the *Juáristas* early (a fact appreciated in Mexico to this day), Lincoln knew that his hands were tied by the Civil War. However, once the Confederacy was defeated (and, unfortunately, Lincoln was assassinated), the newly reunited U.S. government wasted little time in supporting Juárez and his fighters; first politically, with Congress, now under new president Andrew Johnson, condemning the French occupation of Mexico; then militarily, with American guns being shipped across a newly liberated southern border into the hands of grateful *Juárista* guerrillas.

All this logistical American support soon bore fruit: Juárez and his followers started to drive out the French in 1866. By the end of the following year, the French occupation would be a bitter memory.

However, the Mexican heroes who bled and died defending Puebla on May 5, 1862, will always be with us as citizens of both Mexico and the United States celebrate their victory and mourn their sacrifice. This nation owes them our gratitude as well. Had Napoleon defeated the heroes of Puebla that May 5, inevitably his troops would have turned north, and with the French fighting side by side with a belligerent Confederacy, the United States could have become a French possession.

On September 16, 1943, as most of the world was fighting the Second World War, Producciones Rodríguez Hnos, with the full backing of the conservative government of President Manuel Ávila Camacho, released *Mexicanos al Grito de Guerra* (literal English translation: *Mexicans to the Yell of War;* or, as the DVD box says, *Mexican National Anthem*). It was written and co-directed by novelist Álvaro Gálvez y Fuentes and a man who would help define the greatness of his nation's film industry: Ismael Rodríguez.

The Golden Age of Classic Mexican Cinema had already begun. As the world's democracies fought against a ruthless totalitarian enemy, Mexico would use an event from its own history to show them that she too knew how to fight for freedom...

Our story begins in France in the 1850s. We see Napoleon III (Angel T. Sala) declaiming about the state of the world and his armies, chortling over his invasion of the Balkans and the infallibility of his crack troops. The emperor is first seen seated in a chair in his seedy-looking bedroom wearing a robe and in his bare feet as he talks to his aide, Dubois. This is quite a difference from Claude Rains' portrayal of the dictator in *Juarez* in full-dress uniform with his wife and far more advisors with him in his opulent dining room. Still, as we will see, the Mexican filmmakers took quite a bit from Hollywood, particularly *Juarez;* the Warner film was released nationally in America on June 10, 1939, and imported to Mexico a mere 13 days later. In *Juarez,* Rains' Napoleon III will also crow of the greatness of his armies and the right of France to inherit the earth; and, as in the Warner film, the Napoleon in Rodríguez's film (he was the production manager as well as the writer and co-director) will have nothing but racist condensation for the Mexicans he wishes to conquer. When a Mexican Quisling general is announced before entering, despite his appearance, the arrogant Frenchman refuses to put on some clothes or neaten his appearance: "Where I am is the throne of the Empire! Besides, it's about a *Mexican!*"

Certainly, the dialogue makes plain what most historians suspect about where the dictator's ambitions truly lie: "Owners of Europe, the next step will be America!" Dubois says. And, he adds, all Napoleon needs is a "weak point" through which to get there. However, when the emperor is told that his armies would have to sail across the Atlantic to get to North America, he asks, "Where the hell is Mexico?" Then Napoleon goes to a map and points out everything *but* Mexico, emphasizing not only his contempt for the country, but the inescapable conclusion that the great dictator is a bit of a ditz.

In the meantime, in the land of the would-be victims of conquest, there is a contest for writing the most patriotic song. The poet Francisco González Bocanegra (Carlos Riquelme), at the urging of his girlfriend Lupe (Margarita Cortés), writes a patriotic song for the contest. Lupe has this accomplished by locking her boyfriend in her drawing room until he finishes it. Surrounded by paintings of Mexicans in glorious battle, he writes the song, which moves his girlfriend to tears. Previous to this, the two had talked about how the song will show the *real* Mexico that "makes us defend our land with all our strength beyond all internal hatred that now separates all Mexicans."

Luis Sandoval (the great singer-actor Pedro Infante) hopes to make up for his father's fighting on the French side. A musician and singer, he wants his music teacher, who is Spanish, to write the music for his patriotic song and enter it into the contest. Commenting on Mexican patriotism, Luis says, "We Mexicans may suffer a lot with our bad governments, but we won't stand foreign rulers." As we'll see all through the film, especially the first half, Rodríguez and Fuentes have written several scenes with a wicked sense of humor, satirizing the political atmosphere in Mexico in the 19th century. In one priceless scene, a limping President Antonio López de Santa Anna (Salvador Quiroz), who is followed around by a little toadying assistant, comments on his leadership; for instance the fact that his people need him despite the fact that they *didn't* give him unlimited powers, *didn't* bring him back from exile, and *don't* call him "Your Highness." "Mexico has been a republic for thirty years and has had 45 presidents, some lasted just *a few hours.* In twenty years, I have been elected president 11 times." Tragically, this comical figure (who wiped out the defenders at the Alamo and ordered the massacre of Texas soldiers at Goliad) was speaking the truth about the sad state of Mexican politics; in such a nation it was certainly hard for an economically divided and cynical people to be patriotic to a system that couldn't hold onto a worthy leader, and ended up electing crooks who looted the nation's treasury to boot. Santa Anna, no matter how many times he was "elected" president, usually stayed home at his hacienda and had his vice-president do the actual governing. For him, it was a perfect arrangement; he was able to retain his presidential powers at a high salary, without accepting *any* of the responsibilities of office. Coasting on his reputation as a military commander, and without any scruples whatsoever, he always sold his allegiance to whatever party was able to secure victory at the polls.

Meanwhile, Luis has literally bumped into Napoleon's new minister Debois and his beautiful blonde daughter Esther (Lina Montes). Following the entourage to the park, the young man sings to the impressed Frenchwoman. Also at this musical fair selling cakes is Pastelero, played by talented Mexican comic "Chicote" (real name, Armando Soto La Marina), a little guy with a high-pitched voice. In a meeting with Mexican Quislings, Debois and his fellow imperialists are predicting that foreign intervention will mean a "a triumph for the Conservative Party, a triumph for the aristocracy!" Napoleon's hand-picked minister also heaps contempt on the people he hopes his masters will conquer: "Mexico with its revolutions and its anarchy is a child that needs tutoring!" By the end of the film, however, the audience will see just which country is taught a lesson.

Finally the day of the contest arrives, and even though Luis' teacher wins, the victory is hollow since Santa Anna has such contempt for the affair that he merely sends an aide to represent him. It is now 1859, and Mexico has the amazing distinction of having *two* presidents; the liberal Benito Juárez and Miguel Miramón of the Conservative Party each running the country with their own agendas. Rodríguez cleverly shows us a split screen, with each president on his side speaking to an aide and demonstrating how each would handle Mexico's financial mess. Miramón wants to endlessly borrow money from foreign nations while the more austere and sensible Juárez orders wages cut back and predicts that the nation should starve first before asking a loan from foreigners. Whereas Miramón is concerned with getting money and doesn't care how he gets it, the moral Juárez is more concerned with "justice on our side."

Meanwhile, with Juárez as president, Luiz has proudly joined the army; this also gives him a chance to be in the proximity of the lovely Esther. However, in the corridors of power, Debois insists on a French occupation of Mexico, with Spanish and English help, in a three-pronged naval landing at Veracruz. However, this plan to sell out Mexico is heard by Pastelero, who promptly informs the president (*not* Miramón, the *real* president). Of course, instead of throwing him out of his office as some short-sighted leaders might (Pastelero slipped past the guard), Juárez wisely treats the little peddler as an equal, and is *very* interested in the traitorous plot being hatched. Later, Juárez is alerted to the occupation of Veracruz by General Zaragoza (Seguin). Juárez commissions Luis' national anthem to be distributed to all his soldiers. And so, to resounding boos from the Mexican audience, the French flag is raised over Veracruz. In this hour of need, the country turns to President Juárez, who gives a rousing speech before congress. Condemning the invasion in no uncertain terms, Juárez' words, delivered in a film released in 1943, struck a chord *outside* Mexico as well:

> Europe thinks American countries are weak. We would never go and incite them. But if they come to this continent that is our home [and try] to make us their slaves, we'll show to their invincible armies that a small country can be big, that a weak country can be strong, that a young nation can be powerful, when it's encouraged by love of freedom and justice.

Though the speech ends by again mentioning Mexico, it was obvious that the filmmakers were using the invasion of 1862 to comment on the worldwide turmoil of 1943; and that the French dictatorship of Napoleon III is being used to suggest the totalitarian nations then fighting against Mexico's neighbor to the north.

When Esther expresses the desire to marry Luis, Debois angrily says that the young Mexican lieutenant doesn't belong to their "race" or "lineage." Here it is revealed that Esther herself is of Mexican blood, which she is proud of. However, leaving the room, she overhears the generals planning their sneak attack on the city of Puebla, which is set for May 5. Traveling to Puebla, Esther is arrested by Luis as a spy and put in the fort's jail before she can warn him of the attack. Preparing to fight, the troops are given a patriotic speech by General Zaragoza. As the general and his officers prepare for battle, they are met by a contingent of Zacapoaxtlas Indians who are anxious to fight "the blonde ones." This is yet another line which makes a euphemistic comment on World War II. Here, the dark-skinned Indians (who would ordinarily face discrimination from Mexicans) exhibit patriotism against the so-called "blonde ones," a barbed comment that fits the Nazis' claims of Aryan superiority rather than any racial theories proffered by the French (though many French soldiers *were* bigots who hated Mexicans). Continuing this theme, a French general incites his men into battle by emphasizing their racial superiority over their opponents.

The battle begins, with Mexican troops falling left and right, and blood and gore, though restrained, prevalent. In one shocking bit, even the comic relief is seen losing his leg just before Rodriguez makes a judicious cut-away. Though they are being beaten, a mortally wounded Luiz grabs a bugle from the dead bugler and blows out the patriotic tune that won him the contest. Miraculously, despite their being on the edge of defeat, the Mexican soldiers rally (of course, while singing Luiz's song in perfect harmony) and beat back the French. When the Mexican Quislings try to ride over to their now-victorious countrymen, French officers maliciously shoot them in the back.

Though the French are soundly defeated, many of the Mexican troops are dying, including Luis, who survives just in time to see his own father crawl towards him. The now-released Esther is around to witness dying father and dying son clasp hands while crawling in the dirt before both expire. Laughable, yes, but there were nothing laughable about the staging of the rousing action that preceded it.

Again, the acting in this film was flawless (with another standout performance by Pedro Infante), even if the propaganda was a bit heavy-handed. Certainly, no one had to exaggerate the heroism of the defenders of Puebla. For the talented Infante, this is but another Mexican film in which he is thrust against a background of military heroism, this time the Mexican revolution against the French invaders.

Whether playing a soldier, revolutionary, priest, motorcycle cop, Indian, boxer, outlaw, husband, composer or, of course, singer, Infante instilled warmth and integrity into these roles that reflected the decent man that he was off-screen. He was concerned with helping the oppressed, and many of his screen roles dealt with fighting poverty, racism and ignorance. Years before Douglas Sirk's remake of *Imitation of Life,* Infante starred in 1948's *Angelitos Negros.* Dealing with a rich white woman who doesn't realize that she's the daughter of a black maid, the film is a rare attack on Mexican racism of its black population. In *La Mujer Que Yo Perdí (The Woman He Lost),* we not only see the barbarism of the federals under the Díaz regime, but particularly its racist treatment of its Native population. In one scene,

Pedro is an eyewitness to a federal attack on a poor Indian village. It is a brutal and harrowing scene; we see the soldiers beat men and women, abuse children, burn huts and trample anyone who flees. Try to remember this is a movie and that for decades *real* Natives were treated much worse in these pogroms, as we watch this horrifying spectacle with the restrictions on extreme violence a Mexican censorship board would impose.

By the time *La Mujer Que Yo Perdí* was released in Mexico (October 20, 1949), its leading lady, the beautiful Blanca Estela Pavón, had died tragically, lending further poignancy to her role as an Indian who would give her life for the man she loved.

Usually under the guidance of director Ismael Rodríguez, Pedro would return to the world of the Revolution, with 1951's *Las Mujeres de Mi General* (*The Women of My General*) a standout. Pedro plays a revolutionary general whose men take over a town (by an amazing coincidence, he can also sing). He has to deal with the shy Indian girl who loves him and whom he eventually marries, and the evil, rich blonde slut who lusts for him. Towards the climax, when Pedro's fort is attacked by federals, the two women have a violent catfight down in the stockade after the blonde hurls racist epithets at her Native rival. The ending, when Pedro and his wife and newborn baby are facing certain death at the hands of the conquering federals, with both of them laughing hysterically while firing a machine-gun at the enemy, is still a shocker for those expecting the two to survive and escape with their baby.

As for Ismael Rodríguez, he would continue to work with his muse, Pedro Infante, all through the 1950s until the singer's death in a Yucatan plane crash on April 15, 1957. However, though in mourning for the passing of his friend, the helmsman was able to concentrate his energies on his Pancho Villa trilogy, which starred another Pedro, *Armendáriz,* which further mythologized the guerrilla chief.

Meanwhile, back during the war years, another iconic Mexican performer, already having become a star in another country, was returning to the land of her birth…

> I wanted to go the way of the art. Stop being a star and become an actress, and that I could only do in Mexico. I wanted to return to Mexico, a country that was mine and I did not know. I feel the need to return to my country….

This was the great Dolores del Río on making her life-changing decision to return to her homeland. However, it was not as if her fellow countrymen were going to welcome her with open arms. Both the Mexican public and industry professionals (perhaps prodded by a still-xenophobic government) deeply resented the fact that, despite all her talk of returning to her native country for good roles, she had previously spurned all offers from the Mexican film industry until scandal, age and racism ended her Hollywood career. These naysayers forgot that Dolores continued to keep in touch with Mexican artists, actors and writers all through her Hollywood years, and that she would always remain loyal to her family. (Soon, she would mourn the death of her father who passed away around that time.)

Nevertheless, meeting these obstacles head-on, Dolores was nothing if not resourceful. In 1943, she accepted Emilio Fernández's offer to star in *Flor Silvestre* (*Wild Flower*). The shoot was not a pleasant one, with the brutal and sexist El Indio persecuting the former Hollywood glamour queen endlessly. Several times she wanted to quit the production, but Fernández's more mature partners begged her to stay. For their sake, as well her genuine professionalism, she stayed on the production, but she kept El Indio and his violent temper tantrums at arms' length. There was reportedly another reason for Fernández's brutal treatment of his beautiful star: He was in love with her.

It was the spring of 1943, and as the world was at war, *Época Dorada* was entering the beginning of its golden years with the release of *Flor Silvestre*. The film continued a tradition of using the Revolution (as well as other upheavals within Mexico) as a backdrop for melodrama, the nation's tragedy personalized into the tragedies of those brave men and women who lived through those times.

Our story begins when we see the aging Esperanza (still gorgeous even when made up to look like an old woman, Dolores del Río) speaking to her son who's in uniform (Tito Novaro) as they gaze over a resplendent valley. Apparently much has happened here thirty or so years ago, and Esperanza relates to her son in flashback about the people who lived there, including his late father.

It is 1913, and young Esperanza (the now 39-year-old Dolores del Río doing a *very* convincing job playing a virginal maiden in her teens) lives in the valley with her poor family. However, she loves the son of a rich *hacendado* named Jose Luis Castro (Pedro Armendáriz). His father Don Francisco (Miguel Ángel Ferrez) is against his son seeing the daughter of a poor family. However, Jose has the heart of a social activist who treats his workers as equals, and frequently invites them into his home to eat or just shoot the breeze. After Don Francisco physically attacks his son at the local rodeo, Jose defiantly marries his poor but dazzling brunette girlfriend. Doña Clara (Mimi Derba) visits the ailing Esperanza and cynically insists that she leave her son, but the old woman suddenly realizes that the maiden really *does* love him. After the birth of their son, the couple is happy even though the old man has cut him off.

But the times, they are a-changin', and soon President Díaz is overthrown. Though asked by a revolutionary chief to join them, Juan remains with his wife and son. Even though at heart he *wants* to join them, he feels responsible to his family. Sensing this, Esperanza insists he go, that she'll be all right (famous last words). Meanwhile, back at Don Francisco's, his ranch hands are leaving him by the score; he is a hated *hacendado*. Soon, Bandits masquerading as revolutionaries arrive at his spread and hang the old man, but Juan and his men capture the bandit leader responsible. On his knees begging for mercy and claiming to be sick, the man is not believed by an unmoved Juan, who promptly readies the rope. Then, surprisingly, the man *does* die of his illness.

Cheated of his vengeance, Juan has the dead man hanged anyway, directly over his father's grave, a stunning shot composed by director Fernández and expertly photographed by Gabriel Figueroa. In fact, a later anecdote told by the cinematographer concerns a preview screening of *Flor Silvestre,* organized by Dolores del Río, in which the great Mexican painter José Clemente Orozco, seated next to him, commented that he recognized his work on screen. To which Figueroa modestly replied, "Maestro, I am an honorable thief; that is from you." "But you have a perspective I wasn't able to achieve," replied the painter. "You must invite me to watch you work."[6] Certainly, with El Indio lining up the shots, Figueroa's frames become mini-paintings; his shots of the sunset hanging of Don Francisco's murderer and Juan's long ride in the twilight with a companion are visual highlights, fully demonstrating the wonders achieved in cinematography during *Época Dorada*.

In revenge for the man's killing, Juan's home is taken over by the bandit Rogelio Torres (the director himself, Emilio Fernández), who also kidnaps the pregnant Esperanza ("Now

I will have a son," he says proudly). But now his men are hunting Juan, and in record time they catch him and set him before a firing squad. Here, playing the small role of Torres' aide Teniente, was an actor whose seriocomic screen persona would resonate very soon with American audiences: Alfonso Bedoya. Now facing a firing squad, Juan begs not for his own life, but for Torres to take his sobbing wife away before the bullets strike her. After Juan is killed, we come back to Esperanza finishing her story about the people who once existed in a land that is no more. As she walks off with her uniformed son (who, like many Mexican men, probably joined the fight against America's Axis enemies), we see the aged Esperanza, sad but still quite beautiful and obviously very eloquent in her old age.

We also see a vibrant Dolores del Río, rejected by her adopted country, newly reborn in her native land. This would be only the beginning for the aging but still stunningly beautiful actress. Far away from the stereotypical roles Hollywood forced on Latin actors at the time, del Río was offered parts which took full advantage of her talent and demonstrated her versatility for all time.

Meanwhile, as *Época Dorada* continued to grow during the postwar years, three of its major artists would assemble for one of the era's finest films, a work that won awards for its depiction of an unlikely romance set during the chaos of the Mexican Revolution...

In *Enamorada*, the first shots are of cannons firing a volley at some unknown target. It gets our attention right away; it's also a harbinger of the explosive emotions that will dominate the film. While the guns fell silent in Europe and Asia, *Enamorada* (released on Christmas Day 1946 in Mexico City) reminded the world of another war fought for freedom thirty years before. Co-written and directed by Emilio Fernández, *Enamorada* became the Mexican Revolution's version of *The Taming of the Shrew*.

After the cannon-fire, Fernandez gives over-the-top entrances to his two stars, the explosions in the background perfectly complimenting their appearances. Almost immediately, the door of a hacienda is thrown open and the well-dressed Beatriz Peñafiel comes out to see what's going on. It is María Félix giving her patented glare, as if the opposing armies had the audacity to interrupt her at whatever she was doing; here, Fernández puts a "starring María Félix" at the bottom of the screen as soon as she springs into the scene. Then the rebel chief José Juan Reyes rides in on his horse while brandishing a pistol. It's Pedro Armendáriz, with his name appearing as he rides into frame. Also reacting to the explosions is Father Rafael Sierra (Fernando Fernández) praying in his church. Apparently, director and cinematographer are also complimented by the visuals, with Gabriel Figueroa's name coming onscreen as we see a shot of church bells ringing in celebration. Fernández's director credit comes on in a close-up of victorious revolutionaries raising the Mexican flag over the town. Then we see the rebels march past a sign establishing the village's founding in 1821, the same year as Mexico's independence from Spain; this shot alone suggesting a kinship between the heroes who drove out the Spanish with the rebels fighting to free Mexico in the 1910s.

In a nearby basement Reyes and his men force the mayor to sign the town over to the general. This scene gives us a good idea of how powerful Reyes is; and as played by Armendáriz, the rebel's intensity and single-minded rage against the town's *hacendados* and petty politicians is obvious from the start. Seated on the edge of a table, rage distorting his face, angrily shouting orders and issuing personal indictments to those who have exploited the poor, with a lit cigarette between his fingers and a loaded gun at his hip, Armendáriz is a stunning presence. For Mexican film audiences, he would define *machismo,* both as a leading man and an actor who could handle action scenes. After one toadying *hacendado* begs for his life, he is mercilessly dragged out to be shot. At the beginning of this scene, we see that Juan and the padre were old friends; and though he is happy to see Juan, the padre is disturbed by the apparent cruel streak which has allowed him to order executions without mercy. However, the rebel chief has also taken in Adelita, a little orphan girl (whom we never see for the rest of the film). Juan also meets Eduardo Roberts (Eugenio Rossi), a foreigner who has settled in Chohula to educate children. Spared by the rebel chief, he is encouraged to teach his charges the value of equality.

When Beatriz passes in front of Reyes and his men, the general makes the mistake of complimenting her gams, as his men laugh. After Beatriz defiantly shows off said gams, she knocks him to the ground. The battle lines have now been drawn. Yet our tough-as-nails rebel officer is also turned on. He follows her through town on horseback, though the woman bluntly refuses his advances. She even chucks a lit firecracker which blows him into the air in true slapstick fashion; utter hilarity in the midst of war and the class struggle (and remember that this prank is being done by a daughter of the wealthy against a fighter for the poor).

When Juan visits his friend in church, the scene resonates in piety, with the suppressed Catholic boy in Juan gazing about at the paintings of the saints and the ornate ceiling, all as his friend the padre powerfully sings "Ave Maria." Here, under the conservative Camacho regime, in fact, all through *Época Dorada,* we are reminded, as in the Breen Office–dominated films of the United States, of Mexico's pro-clergy stance, especially in the movies' depiction of priests and nuns. With the enthusiastic backing of the administration in Mexico City, the film industry venerated the Revolution as a Holy Mission, but it totally ignored, at the time anyway, the collaboration of the Church with the dictators Díaz and Huerta, not to mention their grasp on power before and during the days of Juárez.

In the basement's workshop where, symbolically, crosses and icons are carved, Juan announces that he is in love with the tempestuous Beatriz and wants to marry her. Father Sierra knows that Eduardo also loves her and wants to marry her. When Juan is about to have Carlos Peñifiel (José Morcillo) killed, he is saved when his daughter shows up. Belatedly realizing that his target was the father of the girl he loves, Juan apologizes as Beatriz pulls her father out of the room, slapping a rebel soldier on the way out as the fabled Félix glare goes on overdrive.

That night, Juan arrives at her front door in full military dress uniform and riding prop as Beatriz answers. This gives the two would-be lovers a chance to slam doors on each other and laugh uproariously at the other's pain, another romantic comedy-slapstick bit that could have easily come out of a Tracy-Hepburn comedy made for MGM or, more likely, a Three Stooges short. However, liberated as Hepburn's screen persona may have been, she still could not match Félix in unrestrained defiance. Days after this, Juan is miserable, unusually smitten and moaning over his lost chances with her. When he corners her going into church, he doesn't take no for an answer, but she compounds the problem by putting on airs and slapping him yet again. Fed up, he reverts to machismo rebel general and knocks her down.

Soon, Juan realizes that he's going about it the wrong way. And so, that night, Reyes arrives with a band to serenade her (the band does the actual singing). Here, Fernández gives Félix some striking close-ups, especially of her beautiful eyes. Her Beatriz is not crazy about being woken up, but the young woman is intrigued, and curiously looks through the curtains to see Juan looking down in humble contrition. The next day when she is on her knees in church, Juan joins her and apologizes for his behavior. Finally, confused by the apology and her own feelings, she leaves, turning back just in time to see him with his head bowed in shame. It's one of the best scenes both actors ever did together.

Roberts comes to Juan and admits his love for Beatriz. Thinking that he has no chance with her, Reyes blesses the union. However, word comes that the federals are in the area and will probably arrive that night. Juan leads his troops to the battlefields outside town as Beatriz is about to sign the marriage license affirming her wedding to Roberts. Just then, the anguished Beatriz rushes outside. Grabbing a maid's shawl, she runs after the now-jubilant Juan as he rides off into battle, walking beside her man as other *solderas* of the Revolution follow their men into war. It's an ending straight out of *Morocco,* with the high-falutin' Marlene Dietrich leaving the permanence of a marriage to successful Adolphe Menjou so she can follow Foreign Legionnaire Gary Cooper into battle along with dozens of other camp followers; indeed, Dietrich's condensation of these women at the beginning of *Morocco* seems to be a harbinger of Félix's arrogant ways in *Enamorada.*

Shot in Puebla, the famous locale of the *Cinco de Mayo* battle, *Enamorada* swept the Ariels (Mexico's Oscars) in 1947, with Félix predictably winning as Best Actress (you had to be good to beat Dolores del Río for her performance in *La Otra*). Fernandez won for Best Direction, Figueroa for Best Cinematography, and a Special Award went to Armendáriz for his long career in Mexican cinema. The film was released in the United States on December 2, 1949, under the title *A Girl in Love.* However, its release was cut short when Hollywood's Eagle-Lion studios bought the rights to the film for an American remake; and though the producers wisely retained the services of Fernández as director and co-writer and Armendáriz repeating his role as Reyes, they could not get the notoriously anti–Hollywood Félix to reprise as Beatriz.

And this is when the story gets a particular savage Hollywood twist…

There are many fundamental differences between *Enamorada* and its Mexican-American remake *The Torch,* released in the U.S. by Eagle-Lion on June 2, 1950, but the major one, of course, is the fact that the associate producer and star of the latter film is Paulette Goddard. That's right, Paulette Goddard, Charlie Chaplin's ex, former Paramount star, and future paramour of author Erich Maria Remarque. She was one of the highlights of MGM's *The Women,* and in her years at Paramount, she was the brunette counterpoint to the bland and blonde peek-a-boo girl Veronica Lake (who, in her screen decline, would *also* appear in a film shot in Mexico around the same time, though it dealt with the reign of Maximilian and Carlota). Goddard was only *slightly* better than Lake as an actress, and where the peek-a-boo girl seemed to merely walk through her roles and let someone like Alan Ladd do all the work, Goddard's style was the opposite, projecting enthusiasm and effervescence whereas Lake didn't seem to project anything at all. Taking this into account, it wasn't a surprise that Paramount released Lake a few years *before* they got rid of Goddard. The attitude of Paramount's all-male studio bosses concerning a woman's age may have had something to do with letting Goddard go, but then again, the studio was already losing interest in her. She tried to instill some life into her role as Lucretia Borgia in her last Paramount film, *Bride of Vengeance,* but she lacked the range for such an iconic part; and her performance in the title role of *Anna Lucasta* for Columbia also didn't spell big office or critical raves either.

In his autobiography *Wide-Eyed in Babylon,* her frequent co-star at Paramount, Ray Milland, said she was "wise, humorous, and had no illusions," and called her one of the hardest-working actresses he ever knew. Far more intelligent and savvy than her sometimes one-note performances would imply, Goddard was another casualty of Hollywood ageism. However, being associate producer of *The Torch* and casting herself as a virginal maiden when anyone with two eyes could see that she was, let's say, a bit *up there,* was a blunder for which she had no one to blame but herself. María Félix was 32 years old when she played the role of Beatriz Peñafiel in *Enamorada;* anyone who saw the film could tell that this was a mature woman (that is, in *age,* not behavior). Still, María had the talent to make us forget for 103 minutes that she wasn't an ingénue any more. Regardless, *any* actress stepping into María Félix' shoes better have some awfully big feet.

The remake was again directed by Emilio Fernández and shot by Gabriel Figueroa, but the screenplay was adapted and written by producer Bert Granet and the co-writer of the original, Iñigo de Martino. Thanks to Fernández, Figueroa and Armendáriz, even Eagle-Lion couldn't screw up *all* of it. It gave Fernandez a chance to re-do the material, adding little touches to his already impressive direction of the original.

"By gun ... by flame ... by force.... He took everything he wanted!"[7] As one can tell from Eagle-Lion's over-the-top tagline, the focus of the film is not on Goddard's overage maiden, but Pedro Armendáriz's revolutionary. In fact, in this film, the actor adds even *more* machismo to his role of General José Juan Reyes, effectively blowing away his more famous leading lady (or perhaps this is what Fernández had in mind all along).

As the film begins, we see the daughter of the town's richest man, María Dolores Penafiel (Goddard), watch the glassblowers at her father's factory create a present for her upcoming wedding to Dr. Robert Stanley (B western and serial veteran Walter Reed). This beginning is significant for two reasons. One is Fernandez and Figueroa's creative use of the glassblowing sequence to add something that wasn't in the earlier picture; and the other is Beatriz Peñafiel's reemergence as *María Dolores* Penafiel, the first two names being Fernández's blatant homage to the two queens of *Época Dorada.*

Not stopping there, the director gives Armendáriz a better entrance than in the original. Since Eagle-Lion bought the rights to *Enamorada,* expensive scenes from the original, like the cannon fire that began the earlier film, end up here. However, instead of having his leading man merely ride into the frame with his name coming up onscreen, the director has Pedro's revolutionary general appear atop a hill out of the clouds of thick smoke, like an angel of vengeance, the imagery complimenting both the Revolution as well as Fernandez's favorite leading man.

From here till about halfway through, the film conforms more or less to the original. However, the *yanqui* producers decided to replace some of the original music with a stereotyped, comical use of "La Cucaracha," with the producers obviously not realizing its significance as a song used during the actual Revolution. This is annoyingly played during Juan and Maria Dolores' door-slamming sequence that was actually funny in the original, but is hard to watch here.

As we go through this film, we also notice something else that will annoy us: Goddard's performance. In her previous films, we could always count on at least a modicum of charm from the gorgeous, Long Island–born brunette, but there is none to be had in this picture. In fact, her former enthusiasm is replaced, literally, by wide-eyed, over-the-top hysteria. The characters in *The Women* didn't act this depraved. With her beautiful eyes practically coming out of their sockets and baring a great number of her beautiful teeth, the actress–associate producer is letting us know that María Dolores is not only angry, but ready to take hostages. The more a great dramatic actress like María Félix got angry in *Enamorada,* the funnier she got as she raged against the annoying general who won't leave her alone. When Goddard's María Dolores gets angry, instead of laughing at her irritation, we're convinced that she's in need of meds.

Of course, this overacting might not be the actress' fault.

With Eagle-Lion owning the American rights to *Enamorada,* it's quite possible that *The Torch*'s associate producer had viewed the earlier film and modeled her performance in the remake on the one and only María Félix. In fact, when one sees *The Torch,* it's hard not to notice Goddard's heavy use of widening eyes and bared teeth, of wildly shaking her fists and angrily stomping her feet, all in imitation of the woman who originated her role. However, the actress did *not* have the patented Félix glare, the look that seemed to literally destroy arrogant men on the spot; her sometimes whiny voice couldn't match Felix's rage-filled, rapid-fire delivery, all carried by a voice that snapped like a whip. Also, the diminutive actress, who stood at 5'4", did not convey as much of a threat as the statuesque Félix who towered over many of her co-stars at 5'9". (Added to this was the eternally proud way Félix carried herself, with shoulders thrust back and standing at her full height, a physical compliment to the strong women she played.) Of course, Fernández might have advised Goddard to view *Enamorada* and suggested that she model her performance on Felix's. Either way, it wasn't good advice. Even Goddard's cinematographer seems to be against her. Shooting the film with his typical brilliance, Figueroa does little to conceal the actress' age, with her wrinkles showing up quite plainly in the sequence in which Juan and his band serenade María Dolores outside her window.

A surprise in this film is the unusually restrained Gilbert Roland. A good actor capable of subtlety and restraint, Roland (playing the padre) is *not* the wily rascal character that the actor would soon make famous, first in Hollywood adventure films, then internationally in the spaghetti western. He was the Mexican star who left his homeland and made his fame with the *Americanos,* and ended up having a longer career than many of his contemporaries. He did not make films during *Época Dorada,* but he was certainly a major player in Hollywood's version of the Mexican Revolution.

Somewhere around the halfway point into *The Torch,* the film takes a radical turn away from *Enamorada.* Juan soon learns that his men, as well as other people in the town, are dropping dead in the streets. It's the time of the horrible influenza epidemic which swept the planet, killing millions of people. Juan's first thought is of Adeli (Antonia Daneem; "Adelita" in the original), the little girl unofficially adopted by the general. In *Enamorada,* the little girl is taken in by the church; in this film, her future is not as secure.

In a way, the sudden introduction of the influenza epidemic into the plot gives Fernandez a chance to expand the characters. The village's tragedy also galvanizes the previously selfish María Dolores to roll up her sleeves and help those afflicted with the disease. In fact, one does wonder what *Enamorada* would have been like had the influenza epidemic entered into the plot. And though one might find it hard to envision the eternally self-possessed Felix persona getting involved in helping the sick, remember that she *did* occasionally play women who sacrificed themselves to help others; one role that comes to mind is her caring teacher fighting rural ignorance in writer-director Fernandez's *Rio Escondido* (*Hidden River*), filmed two years after *Enamorada*. In *The Torch,* the new plotline also gives Dr. Stanley more to do than just being the Ralph Bellamy part in the earlier film, as he dishes out medical advice to stem the spread of the disease. However, the character who benefits most of all from this new storyline is Juan. When Adeli is lying sick and dying, you feel immense sadness for this tough revolutionary general. Powerful and uncompromising in the first scenes, shouting orders, shoving around the village's rich men and ordering executions, Juan is pitiable as he begs the little girl not to die. With tears in his eyes, the formerly strong rebel officer now pathetically offers the girl a chance to ride his horse and fire his pistol whenever she wants as long as she gets well. Armendáriz is such a good actor that when the girl dies, we feel his heartbreak. In fact, we're practically forgetting all about María Dolores' transformation into Caring Human Being, and instead share Juan's despair over his loss.

The epidemic recedes, but with federal troops on the horizon, Juan is back at the head of the column leading his men into battle. However, back at the Penafiel hacienda, María Dolores is about to sign that marriage certificate when—surprise!—she realizes that she's in love with the general. And so, as Félix did in the original, she walks by her man's side as he rides into battle, though I always had the impression that Armendáriz's smile was wider when *Félix* was walking at his side.

While it was still known under its American title *The Beloved* (the English translation of *Enamorada*), the film's original script caused some concern from the Production Code office. In an August 18, 1949, letter to Norman Freeman, producer at Kaldore Corporation which was producing the film for Eagle-Lion, Joseph Breen had his usual reservations:

> As discussed with you this morning over the telephone, we believe it will be essential (particularly for non–Mexican audiences) to make clear that these "camp followers" are not prostitutes, but are, in effect, the common-law wives of the soldiers. We agree with you that can probably be done with a line or two of dialogue.[8]

On page 110 of the script, Breen had another complaint:

> This scene seems too suggestive of attempted rape to be acceptable under the Code. While it has one of violent lovemaking, it should not be done with a bed or cot in the background, or in any way suggest that your sympathetic lead, José Juan, is actually working up to the point of attempting to rape [María Dolores].[9]

Released in the United States on November 14, 1951, *The Torch* failed, and failed badly. Typically, the British would ignore the fact that Armendáriz's character was a *revolutionary* fighting for a cause, and change the title to the insulting *Bandit General.* The *New York Times*, in a predictable comparison, declared:

> Commenting on [María] Félix's performance, we wrote at the time [of *Enamorada*'s release], "Miss Félix has just claim to her reputation of being Mexico's most fiery actress. She is a wonderfully expressive performer." Unfortunately, the same enthusiasm cannot be applied to Miss Goddard's acting. Her tantrums lack spontaneity and live animal vigor. Her whole manner is cheap and coarse and throws the character of a lady of breeding completely off-key.[10]

After this film, Goddard would be trapped in pathetic Bs for Columbia and UA that made her worst Paramount films look like they were directed by Eisenstein. For Fernández, the film's failure also effectively killed off any directing offers from Hollywood (that, and his blatant anti–Semitism), though he would continue to direct films in his native Mexico all through the 1950s, and have his one acting gig during that decade in Ismael Rodríguez's postwar tribute to the Revolution, *La Cucaracha* (*The Soldiers of Pancho Villa*). The one man who *did* benefit from the film was Pedro Aremendáriz. Still steadily employed in Mexican films, the actor would also now branch out into even more Hollywood films, and they weren't solely directed by John Ford either. It was a decade where the actor would play his most iconic role, that of Pancho Villa in the trilogy filmed by Rodríguez, as well as playing Villa in *Vuelve Pancho Villa,* a Spanish-language version of *Pancho Villa Returns* (starring Leo Carrillo as Villa) made in Mexico around the time he shot *The Torch*. Both versions were directed by Miguel Contreras Torres (*The Mad Empress*).

The 1950s was also the decade in which the actor would make a fateful decision to appear in *The Conqueror,* a project that was a tragic harbinger for himself as well as his co-stars.

Now as the Cold War hit the United States and *Época Dorada* was starting to fade into memory in Mexico, both nations continued to film stories depicting revolutionary war Down Mexico Way...

IV

Revoluciónistas, 1951–1959
The Cold War and the Mexican Revolution

There are many things one can say about the films made by Lippert Pictures; big budgets, cohesive plots and good acting are usually not among them. However, there were times when the company that gave us *King Dinosaur* and *Rimfire* could come up with something so unusual that both audiences and critics were too shocked to complain.

As director Steve Sekely wrote to Joseph Breen on March 6, 1950:

> We are preparing a picture in two versions, Spanish and English, tentatively entitled *Stronghold* to be produced in Mexico City by Filmadora Internacional, S.A. The English version will be released by Film Classics, Inc.
>
> I am attaching the first draft of the English version and, although we started a polish job on it several days ago, I would appreciate your comments on it because we intend to go into production within the next three weeks.[1]

There was quite a stretch between Sekely's letter to Breen and *Stronghold's* release in the United States in February 15, 1952. Made around the time of another film with mostly Latino characters, the soon-to-be-banned *Salt of the Earth*, *Stronghold* was not made by members of the American Communist Party at the height of the Blacklist Years, as was the former film. Instead, it was set in Mexico at the time of the French-backed rule of Emperor Maximilian and Empress Carlota. Instead of attacking the U.S. government and capitalist excess, it attacked foreign intrigue in Mexico and those wealthy Quislings who sold out to French colonialists. Set 85 years in the past, and in a foreign country (albeit just over the border from us), *Stronghold* allowed American audiences to thrill to a revolution that overthrew an unjust government without feeling like fellow travelers for having done so.

As Sekely had written to Breen, there indeed *were* two versions of *Stronghold* made, one for English-speaking audiences and one for Mexican audiences called *Furia Roja* (*Red Fury,* an ironic title for a film made during the Cold War). The same sets were used for both films, as well as the lion's share of the supporting cast, which included mostly Mexican actors. Only two top-billed roles would be played by Americans for the U.S. version, with Mexican actors playing these same roles in *Furia Roja*. Former Hungarian filmmaker Sekely was a veteran of Monogram and PRC, and he directed the English-language *Stronghold,* while both he and Mexican filmmaker Victor Urruchua got credit for directing *Furia Roja*. Both versions were written by Wells Root, a former director-writer for MGM crime melodramas, but by the 1950s reduced to writing TV (*Superman* episodes) and low-budget efforts like this one.

In "the year of our Lord, 1865," the Civil War is over and Señora Navarro Stevens (Fanny Schiller), the widow of a Southerner, is returning home to Mexico with her daughter

The Privileged Enjoying Their Privileges: At the head of the table is Zachary Scott as the wealthy pro–Maximilian lackey in *Stronghold*. The film took aim at Mexico's upper classes for having sold out to Napoleon and Maximilian at the expense of the poor.

Maria (Veronica Lake, by the 1950s considered a has-been). In the American version, after introducing the former peek-a-boo girl and her Latina mom, actor-voiceover artist Marvin Miller shows us a guitar-playing black man named Cesar (black Latino actor Jose Laboriel), "a family retainer," which apparently means a slave in a servant's outfit. Why Cesar is traveling with them instead of attempting to escape is a mystery.

One will also notice that the voices of all the actors, except for those who can speak English (like Lake), will be *badly* dubbed and sound as if they're in a soundproof booth speaking dialogue rather than on-location. This is the same type of subpar dubbing usually associated with Cherubuska-Azteca Studios, the same folks who not only produced this film, but gave us the Aztec Mummy and Wrestling Women films (don't ask!). We are told (again by Miller) that the two women are seeing their native land as a haven and a "stronghold" (title!) under the reign of the Emperor Maximilian and Empress Carlota.

Suddenly their ship is boarded by the redoubtable Ignacio "El Nacho" López (the always enjoyable Alfonso Bedoya) and his men. Here, Bedoya chews the scenery with ease, the Mexican performer's entrance speeding up the film whenever he appears, as he attacks his over-the-top dialogue with relish. He introduces himself with a little story: "When I was a small boy, my mother said, 'Oh, that ugly *Nachito,* he looks like a bandit!' Well, I don't want to disappoint my mother!" Capturing the women, the outlaw is also given a history lesson. It must be said that for any screen character to explain history or *anything* to any character played by Alfonso Bedoya is alone worth the price of admission, as the colorful Latino performer usually comes up with his own twisted version of what the explainer is trying to convey. When the women and Cesar (showing remarkable spunk usually not given to black characters in American films) try to explain the Civil War to Ignacio, he smiles and responds with, "Ohhhhh, *revolution!*" Well, not exactly.

Unaware of their capture is her cousin, the wealthy Don Miguel Navarro (Warners' former heel, Zachary Scott), an aristocrat who has become a collaborator in the despotic rule of the emperor and empress.

After escaping El Nacho, the women fortuitously arrive at the home of Don Pedro Alvarez (a veteran of both Hollywood and Mexican films, Arturo de Córdova), whose mother had been friends with Señora Navarro Stevens. Discovering that she is a Southerner, Navarro declares, "Good! We like rebels here in Mexico."

Just as when El Nacho mistakenly refers to the Civil War as a "revolution," the Confederacy's fight with the North is referred to as a "rebellion," justifying it as a war against an oppressive regime, not the act of treason that it actually was. For Don Pedro to compare the Confederacy's fight to keep slavery and perpetuate racism with Juárez's fight to free Mexicans from foreign domination was reprehensible.

The two women are shocked (again) at the appearance of El Nacho at Don Pedro's front door. It appears that the wealthy Don, unlike Maria's cousin, is a rebel in the service of Benito Juárez, and that the forever smiling Ignacio is his sidekick. Señora Navarro damns Don Pedro as "a traitor to his country and to his class!" Speaking to her daughter, the elder woman laments that the two have "turned their backs on rebellion and come home to revolution," without explaining the difference between the two. Besides the sneering "traitor to his class" remark, the Señora injects some racism into the conversation by referring to "the Indian Juárez," as if his ethnicity alone made him a pariah.

Visiting her duplicitous cousin in Tosco, Maria is impressed with Don Miguel's charm and manners. However, during a night coach ride, Don Pedro and Nacho arrive and knock out Don Miguel; then the Juárista aristocrat takes the naïve young woman on a tour through the poor sections of town. The formerly "stone cold" princess realizes that there is another Mexico that the emperor and empress never mention, one where the have-nots have been neglected by the wealthy. At a ball given by the royalty, she and Don Miguel appear before Maximilian (named *Maximiliano* in *Furia Roja*; and played by Felipe de Alba) and the Empress Carlota (the strikingly beautiful María Teresa Piana). In the English-language version, de Alba is badly dubbed; and while Ms. Piana, who appears in both versions, clearly speaks English, her Belgian-born empress definitely has a Mexican accent.

Appearing before the two royals, Maria expresses gratitude for being there, but can't help apprising them of the poor slums she had just seen. While Maximilian pooh-poohs her concerns ("Scum floats on the clearest pools!"), Carlota more aggressively condemns the *Juaristas* as "peons with knives and stones!" After Maria's maid bursts in uninvited to tell her that her ill mother has died, Carlota plots to have Don Pedro hanged, and decides to push Maria into a marriage of convenience with the wealthy Don Miguel; "There is nothing like marriage to amend a lonely woman's heart—and her politics." At times Maximilian could be dangerously naïve and uncaring but he was perfectly balanced by the forceful and charismatic Carlota, though in this film it's obvious which one of them calls the shots.

At her mother's funeral, Maria is shocked when the hunted Don Pedro makes an appearance. Coming unarmed and claiming sanctuary on holy ground, he is allowed to join them

IV—Revoluciónistas, 1951–1959

in prayer without getting arrested. However, after the ceremony, Don Pedro enters a mausoleum and doesn't come out. To the frustration of the emperor's troops ("*Sacre bleu!*" shouts a French captain with an obvious Mexican accent), Don Pedro has escaped through a secret tunnel. Finding where the tunnel leads, Don Miguel has a nearby dam blown up, drowning several rebels, but Don Pedro and Nacho escape. Going to the location of the explosion, the newly compassionate Maria helps the maimed and wounded with bandages and medicine.

Tired and angry, Maria arrives at Don Miguel's to find her cousin and his wealthy friends laughing and toasting their "victory" over the drowned rebels. Furious, the now–socially conscious young woman condemns Maximilian and praises the "real Mexico" as that of "the fields and the mines and old honest families." She also declares that "Maximilian is a feudal Austrian, out-of-work duke, forced on Mexico by the points of French bayonets!" Certainly, *not* historically true. Maximilian was, if anything, a charming, industrious and talented man; but he was also a charismatic thorn in the side of his jealous brother, the archduke of the Hapsburgs. Napoleon's need for a French-backed Mexican emperor was the perfect excuse to get Maximilian out of the way. However, the Mexican nationalists who backed the production, as well as Mexico's government censors, weren't about to say anything good about a foreigner who thought he could rule Mexico, even if that foreigner was plainly Napoleon's pawn.

During this tirade, one is actually stunned by Veronica Lake's excellent performance. Replying to dialogue delivered by actors appearing in the Mexican version, she has a two-shot with her fellow American actor Zachary Scott (who oozes deceit and corruption as the privileged Don Miguel). Without ham or over-the-top facial expressions, the former Paramount star is convincing in her rage as she condemns not only Mexico's foreign rulers but the wealthy native Quislings who welcomed them, especially her double-dealing cousin. She finishes her tirade with, "Live long, Don Miguel, and sleep well with your thirty pieces of silver!"

Captured by French soldiers, Don Pedro and Nacho are condemned to be hanged in the town square, but the peons overwhelm the soldiers. A rider then arrives with a special dispatch which Don Pedro reads to the crowd; he announces that Juárez has returned, signaling the beginning of the end of French rule in Mexico. Interestingly, American aid to the *Juáristas* is never mentioned; it's as if they kicked out the French without the help of American arms.

Though Don Pedro and Maria are allowed to clinch, it is the proclamation of a new freedom in Mexico that takes center stage at the end. Indeed, we don't even see any punishment delivered to the traitorous Don Miguel and his friends.

There is much to be said for *Stronghold*'s politics. Seen as a patriotic tribute to Mexico, the film also blatantly condemned the upper classes as the first ones who would sell their nation down the river. This attack on the rich is clearly coupled with praise for the virtuous peon who is seen as the "real Mexico," a figure who will lay down his life for a free and independent country.

The acting is, if one ignores the bad dubbing of the supporting cast, excellent. Arturo de Córdova, freed from Hollywood, where he seemed to play every ethnicity *but* Latino, is good in the role; back in his native land, and not having to worry about dubbing, he is far more relaxed than in his Paramount efforts of the 1940s. The Texas-born Scott is a master at playing villains like this. Cut loose from his Warner Brothers contract and "unofficially" blacklisted around Hollywood, thanks to the vindictive Jack Warner, the talented Scott was

Duel Role: Mexican and Hollywood star Arturo de Córdova (left) has a machete duel with Zachary Scott (right) in *Stronghold*. The American-Mexican co-production was also shot in Spanish as *Furia Roja* (*Red Fury*).

forced to do low-budget Bs like, for instance, this film. The actor is excellent as the wealthy, traitorous heel, and he works well with his fellow "Hollywood has-been" Lake. He's especially good in the scene where Maria is at Maximilian's court, as Don Miguel uncomfortably gestures for his cousin to restrain herself. In his biography of the actor, author Ronald L. Davis wrote that in this film, Scott "had little opportunity to do more than leer lecherously and look shifty-eyed."[2] In 1961, Scott, one of five investors in the poorly distributed film, filed a lawsuit against the National Financiera, S.A., a corporation controlled by the Mexican government (considering its patriotic plot and execution, this is not a big surprise) for, as Davis put it, "poor services the company had rendered on the picture."[3]

Yet for all the good work by the lead actors (including the usually over-the-top Bedoya, this time on the side of Right for a change), the real surprise is Veronica Lake. The scene where she expresses her rage at Don Miguel is one of the best things she'd ever done, as her character suddenly realizes that for years she's been deceived by her own family as well as her own "class." However, the former peek-a-boo girl would not have nice to things to say about *Stronghold* (which she referred to as "a dog"), nor the director who obviously brought out her talent in front of the camera more than any Paramount helmsman ever had. In her autobiography, she writes that her director was Steve Sekely, "a Hungarian director, with an accent. I laughed through the whole filming of *Stronghold*. Every time the director would give me directions, I'd hear that accent and break into laughter."[4] The actress' anti–Hungarian remarks might have been influenced by her rocky marriage to the bullying, wife-abusing

Hungarian helmsman Andre DeToth. She divorced him on June 2, 1952, four months after the American release of *Stronghold*.

The Mexican version has a performer who fit the part much better: dark-haired Mexican actress Sara [Sarita] Montiel (who would soon marry director Anthony Mann) played Maria. And though the bilingual de Córdova and Bedoya played their roles in both versions, Zachary Scott's role of Don Miguel would be played in the Mexican version by Carlos López Moctezuma. A homely-looking actor, Moctezuma would later play Pancho Villa's second-in-command, Rudolfo Fierro, in Ismael Rodríguez' Pancho Villa trilogy opposite Pedro Armendáriz.

It was the now the early 1950s. With HUAC in Hollywood and Communist tyranny at its height, Elia Kazan thought the time was right to make a film about a revolutionary whose idealism couldn't defeat the treachery of Stalinist traitors waiting in the wings.

It was originally conceived as a tribute to one of Mexico's favorite sons, but once Kazan took over, the film would become more of a commentary on the present than a story set during the Revolution of 1911.

And so, in that turbulent year of 1952, the Mexican Revolution was about to enter the Cold War...

> I know only one actor who could play the part of Emiliano Zapata with veracity and integrity and believableness [sic], and that is Pedro Armendáriz.
>
> Compare a photograph of Armendáriz with that of Zapata, and you'll see the same face, the same fierceness, the same vitality. In addition, Pedro is a good horseman, and he is believable in all ways. In physical structure, he is a little taller and a little broader than Emiliano was, but his face is the same, and his race is the same.[5]

This is the great John Steinbeck in the introduction of his screenplay of *Viva Zapata!* In book form, in the edition called *Zapata: A Narrative, in Dramatic Form, of the Life of Emiliano Zapata*.

An accomplished icon of Mexican cinema, Armendáriz gave a shattering performance in *La Perla* (1947), the Mexican-shot film version of Steinbeck's classic novella *The Pearl*. And in these ruminations, obviously put down on paper years after the filming of *Viva Zapata!*, the prize-winning author was voicing his own regrets about the racial miscasting of Marlon Brando as the Mexican guerrilla.

Viva Zapata! was supposedly based on a book by Edgecumb Pinchon (the author who wrote the book on which Ben Hecht and others based their *Viva Villa!* screenplay), which Fox didn't bother to credit (and which Kazan and Steinbeck barely acknowledged, thus the author got an "original" screenplay credit). MGM wanted to film it in 1947 with Ricardo Montalban as Zapata and with a screenplay by Lester Cole. However, Communist Party flunkie Cole was about to be blacklisted. With the fear that such material would glorify revolution and with HUAC lurking on the horizon, Mayer sold the rights to the book to Darryl F. Zanuck's Twentieth Century–Fox.

To this day, there are those who scoff at the planned casting of Ricardo Montalban as Zapata; the actor was then specializing in "Latin lover" musicals and romantic comedies. Particularly galling is the derisive attitude from Latino film historians in the documentary *The Bronze Screen* in which they condemn the very idea that such a performer, despite his being born in Mexico, should play the Mexican icon. This critique is coupled with fulsome praise for the overweight white actor from Nebraska who eventually *did* play Zapata, all while these so-called historians avoided the uncomfortable subject of the film's obviously racist miscasting.

Director Elia Kazan wanted to film the project (he claimed he had always dreamed of making a film bio on the life of Zapata); and the actor he wanted was the one many believed was his "pet," Marlon Brando. A former Communist who squealed before HUAC, Kazan apparently had no problem with the racist casting choice as long as he got the chance to use his favorite actor. However, one man who *did* have a problem with the casting was the man whose studio was putting up the money.

Originally, Darryl F. Zanuck had wanted Fox contact star Tyrone Power for the role of Zapata; hey, he had played Zorro ten years previously, right? In a disastrous screen test, Brando, of course, did Brando, mumbling his lines because, according to Kazan biographer Richard Schickel, he usually did this when he was "not committed" to the project. (This was certainly the attitude of an *amateur,* not a dedicated professional.) Besides Brando's mumbling freedom fighter, Zanuck had to view the blonde-haired Anglo Broadway star Julie Harris as Zapata's bride. Predictably, Zanuck called the pair "ridiculous" as Mexicans, and who could blame him? Kazan demanded a trade-off (otherwise, without Brando, he wouldn't have made the film): Brando would remain as Zapata, and he would accept Zanuck's choice of dark-haired Fox contract player Jean Peters as Zapata's wife.

Do You Know the Way to Mexico City?: Marlon Brando as Emiliano Zapata (opposite Lou Gilbert) in Elia Kazan's *Viva Zapata!* Kazan insisted on casting a white actor in the lead and New York–accented Broadway actors as Mexican peons.

While casting the role of no-good brother Euphemio, Kazan missed another good bet by passing over Anthony Quinn for the title role. Half-Mexican and half–Irish, born Antonio Rodolfo Quinn in 1915 (as the Revolution was being fought) in Pancho Villa's Chihuahua, Quinn was severely disappointed when Brando got the role he thought he should have played. He certainly would have been a distinct improvement.

In a memo sent to both Kazan and Steinbeck on May 3, 1950, Zanuck wrote: "Not many pictures about Mexico have been financially successful. As a matter of fact, the only really outstanding success was a terrible piece of hoke called *Viva Villa!* starring Wallace Beery. This does not in the least disturb me any more than the commercial failure of John Ford's *The Fugitive*."[6]

In a memo to both Kazan and Steinbeck on December 26, commenting on the scenarist's new revised screenplay, Zanuck revealed another fear about the subject matter in that heady year of 1950:

> Now further about Zapata's *idea:* Certainly it isn't Communism, and we want to make this very clear because frankly, in the present script there is inadvertently a peculiar air about certain speeches, which might be interpreted by the Communists to claim that we are solely working for them. It seems that Zapata is surrounded by a couple of fairly well-informed people. Even though one of them is fairly misguided. I refer to Pablo and Bicho. [Pablo would eventually be played by actor Lou Gilbert; the character of Bicho does not appear in the finished film.—B.H.] Pablo must have told Zapata about a little country called the United States of America. After all, Pablo went to Texas. It seems to me that Zapata must have heard about free elections and a government run by the people for the people. Nowhere in the script do we get any indication that anyone is talking about democracy....[7]

Later in the memo, the mogul questions whether "this is the moment to tell the story of a Mexican revolutionary hero. I do not directly expect it to apply to the world situation today, nor do I expect present-day audiences to learn any great lesson from it."

Indeed, if convincing the man producing the picture was going to be a problem, one can only imagine the comments by the government of the nation where said story was set. Claiming that they wanted to perform a "service" for the *Zapata* company, the Mexican government, according to Zanuck in a memo from May 2, 1951, "implied a threat to the effect that if we disgraced their national hero in any way, they would completely ban the picture from ever playing in Mexico and might even make diplomatic efforts to ban the picture for all of South America."[8] In fact, holding onto the figure of Emiliano Zapata as if he were a copyrighted character only *they* owned the rights to, the Mexican government and its film industry, always jealous of the wildly successful *Americanos* in Hollywood, did whatever they could to block the filming of *Viva Zapata!*

Traveling to Mexico to scout locations for their film (particularly the state of Morelos where Zapata lived), Kazan and Steinbeck were shocked when they hit a roadblock called Mexican xenophobia. Hoping to have the use of those technicians who had done so much for Mexico's film industry during *Época Dorada,* the two men booked rooms in the Hotel Marik in Cuernavaca, bringing along with them Steinbeck's new wife Elaine Scott. Besides being the country's greatest cinematographer, Gabriel Figueroa was also the president of the powerful Syndicate of Film Technicians and Workers; the Americans couldn't possibly use Mexican film personnel unless the SFTW approved of the project.

Figueroa had studied at the feet of Hollywood's Gregg Toland and shot his greatest works for Mexico's Emilio Fernández, Luis Buñuel and Ismael Rodríguez; he had even worked for John Ford on *The Fugitive* and would later shoot *Two Mules for Sister Sara* for Don Siegel. If Kazan (who called Figueroa's work too dark) and Steinbeck thought that this "American connection" would work in their favor, they were in for a rude awakening. According to Schickel in his bio of Kazan:

> [T]he minute he and Steinbeck mentioned Zapata, a cloud passed over the cameraman's face. The man was as close to a saint as anyone Mexican politics had ever produced, he said. It was shameful that no film had ever been made about him in his native land. But ... for his story to be told by gringos, with, doubtless, an American actor playing the role? This would require much thought. He requested a copy of the screenplay. It was given to him, and he promised to read it over the weekend and return it.[9]

Both men suspected that the Mexican film unions were dominated by Communists, though Steinbeck counseled that a sufficient bribe (with the author using the Spanish word *mordida*) might sway the leftists into accepting their screenplay. Again, the two men were mistaken. Figueroa arrived at their hotel room Monday, accompanied by someone from the union who apparently didn't say a word, and informed them that the script was "unacceptable. It would have to be reworked and then vetted by Mexican government censors to match local hagiography."[10]

Steinbeck suggested that he would write a bogus screenplay incorporating everything the censors wanted, and then film whatever they pleased. However, Zanuck was also disturbed by what he saw as Communist influence in the Mexican unions and its government's outrageous insistence on dominating a film made by American artists. The die was cast: Zanuck ordered filming locations to be moved north of the Rio Grande to the small hamlet of Roma, Texas, where the subject of Emiliano Zapata was treated with far less reverence.

Kazan related this incident in a letter published in the *Saturday Review of Literature*, in which he slammed Mexico's premier cinematographer and the strident, narrow-minded politics behind their decision to refuse location filming to the *Zapata* company. He claimed that they weren't pleased by Steinbeck's insistence that Zapata had "Spanish blood and was proud of it," as well as the guerrilla chief's vanity about his appearance and uniform and his reluctance to take up arms; "The Mexicans attacked with sarcastic fury our emphasis on his refusal to take power."[11] Though post–Revolutionary Mexicans weren't exactly going to lose sleep if someone sneaked a derogatory portrayal of Spanish people into a screenplay, what Kazan doesn't mention here is that the guerrilla chief, besides having "Spanish blood," was also a *mestizo,* half–Creole and half–*Indian,* a fact barely mentioned in Steinbeck's shooting script. In fact, in the finished film, the opening titles announce a "delegation of Indians from the State of Morelos," but they never once single out Zapata as a *mestizo*.

Watching *Viva Zapata!,* it's obvious to anyone with a smidgen of knowledge of Mexican history that the film has *huge* inaccuracies. However, if what Kazan claimed was true, then Steinbeck's screenplay is far more accurate than what Gabriel Figueroa and flunkies in the Mexican government and film unions wanted shot. With Kazan publishing his emphatically anti–Communist (and self-serving) letter a mere five days before his own appearance before HUAC on April 10, 1952 (and two months after *Viva Zapata!*'s American release), the director hedged his bets on the screenplay. In fact, shortly after the meeting with Figueroa and the silent union official (an appearance obviously made for purposes of intimidation), Kazan and Steinbeck created the character of Fernando. Traveling with a typewriter, hovering behind the scenes manipulating everyone, Fernando is the symbolic Stalinist fellow-traveler who thrives in the wake of all national chaos, always with an eye towards the Big Lie, the usurper who profits from political turmoil, as well as the power without the noble ideals behind it. Though the Russian Revolution had yet to take hold when the Mexican one began in 1911, Kazan cunningly used this obviously villainous figure as a Latino Stalin, supporting Zapata as long as he forgets his ideals and spreads his power over a victimized populace. Kazan didn't out-and-out claim that Fernando was Figueroa, or any other present-day Mexican official; in fact, he claimed that Fernando was meant to depict members of the Communist Party that he had known in New York in the 1930s who always thought they had all the answers. Still, it's awfully hard not to come to the conclusion that Kazan saw Figueroa and other Mexican officials who tried to control his film, as people who were in love with their own power as much as the fictional Fernando.

As the movie begins, we see Mexico City during the *Porfiriato;* we'll actually see *El Jefe* himself as he sits in his palace and talks down to a group of peons from the state of Morelos. Condescendingly calling them "my children," the dictator thinks he can sweet-talk his way out of their legitimate complaints, but he has the misfortune of running across (drum roll please) Emiliano Zapata (Marlon Brando)! When the upstart complains, the dictator demands to know his name and, in a bit that will be repeated later in the film, he has his name circled in a book. In reality, when a delegation from Morelos did meet with *El Presidente,* Zapata was a junior member of the group and said nothing that made Díaz take notice of him.

Later, after federal troops machine-gun some villagers trying to cross a hacienda's boundaries, Zapata, his brother Euphemio (Quinn), Pablo (Lou Gilbert) and others (including what amounted to a non-speaking bit as a *soldadera* for former Fox contract player Margo) take to the hills to foment their revolution. (Zanuck would say that he hated films that depicted governments being formed on the run in the mountains.) A lone figure follows Zapata and cries out his name, even after Eufemio's uncomfortably close warning shots. It is journalist-*agent provocateur* Fernando Aguirre (Joseph Wiseman). When Eufemio tries

Revolution from Above: Marlon Brando (seated) and Joseph Wiseman in *Viva Zapata!*, made around the time of Elia Kazan's testimony before HUAC. The director used Zapata's life to attack Stalinists during the Cold War and ignored the real-life story of the famed revolutionary.

to throw Aguirre's typewriter down the hillside, he is screamed at by the journalist, with Wiseman's overplaying kicking into high gear. It is also an indication of the naked rage behind the pose of Fernando's cunning scribe. Hearing about a man named Francisco Madero in exile in Texas, Zapata sends Pablo there to meet him and test his sincerity.

Zapata has eyes for the beautiful Josefa (played by the beautiful Jean Peters), daughter of a wealthy merchant. In a memorable scene in a church during prayer services, Eufemio puts his hand over the mouth of the old woman who is Josefa's escort, while Zapata proposes marriage to his beloved. However, the privileged daughter has no intention of living in a ditch and cooking Zapata's food "like an Indian." The guerrilla leader has no money or property and therefore is *not* a good candidate for marriage. However, history proved otherwise. Making Zapata close to the stereotype of the poor Mexican *peon* who can't read or write, Kazan did no favors to admirers of the guerrilla leader; this cliché-ridden conception also fit the rather narrow range Brando was already accustomed to on screen with his previous characters, notably Stanley Kowalski, by continuing the role of "noble savage." In fact, Zapata was the son of prosperous farmers and the manager of the stables of a local hacienda. Not only did his parents provide him with an education (he most *definitely* was taught to read and write), but he was considered one of the best experts on horseflesh in the village. This historical reality, of course, would have made Josefa's snobbery pointless.

After Zapata kills a *Porfirio* policeman for attempting to lynch an old peon, he is arrested and taken away for *lay fuga* (the "official" verdict of being shot while fleeing from the police). His arrest is witnessed by Eufemio, who rhythmically strikes two rocks together, a signal that is taken up by the whole village, and soon they all follow the officers armed with knives and machetes. Out in the wilderness where the lynching is to take place, the officers are intimidated by the growing number of peons (the head constable is Mexican-born Republic serial veteran George J. Lewis) and they're forced to let Zapata go. Typically, Brando's nonverbal "noble savage" does not even bother to thank the old villager who led the crowd to his rescue. Still, the sequence is deserving of all the praise heaped upon it down through the years; in turn, Kazan would praise Quinn for coming up with the idea of his clacking the two rocks together being taken up by the villagers.

Zapata and his group carry out several successful raids on federal outposts; during one attack, our guerrilla hero even risks the lives of several women, thus causing one to question the "nobility" of Zapata's cause. Soon, however, he is a famous man; in the film, Madero makes him a "general," something that never happened. As he is betrothed to Josefa, there comes word that Díaz has resigned and that Madero is president, Steinbeck cutting to the chase here. In reality, a "caretaker government" reigned in Mexico until Madero was actually elected months after Díaz resigned. In the presidential palace we see Madero (Harold Gordon) offer Zapata a new ranch, which the incorruptible guerrilla angrily rejects. Though the scene has its faults, it does bring to light the fact that Francisco Madero, Jr., the great reformer, had no intention of really reforming anything, and least of all correcting any injustices done to the peons of the south concerning land distribution.

General Huerta, a bullet-headed gargoyle in dark-shaded glasses, insists on having his army crush Zapata and all other rebels in Morelos. It's not a big part, but character actor Frank Silvera is chilling in the role; he's not a perfect depiction of the alcoholic and psychopath general, but his coldness and naked ambition make him a truly frightening fascist. Certainly his performance is far better than Herbert Lom's more subtle playing of the role in the later, over-the-top *Villa Rides*. Trusting the general too much, Madero is "taken for a ride" one night and, as the little president pathetically tries to appeal to his officers, he is gunned down. Madero was murdered along with his vice-president José Maria Pina Suárez by Huerta's officers, with the colonel who had them murdered receiving a mysterious promotion soon after.

Now both Zapata's and Pancho Villa's armies finally defeat Huerta. One scene is in the presidential palace where the two rebel chiefs had that famous picture taken with Villa in the presidential chair and Zapata in the vice-president's chair. In the actual picture, we see the garrulous, over-the-top Villa laughing, as if the whole thing were a great joke on everyone; however, Zapata, sullen, suspicious, forever distrustful of all forms of government power, does not even smile. In the film, Villa (Alan Reed; yes, the voice of Fred Flintstone) and Zapata talk under a tree about who's to take control of the country. Villa is sick of it all, and wants the reluctant Zapata to become president. This scene totally ignores the existence of the power-hungry "First Chief" Venustiano Carranza, who had only *one* person in mind for that presidential chair, and it certainly wasn't going to be any bandolier-wearing guerrilla. In fact, contrary to what is shown in the film, both Villa and Zapata were quite reserved with each other in this, their first and only meeting. With both men having trouble starting a conversation, the ice was finally broken when they both discovered their mutual hatred of Carranza. Still, Pancho Villa was *not* tired of the battlefield just yet; that would come when new president Alvaro Obregón bought him off years later. Villa had many battles yet to win (and far more yet to lose), as well as a costly incursion into Columbus, New Mexico, before he would hang it up. In fact, the attitude of the two rebel chiefs towards running the country was basically that the new president would be all right with them as long as he would let them run their own affairs within their own spheres of influence; for Villa, that meant the North, for Zapata, the South. This, of course, flies in the face of real democracy; you can't have a free country if private armies are allowed to exist that mete out their own laws.

And so, in a scene so fantastic it borders on science fiction, we have Zapata as the new president forced to see a new group of peons from Morelos. That John Steinbeck, a man who reputedly knew Mexican history and had spent years researching Emiliano Zapata, had written this scene is still unbelievable. Zapata detested all governments; and instead of worrying about the interests of the nation, his *only* concern was land reform for the South, especially Morelos. It's possible that Steinbeck might have been influenced not by Darryl Zanuck, but by Elia Kazan's growing anti–Communism; and that the scene showing Zapata in the presidential chair he never really wanted was written in to back the director's new outlook that the Revolutionary could easily become the Tyrant.

After he is about to circle the name of a defiant peon (one of the film's few Latino actors, Henry Silva, who towers over Brando), Zapata realizes that he's become like Díaz. He breaks with Fernando, but not before indicting him as one who has "no field, no home, no wife, no woman" and that to destroy is his only love, a very good description of Soviet dictator Josef Stalin, a man to whom *power* was his true opiate. (Steinbeck and Kazan were probably aware of this.) At least, Steinbeck has Zapata mention the names of the two men whose existence his screenplay was, up to then, blissfully ignoring: Obregón and Carranza.

Returning to his village, Zapata has to deal with his wild brother. It must be said that in real life, Eufemio Zapata was every bit the scumbag his brother *wasn't* (though obviously the brooding Emiliano did have his dark side). A drunk, a thief, a bully, and a rapist and abuser of women many times over, Eufemio was the rotten apple in the equation who used his brother's fame and iconic status to rip off everyone he could. Of course, you couldn't tell Emiliano this without him having you shot. In the film, the neglected brother complains of never having profited from his sibling's fame, and then, rushing outside, he is shot dead. In reality, Eufemio was killed by a powerful rebel chief for his having beaten to death the guerrilla's father.

Zapata is lured to the middle of a village square where the turncoat Colonel Jesus Guajardo (Frank De Kova in his film debut) wishes to turn over a large cache of weapons, as well as the guerrilla's white horse. As Zapata reunites with the horse, Guajardo backs out of the way and federal troops riddle Zapata. Of course, Fernando appears, having instigated the whole thing. Even seeing the guerrilla's body, the rather dumb villagers *still* think Zapata is alive. Then we see the white horse, the symbol of freedom, still alive. Kazan reportedly hated the scenes with the white horse that Zanuck insisted upon (the equine is prominently mentioned in the producer's memos to both Kazan and Steinbeck), yet the director still respected Zanuck's judgment enough to give the animal the final shot.

Certainly the guerrilla chief's death was far more complicated, and though Steinbeck points to a government conspiracy to assassinate Zapata, the author amazingly avoids putting the blame on the one man who held power at the time: Venustiano Carranza. Nestor Paiva (another one of the few Latinos in this film), whose character sits in the president's chair, is never referred to as Carranza, and he certainly doesn't even resemble him. In fact, the bid to assassinate Zapata is once again laid at the feet of the evil Fernando, this time conveniently lurking behind a wall in the president's chambers. (How did he get past the guards?)

The real-life machinations behind Zapata's assassination were no less disgusting. A man who had ordered the murders of hundreds of innocent people in Morelos, General Pablo Gonzalez, was ordered by Carranza to get rid of Zapata by any means necessary. The ruthless general found the way when he had his subordinate, Colonel Jesus Guajardo, arrested after a spending a drunken night in a cantina. In a meeting with the disgraced officer, Gonzalez called him a drunk and a traitor and then slyly offered him a way to redeem himself. Treachery had always been a major character in the Mexican Revolution; it was the prime factor leading to the deaths of practically all its main participants, as well as the deaths of thousands of innocents cruelly caught between opposing armies who cared little for the populace, but very much for grabbing the spoils of victory. Knowing that the Zapatistas were chronically short of ammunition, Guajardo posed as a federal officer willing to betray Carranza and deliver weapons to the rebels. After the colonel made a long series of maneuvers to gain Zapata's trust, the day finally came when the officer was friendly enough with the guerrilla chief where he could invite him and his many bodyguards to his home for dinner. After Zapata and his men rode through the gates, they saw what looked like an honor guard, something that might have actually impressed the guerrilla chief. However, as soon as they rode in, the honor guard suddenly turned into a firing squad and Zapata and his men were riddled with bullets from the same kind of government-issued rifles the guerrilla chief coveted.

As history, *Viva Zapata!* is pretty bad; as a western (which is how Zanuck saw it) along the lines of something like *The Robin Hood of El Dorado,* it worked. Kazan had always been considered one of the finest directors of actors in the postwar era, yet for some reason he insisted on casting Broadway actors in the roles of Mexicans, both federals and rebels. In fact, when one Mexican soldier in the presidential palace makes a speech about the fighting spirit of the people in his broad New York accent, it's hard to keep a straight face. Kazan, one of our allegedly greatest directors, is putting his helpless actors on the level of a "Yonder lies the kingdom of my fodder!" B-grade swashbuckler schlock of the type Universal was fond of casting Tony Curtis in at the time.

Brando never really mastered a convincing Spanish accent, and opposite real-life Latino Quinn, his clumsy attempts stand out. To compensate for this, Kazan tries to cut down his dialogue, which, of course, makes him look *more* like Stanley Kowalski rather than Emiliano Zapata. In real life, the rebel chief could be suspicious, but he *wasn't* Calvin Coolidge.

Unfortunately, thanks to friendly witness Kazan (and Steinbeck's kowtowing to his concept of the script), the life of Emiliano Zapata is turned into an anti–Communist tract that has little to do with the Mexican icon and everything to do with absolving its obviously frightened director. Indeed, one can lose count of the many, *many* times that either Zapata or someone else mentions the People, meaning ordinary Mexicans, as being the ones who really count. In reality, it's highly doubtful that either combatants or non-combatants during the Mexican Revolution actually stopped long enough during their shared misery to actually hold socio-political discourse about "the People." They were more likely just trying to get out of the way of flying bullets.

Meanwhile, the B movie would continue to pay tribute to the heroes of the Revolution. However, unlike the schlock of *Stronghold*, this time, Hollywood would turn to the work of a classic author...

The man called Jack London (real name John Griffith) was born in San Francisco in 1876 and died, whether by his own hand or by excessive drinking or drug use or whatever, in 1916. He was an immensely talented—and tormented—writer of adventure stories and novels, many of which would proclaim his socialist viewpoint. He married twice, had numerous affairs, travelled the world as a seaman, gold prospector, amateur boxer, journalist, spokesman for socialism and war correspondent (with outstanding coverage of the 1905 Russo-Japanese War).

One of his classic short stories (originally published in 1913 in a long-forgotten periodical called *Night-Born*), "The Mexican," was that rarity in literature: a story depicting a sporting event that also served as a political tract.

The story has a Mexican youth named

Method Outlaw: Marlon Brando as Zapata in a publicity shot from *Viva Zapata!* The film falsely portrayed Zapata as a Mexican Stanley Kowalski.

Felipe Rivera seeking work in the Los Angeles office of a group of activists for the Mexican Revolution which, pre-1913, would have been working for a Madero victory. In his own rather simplistic way, and perhaps not realizing the full meaning of the word he uses to describe the activists, London calls the movement "the Junta," a word that would have a fascistic connotation rather than one of liberation. Cold and silent to others, Rivera wins no friends among the activists who quickly suspect the antisocial young man of being an agent for Díaz, especially since he wants to sleep in the office itself. Condescendingly ordered to sweep the place, Rivera does as he's told.

The activists are mystified as to several things about him, all of which he doesn't talk about. Sometimes he disappears for days or weeks at a time without explanation, only to return and unceremoniously drop gold coins into the hands of married office manager May Sethby to use for the Revolution. Her assistants Arrellano, Vera and Ramos notice the young man's facial bruises and swelled knuckles and quickly surmise that Rivera lives a life of sleaze and brawling, though the youngster never verifies their suspicions. Certainly, one has to get past London's stereotypical portrayal of Mexican patriots as speaking in a stilted, flowery tongue which belies the urgency of their situation, especially in their observations of their scary new member:

> "I feel like a child before him," Ramos confessed.
> "To me, he is the power—he is the primitive, the wild wolf, the striking rattlesnake, the stinging centipede," said Arrellano.
> "He is the revolution incarnate," said Vera. "He is the flame and the spirit of it, the insatiable cry for vengeance that makes no cry but that slays noiselessly. He is a destroying angel moving through the still watches of the night."

Though there is much debate about London's purported racist views, the author, who's supposed to be honoring his Latino characters, ironically gives his white characters much better dialogue. However, the thrust of the story is not only the heroism of those who fight for the Revolution, but the virulent racism of the story's white characters (excepting the sympathetic Mrs. Sethby, that is). During one of his absences, the brutal "federal commander" and murderer of revolutionaries, Juan Alvarado, is mysteriously killed. London describes the action succinctly:

> Young Rivera was given his instructions and dispatched south. When he returned the line of communications was re-established, and Juan Alvarado was dead. He had been found in bed, a knife hilt-deep in his chest. This had exceeded Rivera's instructions, but they of the Junta knew the times of his movements. They did not ask him.

It seems that Rivera had witnessed his family massacred by *Porfiria* troops, and that he himself survived only by hiding under dozens of bodies and then crawling out to safety after they departed.

It is established that the Revolution will succeed if only the rebels had a new supply of guns for one final thrust at the enemy. Rivera tells May to order the guns, and that he'll have the money for them in three weeks.

Finally, we see that the taciturn young man is a boxer and that he's been giving his money to the Revolution. When a title is arranged, one of the fighters gets ill, and Rivera not only insists on taking his place in the ring, but that the winner take all. His opponent is an arrogant young man whose belligerence is reflected in the game's other white characters whom Rivera has to deal with. To a man, these characters are slimy, greedy, vindictive and most definitely racist, with the words "greaser" and "Mex" making ugly appearances. However, London also has his "hero" stewing endlessly on his Anglo compatriots, with the epithet "gringo" raging in his own thoughts. These moments are certainly quite real, with racist thoughts and racist actions being enacted all through the proceedings, from the so-called civil negotiations down to the actual long, grueling fight itself. Everyone in the crowd, as well as the ring personnel and the referee, are against Rivera and want the young white fighter to win. The referee does a fast count when Rivera is knocked down, but drags the count out when his white opponent hits the canvas.

Much of this was apparently based on fact. Among his many talents, London was also a sportswriter and a boxing enthusiast. He covered the 1910 fight between black boxer Jack Johnson and "Great White Hope" Jim Jeffries. Two years before this, London praised Johnson's "coolness, quickness, cleverness and vast physical superiority.... Because a white man wishes a white man to win, this should not prevent him from giving absolute credit to the best man, even when the best man was black."

In "The Mexican," London uses the real-life racism of the white-dominated sports world against an athlete like Jack Johnson to throw up against bitter Mexican youth Felipe Rivera. In the story, Rivera wins, punching out his bigoted opponent and confounding the white crowd and boxing establishment. In the process he also wins the money to send to the rebels for a Madero victory.

A well-written and compelling boxing tale a half-century before the filming of *Rocky*, "The Mexican" has its flaws, a few already mentioned. As far as the Revolution is concerned, London makes a major mistake. Written before the success of the 1917 Russian Revolution, the story heavily reflects the author's dedication to his socialist beliefs. Unfortunately, London depicts the Mexican Revolution along the lines of, more or less, a Communist one. The story is full of simplifications and Marxist buzzwords, calling the rebels "comrades" more than once and even mentioning the participation of men from the I.W.W. (International Workers of the World, aka "Wobblies"). At another point, he refers to it as a "Red Revolution," again portraying the Mexican Revolution as being inspired by Marxist doctrine.

This next paragraph demonstrates London's shocking naïveté, both about those who fought the Revolution, as well as the Revolution itself:

> The time was ripe. The revolution hung in the balance. One more shove, one last heroic effort and it would tremble across the scales to victory. They knew their Mexico. Once started, the revolution would take care of itself. The whole Díaz machine would go down like a house of cards. The border was ready to rise. One Yankee with a hundred I.W.W. men waited for the word to cross the border and begin the conquest of Lower California. But he needed guns. And clear across the Atlantic the Junta in touch with them all and all of them needing guns, mere adventurers, soldiers of fortune, bandits, disgruntled American union men, socialists, anarchists, roughnecks, Mexican exiles, peons escaped from bondage, whipped miners from the bullpens of Coeur d'Alene and Colorado who desired only the more vindictively to fight—all flotsam and jetsam of wild spirits from the madly complicated modern world.

What "disgruntled American union men," who should be preoccupied with their own fight for recognition, is London talking about? Why would miners from as far away as Coeur d'Alene and Colorado give a damn about what happens in Mexico instead of feeding their own families? These are mysteries only London knew the answer to. Added to the above rousing description, London seems to think that the "conquest of Lower California," meaning perhaps Baja California, as well as the disposal of the Díaz regime, all launched from *this* side of the U.S.-Mexican border, could be handled very easily. London's ignorance of the banning of American gun shipments to all of the belligerents in the Revolution, as well as his total disregard for real-life native Mexican fighters like Pancho Villa, Emiliano Zapata and dozens of rebel armies who have had absolutely nothing to do with American workers, much less members of the International Workers of the World, was shocking coming from a writer with so much knowledge of the international scene.

On May 23, 1952, United Artists released *The Fighter,* a low-budget B based on London's "The Mexican." It was produced by Abbott and Costello's producer Alex Gottlieb and had a screenplay by director Herbert Kline and Aben Kandel. Kandel was a left-wing playwright on Broadway during the Depression who eventually became a scenarist for Warners; he did the screenplay for *They Won't Forget,* and the studio even bought the rights to his novel *City for Conquest* and starred James Cagney in it. However, Kandel's future may not have turned out so prestigious, as he partnered with schlock producer Herman Cohen and then gave the world the screenplays for *How to Make a Monster, Horrors of the Black Museum, Konga, Black Zoo, Berserk* and *Trog. The Fighter* would be perched somewhere between Kandel's period of working for the majors in the 1930s and '40s and his prolific output for Cohen. However, the background of the third point in this triangle is perhaps the most interesting.

Herbert Kline, the film's writer-director, was a member of the Communist Party since the 1930s. He was a radical from an early age and, once he got to New York City, fell in with its leftist theater scene, eventually editing the Communist-backed periodical *New Theater.* He became one of the first publishers of Clifford Odets' plays. As someone with a talent for shooting documentary footage, Kline became the Party's major helmsman for recording the outrages of fascism around the globe. Starting with *Heart of Spain* in 1937, about the victims of the Spanish Civil War, Kline shot his documentaries clearly along Party lines. For instance, showing us Hitler's conquest of western Poland in *Lights Out for Europe,* he conveniently ignored Stalin's conquest of the eastern half of the country. He continued to crank out documentaries like *Crisis!* and *Rehearsal for War* in between submitting stories and screenplays to the majors. He even worked with John Steinbeck when he made *The Forgotten Village,* which was actually shot on location in a Mexican village. Despite the Party looking over his shoulder, Kline displayed incredible talent with his mobile camera that transcended propaganda, and his documentaries, many of them emotionally powerful and shot with a compassionate eye towards the oppressed, won prizes around the world. One wonders why Gottlieb chose a class act like Kline to work on *The Fighter,* a low-budget work that could have been shot without fuss by any B Hollywood hack.

On a street in El Paso in 1913, we see a policeman prevent the beating of Paulino (Frank Silvera in his third film), the editor of a pro–Madero newspaper. After having witnessed the attack, Felipe Rivera (Richard Conte) follows Paulino to his office and, just like in the short story, seeks to work for the Revolution. And, just like in the story, he is rather rudely told to sweep the floors. Also working in the office is Carlos (Rico Alaniz), who quickly accuses the newcomer of being a Díaz agent, an accusation that is met with Felipe's attempt to strangle him. Another pro–Madero co-worker is the pretty *yanqui* widow Kathy (standing in for the middle-aged May Stethby, and played by the cute Vanessa Brown). As time goes on, Rivera sweeps the office one day, disappears for a while, and then returns with much-needed rent money so the paper can stave off eviction. After giving the activists even more money, Felipe's three co-workers decide to finally follow their close-mouthed colleague and find that he is being paid to be a sparring partner in a local gym. Standing at the edge of the Rio Grande one night, Felipe decides to tell the curious Kathy all about himself, including the hatred he carries inside of him.

In a long flashback, we see Rivera as a simple young man of his village with a mother, father, little brother and local gal to whom he is betrothed. The *federales,* under the command of Captain Alvarado (future portrayer of Pancho Villa, Rodolfo Hoyos, Jr.), have been riding the area, killing and bullying the locals. When the wounded guerrilla leader Durango (Lee J. Cobb) wanders onto their land, the family hides him under a pile of corn. After the federals leave, Felipe is detailed to escort the now-rested guerrilla chief out of the area. However, when he returns, Felipe finds that his father has been tortured (he dies soon after), his village burned to the ground (some of Kline's documentary stock footage is used here), and his family and girlfriend murdered (with a heavy implication that two federals raped the girlfriend before murdering her).

Durango is captured and Rivera finds out where he is being held. Rivera hooks up with other rebel sympathizers, frees the grateful guerrilla chief and kidnaps Alvarado and his adjutant. Out in the mountains, sentence is pronounced on the murderous officers and they are shot dead. Now Felipe crosses into America to make money to send back to Durango and his men in order to free Mexico.

A fighter for a championship match is taken ill. With the help of fight manager Roberts (Hugh Sanders), Rivera talks his way into taking the young man's place. When Felipe's opponent calls him a "greaser," the Mexican decks him and the fight becomes personal, with the contest now being billed as "winner take all." With Paulino and Kathy in the audience (with the proper young lady crying out "Kill 'em!" at certain intervals), Rivera triumphs over his young opponent. At the end, we see a forlorn Kathy waiting at the edge of the Rio Grande, with Paulino assuring her that Felipe will return soon. Meanwhile, down in Mexico, Durango is distributing rifles, newly bought with Felipe's winnings, to his men, one of whom now happens to be Felipe. Before returning to his cute *yanqui* sweetheart, he must help free his country from tyranny.

There is nothing of Kline's fabled talent for documentary shooting in this rather mundane, low-budget B melodrama—that is, except in the final scenes in the boxing ring. Photographed by the great James Wong Howe (who shot *Body and Soul*) with uncredited help from Floyd Crosby, and edited by Edward Mann, the sequence transcended the production company's measly budget and put real quality into this one-hour, eighteen-minute B. The rest of the film doesn't even come close to these scenes in the ring. For instance, the scenes in the supposedly poor Mexican village (where no one has money to eat, but everyone can still afford fireworks as well as elaborate decorations for their fiestas) were obviously done on a standard Hollywood soundstage; Kline's legendary talent for documenting the life of a real Mexican village is definitely *not* on display here.

In a letter to producer Alex Gottlieb, dated August 21, 1951, Joseph Breen had his usual complaints about scenes of what he considered "excessive brutality." On page 2 of the finished script, he cited the "action of the thug kicking Paulino as unacceptably brutal," and didn't care for the violence in the climactic fight scene. The horrified Breen also insisted on deleting a scene on Page 61 "where Felipe's father is shown crucified." Then, in a nitpicking mood, he reminded Gottlieb of Scene 252 on Page 103: "Please take notice that the actual word 'raspberry' is forbidden by the Code."[12]

Poster Boy for the Revolution; Richard Conte (holding rifle) starred in *The Fighter*, the film version of Jack London's short story "The Mexican." London's plot dealt with a Mexican teenager who became a boxer and turned his winnings over to activists fighting for the Revolution. It was directed by prize-winning documentary filmmaker Herbert Kline.

IV—Revoluciónistas, 1951–1959

The casting is clearly along B melodrama lines of the early 1950s. Though praised by papers like *Variety* for "etching a standout characterization," Richard Conte is not what most folks at the time would call a gangly youth; and one almost cringes while watching the 42-year-old actor go through his paces in the climactic fight scene. In the story, the dislikable Felipe is a Mexican teenager, and one wonders, even with the racist casting choices of the day, why the producers cast a middle-aged Italian-American for the role. Vanessa Brown's casting gives our hero someone he can end up with—or rather *not* end up with, since Felipe puts his arms around a rifle at the end, not Kathy. Brown herself was a talented actress who was also smart enough to return to Broadway for better parts. It was she who played "the Girl" opposite Tom Ewell in the play *The Seven Year Itch;* of course, when Fox decided to make the film, they cast superstar Marilyn Monroe, not Vanessa. Born in Vienna, Brown was the daughter of Austrian Jews (her real name was Smylla Brind) and eventually she starred in *Tarzan and the Slave Girl,* making her the only Jewish actress to ever play Jane in the whole Tarzan series. She had made her film debut (as Tessa Brind) in a B film of 1944, RKO's *Youth Run Wild,* where she first met the film's writer, Herbert Kline. Vivacious and extremely intelligent (it was said she had an IQ of 165), she always brought more to her Hollywood roles than they deserved; case in point, the thankless part of Kathy in *The Fighter.*

Frank Silvera was a different story. A light-skinned black man born in British-dominated Jamaica in 1914, Silvera was forced by racist Hollywood to deny his ethnicity and play almost everyone *but* a black man. For the next twenty years, he would have a long career playing, ironically, Latinos. Before Kline's film, Elia Kazan had cast him as a sunglasses-wearing General Victoriano Huerta in Fox's *Viva Zapata!,* with the actor giving a terrifying performance that was far different from his gentle newspaper editor in *The Fighter.* The one exception to Silvera's racist miscasting was his later performance as the black chauffeur in the film version of *Toys in the Attic.* In this film, he's allowed to be a black man—with the filmmakers obviously thinking they were casting a Latino as a black man and not realizing Silvera's true ethnicity. Besides this off-screen dissembling, his character is pretending to be Gene Tierney's chauffeur, but is in reality her lover. Silvera's last role before his untimely death in a freak accident was as a Latino gunfighter in *Valdez Is Coming* (talk about racial miscasting, it has Burt Lancaster as a Mexican gunfighter).

Herbert Kline's future would not be as tragic as Silvera's, but he *was* blacklisted soon after the film's release. Denied employment in Hollywood, he returned to New York and continued to sharpen his skills in photography, eventually returning to documentary work by shooting *Walls of Fire,* a film about Mexican artists Diego Viega and David Alfaro Siquerios.

At the dawn of 1953, as the Cold War heated up around the globe, Universal-International took a brief hiatus from their cinematic chronicles of the Indian Wars and shot their one and only film dealing with the Mexican Revolution. Though it again starred an Anglo as the main protagonist, at least the film would be shot by a *yanqui* director who loved Mexico...

There are very few directors, even those who had filmed the west, who can sincerely call themselves Mexico-philes. Much of the western genre sets its stories in places like Texas, New Mexico, California and Arizona, locales bordering the sovereign nation of Mexico However, unlike many directors of the western film, Oscar "Budd" Boetticher, Jr., had actually lived in Mexico many years *before* he would cement his fame as a western director.

As a college student, then as a young bullfighter who applied his own *yanqui* methods to the sport of bullfighting in some of Mexico's largest arenas, Boetticher learned the language and customs of Mexico, as well as a feeling for its people. It was this innovative point of view *vis-à-vis* the Mexican people that always separated his south-of-the-border–set films from that of his Hollywood contemporaries. Every western director worth his salt had featured Latino characters in his films, from Howard Hawks to John Ford, yet very few of them would feature Latinos as major figures who help drive the story, or portray them as human beings who had thoughts, feelings, ambitions and passions every bit as honest and legitimate as those of the mostly Anglo characters who populated the genre. For instance, unlike Ford or Hawks, there were no "lazy Mexicans" in Boetticher's films. If there *were* any "villainous" Latinos, their villainy was usually balanced by positive Latino figures whose strong principles were beyond reproach.

In 1953, *Wings of the Hawk* starring Van Heflin would be Boetticher's final film for Universal, and the only one in which he uses the Mexican Revolution as his backdrop. Here, the self-styled Mexico-phile would depict the single most tumultuous event of that nation's history in his own inimitable way.

Based on the novel by scenarist Gerald Drayson Adams, *Wings of the Hawk* stayed far away from the political dynamics leading to the Revolution; in fact, with a slight change of

Guerrilla My Dreams, Part II: Soldiers (played by extras) have the drop on *soldera* Julie Adams and *yanqui* Van Heflin in Budd Boetticher's *Wings of the Hawk*. Based on the novel by Gerald Grayson Adams, the film was one of only two attempts during the 1950s by Universal-International to depict Revolutionary Mexico.

locale and characters, the film had the same evil oppressors vs. noble rebels plots that characterized too many Hollywood products, particularly *The Adventures of Robin Hood*. The film became a rousing adventure tale, not an incisive discourse on Díaz-era political turmoil. Another impediment was Universal's sometimes chintzy budgets. Pancho Villa and his contemporaries fought Díaz with thousands of men; in *Wings of the Hawk,* there seems to be just a handful of sombrero-wearing men and one lady, not including Van Heflin's *yanqui* miner.

But perhaps the major problem with this film, certainly to Budd Boetticher's thinking, was the studio forcing him to cast white actors in Latino roles. Though the helmsman was able to get his way on casting Latinos in supporting roles, all the top-billed Latino roles were played by Caucasian actors who had to dye their hair jet-black.

Our story begins in the Mexican countryside in 1911. Mine owner "Irish" Gallagher (played by the non–Irish Van Heflin) has remained neutral as the Revolution tears apart the nation's cities. His relationship with Colonel Ruiz (born in Austria-Hungary, George Dolenz) is one of mutual respect: Gallagher will not aid the rebels if Ruiz lays off his mine. The double-crossing Ruiz suddenly orders his troops to confiscate the mine for themselves. After a fight with Ruiz (Joseph Breen pointed out that the "gouging in the fight between the two men seems excessively brutal"[13]), Irish escapes, but his Latino partner is killed. After chasing the now-horseless miner to a nearby mountain range, the Federals are fired upon by rebels led by the cutest *soldadera* this side of Sunset Boulevard, Raquel Noriega (her dark-blonde hair bleached uncomfortably black, Julie Adams).

However, the soldiers had wounded Raquel in the shoulder. Since no one in the rebel band can remove a bullet, they're forced to let the *yanqui* mine-owner do it. This begins the predictable bonding between them. Trying to melt the *senorita's* icy reserve, Gallagher's sexist remarks don't help: "Why don't you stop playing soldier and go back to your sewing basket and let the *men* do the fighting?"

Taking an immediate dislike to Gallagher is Raquel's jealous suitor Arturo (Rodolfo Acosta), a weak man whose "leadership" of the band is hardly inspiring. The other part of this soap opera, Raquel's sister Elena (nice Jewish girl from Brooklyn, Abbe Lane, originally Abigail Francine Lassman) is married to the evil colonel. He murdered the parents of Raquel and Elena but she steadfastly believes his story that another officer ordered their deaths and he was powerless to stop it.

Gallager and Raquel are captured by Ruiz's men. When the other rebels, led by Arturo's lieutenants, Marco (Paul Fierro) and the comical Tomás (Pedro Gonzalez-Gonzalez), both of whom like the *yanqui,* break them out, a shootout starts. Gallagher rolls a hay-wagon right into their gun emplacement and gives the edge to the rebels, who are victorious. In a celebration, Arturo gets into a fight with Gallagher, but when the frustrated rebel attempts to draw his gun on the Irishman, it is the comical Tomás who stops him. Joseph Breen insisted that the violence in this scene be watered down, reminding producer William Gordon that "the use of a broken bottle as a weapon is extremely dangerous screen entertainment."[14] Now having lost the band's respect, Arturo leaves the room. In record time, he rides to Ruiz's compound and squeals like the yellow rat he is.

Earlier, the band had been visited by revolutionary bandit Pascual Orozco, played by the totally miscast Noah Beery, Jr. The actor son of Noah Beery and nephew of Wallace was a talented actor in his own right, and though he had played Latinos before (and had given a memorable speech about anti–Latino racism at the climax of Paramount's *The Light of Western Stars* in 1940), it was obvious that Universal (with Boetticher's obvious approval) cast the actor because he had dark hair. In his *only* scene in the entire film, Beery's performance as Orozco is convincing, if not his accent. However, his five-minute scene barely gives the actor any time to attempt to portray the highly complicated Mexican general and traitorous rebel leader.

The son of a successful middle-class family (as were practically all of the major revolutionaries), Pascual Orozco, Jr., was himself a successful miner, freighter and merchant. Attracted to the revolutionary ideas of the Flores Magón brothers, and chafing under the restrictive dictates of the Díaz regime, Orozco was arrested when he was caught with anti–Díaz literature in 1906. By 1909, he had partnered with revolutionary José Inés Salazar to smuggle guns from American arms dealers into Mexico. At the behest of the rising Francisco Madero who called for an armed uprising, Orozco was put in command of revolutionary forces in Guerrero on October 31, 1910. Ironically, for a man with absolutely no military training, the former miner and precious metals merchant became a successful commanding officer, and his men roundly beat Díaz's armies again and again, especially in the state of Chihuahua, where he was hailed as a hero. In March 1911, Orozco was promoted to brigadier general (Madero had already made him a colonel). On May 10, he and "Colonel" Pancho Villa captured Ciudad Juárez from Díaz troops, no mean feat for rebel armies with little or no military training.

After Madero's victory and Díaz's ouster, the new president appointed the arrogant Venustiano Carranza, a man who never fought on the battlefield, to his War Ministry (*Ministerio de Guerra*) rather than the proven soldier Pascual Orozco. Fuming over the rejection, and disillusioned that Madero wasn't initiating the land reforms the new president had promised, Orozco refused his order to lead his forces against the still-rebelling Emiliano Zapata. By the spring of 1912, the former Madero supporter had openly turned into a Madero-hater. Defying President William Taft's ban on arms shipments to Mexico, the miner turned brigadier general smuggled guns across the border from Texas, a move partly financed by the theft of cattle and horses. His under-supplied *Orozquistas* were defeated several times by General Victoriano Huerta. After Huerta took over the government (and had Madero and his vice-president murdered) Orozco agreed to support the new president if he put forth the land reforms Madero didn't. After Huerta was deposed, both men fled to the United States. On June 27, 1915, they were arrested for violating American neutrality laws. This was around the time when German espionage agents promised to reinstate Huerta as the president of Mexico to subsequently use the country as a base of operations in which to launch German attacks on the U.S.

Escaping house arrest in El Paso, Orozco returned to Mexico and raised another army, though a much smaller one that he had been used to commanding. But it was too late. In an attempt to steal the cattle of Texas rancher Dick Love, Orozco was killed on August 15 in a gun battle between his men and Love's crew.

Ironically, despite Beery's brief bit as the revolutionary general (here not portrayed as a general, but instead a Pancho Villa–like bandit), his Orozco moves the plot forward and subsequently puts some actual history in the contrived plot—with one major omission: Though the film will make much of Orozco's victory over Díaz forces in Ciudad Juárez (justifiably), Boetticher and his screenwriters neglect to mention the crucial participation of

Pancho Villa. Perhaps Universal wanted to keep Villa as a stereotyped bandit with no military talent of any kind (a persistent Hollywood prejudice whenever the rebel leader was depicted on screen). Or perhaps screenwriter James E. Moser and adaptor Kay Lenard felt that by portraying Orozco as a bandit leader, they could afford to remove Villa's presence.

Beery's Orozco needs money to buy 200 rifles and ammunition from Americans across the border and the rebels must come up with the aforementioned cash. This dialogue also simplifies the revolution's dynamics *vis-à-vis* purchasing arms in Texas. In real life, after his break with Madero, Orozco did have trouble adequately supplying his men with enough arms, but the purchase of 200 rifles was hardly going to make a dent in battles that commanded the participation of thousands, as well as the frequent use of artillery pieces (a particular obsession of Pancho Villa's). Though the lazy Arturo refuses to help Orozco, Marco and Tomás are more than willing to listen. With Gallagher's help, they decide to raid the American's own captured mine and blow up the rest of it.

In the meantime, the murderous nature of the Díaz regime, as personified by Colonel Ruiz, rears its ugly head. Hidden in the basement of the local church after their escape, Irish, Raquel and Tomás are forced to watch, through the basement window looking out onto the street, Ruiz's men liquidate innocent civilians via firing squad, including Tomás' mother. Gallagher is forced to punch out his friend to stop him from rushing outside.

Despite the fact that Ruiz has a lot of men guarding the mine, our heroes can sneak in and sack the place with no trouble at all. Raquel is captured when she lures Ruiz' men away from Gallagher's crew. At the colonel's home, the *soldadera* tries vainly to get the rather dense Elena to leave him. When the treacherous Arturo (whose squealing on the location of the rebels' hideout cost the lives of many of them) interferes, Ruiz orders him shot.

After the guns are purchased from an American rancher (a walk-on by former WB star of the 1930s, Lyle Talbot), Gallagher and the rebels learn from the dying Arturo of Ruiz's plans to take Raquel back to the mine (and for some strange reason, Elena goes along as well). Using a massive amount of explosives, the audience previously didn't know they had, the rebels blow the hell out of Gallagher's mine and, backed up by their newly acquired American-made Winchesters and Springfields, decimate Ruiz's men. When the colonel himself attempts to escape, he is riddled with bullets by Tomás' rifle, the little caballero avenging his mother's execution. As Gallagher and Raquel clinch, it is announced that, thanks to the smuggled rifles, Orozco and his army (*without* Pancho Villa) have captured Ciudad Juárez, spelling doom for the Díaz regime.

With this trumped-up ending in the story of the Mexican Revolution, both Boetticher and his writers were allowed to ignore the madness that would follow, including the hope that would be crushed with both Madero's lackadaisical leadership, and then Huerta's takeover, culminating in the little man's murder. In *The Man from the Alamo,* Boetticher showed the anti–Latino racism beneath the surface of a wagon train containing "civilized" Anglos, and their vindictive hatred of one of their own when it looked like he ran out on his brethren at the Alamo. In almost a reverse of this plot, in *Wings of the Hawk*, we see Latino guerrillas whose rebellion is in limbo until a *Yanqui* mine owner happens along and shows them the way. Though there are parallels between these two Boetticher films, particularly their depictions of Mexican history, the casting would have linked these two films even closer. Both films not only have Julie Adams as their leading lady, but had he not been recovering from injuries he suffered while filming the Alamo production, we would have seen Glenn Ford, not Van Heflin, as "Irish" Gallagher. In just four years, the two actors would finally get a chance to work together on the classic *3:10 to Yuma*.

Another interesting side-note to this film is its title. What "wings" and what "hawk" are the filmmakers talking about? Before you can say "Call the Audubon Society," you'll notice that when Gallagher first meets Arturo at the rebel camp, he has a rather big hawk perched on his shoulder (or maybe it's a falcon). As he speaks to the new arrival, Arturo barely acts like the bird is there, like it's some kind of big feathery boil that appeared on his shoulder and will just go away in a few days. And sure enough, by the next scene the bird disappears from the film and never shows up again. Maybe the thing flew over to Díaz's side.

Despite the film's oddball title (which came from Adams' novel), controversy existed behind the camera, most of it centering on the usually feisty helmsman. Ordered by Universal executives to shoot *Wings of the Hawk* in 3-D, he refused, guessing correctly that 3-D was a fad (though it would make a kind of dubious cinematic comeback half a century later). U-I executives were not happy with Boetticher's decision, a fact reiterated by the helmsman himself: "So I didn't do it. I thought [3-D] was absurd. They brought in another director after I left Mexico and he shot ten days of 3-D stuff."[15]

Though the director heavily implied that *Wings of the Hawk* was filmed on location in Mexico, in reality it was shot on the Universal backlot and the Corrigan Ranch in Simi Valley, California; this was a fact Boetticher himself emphasized when he boasted in the

Target Practice: A Mexican (actor unidentified) aims his Winchester at a federal target as Van Heflin watches in *Wings of the Hawk*. As usual, a *yanqui* adventurer finds himself helping the rebels, a common plot device in many a Hollywood film depicting Revolutionary Mexico.

documentary *Budd Boetticher: A Man Can Do That* that the final explosive pyrotechnics in the film's climax effectively blew up Universal City.

Viewing the film today, one is still entertained by it without the use of 3-D, but there *are* times, though not many of them, when objects *do* seemingly fly towards the camera 3-D style. Author C. Courtney Joyner, who had interviewed the helmsman many times, has written that studio contract director George Sherman did a few days of extra shots, and that it was *he* who was the other director the irritated Boetticher refused to mention by name.[16]

Another gripe from the helmsman was the fact that he wanted two weeks' vacation and the studio was overworking him. Boetticher directed four films in 1952, the first full year of his contract, and then a whopping *five* films in 1953 (all of them were not B quickies, but A caliber films with major stars). In fact, *Wings of the Hawk* had a Los Angeles premiere on August 26, with another Boetticher-directed U-I film, *East of Sumatra,* released practically on top of it on September 23. This info backs the director's claim that he desperately needed a rest.

Having had it with the studio, Boetticher called for a release from his contract, which caused Universal to rather vindictively announce to the press that it was "dropping his option"; in other words, making it look like he was canned.

Wings of the Hawk was one of the first major Hollywood studio attempts to film the Revolution from the perspective of the Communist-hunting 1950s. As the decade went on, even more *yanquis* would head south of the border, like "Irish" Gallagher, at first looking for riches, but ending up helping the downtrodden fight a dictatorship. Consequently, because the guerrillas were, for the most part, *not* instilled with Marxist doctrine (especially in a devoutly Catholic nation), these films allowed American capitalists to side with revolutionaries in a way the anti–Communist films of the Blacklist Years would never do…

THEY HAD A DATE WITH DESTINY IN THE
POWDERKEG OF THE WEST … ZONA LIBRE!

So shouted the tagline to Universal-International's *Border River.*

At the beginning of the film, a title tells us that it is 1865, at the time of the French occupation of Mexico and the *Juáristas*' war against the occupiers. It is also towards the end of the American Civil War; hence, like *Stronghold,* our Civil War is shown in contrast to another conflict just over the border in Mexico. Unlike *Stronghold,* however, *Border River* will avoid heavy political issues and condemnation of Maximilian in favor of good old-fashioned western adventure. Instead of attacking French imperialism or the gluttony of the Mexican aristocracy, it reserves its condemnation for a typical Hollywood villain whenever the film industry deals with the Mexican Revolution: the usual black-hearted (and black mustachioed) renegade general who runs his own little town like a dictatorship. In this case, said town is a hamlet situated on the border just over the Rio Grande called Zona Libre (free zone). Here, like the future Cherokee Strip in the Oklahoma Territory, Zona Libre is a haven for American outlaws. Unlike the Cherokee Strip, these outlaws have to pay the usual "renegade general" a fee to be protected from American lawmen.

Union cavalrymen chase a lone rider splashing across the river (the Colorado River doubling as the Rio Grande). It turns out that the quarry is Confederate officer Clete Mattson (Joel McCrea). Watching from a carriage are General Eduardo Calleja (Pedro Armendáriz),

Carmelita, his paramour (he *thinks*!—and played by the gorgeous Canadian-born Yvonne DeCarlo), Calleja's over-the-top sidekick Captain Vargas (the usually over-the-top Alfonso Bedoya), and American expatriate Newlund (Howard Petrie). Carmelita insists on the southerner's rescue and so, to the frustration of the pursuing Union commander, Vargas rides out and tells him that the officer and his men have no jurisdiction in Zona Libre. It is a wonderful scene, Bedoya using his character's poor pronunciation of English words to parody those of the Union captain. When the blue-belly tells him that Calleja is an outlaw to the government, Bedoya sarcastically asks (as only Bedoya can), which "government" is the officer talking about? The one run by Lincoln, or the one run by Jefferson Davis?

It seems that Mattson's landing in Zona Libre is no accident. He is planning to buy guns, ammo, clothing and food from the general for two million in Confederate gold, which originally was Union gold stolen by Mattson and his men from a shipment in Colorado. In a meeting in the general's office, whenever he is on camera, Pedro Armendáriz neatly steals the show from the *yanqui* actors. When he is told of *Juárista* agents seeking to overthrow him, the wily and grinning imp gives way to the murderous psychopath in full dress uniform and epaulets. "*Everyone* wants to get my little country!" he fumes while crumpling an Austin newspaper.

Mattson wants to get closer to the lovely Carmelita, but the gorgeous north-of-the-border actress, pretending she's a south-of-the-border babe, rejects his overtures. In the saloon she co-owns with Calleja, Mattson pulls her out of the way as Vargas guns down two *Juárista* agents. Confronting one, Calleja condemns his mission: "My people love me! I've always been fair! I dominate no man!" However, this self-justification on what a lovable Teddy bear he is takes a dive when he tells Mattson and Carmelita, "We will give them a fair trial, then shoot them in the morning!"

After Mattson beats up two men who broke into his room, the general orders his soldiers, including the sadistic Captain Sanchez (the Mexican-born and American-raised George J. Lewis) to deposit the two badmen across the river, where Texas authorities will arrest them for cattle rustling. This gives the general a chance to ponder man's inhumanity to man: "It's strange what greed does to a man's mind. A very sad thing too."

Up in Carmelita's room, Mattson despairs that the *señorita* is no longer fighting for an ideal as, it is implied, he is. Again, like *Stronghold,* the film's misguided ethics portrays the Confederate cause of fighting for a slave state as an "ideal," instead of the perpetuation of oppression.

In the local saloon, a pro–Union loudmouth named Fletcher (serial and western veteran George Wallace) beats up a pro–Rebel young man until Mattson punches out the "yankee." Later, in Mattson's room, it is revealed that Fletcher and the youngster he beat up are Reb spies who have the gold across the river and are ready to transport it after the purchase for arms is made.

Riding over to the purported location for the gold landing, Mattson almost loses himself and his horse in a huge quicksand bog. It is a frightening scene, with the poor animal almost drowning in the bog. Later, after returning the horse to the rental outfit, the hostler, noticing mud all over his animal, reports to Captain Vargas, who happens to be making the acquaintance of bottle after bottle of tequila. There are very few moments in the history of cinema as enjoyable to watch as a drunken Alfonso Bedoya. Already making a mockery of English words in his natural style of speech, imagine his patented imitation of drunken slurring *on top of that!*

When Vargas rides out to the river to trap the Rebs, one of them throws a Bowie knife into the drunken captain's back and kills him. Afterwards, Newlund appears unannounced in Mattson's room and reveals himself to be a private detective hired by the Union to get the gold. Mattson seems to meet more people in his hotel room in the middle of the night than he does during the day in the entire film!

Calleja, Carmelita, and Sanchez and his men ride to the river to look for the gold. To stop them, Mattson follows them with his two Reb assistants and Newlund. During the subsequent shootout, Newlund and Sanchez are killed and Mattson tackles the general, with both men predictably tumbling into the quicksand bog (Bobby Hoy is doubling for both McCrea *and* Armendáriz). Of course, only Mattson survives.

In a letter to producer William Gordon, dated May 29, 1953, Joseph Breen objected to an earlier version of this scene: "Page 127: This final fight scene between Clete and Calleja seems to suggest that Calleja is actually beaten to death. This is unacceptably brutal, and we must ask that some other means be found for Calleja's elimination."[17] Zona Libre's quicksand corrects this situation.

At the end, Mattson and his men get the guns, clothing and food courtesy of Juárez's victorious troops. In fact, grateful for Mattson's disposal of the despotic general, the new *Juárista* commander of Zona Libre even wishes the Reb officer "great success"! This is amazing, since President Lincoln supported Juárez and vice versa, with the Mexican leader heaping scorn on Southern slavery and oppression.

And this might be the crux of the film that leaves a bad taste in one's mouth. Despite the wonderful performances of Armendáriz and Bedoya, *Border River*'s politics are, at times, dubious. Much of this is due to the character of Clete Mattson (played woodenly and without a trace of Southern accent by the California-born McCrea). Arrogant, sometimes brutal, and justifying the Southern cause as an "ideal," Mattson is supposed to be the hero. Yet his brave deeds against the murderous General Calleja mask the fact that he is fighting for a slave state; an irony is that he frees Zona Libre only so that he can aid a dying South destroy even more enemies of slavery in the United States. The pro–Southern sentiments expressed in the film, as well as making the Reb the hero, is a sop to a Southern audience still practicing Jim Crow; indeed, the film was shot (from June to July 1953) a full three years before *Brown vs. Board of Education*. As directed by George Sherman, *Border River* is an apology for a south that still refused to change its racist ways and revisionist history *vis-à-vis* their defeat in the Civil War.

The history is also somewhat skewed from the Mexican angle. Immediately after the end of the Civil War, President Andrew Johnson, succeeding the murdered President Lincoln, ordered newly minted Supreme Commander of the United States Army, General Ulysses S. Grant, to assemble 50,000 American troops along the Mexican border. Lincoln's support for Juárez's Republican army would continue under the administration of President Johnson and his "Radical Republicans." The troops' dual purpose was to threaten French forces close to the border, as well as supply the *Juáristas* with American guns (with muzzle-loaders soon to be made into "repeating rifles" and Navy Colts soon to be turned into double-action six-shooters). While they were at it, the now-victorious Union Navy blockaded French ships from providing any reinforcement, either in men or weaponry, to their troops on Mexican soil. On February 12, 1866, the U.S. officially protested the presence of French troops in Mexico (on April 3, 1864, they had already protested the establishment of a Mexican monarchy). On May 6, they protested the use of Austrian and other foreign volunteers in Mexico. On the 31st, Napoleon III, frightened that the United States seemed far more powerful after the war (and without the war to distract it), announced the withdrawal of French troops from Mexico.

However, besides the U.S. watching its back, Mexico got plenty of help from Juárez's own crack troops, brave men in their own right. His Republican army took Chihuahua on March 25, Guadalajara on July 8, and made a clean sweep by the end of the month, conquering Matamoros, Tampico and Acapulco. Four months later, the *Juáristas* captured Oaxaca and parts of Zacateas, as well as San Luis Potosí and Guanajuato.

Yet all these great victories, justifiably cherished by Mexicans to this day, were accomplished in 1866, not the spring of 1865, when *Border River's Juáristas* were supposed to have conquered large parts of Mexico, including the mythical Zona Libre.

Still, despite its oddball mixture of inaccurate history and even more inflammatory pro–Confederate ideology, there are the film's performances. McCrea is, of course, McCrea, his character humorless and unbending as usual. Having played "the girl" in numerous period adventures for U-I, DeCarlo tries to instill feelings of confusion about Mattson, as well as bitterness, in her character, but the performance doesn't quite come off. The actress, whose colorful ancestry was Scottish, Sicilian and Russian-Jewish, may be dark-haired and look exotic (she'd portrayed many exotic women since the mid–1940s), but she's no María Félix. Again, it is the native-born Mexicans who best played native-born Mexicans. Bedoya dangerously crosses the line from murderous bad guy to slapstick comedian—and back again—so often and so well, that he fairly blows away McCrea and DeCarlo. At one point, the poor actress has to stand by as Bedoya, drunk on tequila, gives a disgusting belch to the camera. Tragically, this bit might have been based on reality; the talented Bedoya was a heavy drinker, and he would die of cirrhosis of the liver four years later, on December 15, 1957, in Mexico City at the age of 53.

However, it is the man who plays his boss who again shows what a fantastic performer he always was. In the language of Mexico, Pedro Armendáriz had *macho,* a true manly charisma that dangerously threatened to blow his American co-stars off the screen. His presence was almost always severely restricted in his Hollywood films from overtaking that of the American stars. Even in his John Ford films, he is obviously in support of Hollywood top-liners, though even he couldn't steal a film from John Wayne (a man who, coincidently, always loved and married Latinas). In *Border River,* Armendáriz can't help but show Universal and the rest of Hollywood the enormous acting experience he attained while performing in his native land. Though Calleja is written as the typical clichéd adventure movie villain, thanks to Armendáriz, the general is far more versatile than the role was on paper. The actor's change from good cheer and wry humor to murderous hatred is quick and sometimes shocking. Displaying irony, he condemns greed and violence while enjoying his own dictatorship of the town; he cheerfully tells Vargas how volatile dynamite is just at the point where the captured rebels are shot by his firing squad; to a captured *Juárista,* he almost wistfully claims that the people love him and that he is always fair, just before predicting their execution after a "fair trial"; scheming to steal the gold from Mattson, he also laments, quite convincingly, the bottomless greed of men. Thanks to the actor, every one of Calleja's contradictions is played out to the fullest, making him far more interesting (and likable) than the film's designated hero. *Variety* called Armendáriz a "a topflight Mexican actor (who) shades his role skillfully and colorfully."[18]

IV—Revoluciónistas, 1951–1959

By the mid–1950s, Universal was done with Mexican history and instead continued their cinematic chronicle of the Indian Wars. However, over at United Artists, the Mexican Revolution would be the subject of *several* of their films of the 1950s…

On February 7, 1954, United Artists gave new independent company Hecht-Lancaster $12 million to make seven films, five of which were to star co-producer Burt Lancaster. Columbia's *From Here to Eternity*, starring the dynamic actor, had been a box office smash the previous year, and UA wanted to ride the gravy train. They financed *Apache*, which starred the blue-eyed Caucasian New Yorker as real-life Apache mass murderer and rapist Massai. However, as filmed by Robert Aldrich, Massai's brutal treatment of "his woman" is seen in a positive light, and his real-life murders of innocent people seen as Native American "resistance." In the next Lancaster-Aldrich collaboration for UA, both men would reduce the sexism shown in the previous film, if only slightly, and instead concentrate on the macho pairing of two male stars of the western genre. The screen story for the new film, *Vera Cruz*, was written by veteran Borden Chase.

In 1866 Mexico, ex–Confederate colonel Ben Trane (Gary Cooper), riding a sick horse, spots another tied outside a cabin. Suddenly, another *yanqui*, Joe Erin (Burt Lancaster with megawatt grin), appears. The need to outdo each other in manly behavior begins when Trane suddenly shoots his horse dead, prompting a fast-draw display from Erin. After purchasing the new horse, Ben rides off, but soon finds Joe riding fast ahead of him; both are now being chased by French troops. Ben, wondering why the fancy-dressed colonialists are chasing him, gets his answer when Joe admits that the horse he just sold him belongs to the officer chasing them. It is certainly an audacious way to begin an audacious western.

After knocking out Erin when the outlaw tries to rob him, Trane meets Joe's gang in a cantina; they are a cinematic potpourri of western hellions of the 1950s; Charles Bronson (still being billed as Charles Buchinsky), Ernest Borgnine (who would win the Oscar the following year in the Hecht-Lancaster produced *Marty*), James Seay (usually cast as army officers in sci-fis of the '50s), Charles Horvath, Jack Lambert, and the very busy Jack Elam. When the gang tries to beat up Trane, the assault is stopped by Joe, who, despite the punch, admires the ex–Reb's spunk.

When a young senōrita named Nina (Mexican actress and future wife of director Anthony Mann, Sara [Sarita] Montiel) is manhandled by Anglo louts, the gentlemanly Trane rescues her. Typical of Aldrich, the young woman shows her gratitude by swiping Ben's wallet while giving him a kiss. The rescue is followed by the pompous arrival of the Marquis Henri de Labordere (Cuban-American actor from New York, Cesar Romero). The marquis wants to hire the American mercenaries to work for the Emperor Maximilian. This offer is "countered," in a way, by *Juárista* rebel chief Ramirez (nice Jewish boy and veteran general from '50s sci-fis, Morris Ankrum).

During the ride to Mexico City to meet Maximilian (Joe archly refers to him as "Max"), Erin introduces Ben to Ballard (African-American dancer Archie Savage). Pointedly, the intro barely gets a nod from the uncomfortable ex–Confederate officer, all to the enjoyment of an unusually tolerant Joe.

At the ball, the appearance of the uncouth *Americanos* opposite the cultured European imperialists is obvious, with both Ben and Joe turned off by the pompous and arrogant French officer Danette (played with supreme hauteur and incipient snobbery by gay actor

"Yep...": Gary Cooper as the ex–Confederate officer seeking Maximilian's gold in Robert Aldrich's *Vera Cruz*. Instead of the heavy polemics of *Juarez* and *Stronghold*, the film took the French occupation of Mexico and turned it into macho adventure.

Henry Brandon). Soon they meet the emperor (the 54-year old Rhode Island native George Macready portraying an Austrian who died at the hands of a *Juárista* firing squad at age 34), as well as the lovely Countess Marie Duvarre (the lovely Denise Darcel—the only French actor in the entire cast actually playing a French character). Less to impress the emperor than to stir things up, Joe and Ben show him and the fancy guests their shooting skills, accurately shooting the tops of lances and the flames of candles—all with double-action Colts that couldn't possibly have been in use so shortly after the Civil War. To top them in "manly" behavior, the emperor fires at a target with a Winchester "repeating rifle" that also didn't exist in 1866.

With the marquis in charge, Ben and Joe (and their gang) are offered $50,000 in gold merely to escort the countess through *Juárista*-held territory to the port city of Vera Cruz (reportedly spelled as two words at the time the film was set), and she will return to France. Later than night during a stopover, Ben and Joe discover that the coach has a secret compartment containing three million dollars, all to be used to hire more troops to take over Mexico and beat the *Juáristas*.

Joe visits the countess and lays down his rules in true misogynistic Aldrich style, with Joe slapping the noblewoman and pulling her hair. It seems that Marie wants to depart for France with the gold, but not to pay for any troops; Nina reveals herself to be a *Juárista*, and wants the gold for the rebels; Ben and Joe want to swipe the gold and escape to Vera

Cruz, effectively cutting out Joe's gang. To fully understand all the planned double-crosses in this amoral film, one needs a scorecard.

Having heard of the plot, the marquis, accompanied by Danette and their men, race off with the coach one night, wounding Erin in the arm. This prompts the manly outlaw to insist that Ben cut the bullet out with his knife fast so they can give chase. When one of the outlaws interrupts, Ben says, "Don't bother him now, can't you see he's suffering?"

When the coach is overturned in a *Juárista* ambush, Ben and Joe discover that the boxes are gone. Now Ramirez must join forces with the *yanqui* outlaws to get back the gold, and offers them a portion of it for their help. After catching up to the French, Joe pays Danette back by impaling him on his own lance. The big shootout begins and the marquis and all the members of Joe's gang are wiped out. After gunning down the innocent Ballard, Joe is about to steal it all until Ben stands in his way; the Southerner hopes to give the gold to the *Juáristas*. "That old soft spot," says the black-clad outlaw with contempt. Though holding a rifle on him and saying he was going to give Joe the same treatment he gave Ballard, the actor playing him is still Gary Cooper, so he tosses the long gun away and the two draw their 1860s model single-action pistols. Joe has enough time to fire, twirl his gun and holster it before he dies, a killing the ex–Reb did not want to do. Nina appears and it is implied that instead of using the gold to revitalize his old plantation, Ben will stay in Mexico and fight against the French aside his half-his-age *senõrita* cutie. This was *not* the original ending. According to correspondence between the Production Code office and Hecht-Lancaster, Erin is allowed to live and go unpunished, with he and his pal Trane shrugging off the loss of the gold. Indicating Erin, Breen complained loudly that an early draft of the script had "a cold-blooded murderer, thief and professional gunman going off scot-free...."[19] Therefore, Coop *has* to blow him away.

Some cineastes, including neophyte helmsman Sergio Leone, have called *Vera Cruz* the first spaghetti western. There's no doubt that the film is fun, with appropriately smarmy acerbic dialogue by veteran western screenwriter James R. Webb and his partner, Roland Kibbee. At the time, Cooper was enjoying a comeback after his Best Actor Oscar for *High Noon*. As a tax shelter, the star had to work outside of the United States for eighteen months to save on paying the IRS, and so 1953 to '55 became his international years, with *Vera Cruz* following the Mexican-shot *Garden of Evil*. Cooper was also smart enough to know that he had to appear in more violent, amoral material (though he didn't necessarily like it) in order to appear "relevant" to younger audiences who had no idea of the censorship in American films under the Production Code.

However, he insisted that his character still be "moral" and be the good guy, ultimately a wise choice. Aldrich would grumble that Cooper insisted on these rewrites, while Lancaster, grateful to add Cooper's box office presence to his own, wisely saw that the actor was right to make those changes. Indeed, the script was reportedly written *as* the film was being shot, never an ideal situation. Aldrich would later claim that the movie was "made up, improvised." Added to this, co-producer Lancaster, a hands-on performer every bit as concerned with details on a production as his friend Kirk Douglas, practically co-directed the film (something Aldrich *doesn't* say). Meanwhile, Cooper had to endure working in close proximity to Sarita Montiel, whom he had to kiss (once quickly on the lips), a collaboration the star claimed was brutal due to the actress' alleged lack of hygiene (smelly hair and never bathing, according to Coop).

The film is an amoral, take-the-money-and-run masterpiece. Lancaster's dressed-in-black outlaw, who grins every time he's happy (and sometimes when he's unhappy), is so charismatic that we understand Cooper's pained expression after he's forced to kill him. Cooper's character, however, is not as good as the actor himself wanted him to be. A reactionary in the days of the Cold War, the Montana-born star (who had been accused of making anti–Semitic comments) apparently had no problem playing an ex–Confederate officer who wanted to revive his plantation. Of course, after the North won, this was impossible since he could no longer procure slaves to work it. One must at least give Aldrich and the liberal Lancaster credit for including the scene with black actor-dancer Archie Savage, in which Joe Erin gleefully introduces Ballard to the ex-colonel, the chilly response underlining the fact that that the alleged "good guy" still perpetuates a racist culture.

Juáristas are clearly seen as heroes in this film, though you'd never know that from the reaction of the Mexican government. Years later, Eli Wallach, the Bronx-born Jewish actor who became the genre's favorite Mexican bandit, would claim that the government, then run by the administration of President Adolfo Ruiz Cortines (of the left-leaning Institutional Revolutionary Party), complained of the film's portrayal of Mexicans, and apparently ignored the even worse portrayal of non–Latinos. Because of this allegedly negative depiction, the new government of Adolfo López Mateos (also from the left-leaning Institutional Revolutionary Party) demanded that a Mexican censor observe the portrayals of Mexicans on the set of the Mexican-shot *The Magnificent Seven* six years later.

Pardon My French: The lovely Denise Darcel poses between Gary Cooper (left) and Burt Lancaster in *Vera Cruz*. Out of all the actors portraying members of Napoleon's court, Darcel is the only French performer in the entire film.

Despite all this in-fighting and controversy *Vera Cruz* (where absolutely *none* of the film takes place), produced on a budget of $3 million (some say $1.7 million), grossed upwards of $11 million (some reports say $9 million) in the United States alone.[20]

Now freed of the restrictive Breen Office by the mid–1950s, Hollywood was allowed to focus on the upheavals suffered by our neighbors south of the border. And so, in 1956, the dying RKO studios would shoot another tale of *yanquis* and gold, though this time the film would be set back in the 1910s, and even have the name of a major figure of the Revolution in the title...

In his huge catalogue of films, producer Edward Grainger never once touched the subject of the Mexican Revolution. Then, with the sudden revival of the topic in many Hollywood products, Grainger, through RKO, filmed a treatment written by veteran scenarists J. Robert Bren and Gladys Atwater, and wisely hired western novelist and screenwriter Niven Busch (he wrote the novel *Duel in the Sun,* among many other works) to do the screenplay.

The die was already cast in Hollywood's 1950s versions of the Revolution and, unlike Boetticher's *Wings of the Hawk* shot at Universal City, it was a given that these films would be shot on location. This, of course, meant hitting a roadblock much bigger than the Breen Office—the Mexican government. Fiercely nationalistic, the Mexicans had long held sway over their portrayal in Hollywood films. Certainly the administration of Presidente Adolfo Ruiz Cortines was not going to be any different. When United Artists shot *Comanche* on location in Durango in 1956, this American-Mexican co-production *had* to make sure the depiction of Mexicans in the screenplay met with the approval of higher-ups in the Mexican government. Therefore, the real-life Mexican suppression of the Comanches in the 19th century would have to be ignored, and Mexican officials would be portrayed as honest, fair-minded men who despaired of the needless waste of life. At the beginning of *Comanche,* a Mexican official claims to our heroic American scouts that Mexico had long ago outlawed the policy of paying bounty on Comanche scalps—a boldfaced lie. Indeed, with the history of on-location shooting in Mexico, a Hollywood production company would *have to* have a positive portrayal of Mexicans in their screenplays, for how else would their crews be able to use those great panoramic locations without permission?

In *The Treasure of Pancho* Villa, our story begins somewhere near a mountain range in Mexico in 1915. American mercenary Tom Bryan (taking a break from his Universal, Columbia and Fox westerns, the very busy Rory Calhoun) and his *Villista* friend Colonel Juan Castro (the wonderful Gilbert Roland) are taking cover behind a solid wall of canvas bags filled with gold coins as they are surrounded by a troop of Federales. In a corny voiceover narration, Bryan wonders just what got him to this decisive moment in his life, and we flash back to a little Mexican town where his present voice comes up with some trenchant observations: "Well, this happened in the days when Mexico was fighting for freedom. There had been two liberators, but one of them turned dictator. It's a habit liberators often get into ... and it tends to confuse the people it liberated...."

Certainly, during the Cold War era, the comment about the liberator turning into the dictator could have been a sly reference to Lenin and Stalin. However, one also wonders about the identities of the Mexican figures Bryan is alluding to.

Bryan also tells us that "it was not healthy to be known as a friend of Villa's" and that Villa himself had been chased back into northern Mexico. Indeed, at the time, repudiated by Carranza and losing on the battlefield to Obregón, Villa was now watching his men abandon him by the thousands. He was losing face, prestige and material (guns, horses, money). This is where, Bryan tells us, *he* comes in: Claiming to be in "the finance business," Bryan intends to supply Villa with money for the supplies he needs.

At this point, as Bryan's buckboard stops at a certain corner, the audience can clearly see a big red Coca Cola sign over the mercenary's shoulder that was impossible to see on a real Mexican street in 1915. When a group of men hold up the nearby bank, Bryan aids them by gunning down approaching Federals with an unusual weapon that looks like a hand-held Gatling gun. Afterwards, Bryan meets up with a *Villista* agent and, despite an offer of twice as much pay for another job, tells him the Revolution is washed up and that he's planning to quit and "live high on the hog." Certainly, the role of cynical and amoral mercenary only working for a buck is right up Rory Calhoun's alley. His usually bitter but black-humored cowpokes rarely used his gun for an ideology outside that of protecting his own skin; this ability to play a sometimes greedy anti-hero would also help him in his villainous characterizations, like his roles in *River of No Return* and Universal's 1956 version of *The Spoilers*. In fact, Calhoun's (as well as Mitchum's and others in the 1950s) version of the *yanqui* mercenary down in Mexico working for gold to supply the rebels with guns, would be a harbinger of the spaghetti westerns of the 1960s and beyond (which were usually set in either the west or revolutionary Mexico).

Reluctantly, the mercenary is forced to reconsider when he hears that the man who wants his services is his old friend, *Villista* colonel Juan Castro. Unlike the Castro of a later day, this one is interested in liberating his people. We see him meet up with rebel Captain Pablo Morales (played by Italian-American screen bad-guy Joseph Calleia). The colonel dislikes the greedy Morales and thinks he'll betray the movement at any minute. But Castro needs the *capitan* as a guide and to help him blow up a train with federal troops and relieve it of some gold. Castro also meets with a schoolteacher and daughter of a murdered American mine owner, Ruth Harris (the usually brassy and dysfunctional Shelley Winters). Ruth tells the colonel she wants to help his people, though her pompous platitudes are clearly uttered from the perspective of a liberal activist from the 1950s rather than a boots-on-the-ground rebel from 1915.

After the successful raid, the money-hungry mercenary meets the idealistic teacher, and music swells up on the soundtrack whenever they get close—which seems to be often. Winters was no social activist off-screen, and, if one can believe her autobiographies, she was also one of the most sexually active women in this or *any* century. These little off-screen details, however, do not help her in her role of a sexually shy, socially conscious daughter of a mine owner. Practically everything she says about fighting for a cause not only fails to impress the mercenary Bryan, but fails to impress us as well. Bryan wants to have lots of money and live high on the hog, an ambition which immediately repels the idealistic would-be schoolmarm. However, no matter how many times Bryan turns her off with his cut-throat way of living, like a bad penny, she keeps coming back so he can alienate her even *more*. Oh, and all this happens between some bouts of passionate kissing.

The aim of the trip is to meet up with Villa in Yaqui country and give him and his men the gold (for the usual guns, food, clothing, etc.). The rebel caravan is being trailed by *Federales* led by Yaqui trackers, an interesting sight since the nation's Indians fairly spat contempt at federal troops who had traditionally burned their homes, raped their women and murdered their children.

IV—Revoluciónistas, 1951–1959

Mexican Standoff: *Yanqui* mercenary Rory Calhoun (left) and *Villista* officer Gilbert Roland (second from left) face the treacherous Joseph Calleia (standing opposite) and his gun-toting men in *The Treasure of Pancho Villa*. Again, a money-hungry *Americano* helps the rebels only for the love of gold—that is, until he sees the light. Pancho Villa is talked about, but never once appears in the film.

When they arrive at the appointed spot to meet Villa, the Centaur of the North is not there. Further down the valley, Morales has taken some of Castro's men to seize the gold (packed on twenty mules). "You dirty traitor!" says Castro, stating the obvious. Then the Reb colonel threatens him with the specter of Pancho Villa's revenge upon traitors (shooting, being staked out on the ground for ants; you know, the usual). Soon, with Bryan's help, Castro is able to have a machete duel with Morales as everyone hangs back and watches. Victorious, and backed by Bryan's big gun, Castro orders Pablo and his band to leave—and to take Ruth with them and out of harm's way.

There is a further betrayal as Bryan turns his gun on Castro. Planning to steal the gold for himself, he has the colonel disarmed and they all travel through the mountains. Meanwhile, the treacherous Morales gives himself up to the nearest federal garrison where he instantly betrays the whereabouts of Castro, Bryan and the gold. The men who rode with him are immediately shot by firing squad, and Ruth is about to be sent to the American consulate in Tampico—but not before the annoying deb calls the federal commandant a "killer" and lambasts Pablo as a traitor (big surprise). "In spite of men like you," *Senorita* Winters declaims, "the ideals and the cause of the people will win, and then you will have no place to hide!" Despite this speech, she's *still* going to Tampico and, thankfully, we never see her in the picture again.

When Bryan sees that they are being closely followed by federal troops, he unties his friend and gives him a gun. Then and there the two renew their friendship and decide to destroy the gold rather than let it fall into the hands of the federals; they build a wall of gold bags as a buffer against gunfire, a little million-dollar fort. Meanwhile, the commandant, at gunpoint, forces the treacherous Morales to go out into the open and beg for their surrender. A bullet from Castro kills the traitor. Now the two old compadres make their last stand. As the troops ride in shooting, the two kill the commandant and lay waste to his men. However, one soldier has snuck behind them and shoots Castro dead. Bryan avenges him by killing the soldier.

Realizing their fight is lost, the two old friends had set dynamite charges by the wall of gold. After Castro's death, Bryan now pushes the plunger down just as the greedy troopers arrive at the gold wall to stuff coins into their pockets. With all the *federales* dead, the formerly cynical mercenary buries his friend and, gazing up at the frustrated buzzards overhead, says, "You've tasted everything, you buzzards, but if you'd ever tasted Juan Castro, you've tasted a man!" Not exactly a final line on a par with "Rosebud!" or "'Twas beauty killed the beast," but we get the point.

In the last shot we see Bryan walking off, possibly to make his way to Tampico and reunite with an obnoxious strawberry blonde social activist with an out-of-place Brooklyn accent.

The Treasure of Pancho Villa (which we now see was *not* his treasure after all) was a last gasp of western action from the dying RKO studios, emphasizing the studio's decline with some pathetic color photography. Gilbert Roland does not look comfortable playing the loyal Villa idealist, and he only seems to really come alive when he's being playful and anarchic. Peering at the cowardly Morales from behind his fortifications, he says, "Isn't he cute! And he has a little white flag!" Or the last moments when he and Bryan just shoot the breeze before the federals' last charge, Gilbert is the wily Latino rascal we all know and love. Certainly no one in the history of the adventure film was more fun to be with on a caper than Roland (a favorite of my spaghetti western-loving father, by the way). Calhoun is excellent, playing his signature heel who ends up doing the right thing. Only Winters sounds the wrong chord. With activists like her, the followers of Huerta would *still* be in power.

However, you'd never know this from Winters. According to her bio, *Shelley II*, the actress showed her contempt for the film by mistakenly writing "the plot is about six mules carrying a great deal of gold to Pancho Villa from the Pacific to the Atlantic side of Mexico or maybe vice versa." However, the Oscar-winner did admit that it was "one of the funniest films I had ever done, although at the time I didn't mean it to be." Expanding on her participation, and that of her co-stars, she wrote:

> Rory Calhoun, Gilbert Roland and some other fine character actors in the cast were doing a cowboy picture. I was doing a revolutionary film about the exploitation of Mexican peasants. I think I modeled my character on Emma Goldman. They acted; I made speeches. Howard Hughes (who ran RKO), who was very anti–Communist, must have had a fit when he saw it.
>
> From the neck up, I was Universal's blonde bombshell, with every curl in place and long black eyelashes. From the neck down, I was a revolutionary. I wore a man's shirt, with the sleeves rolled up, Mexican worker pants, old boots and a gun. So maybe I rewrote a few of the lines. The producer, Edward Grainger, let me.[21]

In fact, Shelley's "Emma Goldman" is emphatically *not* given a gun, even though her character begs Castro for one. Also, her claim of making up her lines probably explains why she's allowed to verbally indict the traitorous Pablo without the ex-*capitan* making any effort at an appropriate comeback.

IV—Revoluciónistas, 1951–1959

In the meantime, south of the border, Mexico's Dark Queen of Cinema was kept busy leading valiant revolutionaries astray. Once again, a scheming woman compromises the Noble Cause, as only the great María Félix can...

La Doña herself, María Félix, had buried her late husband, iconic singer-actor Jorge Negrette, who died in December 1953 of cirrhosis of the liver at age 42. In 1956, it seemed like the right time to marry husband number four, Alex Berger. The happy union lasted until his death in 1974.

On July 18, 1956, Mexican audiences saw the release *La Escondida* (*The Hidden One* or *The Hidden Woman*), based on the novel by Miguel Nicolás Lira, and starring Maria and Pedro Armendáriz. Directed by Roberto Gavaldón and shot by Gabriel Figueroa in Tlaxcala and the Churubusco-Azteca Studios in the fall of 1955, *La Escondida* returned Félix to the turbulent world of the Mexican Revolution in a work that reaffirmed Mexican identity and revolutionary idealism at a time when the country's successful middle-class was starting to forget what the Revolution was fought for in the first place.

Our story begins in 1912. Gabriela, a woman of privilege (an older, but still strikingly beautiful María Félix), is looking through the window of a train, temporarily stopped at a station, and sees a female peon offering to give her a drink of Aguamiel from her homemade porcelain jug for a few pesos. The woman's appearance repels Gabriela and she pulls down the shade. Then she flashes back to the time three years ago when she herself used to be one of those sad, desperately poor women.

It is 1909, and the nation is still under the iron heel of the Díaz dictatorship. Selling the drink, she has the advantage of actually boarding the train and using her feminine wiles and natural beauty to her advantage in her "sales pitch" to the *Porfiria* army officers. The other girls are scandalized by her "boy games" and "shameful behavior." When Gabriela suggests that they do the same, they surround her and beat her up, giving her a nice crack on the skull to boot. Out in the fields, she meets her beau Felipe (Pedro Armendáriz) who, like his father Tata (the Pancho Villa of *Let's Go with Pancho Villa,* Domingo Solar) and his buddy Máximo (Jorge Martinez de Hoyos), are peons enslaved by the dreaded *hacendados*. Gabriela wants Felipe to marry her so they can leave for a better place, a quite reasonable wish. Yet the men have contempt for Gabriela, with a not-so-subtle example of Mexican racism demonstrated to show their feelings. "The truth is," one says, "she's as conceited as her *blonde mother*," as if the old woman's hair color or genes dictated the kind of person her daughter would be. And though it *is* hard to accept the eternally dark-haired María Félix as the daughter of a blonde, at least she goes through these early scenes of peon poverty wearing some tastefully applied makeup and lipstick.

When *Federales* show up, the hacienda store manager leaves his place and Gabriela steals the profits he just shoved behind the counter. Meanwhile, outside, the federal sergeant shoots dead a fleeing peon who was caught with "subversive propaganda," the man's death prompting an officer to wryly proclaim the government's "good intentions." That night, as the man is buried by the mournful villagers, the rich *hacendados* dance and party at a nearby ball. Gavaldón cuts back and forth between the sadness and reverence of a poor peon's funeral and the useless frivolity of the wealthy partygoers as they drink, shout and play infantile games. Gavaldón's genius here is in constantly contrasting the activities of the classes as they are sucked into the maelstrom of the Revolution.

The peons, all of whom are *Revoluciónistas,* want to send Felipe to see Dr. Herrerias (Carlos Riquelme), their leader, to find out what to do next, arm themselves and fight or sit it out. However, Felipe needs money to get to see the doc; at this point, Gabriela shows the shocked young man the stolen money and offers to join him if they both flee together. When the creepy storekeeper tries to rape Gabriela and she fights him off, he informs the federals, but Felipe saves her by confessing to the crime. After Gabriela begs a local *hacendado* for mercy, Felipe's punishment is knocked down to conscription in the military: "Two years marching in the National Valley. You won't see him again."

As the train pulls out, we see Felipe in a crowded cattle car as Gabriela chases the moving train, promising to throw herself under its wheels should Felipe never return. The young man begs her to wait for him. Gavaldón cleverly fades out on the train heading one way, then fades into the new scene with the train heading in the opposite direction: two years have sure gone by fast! However, when Felipe returns, he is in a federal uniform, shocking his father and friends. But Felipe is still a revolutionary ("The snowball has already started in the North, headed by Don Francisco Madero!"). After ditching the federal outfit, he hopes to get the peons together and link up with their *Zapatista* brethren in the South. Unfortunately, Tata delivers the bad news: Gabriela emphatically did *not* throw herself under a train; instead, she "left with the fancy people," and is probably busy "rolling around, what else would they take her for?" Felipe is justifiably bitter, but the fight for freedom must come before his personal anguish.

The next day, the villagers of Vergel are ordered to receive the new *Porfirista* governor, General Nemesio Garza (Andrés Soler), a reputed "hero of the Yaqui War," which, in Mexico-speak, usually means a brutal extermination of the Yaquis. After the general's train pulls in, there is much pomp and celebration with the peons ordered to look happy as they welcome the new governor. Also in one of the cars, dressed to the nines, is the formerly poor Hortensia (Sara Guasch) and her wealthy pal and former peon's babe Gabriela, now the general's mistress. Gavaldón turns Gabriela's reappearance as an aristocrat into a stunning second entrance into the film. Inside the car, the now pampered woman tells her liquor-guzzling friend (Hortensia is attired in flaming red) how much she hates being back, and she hopes her ambitious nature will not only get the general to marry her, but push the mass-murdering *Porfirista* into even greater heights.

Later that evening, as Garza meets with officials in Puebla, there is a huge celebration put on by the town's elite, including a towering, 100-foot tall effigy of the general in the town's main square. In a building close to the structure, Felipe is meeting with Dr. Herrerias and the other rebels, with the physician–rebel chief counseling patience. On the other side of the giant Garza figure, a bored Gabriela goes out on the terrace and looks at the display at the same time Felipe goes out on *his* terrace. And so, as the fireworks go off and the effigy is lit with glowing lights and smoke, the two former lovers actually find themselves staring at each other across the wide distance, but the lights and haze are thick and they obscure their view. Then the smoke clears and their vision focuses, emphasized by Gavaldón's sweeping close-ups, first of Felipe, as he suddenly realizes who the wealthy woman is that he's been staring at, and then to Gabriela. At first, she registers shock, then fear, and as he cries out her name, she flees back into the room and slams the door shut. It is an excellent scene, the director taking full advantage of Figueroa's shot, with the cameraman purposely using the general's iconic effigy as a barrier obscuring the former lovers from rediscovering each other, then closing in on their strong facial reactions when they realize just who's spying at them from across the courtyard.

IV—Revoluciónistas, 1951–1959

The sight of his beloved Gabriela triggers the bitter peon to ignore the doctor's advice and he orders his friends to launch a full-fledged guerrilla war. Gabriela also has a strong reaction to seeing her former lover; she decides to ignore Garza's insistence on remaining in Clascala. The next day, as the general's train heads for Puebla, with him and his officers interrogating Dr. Herreria, in another car is Gabriela and Hortensia, the former escaping Felipe, the latter just escaping into booze. Soon, the rebels damage the tracks, halting the train. But when they attack, many of them are mowed down by machine-gun fire, including Tata, and the *Porfiristas* capture Felipe (with the Indian-killing general showing us a truly insane smile as he boasts of his victory). When the formerly moderate Dr. Herrerias orders the rebels to attack, he is shot dead by the federals.

It's taking some time to repair the tracks, so that night, as Felipe is being tortured to reveal the rebels' plans, the young man's friends return. In a wild battle, the rebels kill off the federals, forcing the general to man a machine-gun. But before he does so, he gives the frightened Gabriela a loaded gun to use on herself if the "mob" takes over the train. And so, as Garza fires at the rebels, Gabriela fires at the old Indian-killer, emptying the gun into her meal ticket of the past three years.

Now freed, Felipe goes to the car where they imprisoned Gabriela, supposedly to kill her. However, his declaration of hate doesn't fool the wise Máximo, who knows that his friend is still in love with her. Once in the car, Felipe demonstrates his country's typically brutal machismo and slaps his former lover around before he finally embraces her. Looks like the romance, for what its worth, is back on.

The next day, further down the track, federal officers ride up and offer amnesty to the rebels, Díaz is now gone and Madero is in charge. But Máximo rejects this optimism, saying that the Revolution is *not* over. "The Revolution is too large for us to pretend to be above it," he says.

Now a despised general himself, wearing a federal uniform, Felipe shares his bed with Gabriela in an opulent mansion in Mexico City. Not only does Gabriela return to a life of luxury, but things are hotter between the couple than before. Colonel Montero (Carlos Agosti), who also pines for Gabriela, arrives and reports that Máximo, who has never signed any pact to lay down his arms, is raiding again—and since he's still officially a part of Felipe's command, the officer insists that the new general go and see him. Felipe at first refuses, but then rides out to meet his ex-friend before his *Zapatista* rebels take Clascala. At their meeting place, it is not only Máximo, but the sight of *Zapatistas* riding up from everywhere in magnificent splendor which thrills the new general. It is a rousing scene, and the viewer is actually glad that the smiling Felipe tosses his federal cap and uniform coat away and decides to ride with his friends. Indeed, despite Madero's victory, Emiliano Zapata and his guerrillas never really surrendered, the rebel chief realizing that Madero definitely *wasn't* going to grant land reform to Morelos.

Seeking to follow Felipe, the impatient Gabriela takes a train to be with him. But Felipe and his men, seeing what they think is a federal transport, attack the train, with one of the flying bullets hitting Gabriela in the head, killing her instantly. Though Felipe mourns her death, he continues to ride for the Revolution.

Literally translated, *La Escondida* is *The Hidden One* or *The Hidden Woman*. Gabriela certainly carries in her psychological makeup two different women, the sincere peon who loves Felipe, and the ambitious, grasping social climber and mistress of a powerful general.

When she arrives in Clascala, villagers refer to her as "the hidden woman," the mistress and kept woman shunted away from the public's disapproving eye. (The general being a mass killer apparently means nothing to them, but the widower's affair with a young woman scandalizes them.) In the beginning, when she looks through the train window and sees the poor woman selling her drinks, Gabriela sees what's she's running away from, her own hidden self from the past. When she sees the people of Clascala through her train window as they "celebrate" Garza's arrival, again she pulls down the shade, hiding from those she knew. And when she and Felipe spot each other from their respective terraces, it is significant that Garza's effigy, a huge, tacky, smoke-filled ghost, is obscuring their view of each other. But when they actually focus on each other and she sees Felipe, she hides behind a closed door, again thinking she can put up a physical barrier to her past. Her refusal to embrace her own roots and hide herself behind closed doors and window shades stands in sharp contrast to Felipe, who's *never* hidden who he was. It is relevant that during the course of the film, he discards his federal uniform not once, but *twice*—both times when he is back among his own people and is ready to return to the fight.

Gavaldón makes good symbolic use of trains all through the movie, making them every bit as important as any character; mostly, however, they are bringers of death and pain. In the beginning, flashing back to her past, Gabriela's base motives are revealed by flirting with federals on a train, an action which brings about a beating from the jealous women. Ordered out of Vergel with hundreds of others, Felipe rides a cramped train as the heartbroken Gabriela follows; it is significant that she promises her lover that she will throw herself under the wheels if he never returns. But after two years he *has* returned. However, Gabriela has broken her promise, thereby she has also figuratively cheated not only Felipe, but the Train as well. Gavaldón increases the symbolism of this vehicle by having it return the now uniform-clad Felipe to Vergel where he learns of Gabriela's desertion. Later, it is a train that will bring the mass murderer General Garza, as well as the heartbreaking Gabriela and the drunken Hortensa, to Clascala. The next day, rebels attack Garza's train, with many deaths occurring within its vicinity, including the drunken Hortensia who is shot in the head innocently looking through the train's window. That night, more deaths occur near the train, this time federal troopers when the rebels gain the upper hand. When Garza mans a machine-gun placed between the cars, Gabriela kills him with his own gun. At the film's climax, Gabriela happens to be on another bad-luck train when a bullet strikes her in the head.

The train is also used to heighten both passion and violence within the narrative. Gabriela is in a train car when Felipe first beats her, then makes love to her. The rebels are on the captured federal train when they learn that Madero has triumphed; and Felipe happens to be right near it when he and Máximo split up, each deciding to fight the Revolution in his own way. It is significant that the two men reignite their revolutionary partnership by attacking a train at the end.

In the future, both Félix and Armendáriz would return to the world of the Mexican Revolution on screen, but *La Escondida* certainly stands as one of their best collaborations on the subject.

Meanwhile, as the Revolution symbolized passion and idealism to the Mexicans, the *Americanos* in Hollywood had their own take on it. Finding or losing one's soul during the conflict would take a definite backseat to thrilling adventure and action-packed shootouts. United Artists rudely ignored the heavy melodrama and confused loyalties of *La Escondida* and continued depicting the Revolution as a combination Mexican and American boys-only adventure.

And when the cast was headed by the likes of macho actors Robert Mitchum and Gilbert Roland, Revolutionary idealism was about to be thrown under the train...

Earl Felton was a screenwriter of adventure movies since the 1930s; westerns, jungle pictures, thrillers, espionage. He wrote a couple Lone Wolf Bs for Columbia, Gene Autry pictures at Republic, and a few comedies and romances here and there. Very few of his screenplays stood out, that is, with the exception of the ahead-of-its-time western parody *The Beautiful Blonde from Bashful Bend* for Preston Sturges, and the classic film noir *The Narrow Margin*. Born in Sandusky, Ohio, in 1909, Felton suffered from polio since he was a child; it was an illness that robbed the sensitive future scenarist of much of his self-esteem. His Bible-thumping mother used to take him to revival meetings where it was hoped that they would cure his illness; unfortunately, these trips to revival tents did little for the youngster: "Dragging myself up to that pulpit was embarrassing enough. It was the crawling back down the aisle that was so humiliating."[22]

Defiantly, young Earl refused to use a wheelchair and instead hobbled about on crutches or used canes the rest of his life, always wearing leg braces which sometimes caught the stares of passersby. He became a contract writer for RKO in the early 1950s; in early 1951 he had already written the screenplay for *The Narrow Margin*, and the script received positive buzz around the studio before it was released the following year. On the strength of *Margin*, and on orders from Howard Hughes, Felton would be assigned to rewrite the ending to John Farrow's *His Kind of Woman*. Directing another film, Farrow was unavailable to reshoot the climactic battle on a ship between hero Robert Mitchum and a crew-load of gangsters, forcing Hughes to assign another noir specialist, Richard Fleischer, to direct the scene. It was the first collaboration between these three men, and the first meeting between Mitchum and Felton. The two became an unusual pair, with the lonely and usually depressed Felton enjoying the company of the hell-raising actor. It was reported that the two closed many a tavern in the film capital.

In 1955, Felton wrote a treatment set at the time of the Mexican Revolution in 1916. Originally called *Horse Opera*, the story concerned an American soldier of fortune helping Pancho Villa, all while a Hollywood movie crew is filming the guerrilla leader as he embarks on his raids. The story had the definite satirical tone that Felton brought to his screenplay of *The Beautiful Blonde from Bashful Bend* for Preston Sturges. When Felton's pal Mitchum and former RKO collaborator Richard Fleischer read his treatment, they quickly signed onto the project. With Mitchum co-producing, the film was originally to be released by RKO.

After doing the screenplays for the underrated *The Marauders* at MGM, as well as the film version of Norman A. Fox's novel *The Rawhide Years* for Universal, Felton returned to *Horse Opera*, but somewhere along the way, for some reason that was not fully understood by his collaborators, he abandoned the story's tongue-in-cheek humor and wrote a more-or-less straight action picture. Retitled *Bandido*, the script removed Pancho Villa and replaced him with a fictional revolutionary named Colonel Escobar. Since Villa was gone, also gone was the subplot of the film crew. The project now became a standard piece about rival gunrunners that could have been mistaken for any one of Mitchum's early RKO efforts. When the actor read Felton's new script, he wanted to know why it was changed. Felton's response:

"The idea which looked so good over Mexican beer hadn't come out when bathed in typewriter ink, and this current plot had reared its exciting head instead."[23]

Fleischer rejected the new script and wanted to back out of the project, but the studio that took it over, United Artists, threatened the helmsman with a lawsuit. (Mitchum would never return to RKO, which by the mid–50s was run into the ground by the eccentric Howard Hughes, and would close its doors by 1959.) Angrily, Fleischer insisted that the handicapped Felton accompany the cast and crew on the arduous Mexican shoot. Felton was reportedly banging out new pages while the cameras were being set up for the next shot.

Felton took advantage of the demise of the Production Code as it was enforced by Joseph I. Breen, and his script was violent as well as action-packed. In a letter to RKO executive Frank McFadden, dated October 18, 1955, new Code czar Geoffrey Shurlock criticized the "excessive slaughter of human beings in the various battle sequences,"[24] as if somehow there would be battles *without* excessive slaughter of human beings.

Nevertheless, Felton probably didn't realize that 1916 was a terrible year for *yanqui* soldiers of fortune to travel to Mexico. In March, General John J. (Blackjack) Pershing's Punitive Expedition into Mexico was underway, causing violent anti–American rage to spread throughout the country; *not* a good time for rugged *yanqui* mercenaries to drop by, even when played by hell-raising, no-expression, bar-closing actors. However, the newly titled *Bandido* dealt less with history than thrilling adventure in which the revolutionaries are the good guys, the *Federales* (called "the *Regulares*" here) are the bad guys and ideologies are buried in explosions and gunsmoke.

"Big! Bold! Blasting" cried the film's taglines. Another shrieked, "THE CRY THAT ROCKED THE WORLD'S HOTTEST STRIP OF HELL!"[25] This little catchphrase, neglecting to mention that the film was set in 1916, seems to have ignored the far more bloody "strips of hell" then being fought over in war-torn Europe at the time.

As the movie begins, Fleischer's camera shows us a quick shot of soldiers and rebels shooting at each other. After the credits roll (Max Steiner's noisy score is surely one of his worst), the titles tell us it's 1916, and says that Mexico is torn by war, without mentioning its origins. An American border officer says that Mexico is in the midst of a "civil war" and never *once* mentions the word "revolution." *Yanqui* arms smuggler Kennedy (Zachary Scott, again returning to the world of Revolutionary Mexico) and his fed-up bride Lisa (Ursula Thiess; at the time, Mrs. Robert Taylor) are crossing the border into Mexico as Mexicans are going the other way and fleeing the war zones for the more settled atmosphere of the United States. They meet *yanqui* lackey Gunther (Henry Brandon) who is aiding *Regulares* commander General Lorenzo (Victor Junco). They go to a hotel restaurant where Kennedy is to sell the federals a shipment of weapons. Lisa is sick of being a trophy wife brought along as eye candy for Mexican officers so that they can seal the deal for her husband. At a nearby table is American soldier of fortune (gunrunner) Wilson (the usually sleepy-eyed Robert Mitchum). Quietly joining him at his table, as well as swiping his drink, is seedy, Irish-accented informant McGhee (an outstanding cameo by the underrated Douglas Fowley). When Wilson follows the disgusted Lisa outside, it seems that he's out to swipe more from the cold-blooded Kennedy than his guns.

Realizing that he has to make contact with revolutionary Colonel Jose Escobar (the far less famous Pancho Villa clone) and that the colonel's forces are fighting the *Regulares* at the small town of Villa Hidalgo, Wilson, in true unorthodox fashion, pays a frightened cab

IV—Revoluciónistas, 1951–1959

Amigos: Robert Mitchum (left), Ursula Thiess and Gilbert Roland in a publicity shot from Richard Fleischer's *Bandido*. It was originally written as a satirical adventure set during the Revolution; screenwriter Earl Felton inexplicably turned it into a straight melodrama. Still, the film became a box office hit.

driver to take him to the war zone. Registering at the local hotel as bullets are flying outside, Wilson's threat of a grenade tames the anti–American desk clerk. After a bullet tears open Wilson's pilfered bottle of whiskey, the white-suited mercenary casually goes out onto his balcony and lobs grenades onto the federal garrison, effectively blowing up their cannon and winning the day for the rebels. Witnessing this twist of fate that gave him so easy a victory, Colonel Escobar (a man made for this kind of film, the wonderful Gilbert Roland) and his usually skeptical aide Sebastien (played by Rodolfo Acosta, who played a similar role in *Wings of the Hawk*) burst into Wilson's room and confront him. The *Americano* offers an unholy partnership: Wilson and Escobar are to steal Kennedy's stash of guns, giving the rebels half and half to Wilson so that he can sell them to others at a profit. Intrigued by Wilson's offer as well as his cheek, Escobar agrees. What Mexican revolutionary commander could ever resist the usually audacious charm of a roguish *yanqui* gunrunner?

With Wilson along, Escobar and his men attack the train carrying Kennedy and his wife. The unctuous gunrunner claims that the guns are at his fishing lodge (of course they *aren't*). Accompanied to the lodge by Escobar's men, Wilson and Lisa escape the band, are captured by *Regulares*, and are then rescued by Escobar. Verbally ripped a new one by the colonel, Wilson is thrown into a fortified compound along with the treacherous Kennedy. However, the rebels failed to search the resourceful mercenary and, using a couple grenades, Wilson blows their way out of their jail. Kennedy is shot and wounded by Escobar's men.

Crawling through swamps, Wilson and Kennedy escape the rebels and end up at a fishing village where an enterprising priest removes the latter's bullet, but not before Wilson coerces Kennedy to admit that his guns are stored at the shoreline of Playa Blanca. When Lisa reunites with Wilson outside the church, the two would-be lovers are saved from the now-revived, gun-toting Kennedy by Escobar, who shoots the gunrunner dead. After sending Lisa north to reunite with her later, Wilson and Escobar go to Playa Blanca and find the guns. There, the two men foil the *Regulares'* ambush of the rebels using Kennedy's gun stash (which includes the now-mandatory use of a mounted machine-gun). Triumphing over the federals, the rebels can use the guns to free their people as Wilson, now mounted on a horse, tells his new friend Escobar that he's riding north, obviously to meet up again with Lisa.

Variety's review of August 14, 1956, declared:

> While the yarn is a dime thriller, it is also presented with some above-average touches here and there, plus some frank birds-and-bees byplay between Mitchum and the heroine (Ursula Theiss) that adds spice to the action. Film has slow spots, mostly due to occasionally draggy direction by Richard Fleischer and a need of tighter editing.[26]

In fact, Fleischer moves the action so fast that one doesn't think much of the screenplay's many inconsistencies—but remember that Fleischer had Felton writing scenes so fast, there was barely enough time before the next camera set-up. *The Hollywood Reporter* opined, "Fleischer's direction has the sharpness necessary for pace as well as diverse characterizations important for mood … Felton's talent for sharp and original dialogue is displayed again and again."[27] Shot on location in Acapulco, Cuernavaca, Yaltapec (where Emiliano Zapata was killed) and with interiors done at Churubusco Studios in Mexico City, *Bandido* pulled in the customers. Very much like *Vera Cruz,* the film exudes the kind of macho, boys'-only adventure that foreshadowed the Mexico-set spaghetti westerns of the 1960s and '70s. But getting it onscreen and past Geoffrey Shurlock's censors wasn't easy, as correspondence from the censor's office to RKO studios (before the project ended up at UA) reveals.

In a letter from October 18, 1955, Shurlock insists to RKO executive Frank McFadden that "the action of Wilson throwing the hand grenade into the lobby of the hotel is unacceptable," and that "extreme care must be exercised in photographing the action of Lisa about to enter the shower."[28] In the finished film, Wilson attacks the federal garrison from the balcony. As far as Lisa's shower, the original script has Escobar's man Gonzalez pull back the shower curtain and get a good look at the naked woman before she slaps him; in the finished film, as insisted upon by the censors, Gonzalez gets slapped as he's *about* to pull open the curtain. Also, in Felton's original script, Lisa steps out of the shower naked as Wilson wraps a robe around her, but thanks to Shurlock, the scene is now cut.

Three weeks later, on November 8, Shurlock had another note:

> We would like to suggest that you eliminate the dialogue between Wilson and Lisa where they're about to meet at the border hotel at a later time. It is possible that you can transpose this dialogue to the conclusion of the sequence by which time her husband has been killed. In its present position this dialogue amounts to an immoral proposition of the leading woman by the leading man and one that is made to appear perfectly right and acceptable.[29]

In the finished film, with Kennedy conveniently shot dead by Escobar, the two lovers can reunite at the end without guilt.

Shurlock and his army of blue-noses couldn't hold a candle to the Mexican government and *their* usually dishonest army of soldiers and police, as the film's wrap-up irrevocably proved. The night before cast and crew were to fly back to L.A., Mitchum and Felton were in the actor's chauffeured car on their way to a restaurant when they were cut off by a big black sedan. Four large Mexican men jumped out and menacingly surrounded the car; as an afterthought, and perhaps in an unconscious rebuttal to Alfonso Bedoya's character in *The Treasure of the Sierra Madre,* they *did* flash their stinking badges. They ordered the driver to open the trunk, which he did. In surprisingly little time, considering they supposedly didn't know where to look, the policemen suddenly found a bag of marijuana. Mitchum, who had famously been arrested for marijuana possession in Hollywood in the late 1940s, said to Felton, "This looks like a setup." The policemen said they didn't believe the denials of Felton, Mitchum or his driver. In this case, the somnambulistic actor was right: the fix was in. Though these "police" wanted to take the two Hollywood people to the local calaboose (apparently the driver wasn't considered important), Felton, who knew a little Spanish, pleaded with the *policia* to take them all back to their hotel where the entire matter could be "straightened out," though Felton didn't specify how this would occur. Perhaps these thugs—er, police officers had sympathy for the handicapped scenarist, or perhaps it was Mitchum's fame, or perhaps they merely put on an elaborate act of playing bad cop-bad cop before they agreed to Felton's suggestion, knowing full well they *were* going to agree with Felton's suggestion of accompanying them to the hotel beforehand.

At the hotel, Mitchum and Felton were placed under guard while people from Churubusco huddled in the hotel lobby. Then a group of police officials arrived and went up to their rooms. Production manager John Burch was able to talk to Mitchum, and then a conference was held with said police officials. Production manager Burch was in charge of per diems and other such duties of money distribution for the company. Ten thousand dollars was soon packed into a small suitcase and, miraculously, the police officials, as well as the goons guarding Mitchum and Felton, left the hotel, got into their cars and sped away never to be seen by the *Bandido* company again. As Fleischer said, "No one was late for their plane back to L.A."[30]

In 1954, after filming the low-budget *Sitting Bull* at Churubusco, Iron Eyes Cody claimed in his autobiography that policemen sent by the government tried to kidnap him and other actors until money was paid to the kidnappers; they also wanted to hold onto the location footage until a "fee" was paid. Fortunately for the Americans, cast and crew fled the country before this could happen. Certainly, the above examples painted a very disparaging portrait of the Mexican police that, unfortunately, was proven to be true.

In the meantime, Mexican filmmaker Ismael Rodríguez had his own uses for Churubusco-Azteca Studios. He embarked on the first in a trilogy of pictures featuring one of Mexico's enduring revolutionary icons, and it would return the great Pedro Armendáriz to the role he would be most identified with in his native land...

There is certainly a world of difference between Fernando de Fuentes' *Let's Go with Pancho Villa* and Ismael Rodríguez's *Así Era Pancho Villa* (*This Was Pancho Villa*). From the 1930s on, Mexico's post-revolutionary governments ordered its film industry to use the Revolution to redefine Mexico on-screen; to idolize its fighters as flawless icons; to portray its enemies, the *Porfirios* and *Huertistas,* as murderous fascists; and to constantly remind the audience that the Revolution was a fight for freedom and equality. The fact that post–Revolutionary regimes continued to act as if *Porfiriato* was still in place was beside the point (even Madero had no intention of instituting land reform for the peons). The new post–Revolutionary bureaucracy, to take the public's attention off the country's usually terrible economy and systematic corruption, had the entertainment industry promote the Revolution's heroes as men and women to emulate, with the main figure of the Revolution to admire being Pancho Villa himself, "Mexico's Robin Hood (according to Hollywood coming-attraction blather anyway)," etc. The government wouldn't even consider the notion that Álvaro Obregón, one of the Revolution's heroes who became its president, probably ordered the Centaur of the North assassinated.

Like many of the performers and production personnel who would usher in the *Época Dorada,* Ismael Rodríguez (real name, Ismael Rodríguez Robles) was born between 1910 and 1920, as the nation was still fighting the Revolution. He began his show business career as an actor in the mid–1930s, around the same time as a performer whom he would come to admire and use numerous times in his own films: Pedro Armendáriz. The actor had already played Pancho Villa in the Mexican-shot, Spanish language–version of the Hollywood B *The Return of Pancho Villa* in 1950 (*not* directed by Rodríguez). An early admirer of the revolutionary icon, Rodríguez embarked on his famous Villa trilogy. Following government dictum and his own ideological bent, his films became valentines to the former bandit chief turned hero; and in a broader sense, the Revolution continued to be portrayed as the Noble Cause, much as our own films featured democracy's triumph over tyranny.

The movie begins with a voiceover from the dead Pancho Villa (Armendáriz), whose body is buried in the town of Parral where he was killed, and the head preserved in a glass case filled with wine ("where some foreign people took it," the head tells us). As Rodríguez shows us clips of the *real* Villa wearing safari hat and fatigues, his cut-off head tells us about "bits of my life, so you get to know me as a person, more than as a guerrilla man or a bandit." This was, of course, letting us know up front that Villa's life of violence was going to be watered down considerably.

Producer-director Rodríguez got credit for the final screenplay, though he was assisted by four other writers. As it turns out, the multitude of scenarists worked on their own separate sequences, with Don Ismael applying the unifying polish to their work that turned it all into a cohesive whole. In the first sequence, *Thou Shalt Not Kill,* after the execution of several federals, Villa and the gentle Madero are in the guerrilla's tent where they argue about using mass executions against those who use mass executions (actually Villa is arguing, Madero is *reasoning*). It shows the real-life problem between the "eye for an eye" rebel chief and the all-too-forgiving Madero. Unfortunately, as with every portrayal of the so-called "gentle president," movie audiences in both Mexico and America never once see Madero's treacherous side. Though not on the level of a brutal Victoriano Huerta, Madero purposely kept putting off reforms and at times kept his best general, Villa, at arm's length.

In the next sequence, *The Heretic,* we see Villa pray to the Lord for luck in winning a battle. In *Creepy Wedding,* a Villista corporal manhandles a señorita with three kids and shoots her husband dead when he interferes. Flanked by his aides, Fierro (veteran *Época Dorada* bad guy Carlos López Moctezuma) and the bespectacled Luisito (Humberto Almazán), Villa orders that the murderous corporal and the new widow be married. Having read a book on the wisdom of Solomon (despite the fact that the real Villa supposedly couldn't read or write), the guerrilla chief then has the murderous Fierro take the corporal into an adjoining room and deliver his "wedding present." Three loud gunshots later, Fierro emerges and Villa orders that the poor widow will get the late corporal's salary. And so, to the tune of comical music on the soundtrack, the two laugh over the corporal's death. In *What a Cute Brat,* Villa is forced to execute a federal officer whose courage and defiance he admires. In *My General's Women,* Rodríguez takes gentle aim at Villa the ladies' man, with the guerrilla chief promising marriage to all the three women featured in this sequence. "When I marry this time, it'll be forever!" he declares in a promise *no one* in his right mind will take seriously. Unfortunately, Rodríguez shoots this sequence as a celebration of Villa's *machismo* and that of the typical male in a sexist Latino culture. Never addressed once is the fact that the filmmakers find Villa's playing with the feelings of these various women as anything but comedy for Mexican males in the audience to laugh at. At the end of the sequence, we see Villa striking up a conversation with yet *another* young woman at a train depot, already forgetting (and betraying) the other three he promised to marry.

In *My Colonel, the Priest,* Villa is forced to order the execution of a rebel priest when the pontiff refuses to divulge where a cache of federal weapons is buried (a dying officer, in a private confession, admitted the whereabouts before expiring). By not violating the oath of confession, the priest is unfortunately also violating his loyalty to Villa. In *Jesusita in Chihuahua,* a barroom temptress causes friction between two of Villa's trusted lieutenants, Fierro and Luisito. Just in time, her game is exposed and the Luisito re-joins Team Villa.

However, the errant Fierro can't do this because he will drown in the middle of a lake while trying to cross it on horseback. Despite the spat with his boss, Fierro shouts "Viva Villa!" as he's riddled with bullets by federal troops. Here, Rodríguez totally whitewashes Fierro's real drowning in quicksand that had nothing to do with bravery or defying federals or even loyalty to Villa, but rather his own arrogance. When his men refused to cross what they immediately saw as quicksand, Fierro called them cowards and, to prove it, spurred his unfortunate horse across the bog—only to drown in the middle of it. His men did nothing to help him, and were reportedly glad to watch the psychopath get his just deserts.

At the end of the film, the head signs off, promising further adventures in the future. Armendáriz is his usual charismatic self, though Rodríguez allows him to go a bit over the top at times. His Villa is a shouting, glowering bundle of revolutionary energy, though the helmsman does try to emphasize his wisdom and compassion. The homely Moctezuma *does* resemble the hatchet-faced Fierro; however, Rodríguez waters down the sidekick's real-life homicidal behavior and replaces it with slavish loyalty to his boss. In reality, Fierro shot down innocent people right and left, with Villa hardly ever complaining about it.

Meanwhile, as Ismael Rodríguez's first Pancho Villa film was playing to packed houses in Mexico, Twentieth Century–Fox gave us a truncated B version of the revolutionary's life that instantly reminded us of their old Cisco Kid series rather than de Fuentes' *Let's Go with Pancho Villa...*

Shot from late February to late March 1958, *Villa!!* is the first time the iconic revolutionary has his name in the title followed by *two* exclamation points—probably an attempt to increase the picture's level of excitement. Produced by Plato Skouras, the son of the head of Twentieth Century–Fox, Spyros Skouras, and directed by contract director (and former editor) James B. Clark, this B film unusually broke new ground in its depiction of the Mexican Revolution. With the casting of Rodolfo Hoyos, Jr., for the first time in a film made by an American company, the role of Pancho Villa was played by an actor who was actually born in Mexico. Perhaps this might not seem like much, but after having over forty years of Hollywood films in which the character was played by everyone from the Midwest-born Wallace Beery to the Spanish-blooded but California-born Leo Carrillo to Fred Flintstone voiceover artist Alan Reed, this modest little B had broken ground in its own quiet way. Soon, however, Hollywood and Europe would revert to type and cast Anglo actors like Yul Brynner and Telly Savalas as the Centaur of the North.

With an original screenplay by Louis Vittes, the film clearly plays on the box office name recognition of Pancho Villa to bring in western fans (and let's not forget those two exclamations points for added box office insurance). The cynicism in presenting the film is obvious, for while Villa is supposed to be the focus of the film, top billing is given to American Brian Keith, then New York–born Latino Cesar Romero (back at his old studio), then American heroine Margia Dean, and *then* Hoyos gets special billing "as Pancho Villa."

The film opens with a group of peons being herded like cattle by horseback-riding *hacendado* henchmen. Villa and his men ride out of the hills to the rescue; we even have a closeup of Hoyos shouting some Apache warrior-like yell before the attack, then the title comes up over his face. Clue: We're supposed to be impressed.

Hoyos turned 42 as the film was being shot, a few years older than the real Villa was when he joined Madero (though the film starts *before* he joins up with him), and the balding Latino actor is forced to wear a sleek black toupee to make him look younger. Shot on location in Mexico, the film had to go through the usual neurotic censorship from government bureaucrats. However, though the Mexican government was always the first to disparage Hollywood's usually phony, namby-pamby depiction of Villa, they never bothered to mention that *they themselves* always insisted on this portrayal; for had the studios actually showed Villa as he *really* was, it was a certainty that the Mexican government would not have approved of it and angrily denied the company the privilege of filming on location. (And no matter how much Hollywood tried to duplicate them, there was no way they could come up with those wonderful adobes and old forts set amidst some of the most picturesque mountain and desert locations in the world.)

After the raid, Villa and his second-in-command, Tomás Lopez (Romero, playing a kinder, gentler version of Villa lieutenants Rodolfo Fierro and Tomás Urbina) decide to temporarily split from the band and go to a local cantina. Already Villa is smiling at the señoritas and focuses on one in particular, an American singer with a husky voice named Julie (Dean, not only doing her own singing, but singing her own lyrics!). Impressed by the American's beauty, Villa invites her to sing at his cantina in San Pablo; then he and his men scram before the federals show up.

For the most part, we will see a kindly, cheerful, fun-loving Villa; that is, except when crossed. Thanks to a tip from an informant, Villa and his men are able to stop a federal train and lift a gold shipment. Manhandling a young woman and about to kiss her, he is chided by Tomás and the kiss is never placed. This is obviously a Pancho Villa the Breen Office would have loved. When a Mexican law enforcement officer tries to shoot Villa, the American criminal next to him deflects his aim and Tomás kills the cop. The *Americano* is Bill Harmon (top-billed Brian Keith), who has been running guns to the rebels. Grateful, Villa allows the American to join him. This subplot would be duplicated in the 1966 Euro-western *El Chuncho Quien Sabe?*, released in this country as *A Bullet for the General*. In the Italian-made production, a young American on a train helps kill federal troops to ingratiate himself with

Chuncho, a Villa-like bandit-revolutionary, and then offers his services to the guerrilla band. However, unlike Keith in *Villa!!,* in the Italian film the young *Americano's* motivations are far more sinister.

In San Pablo (after Clark gives us interminable time-padding shots of Villa and his band riding through the mountain passes), two middle-aged men see Villa coming and agree to lock up their eligible daughters. In the local cantina, we're treated to a singer who warbles off-key, though Villa is not concerned with her vocal range. Claiming to be unusually ill-at-ease with *Americano* girls, Villa orders Bill to travel to Chihuahua City and bring Julie back with him. After Bill leaves, Tomás despairs of having "two *gringos* along," but to appease his right-hand man, Villa threatens to kill them both if they get out of line.

In Chihuahua City, the audience in the cantina (and unfortunately, the audience viewing the film) have to endure Dean's awful version of a popular Mexican folk song (with her own rewritten lyrics) before a fight scene starts, with Bill soundly beating his opponents. However, in the dressing room, we find out that Bill and Julie have a history—and perhaps a little biology—in their relationship. They were to marry, but the seedy gunrunner left her, knowing that there was no future for a woman married to a lowlife like him.

With Julie now part of Villa's steadily growing legion of conquests, the raids continue. After a young *hacendado* named Don Octavio (Felix Gonzalez) rapes Villa's sister Marianna, the guerrilla chief arrives and forces the young man to marry her so she can avoid dishonor. *Then* he forces the rapist to dig his own grave and has Tomás shoot him dead as he stands in it. However, while the guerrillas are away, the *Americanos* play, though not physically. Instead (this is the 1950s), the two declare their love for each other and make plans to escape from Villa.

After Madero (one of the few American actors in the supporting cast, Ben Wright) is elected, the socially conscious bandit offers his services to the new leader, and even makes a speech about helping the peons achieve justice. Of course, this was nonsense. Madero had Abraham Gonzalez seek out Villa, not the other way around. Also, Villa wouldn't be caught dead making speeches about social justice, and he had very little political idealism concerning the Revolution. He was there as a *warrior,* period.

When Madero's newest general and his men attack a federal garrison, Bill and Julie have a chance to escape, yet the American is loyal to Villa and rides down to help him. Bill is wounded for his trouble. After the battle, Villa takes note of Julie's caring for his American friend and magnanimously orders the two lovers to be dropped off over the American border. At the close, we see "General Villa" now in charge of an army which will help free Mexico. In fact, in some versions of the film, at the end, a voiceover informs us that the people of Mexico will fight until they have defeated those who have been unjust to them.

The film's performances are generally good, despite the fact that the script isn't. As usual, Keith underplays, and his character is more real because of it. Margia Dean plays Margia Dean, the usual B sagebrush heroine of the 1950s, though this time she has a chance to double as both singer and songwriter, not exactly succeeding as either. As she said in an undated interview with *Western Clippings:*

> In *Villa!!,* we were on top of a rocky hill. I was on a horse with the entire Mexican cavalry behind me. I never should have agreed to do it, but rode that horse down that rock-filled hill! If I had slipped, I would have been crushed by all those other horses behind me. A couple of them did slip and fall. I was later told, by a professional stuntwoman, that she would never do

something a professional wouldn't do. Also, the director, James B. Clark, was a former film editor. He'd fill the camera with pictorial things, unnatural things.[31]

(In the film, however, we don't see Julie in danger, on horseback or otherwise, for even a moment.) As for Dean's co-stars, she said, "Cesar Romero was terrific, charming, so witty, so humorous and down-to-earth. He was the only one good in the picture—I didn't like myself or Brian Keith, but of course, we had the terrible direction."[32]

Unfortunately, Dean seems to have left out Rodolfo Hoyos, Jr., who, after all, played the title role. Hoyos also played opposite Dean as the bandito villain in Fox's *Stagecoach to Fury* (1956). If there's anything wrong with Hoyos' portrayal of the iconic Villa, it was the actor's too-fluent command of English. Having worked in Hollywood for many years, the actor, born in the Federal District (*Distrito Federal*) of Mexico City, made Pancho Villa sound more American-sounding than New York–born Latino Cesar Romero did his character. One wonders why Fox didn't have *Romero* as Villa.

There are the usual historical inaccuracies and cutesy comedy moments that remind one of Wallace Beery (Hoyos' Villa even has the same line as Beery that he believes in marriage and is very religious). One of the film's taglines announces, "Out of the mountains stormed Mexico's raging Robin Hood!" This tagline was obviously for American audiences since Mexican audiences rarely used the British character of Robin Hood as a yardstick for heroism. Still, the result was the same—white-washing Villa as a man who simply took from the rich and gave to the poor. Certainly, Robin Hood didn't execute his enemies by lining them up and firing one bullet into them. In the film, Villa also has an eye for every female in the cast, with his sidekick Tomás despairing of his boss giving his concubines money before hooking up with them. Indeed, Tomás is almost a comic version of the psychotic Fierro. At the end, when Villa wants Bill and Julie escorted to the border, he stops Tomás from going with them because he fears that the two lovers won't get to the border alive. Tomás shrugs off his disappointment and the two men laugh over the whole thing. In moments like this, Rodolfo Fierro's thirst for killing people is dismissed as comedy; for Romero, it is a reminder of his own Cisco Kid B pictures he used to make at Fox in the early '40s, as if the actor had done nothing between then and *Villa!!*

As usual in a Hollywood depiction of the Revolution, despite all the Mexican characters (sometimes even played by Mexican actors), the studio focused their attention on the script's *Anglos*. Keith was good in almost any role he played, and though Margia Dean can sometimes be a pill, she was a good B heroine. However, the character of Bill Harmon is still the typical *Americano* riding side by side with the Mexican protagonist, if only for the subtly racist reason of giving *Anglo* audiences someone to identify with, since the studios were not interested in giving its audiences a Latino hero. This oddity would still be in force in 1968's *Villa Rides!*, as well as the 1972 leftist Euro-western *Pancho Villa,* among far too many other films which depicted the Revolution.

Meanwhile, south of the border, director Ismael Rodríguez would return to the subject of the Revolution, but with a new approach. In fact, it was one of the extremely rare times Mexico would view its Revolution through the eyes of its women...

On November 12, 1959, as America grooved to rock 'n' roll and AIP was releasing teens vs. monsters schlock like *Invasion of the Saucer Men,* Mexico saw the release of Ismael Rodríguez's *La Cucaracha,* a love-triangle melodrama with the background of the Mexican Revolution.

Certainly, there were very few actresses, in both Mexico and Hollywood, who could have matched María Félix, *La Doña* herself, in smoldering sexuality and raw charisma. To film a love triangle in *La Cucaracha,* Rodríguez needed an actress whose own presence was as strong, in her own way, as Félix's. With this in mind, Rodríguez went to a star who had already triumphed in Hollywood, but always returned to perform for her beloved Mexico. It was now the right time for an on-screen meeting between the two most sexually powerful female icons of Mexican cinema.

Doña Barbara was about to meet *Doña Perfecta.*

Dolores del Río continued to be an icon of Mexican cinema. Between the release of *Las Abandonadas* in 1945 and the mid–1950s, she mostly remained in her native land, performing in films, TV and the stage. She won her first Silver Ariel (Mexico's Oscar) for Best Actress for *Las Abandonadas* in 1946. That same year, she starred in *La Otra (The Other One),* a classic melodrama of the type which made *Época Dorada* so great. Originally a story by Rian James, the property was owned by Warner Brothers in the 1940s; slated as a vehicle for Bette Davis, it was nixed by Jack Warner because the dual roles to be played by Davis seemed too close to her dual role in 1946's *A Stolen Life.* Yet anything Warners and Davis would have done with the story couldn't hold a candle to *La Otra.* As the put-upon, working-class girl who murders her wealthy twin sister and steals her identity, Dolores was outstanding in the kind of role that demonstrated that she had to leave Hollywood and return to her homeland to be an actress again. When her character belatedly realizes that she really was better off than she thought and ultimately goes to prison for, ironically, her own "murder," del Río the actress had never been better. It is a heartbreaking performance of a lost woman who left all she had to take on a different identity. In this dual role, one can almost see the real-life talented performer who belatedly realized that only in her homeland was she ever going to really find herself. She was nominated for the Silver Ariel in 1947, but lost out to María Félix (it was the year of her *Enamorada,* a hard performance to beat). To this day, it is *Dolores,* not Bette Davis in *Dead Ringer,* who perfectly captures Rian James' tragic heroine, as well as her duplicitous twin sister. The always stunning del Río had no problem convincing us that these sisters were still in their twenties despite the fact that she played this dual role at age 42.

Let's take a quick look at Dolores' only Hollywood production of 1947, mainly because the film was based on a novel set in Mexico. As a favor to her friend John Ford, she appeared as a nameless Indian woman (opposite frequent leading man Pedro Armendāriz as a nameless military officer) in *The Fugitive,* the film version of Graham Greene's *The Power and the Glory.* Though set in a fictional Latin American country (thanks to Breen Office censorship), the production ignored Greene's version of Mexico and its protagonist, a "whiskey priest." Instead, the film turned its hero into a hapless clergyman who bravely went about his priestly duties despite the totalitarian government's hostility to religion. In the late 1940s, with evidence of Soviet belligerency in Eastern Europe and elsewhere, Ford and RKO gave us what seemed to be a pre–Cold War version of what the Church was going through in the Eastern-bloc nations—something the left-wing Greene emphatically did *not* have in mind. However, with Emilio Fernández as assistant director and photographed by the great Gabriel Figueroa, the Mexican-shot film packed a nightmarish, noirish punch. Thanks to the Mexican artists behind the camera (which proved that *Época Dorada* could even travel up north), Ford's work was *never* like this. However, *was* the film only about

Round Up the Usual Suspects: John Ford's *The Fugitive* was shot in Mexico with the assistance of *Época Dorada*'s Emilio Fernandez and Gabriel Figueroa. Based on *The Power and the Glory* by Graham Greene, the film is Ford's attack on Mexico's anti-clerical stance during the Cristero War of the 1920s.

Communist bigotry against religion? The knowledgeable Ford might have used Greene's novel to take an actual look into Mexico's recent past—not the one dealing with the Revolution itself, but the battle between a leftist government and its Catholic population, the Cristero War. In *The Fugitive*, Fonda may portray a Christ-like figure who dies for his faith, but even more interesting is Armendáriz' NKVD-like military commander, a man whose fanaticism against Christianity immediately brings to mind the anti-clergy stances of liberal presidents Obregón and Calles. Thousands died during the Cristero War, a historical event rarely put on celluloid. Giving a powerful performance as a fanatical yet personally conflicted officer running away from his own religious upbringing, Armendáriz easily steals the film from the taciturn Fonda. His officer is still in love with the pious Indian woman played by his frequent co-star del Río, yet the hatred he harbors has gone in too deep for him to change his ways. Still, there are cracks in his supposedly impenetrable armor. When Fonda's priest sacrifices himself to the firing squad, Ford doesn't focus on the American star during his death scene, but on Armendáriz's commandant in his office overlooking the killing field. As we hear the bullets being fired, instead of them striking the priest, Armendáriz's officer grabs his own chest in intense pain, as if he himself were experiencing another man's crucifixion. It's the best moment in the whole impressive film.

In an interview with Hedda Hopper shortly after the film premiered, Ford praised Dolores as "a sparkplug for Mexican pictures" and said that the crew "adored her."[33] Fourteen years after *The Fugitive*'s release, she returned the compliment. When asked to name her favorite director (and in a not-so-subtle swipe at the brutally macho Emilio Fernández), she replied, "John Ford. He's marvelous." In an undated letter from Ford to del Río, shortly after the film's release, the helmsman praised her as "wonderful," and then closed with an intriguing sign-off: "When are we doing Carlotta [sic]?"[34]

It seems that Ford wanted to do another film in Mexico, this time dealing with the short-lived reign of the Emperor Maximilian and Empress Carlota. With del Río portraying the tragic royal (which would have given Dolores an intense scene of her going insane), the project would have returned Dolores to Revolutionary Mexico. Unfortunately, nothing further was ever heard of the project and she wouldn't work for her "favorite director" again until Warners' *Cheyenne Autumn* (1964).

In 1951, del Río gave one of her finest performances as an arrogant matriarch in the title role of *Doña Perfecta* (*The Perfect Lady*). As a wealthy aristocrat at the time of the *Porfiriata*, she is dead-set against her forward-thinking, reformist nephew falling in love with her own daughter. With the backing of the local reactionary elements, she has the young man shot dead; but with this treacherous act, she forever loses the love of her daughter. Even while playing this horrible woman, Dolores still commands both respect and sympathy in the role (though one *does* approve of her "punishment" at the end). A year after the film's release, the star won the second of her three Silver Ariels as Best Actress.

When Dolores was slated to return to America to co-star as Spencer Tracy's Native American wife in Edward Dmytryk's *Broken Lance* (1954), the State Department denied her a visa application to enter the country for the company's on-location shooting in Elgin, Arizona. It seems that McCarthyism was rearing its ugly head, and some in our government reacted very badly to Dolores' signing the Stockholm Peace Appeal in 1950. This petition, which contained language clearly against the proliferation of nuclear weapons (by the western democracies, that is), was presented to her by the so-called "Permanent Committee of the Partisans of Peace."[35] Dolores had good intentions and it's obvious that she didn't fully understand the Soviet habit of affixing the words "peace committee" or some other altruistic term onto organizations they promoted (and whose financial contributions immediately went into Communist Party coffers). With del Río denied entrance into the United States, Katy Jurado, a Mexican leading lady who worked many times in Hollywood (while never attaining del Río's stardom), took the *Broken Lance* role.

Dolores again returned to the film capital in 1956. McCarthy had been discredited in 1954 thanks to the Army-McCarthy hearings and Dolores was now able to get a visa to travel to Hollywood. And so, somewhere between her performance in an episode of the *U.S. Steel Hour* and her performance as Elvis Presley's Indian mom in Fox's *Flaming Star,* Dolores starred as the third point in the love triangle in *La Cucaracha*.

With both del Río and Félix starring, the Revolution never looked like this.

At rise, Colonel Zeta (the miscast Emilio Fernández) and his army, march on foot across the desert to a pro–Villa town where the martinet officer quickly accuses another *Villista* of not supporting his attack against the victorious federals. In record time, the traitorous officer is shot by Zeta's firing squad. It seems that the town's revolutionaries have had it too easy, sitting back and drinking the rebellion away. A good example of revolutionary hedonism is Refugio, aka *La Cucaracha* (María Félix), a soldera to end all solderas. Sexually active, boisterous, brutally frank and non-conformist, she is an insult to everything that is disciplined, reverent and conventional. Her direct opposite is the churchgoing Isabel (Dolores del Río), the wife of the local teacher. After his entrance into town, Zeta and his martinet ways are mocked by the defiant Refugio. Unfortunately, with his forces depleted, Zeta is forced to press-gang the local male populace, including young boys and intellectual conscientious objectors like Isabel's husband, into his army. Isabel begs Zeta to spare her husband, but he coldly refuses. She curses at him bitterly.

That night, Zeta and his soldiers, including his reluctant new recruits, face a federal bombardment on the outskirts of town. Rodríguez's approach throughout the film is quite different than what had been depicted in the Mexican Revolutionary films of the past, for at no time does he show us the attacking federals. Instead, in almost a harbinger of the films of Robert Altman, Rodríguez gives us a series of fascinating character vignettes playing out on the battlefield. We see the priest fighting for the Revolution with his antiquated rifle; we see a soldera about to give birth, only to be coldly told by Refugio that it would be better not to have it since it will grow up either murdered by the federals or killed on the battlefield; we see Isabel finding her husband's distinctive shawl worn by another fighter, who matter-of-factly tells her that her husband was killed; we see the funny Trompeta's (Lupe Carriles) loyalty to Refugio, and her death from an exploded shell; we see the brave Captain Ventura (Antonio Aguilar) question Zeta's delaying action and insisting on taking command rather than sitting where they are and facing certain death from federal bombardment; and we see the boisterous Refugio defying Zeta's orders and saturating her charges with booze and song. In lieu of showing the federal enemy and *their* preparations, Rodriguez keeps us focused on his fiercely loyal and idealistic, but far from perfect, revolutionary warriors. Whether we agree with them or not, we certainly respect them; in time, we will also have affection for them, with perhaps none getting that affection more than that iconic revolutionary party girl, *La Cucaracha* herself, Refugio. Just as Ventura insists on taking command, the federals themselves are bombarded into oblivion when Villa's forces finally arrive.

The celebrations continue in the newly conquered town. Refugio coldly refuses Zeta's gift of a bottle of booze and even an offer to buy her a shawl. Fed up, the colonel decides to do things the *macho* way and bursts into her room uninvited (*this* is the only action in the entire film which perfectly fits in with Fernandez's casting). After she angrily discards his flowers, her forces her to the floor and orders her to take off her clothes, which she does, though with a defiant sneer. The scene then fades out. The next morning, the two are holding hands like lovebirds and visiting the marketplace. Now that Refugio has laid claim to Zeta, she bristles with jealousy when he shows interest in a now-forgiving Isabel.

Just as Isabel is getting closer to Zeta and Refugio farther away, who appears in town but *La Cucaracha's* former paramour, Raza (specially billed Pedro Armendáriz). At the local cantina, the tormented man tells Zeta who he is and that he's willing to kill him to get her back. Up in her room, Refugio denies that Raza was ever her lover, though Zeta knows that she's lying. Called out by the lovesick revolutionary, Zeta goes down in the street and, before Raza can kill him, guns down his rival. The killing causes Zeta to break it off with the promiscuous soldera, which causes him to fly into Isabel's waiting arms.

Now alone, Refugio gets drunk with her new bud, cantina trollop Lola (Flor Silvestre). Of course, being Maria Felix, she berates and physically assaults several of the men in the cantina watching her get drunk, when in reality they would have pummeled her in two seconds for shoving them around. The next day, feeling no pain, the angry Refugio sees Isabel wearing the cross Zeta had given *her*. The two women start a catfight. Unfortunately, Rodríguez doesn't allow us to see it since he has a crowd form to block our view (which includes a little boy who delights in watching the fight). When told that "his women" are fighting, Zeta orders that his men advance to the next town. Though loyal to Carranza and fully aware that he had turned against Villa, Captain Ventura himself remains loyal to *Villista* officer Zeta and follows his commands.

Soon, Refugio is pregnant with Zeta's child. Going to an ancient woman who will act as a nurse, Refugio is forced to listen to the hateful crone tell her *not* to have the child in such a dangerous world, just as the soldera herself had berated the pregnant woman not to have her baby earlier in the film for the same reasons. Then, just as Refugio is having trouble giving birth, the old woman takes a hot poker to her as the soldera screams and Rodríguez fades to black. That moment is actually far more violent and disturbing than any of the film's battle scenes. Now with her baby, Refugio arrives at the town Zeta is to set to march into and, previously mocking religion, now has her baby baptized by the local priest.

Zeta's army is indeed victorious; however, when Refugio asks a rebel where he is, she is told that he was killed in the battle. Isabel suddenly appears and the two women briefly stare at each other. Refugio is wearing a shawl and a crucifix and holds a baby, and Isabel is now holding a rifle, wears a sombrero and has a bandolier of bullets across her chest. Madonna has become whore and whore has become Madonna. Isabel turns away and goes with the rest of her people, following their men into revolutionary battle against their oppressors. With her child in her arms, Refugio hesitates, but only for a moment. She then follows her people as they move across the countryside; and with them is the implication that Refugio's child will witness the birth of a new Mexico.

For all the corruption and failed dreams to come after the success of the Revolution, Rodríguez found the perfect ending for this tale of transformation and rebirth. The irresponsible and irreverent Refugio discovers a commitment to her child and renewed dedication to a cause; the cloistered Isabel abandons her self-centeredness and isolation and fights for her people. With the men in their lives now dead, both women, off-screen icons of femininity in a traditionally *machismo* Latin culture, find shared happiness by forging an alliance to fight for a new Mexico.

If the film hits a sour note, it is Rodríguez's immense blunder in casting the limited Fernandez as his leading man. Instead, one can see the two women fighting over *Armendáriz*. Better yet, why didn't the director cast the Mexican cinema's ultimate *charro* actor (a skilled cowboy dressed to the nines) Antonio Aguilar as Zeta? Talented, ruggedly handsome, and an amazing horseman, he would have been better casting than the usually taciturn El Indio (at one point, as he's deciding whether to follow Zeta or return to Carranza, Aguilar expertly dances his mount in a circle, as if expressing his indecision through his horse). Perhaps casting El Indio was done as a favor; Fernandez's directorial efforts of the 1950s and '60s were box office failures, and to keep working he was forced to be an actor again. In more than one tempestuous interview, Fernandez raged that Hollywood's Jews were responsible for the box office failure of his films, a remark that alienated most professionals in the Mexican film industry.

Released as *La Cucaracha* in Mexico on November 1, 1959, the film made its American debut in New York City exactly two years later. Renaming it *The Soldiers of Pancho Villa*, the U.S. distributors were obviously hoping the more famous name of Villa in the title would ensure its box office success. (Had the distributors actually viewed the film, they should've called it *The **Solderas** of Pancho Villa*).

In his *New York Times* review of November 2, 1961, Howard Thompson wrote:

> Although the film never rises in stature above its melodramatic plane and romantic embellishments, it is well-acted, crisply directed by producer Ismael Rodríguez and graphically photographed by Gabriel Figueroa. The incidents unfold in a steady blend of earthy sensitivity and grittiness. In the first, bloodiest and best part of the picture, the hero prods some quaking villagers into battle. Here, Señor Rodríguez, through Señor Figueroa's color camera, has created a crackling fray that looks like the Fourth of July in an Orozco art gallery.
>
> This physical vigor and biting pictorial edge ... do much to substantiate the nub of the picture—the two women squaring off over the hero. If the final portion seems, after the dust settles, somewhat like a Western, the tone is pensive rather than sentimental.[36]

The esteemed critic ended his review with, "Neighbors below, let's have more."

On the heels of the release of *La Cucaracha,* María Félix and Pedro Armendáriz reunited in the comedy *Café Colón.* Instead of the heavy dramatics of the Rodríguez film, Félix played a tempestuous nightclub singer and Armendáriz played (what else?) a fiery revolutionary general, though this time for laughs. Ultimately, the film was no *Enamorada* (or even *The Torch*).

As the new decade dawned, Howard Thompson had his wish for more Mexican imports, though the second and third installments of Rodríguez's Villa tribute would never hold a candle to *La Cucaracha.* In fact, both Hollywood and the Mexican film industry would return again and again to the subject of Revolutionary Mexico. However, in the next decade, they would be joined by filmmakers from Italy and Spain. With the destruction of the Production Code in America and the growing popularity of violent European westerns, revolutionary idealism would now be paid for with plenty of on-screen blood...

V

Caos Internacional, 1960–1969

Hollywood and Europe Film the Revolution

On June 9, 1960, Churubusco-Azteca released in Mexico *Pancho Villa y la Valentina* (*Pancho Villa and Valentina*), the second in Ismael Rodriguez's trilogy on the revolutionary icon. *Cuando !Viva Villa! ... es la Muerte* (literal translation: *When "Long Live Villa!" ... Is the Death*) was released in Mexico a little over a month later, on July 14. Both films continued the adventures of our favorite iconic revolutionary, with Rodríguez again directing and co-writing the screenplay. Armendáriz was back, with Moctezuma returned to life as the psychotic but lovable Fierro, and Humberto Almazán as the bookish Luisito. In these rather predictable sequels, the whitewashing of the guerrilla chief takes on rather pathetic fantasy aspects, with the helmsman playing Villa's abusive and violent behavior for laughs. Only in the final part of the third film, the one dealing with Villa's assassination, does Rodríguez delve into controversial material. It's still a hackneyed sequence which twists the ugly truth into optimistic guesswork, yet it also levels an accusatory blast at the *real* man who was behind Villa's murder (even if Rodríguez shows the man ordering the hit as having *two* arms—not one arm like Álvaro Obregón).

Far more interesting was a new release in 1961 that depicted the life of a fictional *soldera*.

At the beginning of *Juana Gallo,* the titles state clearly that this film has the backing of the government of *Presidente* Adolfo López Mateos (who led the Institutional Revolutionary Party) and several other officials, including those of Zacatecas where the film was shot. This "blessing" upon the production from the higher-ups will again anoint the Revolution as a holy mission and its fighters as flawless gods. However, this Mexican production, coming as it does from an infamously *macho* culture, was the only film at the time to give the world a female warrior who successfully led men into battle.

Angela Ramos (María Félix) is a farm woman driving a cow before her as she plows the fields. When the usually evil federal troops try to press-gang men of the village to help them, Angela's father and fiancé protest. Angela soon discovers their bodies swinging from a tree. The shot is a grim tableau, typical of cinematographer Gabriel Figueroa's genius. Angry, Angela goes to a gravesite on her property and unearths a cache of weapons. Indeed, what kind of farm girl is this Angela Ramos? Soon she is laying for the federal column atop a hill with a loaded rifle, and when she has a bead on the commander who ordered the hangings, she opens fire, hitting him dead center. Then, as confusion reigns below, she expertly guns down several more soldiers with pinpoint accuracy. At her shouted order, the peons attack the troops and take the survivors captive. Angela Ramos, hard-working farm woman, has once again returned to her revolutionary alias, Juana Gallo!

One guerrilla wants to kill all the captured soldiers but Juana sees no need to mindlessly murder men who were only following orders. She spares one wounded officer, the brave (and handsome) Captain Guillermo Velarde (Jorge Mistral). Aided by her right-hand man (and semi-comic relief) Pioquinto (Ignacio López Tarso), she and her band of rebels plan to give the federals a very hard time. Later, at a meeting place in the hills, Juana meets rebel colonel Arturo Cabellos Rico (actor-singer Luis Aguilar), who laughs at the sight of the female general and delivers the usual sexist remarks (though they do stop short of Van Heflin's "go back to your sewing basket" advice). That night, when the colonel (who, like the actor playing him, has a talent for singing ballads) tries to get a little randy with our guerrilla heroine, she orders him out of her hut. Throughout their successful campaigns, the revolutionaries expertly take one goal after another, thanks in large part to the bravery and military smarts of their leader, the beautiful Juana Gallo.

But there is trouble in revolutionary paradise. When Velarde argues with her plan to take the federal garrison at Zacatecas (and inferring that a woman general couldn't possibly succeed), she slaps him and orders him out. Soon, the battle is on, and though many rebels are killed, Juana's leadership (with her personally taking over a machine-gun emplacement) spells victory for her men. Colonel Rico is mortally wounded, taking a bullet meant for Juana. Dying, his final wish is for a kiss from his cute general (even when dying, Rico still has just *one* thing on his mind!). She kisses the dying man, but this is witnessed by Captain Velarde, who rides away in anger. The loyal Pioquinto promises Juana he'll ride after him and get him back, but after the rebel disappears over a hill there is a tremendous explosion.

After the battle is over, a distraught Juana buries Velarde, Rico and Pioquinto, the three closest men in her life, and then rides on with the others to win back Mexico. At the end of *Juano Gallo*, we hear the speech Captain Velarde had made earlier repeated on the soundtrack, stirring words that told of how the great triumph of the Revolution would give birth to cities and industry, homes and businesses, a great culture dominated by freedom and equality. Needless to say, the speech fails to mention systematic corruption and grinding poverty.

Juana Gallo (known in the United States as *The Guns of Juana Gallo*, and on American TV as, ridiculously, *Wild Stampede*) delivered the revolutionary goods, despite its ignorance of history. The idea of a woman commander was never put into practice by either the federal government *or* the revolutionaries, and the battle of Zacatecas was won by a man—a man who was an actual icon in Mexican history.

Known in Mexico as *Toma de Zacatecas* (Taking of Zacatecas), the battle was fought by Pancho Villa and his *División del Norte* (Division of the North) against the forces of Huertista commander General Luis Medina Barrón. The federals reportedly had between 7,000 and 15,000 men stationed at Zacatecas, though historians basically settle on the number of 12,000; the Villistas numbered over 20,000. Ordered by the arrogant "First Chief" Venustiano Carranza to take the non-essential target of Coahuila, Villa was anxious to attack Zacatecas, a major pathway to Huerta's seat of power in Mexico City. Carranza detested the guerrilla chief, and he had even ordered an inferior rebel general (Panfilo Natera) to capture Zacatecas so that Villa would not receive the glory. A silver mining town of about 30,000 inhabitants, Zacatecas was ringed by hills oddly named *La Bufa* (the Buffoon) and *El Grillo* (the Cricket). Commanded by General Barrón, a combined force of Huerta's federals and Pascual Orozco's Colorados had no trouble beating Natera's ragtag guerrillas.

Rebelling against Carranza's orders, at 10:00 a.m. on June 23, 1914, Villa attacked Zacatecas anyway. The battle may have been the final breach between the mercurial Villa and his "First Chief." Nevertheless, it got results; *Villistas* seized the federal artillery from *El Grillo* that overlooked the town proper and overran Barrón's troops. *El Grillo* fell around 1:00 p.m. with the more fiercely held *La Bufa* falling in late afternoon. Expertly planned by the talented rebel general and Villa favorite, Felipe Ángeles, the fight continued when *Villistas* pursued Barrón's men to Guadalupe. Blocked by 7,000 more *Villistas* (again, flawless planning by Ángeles), the federals were slaughtered. Barrón himself would be one of the few federal generals to survive the Revolution and even outlived Villa by 14 years. After serving in the government for many years as an ambassador, the former commander died in 1937.

Villa's great victory at Zacatecas did the trick. Huerta resigned on July 15, some three weeks after the battle. Soon, the curtain would rise on the equally bloody battle between Villa and Carranza.

However, as personified by the beautiful María Félix, her revolutionary general was a hero one didn't easily forget. And though she was hardly based on fact, her Juana Gallo was one of the few female commanders successfully winning wars depicted in films made by *any* nation, much less any film made in a supposedly enlightened Hollywood.

And what other way was there to trump the perpetually sexist Pancho Villa than have his real-life military victory credited to a woman?

If *Época Dorada* hadn't ended long before the early 1960s, its doom was probably sealed on June 18, 1963, a day when one of Mexico's greatest actors shot himself in the head.

Somewhere amidst his copious film output in both Mexico and Hollywood in the mid–1950s, Pedro Armendáriz traveled to the Escalante Desert outside St. George, Utah, along with his usual co-star in his John Ford westerns, John Wayne, and other actors and crew members. As directed by former actor Dick Powell, *The Conqueror* became a box office smash for RKO, one of its last before closing its doors for good in 1958. Today, the film is considered one of the Duke's few camp efforts, a cornball laugh riot whose major claim to immortality besides its risible dialogue and over-serious acting is the fact that it was filmed on desert locations very close to where A-bomb testing had been performed years before. As time went on, through grisly coincidence or not, cancer ultimately took the lives of many of its performers and personnel, with director Powell being one of the first to die of the disease on January 2, 1963. Opposing this argument was John Wayne's wife Pilar, who had visited the location many times and, along with many other people, did *not* contract cancer. In her estimation, many of these performers got cancer from too much smoking.

In early 1963, Armendáriz was cast as James Bond's Turkish contact Kerim Bey in the film version of *From Russia with Love*. Learning from doctors at the UCLA Medical Center in Los Angeles that his illness was terminal, the actor apprised producers Harry Salzman and Albert "Cubby" Broccoli and director Terence Young of his ailment. The upshot was that the actor's scenes were squeezed into two weeks; Armendáriz made this request so that his wife would receive his pay. Typically, the actor was a model of professionalism despite his illness (which included pains in his hip where the disease had spread), and he was his usual likable and easy-going self throughout the shoot. Young liked him so much that he threw a special going-away party for him after his scenes were shot in mid–May. Armendáriz had gotten along famously with Bond's creator Ian Fleming. In a truly ghoulish conversation, these two men, both dying of cancer, reportedly discussed Ernest Hemingway and his decision to commit suicide by self-inflicted gunshot in the head rather than die slowly of the disease. It'll never be known if Hemingway's tragic suicide was on his mind when Armendáriz took a loaded gun from beneath his pillow and shot himself in the head a month later. Ironically, in scary moments from both Columbia's *We Were Strangers* of 1949 and the Mexican-made *La Bandida,* released in 1963, Armendáriz's characters play Russian roulette.

In Mexico, Armendáriz was truly an icon of film, especially in the genre depicting the Revolution. In America, he provided much-needed color opposite many of his *Anglo* co-stars, with *Border River* being a good example of this. His talent, his charisma and his image as a portrayer of strong men, especially his memorable performance as Pancho Villa, will live on.

In a letter to John Huston, dated June 25, close friend Alberto J. Misrachi wrote from Juárez: "You cannot imagine how sad we feel as a consequence of Pedro's death. In addition to being one of our greatest actors, you know he was one of my best friends."[1]

Audiences around the world felt the same way about him.

By 1964, Sam Peckinpah was Hollywood's Golden Boy. He wrote and directed the groundbreaking TV series *The Westerner.* Of course, since it *was* groundbreaking, the show barely lasted one season.

His directorial film debut, *The Deadly Companions,* based on A.S. Fleischman's novel *Yellowleg,* didn't make money at the box office or garner him any critical raves, but it broke the ice and proved he was not merely a "TV western director." However, with his direction of MGM's *Ride the High Country* starring western icons Joel McCrea and Randolph Scott, Peckinpah transcended the TV western label and gave us a powerful and moving film.

In 1964, Peckinpah was offered a chance to direct a third film, but instead of a piece about the cowpoke of the past uncomfortably stuck in the early twentieth century, like the McCrea-Scott picture, this particular film was a cavalry western set at the time of the Civil War. What made it so fascinating was the fact that the bluecoats were not fighting in the hub of battle around the eastern states, but situated in a fort–military prison in the west. Added to this was the fact that the plot forced Union soldiers to unite with Confederate prisoners against Apache marauders, and *then* to pursue said Apaches into a Mexico dominated by the French troops of Emperor Maximilian. In a screen story by Harry Julian Fink, who would write *Dirty* Harry and two John Wayne scripts (*Cahill, U.S. Marshal* and *Big Jake*) and a screenplay by Fink, Oscar Saul and Peckinpah, *Major Dundee* became one of the most iconic westerns of the 1960s. In an era which saw the first involvement of U.S. troops in Southeast Asia, *Major Dundee* became a euphemistic comment on both the folly and the wisdom of pursuing hostiles into foreign territory.

Throughout the late 19th century, the American military had tentatively chased hostile Apaches and Comanches across the border into Mexico, where the natives thought they'd be safe from pursuit by cavalry. Much of this cross-border policy was successfully enacted by the army's Colonel Ranald S. Mackenzie, referred to by the Natives as "Bad Hand." Mackenzie's tenacious pursuit of the Lipan Apaches and Kickapoos, as well as the violent Comanche tribes of Chief Quannah Parker (called the "Antelope Eaters"), brought peace to the Texas frontier. (After the defeat of the Comanches, Parker would become a close friend to his former antagonist "Bad Hand.") But all that would be in the future; at the time of the Civil War, the western and southern tribes took advantage of the white man's War

Between the States to mercilessly attack all non-combatants, meaning settler families and undermanned cavalry patrols left unprotected due to the deployment of troops to fight the Civil War in the east. However, between the years 1862 and 1867, the government of President Benito Juárez was on the run, and French troops ran the cities. With Lincoln's government coming out uncompromisingly on the side of Juárez, French troops had no trouble ignoring Indian raids onto U.S. soil that killed American citizens.

But what if there was an officer who bucked the status quo, said he was mad as hell and wasn't going to take it any more? With *Major Dundee,* Peckinpah took his cast and crew into a Mexican desert of heat and dirt and bugs in much the same way Dundee took his multi-ethnic, multi-regional crack soldiers into Mexico, here depicted as both Heavenly diversion and hellish danger, to destroy a Satanic enemy. In this film, Revolutionary Mexico becomes the litmus test, the tumultuous locale where at the end of their quest American soldiers must either find their souls or lose everything.

Major Amos Dundee (Charlton Heston) is a Union commander who made a blunder at the battle of Gettysburg and, as punishment, is put in command of a prison stockade in New Mexico Territory. In charge of the Confederate prisoners is Dundee's former friend, Captain Benjamin Tyreen (Richard Harris in his first western). When Apache chief Sierra Charriba (Australian actor, director and playwright Michael Pate) and his band attack a ranch, murder the inhabitants as well as the soldiers guarding them, and kidnap three children, Dundee must rely on the only manpower available, his condemned Confederate prisoners. Bugler Tim Ryan (Michael Anderson Jr.), the only survivor of the raid, joins Dundee's motley group, which include the spit-and-polish Lieutenant Graham (Columbia contract player Jim Hutton), one-armed scout Samuel Potts (in his first film for Peckinpah, James Coburn), Sergeant Gomez (Mario Adorf), black soldier Private Aesop (Brock Peters) and even a preacher, Reverend Dahlstrom (Peckinpah regular R.G. Armstrong). On the Reb side, there are more of the director's favorites, including L.Q. Jones, Ben Johnson and Warren Oates (all later cast in *The Wild Bunch*).

The troops are represented by a huge cross-section of American humanity, northerners, southerners, Mexican-Americans (Sergeant Gomez), African-Americans (Private Aesop and his "Negro" troopers), Native Americans (Christianized Indian scouts), the handicapped (the one-armed Potts) and an Irishman (Captain Tyreen). Needless to say, there are the usual conflicts.

Advancing deeper into Mexico, Dundee and his men spot a village under the control of a French garrison and, when the arrogant Europeans refuse to surrender, Dundee orders a barrage of their headquarters with his mountain howitzer. The villagers don't have food or horses for Dundee's tired men, and ironically, it is the major who ends up feeding the villagers as well as liberating them from the French troops. In response, the Americans are welcomed as heroes and invited to their festival. This situation is in nearly every film set in a poor Mexican village. We are told that the villagers are far too poor to have food, yet they always seem to have money to purchase fireworks, including skyrockets, and hire huge bands to play music for their liberators. Part of the benefits to the Americans' liberation of the village is the eternal "gratitude" of the local female population. This would translate into the young bugler's affair with local gal Linda (a sweet young Mexican actress who would become Peckinaph's second wife, Begoña Palacios); and Major Dundee and Captain Tyreen's flirtation with European-educated, English-speaking doctor Teresa Santiago (Santa Berger), whose husband had been hanged by the French.

During their journey, the troops are able to find the children, and soldiers are detached from the command to return them to America. However, Charriba is still at large, and so the hunt continues. At one point, the men receive distressing news: French troops, finding out that the villagers helped Dundee's men, tortured and massacred everyone. Sergeant Gomez notes that the dead villagers look worse than any victim of Apache torture, with Sergeant Chillun (Ben Johnson) wryly observing that it's all part of "a European education." Here, even the dreaded Apaches can't hold a candle to Napoleon's murderous soldiers. One wonders what the Mexicans themselves had to put up with under the reign of these brutes.

However, the Apaches are still a formidable enemy, and a violently sadistic one. A later scene in which Dundee, Tyreen and Potts discuss strategy at an abandoned Apache campsite ends with a comment about Riago (José Carlos Ruiz). Then Peckinpah shocks us by cutting to the now-dead Christianized scout crucified on a huge makeshift cross.

Inner turmoil still dominates the obsessed major. After his wounding by an Apache arrow and Teresa catching him with the whore who helped patch him up, Dundee gets royally drunk. Ironically, he is rescued from self-destruction and self-pity by, of all people, Tyreen, who returns him to the troopers. Recovering quickly, Dundee decides to think like an Apache and lures the tribe into an attack. When the sadistic Charriba taunts the soldiers with "Who will you send against me now?" the murderous chief is suddenly shot dead by young Ryan, the only survivor of a Charriba massacre, now avenging his comrades. The troopers kill the remainder of the Apaches and, now that "the Apaches are either captured or killed," Tyreen and Dundee plan to keep their earlier vow to kill each other. However, their big gundown is rudely interrupted by the arrival of French troops. With the "frog-stickers" (as Chillun refers to them) now massed on the Rio Grande and blocking the Americans from crossing the border back into their own country, Dundee's coalition of Union and Confederate troops must break through their skirmish line. The opposing armies have a bloody clash in the river itself, but when the Yankee flag-bearer is killed, Confederate commander Tyreen rides forward and keeps it aloft, getting himself mortally wounded in the process. After turning the flag over to an astounded Dundee, the cutlass-wielding Tyreen sacrifices his life by riding into the French line. Humbled by the sacrifice of his former friend, and with the help of their mountain howitzer, Dundee and his men decimate the French and, unopposed, cross the Rio Grande. Dundee's mission is now completed exactly a week before Lee's surrender at Appomattox. He had started with a ragtag group of men who hated each other far more than their French or Apache enemies. At the end, however, the major, hoisting the flag high, leads not a group of Northerners and Southerners, or blacks and whites, or Anglos, Mexicans and Indians, but Americans. It is one of the most uplifting endings to any film released during the cynical 1960s.

In a March 29, 2005, *Village Voice* review of the new, expanded version of *Major Dundee* which included 12 minutes originally cut by producer Jerry Bresler, Michael Atkinson gave the film backhanded praise. Cutting through the critic's convoluted prose, one sentence does stand out, *vis-à-vis* the director's treatment of his Mexican characters: "The natives are, of course, fodder; Peckinpah might have decried the Mexicans' subjugation in film after film, but he was also never very interested in them as people."[2]

Setting many of his films in Mexico, Peckinpah would boast of his knowledge of the country; or, as he would loudly declare to anyone who'd listen, he *married* a Mexican woman, didn't he? Of course, he'd be less boastful about his beatings of Begoña; with at least one phone call she'd make to a friend crying that she loved Sam, but oddly repeating several times during the conversation, "I broke my arm."[3] Still, as far as Peckinpah's films are concerned, Atkinson was right in this respect. From *Major Dundee* to *The Wild Bunch* to *Pat Garrett and Billy the Kid,* Peckinpah would protest about Hollywood's ignorance of Mexicans and then focus his films on his white characters. Possibly an exception to this was actress-director Isela Vega's character in *Bring Me the Head of Alfredo Garcia,* Vega being the only Mexican performer with a prominently billed, co-starring role in *any* Peckinpah film.

However, at another point in Atkinson's rather oddball review, he writes, "As far as I can determine, this is the only American film to even acknowledge France's Mexican presence during both countries' civil conflicts."[4] This statement completely ignores the existence of films like *Juarez,* U-I's *Border River, The Undefeated* with John Wayne, and Robert Aldrich's *Vera Cruz* (and, in a lesser-known capacity, *Stronghold*).

There are many stories damning producer Jerry Bresler and Columbia Pictures for destroying Peckinpah's masterpiece with their cutting of the budget in the midst of a change in the studio's hierarchy, as well as Bresler's constant pressure on the helmsman to get the job done. The director's friends, enablers really, who have excused his alcoholic and misanthropic behavior throughout the years, probably knew better. Peckinpah was clearly too inexperienced and incompetent to direct what he envisioned as an epic. An example of Peckinpah's lack of experience at the time is clearly shown in David Weddle's biography of the director, *If They Move, Kill 'Em: The Life and Times of Sam Peckinpah:*

> After nailing down contracts with Churubusco Studios in Mexico City, Sam plunged into the country's interior to search for locations for the picture. Normally locations are chosen in closely grouped clusters that offer a wide variety of terrain, thus minimizing the number of times the company has to make a major move. A production of this size would require hundreds of crew members, actors, extras, horses and mules, and trucks full of props, costumes and equipment. Transporting such a mammoth operation from one far-flung location to another would require costly days to the shooting schedule and send the budget skyrocketing.
>
> But this seemed of little concern to Sam while he selected a series of remote spots strung out across the length of Central Mexico, from the mining town of Durango to the north to the sizzling Guerrero desert southwest of Mexico City and the tepid waters of the Rio Balsas, where Sam decided the final battle with the French cavalry would take place.[5]

Drunk and abusive much of the time, terrorizing and firing technical personnel at the drop of a hat, even antagonizing the even-tempered Heston into attacking him with a saber, Peckinpah went a week over schedule and over one million dollars over budget. Thinking that somehow he was doing his producers a favor by squandering their money or helping his skilled workers by verbally abusing them, Peckinpah was always enthralled with his own genius. Yet even with these definite fault lines in his personality, he managed to make a powerful if disjointed film. His battle scenes show far more violence than audiences would see up to that time. There are quick flashes of this violence and gore when we discover Riago's crucified corpse, and when Captain Tyreen is practically ripped apart by the French troops when he rides into them. These bits would be a harbinger of the so-called Battle of Bloody Porch in *The Wild Bunch.*

Cut to the bone, *Major Dundee* was released on April Fools' Day, 1965, though it seemed that the joke was on both the audience and its thin-skinned director. The film was released at 123 minutes, far short of Peckinpah's original cut. When the confusing, butchered version came out, critics attacked Peckinpah:

> Hollis Alpert of *Saturday Review*: "*Major Dundee* left me with the impression that I had seen a movie of no distinction whatsoever...."
> *Time*: "Sam Peckinpah lets *Dundee* ramble so freely that the Apaches are soon lost in the subplots."[6]

Major Dundee is not a bad film at all, and certainly holds your attention far better than Peckinpah's eccentric and self-involved *The Ballad of Cable Hogue*.

Time magazine was right in one respect. The many subplots of *Major Dundee* almost swallowed up the film's take on Mexican history, especially concerning the nation's subjugation by French imperialists. In fact, though traveling throughout northern Mexico and going ever deeper into the country, Dundee's men never *once* run into any *Juáristas*, nor any other patriotic, anti–French faction fighting for their country; the Mexicans we see are always helpless villagers, mostly old men and nubile women. The film has no young Mexican rebels who could hold their own against the French; their people must always be saved from their colonial occupiers by the Americans. This is an odd omission, especially in dramatic terms, coming from a director who kept boasting of his love for Mexico and its people.

Despite the failure of this film, Columbia was not through yet with depicting Revolutionary Mexico, and in 1965, the studio found the perfect western novel which set its story south of the border and guaranteed good roles for four of Hollywood's top action stars. Based on a novel by veteran pulp writer Frank O'Rourke, this film would tell the story of four mercenaries on a mission to rescue a kidnapped beauty from the clutches of a Pancho Villa–like Mexican revolutionary and bring her back to the United States.

However, like the many participants of the Mexican Revolution, as well as the Revolution itself, nothing was as it appeared to be...

> I have read the book *A Mule for the Marquesa* and found it very interesting. Should be able to get a good script from it.
> Now about the censorship. I hesitate to give this book to them because so much of the beginning is devoted to descriptive material, building up the main characters of the story. While this descriptive matter actually has nothing to do with the story, I am afraid it might be misunderstood by the censors.[7]

So wrote Columbia Pictures' James L. Fields to studio executive Hal Fisher, in a letter (with the letterhead of Churubusco-Azteca Studios) dated January 26, 1965. Fields was talking about a western novel written by veteran sagebrush author Frank O'Rourke. Hollywood had already filmed O'Rourke's 1957 novel *The Bravados* with Gregory Peck as the vengeance-crazed cowpoke out to avenge the murder of his wife, and Joan Collins, of all people, as the señorita he encounters on his quest.

O'Rourke was born in Denver in 1916, smack dab in the middle of the Revolution; and though he became one of the more original and talented of pulp western authors, many of his novels were set, not necessarily west of the Pecos, but south of the Rio Grande. O'Rourke had visited Mexico and absorbed all he could about its culture. His unique perspective of the Revolution, which was that of showing great compassion for its goals while at the same time readily acknowledging how easy it could become corrupted, gave his novels a cynical thrust perfectly in sync with the postwar era. He knew the many barriers the guerrillas had to break through to defeat the Díazes, Huertas and even the Carranzas who took power—and he also realized that what came after was almost always a replay of what had been before. Still, in his novels, he made it clear that the Revolution *had* to be fought; if

The Fab Four: Burt Lancaster, Lee Marvin, Robert Ryan and Woody Strode (left to right) in a publicity shot for Richard Brooks' *The Professionals*. Based on Frank O'Rourke's novel *A Mule for the Marquesa*, the film was a box office smash for Columbia. Adding to the realism, it starred four men who were World War II veterans.

anything, so that Mexico could find its soul. In *A Mule for the Marquesa,* for all its action content, O'Rourke never lets us forget that the rescue mission (the focus of the book) is set against the background of the Revolution. Without hitting us over the head, the author makes us identify with its goals; we are constantly reminded that all of the novel's *yanqui* heroes also fought for it and were on intimate terms with some of its leaders.

O'Rourke's grasp of Mexican history, was flawless; he had a refreshing talent for researching his subject matter one rarely finds in those dealing with Mexican history—on screen or in genre fiction. This is brought home in a later passage in Fields' letter to Fisher:

> [T]he reference to Díaz and Obregón might cause trouble because the author gives his views of them. Here again this does not affect the story. All reference to politics is dangerous.[8]

This is typical Hollywood timidity concerning international politics which was certainly not new by 1965. Fields was implying there would be trouble from Mexican censors, especially if it was decided to film the story on location. There were good reasons for this fear: For decades after the actual Revolution, the Mexican government would always treat its icons as fabled characters.

Fields suggested that the novel should be broken down to a synopsis of 15–20 pages "which would tell the story but omit the objectionable material." Emphasizing this need for approval from the Mexican government, enclosed in Fields' letter was a to-do list, one section of which, subtitled MEXICAN CENSORSHIP, insisted that

> two Spanish-language copies and two English-language copies of the script must be submitted to the Mexican Government Censorship Department for approval.... When film exposed in Mexican territory is sent outside of Mexico for processing, then it is required that a government censor be on the set at all times during filming. The salary of the censor is $1,500 (pesos) paid per week by the Producer. If the film is processed in Mexico, then a censor projects the positive film when ready for shipment. A nominal charge is made for this service.[9]

The Mexican government's thriving business in bestowing "work permits" to foreigners was also was active as ever. Though the country's actors union "makes no charge for actors who will come to Mexico," a $500 legal fee was charged for all other permits. This meant a charge of thousands of dollars for the crew and all other non-actors, not to mention other fees and surcharges tacked on *in addition* to the nominal fees. Is it any surprise that the company ultimately decided to shoot on location in Valley of Fire State Park and Lake Mead in Nevada, Death Valley National Park in California and interiors at the Columbia-Warner Brothers Ranch in Burbank?

Richard Brooks was hired to direct and write the screenplay. He had helmed the groundbreaking films *Blackboard Jungle, Elmer Gantry* and *Cat on a Hot Tin Roof.* He was a veteran of World War II (U.S. Marine Corps), a ballplayer, sports reporter, radio writer, novelist (he wrote one of the first books dealing with anti–Semitism, *The Brick Foxhole*), scenarist of B movies, then made his directorial debut with a hard-hitting film of Latin American revolution, *Crisis* starring Cary Grant and Jose Ferrer. Brooks was a filmmaker who strove for tough, uncompromising stories and guided many of his performers to either Oscars or Oscar nominations.

For the helmsman, the newly titled *The Professionals* would be his first western since MGM's *The Last Hunt* (1956) with Robert Taylor and Stewart Granger (thanks to Brooks' direction, Taylor gives an outstanding performance as a villain that was quite different from the stalwart heroes he usually portrayed). The basic plot of *A Mule for the Marquesa* dealt with the young Mexican wife of a rich American kidnapped by a revolutionary named Raza. Grant, the rich American, hires five mercenaries to cross the border into Mexico and kidnap the woman back from Raza—all for a huge fee for the rescuers that none of them would ever get in their entire lives of fighting, smuggling and blowing things up. Brooks' job was to hire Hollywood's veteran action stars to headline this sagebrush mayhem.

However, as one can tell from the finished film, there are *four* mercenaries going down to Mexico to rescue Grant's young wife. Somewhere along the way from novel to film treatment to finished script, Brooks combined two of them into one.

Certainly the end result on film differs somewhat from O'Rourke's conception of his original characters. As I stated before, all of the mercenaries had fought for the Revolution, with most of them being veteran *Villistas*. Early in the novel, after he's hired by Grant, the head of the group, "Rico" Fardan, is told just why he was hired by the mogul himself:

> You lived sixteen years in Mexico. You speak the language like a native, including dialects. You lived all through the north, in Mexico City, in Tampico, you traveled this desert country around Dolores [Ranch]. You joined Villa early in the Revolution, your reputation is known to more people than you think. You worked with Rodríguez, Villa's chief of staff, but mostly you were with [former Carranza officer, General Felipe] Ángeles, you helped plan strategy and battle tactics, and you did other things.

Again, O'Rourke's research is flawless, particularly in the naming of actual *Villista* officers. Earlier, when Grant describes Raza's guerrilla background, he makes a point of reminding Fardan of his having been "with [Rodolfo] Fierro and Villa from the beginning," and also mentions the time "Villa joined [Pascual] Orozco." The latter, of course, was the revolutionary who fought Díaz but eventually sold out and turned against Madero as well as Villa. In his letter to Fisher, Fields said that referring to politics in the story was dangerous; for example, these sentences from the novel concerning Raza: "Carranza and Obregón have [Raza] high on their list. If Villa ever catches him, he's a dead man."

The description of Fardan's group certainly changes from novel to film. Hans Ehrengard is a former cavalryman at Fort Bliss, "short-legged and chunky," who, after buying his way out of the army, "appeared in Juarez with a lieutenant's commission in Villa's Army of the North (or *División del Norte*)." This is quite different from Brooks' finished screenplay, in which Ehrengard is hired by the team as a horseman, former wrangler, ranch foreman and packer, with no mention of his having also fought for Villa.

The rest of the team also go through some changes from O'Rourke's original conceptions. One is Fred Bisley "who joined the Carranza-Obregón forces in Sonora," and who "trailed a legend of intelligent violence, the reputation of sympathy for the underdogs, and outspoken hatred of the Díaz regime." But most of all, Bisley was inspired in "the art of creating bombs from scrap."

Third man on the list was a tall man in khakis with "the look of a high-born Mexican" named Danny Rios. He's the offspring of a Mexican father "of good blood [and] a lost Irish girl from the Mormon settlement in Chihuahua." However, as to his main asset as a fighter, "[H]e was a wizard with the rope, superb with all weapons, and a master of a dying skill—the bow."

Number four on the list: "Bill Dolworth was made of bold strokes and unshaded colors, a merry vagabond who had been everywhere and done everything with every kind of man and, as a result, nursed no pipe dreams about everything." In other words, a character just right for a larger-than-life actor like Burt Lancaster.

At the end of these introductions to the team, O'Rourke's prose not only makes a point of wrapping up their combined experiences into one action-filled portfolio, but he wryly comments on the hellish madhouse that was Revolutionary Mexico:

> Dolworth, Bisley, Ehrengard, Rios; they summoned up the memory of horses stabled in palaces, pigs in churches, soldier women giving birth in cathedrals; of the dead and the drunk in commingled heaps; of cowards and opportunists, complete bastards who served one leader today, another tomorrow, what difference does it make, get it while you can, come into the town, grab the horses and guns, let the jailbirds out, give the bugle to a fool and plaster the mayor's diamonds inside your shirt; of the men hanging in bunches, like gourds, it was easy to remember the men hanging, the feet were always bare, and always dirty; shoes were more valuable than life; but most of all, they returned the memory of the Mexican soldier of the Januslike courage and cowardice, ignorant of why he fought, filled with insatiable bloodlust and ancient Indian cruelty, turning his drunken rapes and wild looting upon his own kind, ruthless as the earth itself, stoically accepting any fate, living with irrepressible joy—the men in dirty khaki wearing wide hats and death.

On April 15, in a letter to Brooks written from his home in Medina, Washington, O'Rourke gave the director paragraphs of advice about on-location shooting in Mexico. He ended his letter with: "Both my wife and myself will look forward to this film. We've wondered how you will cast it and, abusing our amateur status, want to register our choice for Rios, the halfbreed. We have admired Charles Bronson for a good many years, and consider him one of the excellent, rather unknown actors, of today."[10]

O'Rourke was right about admiring the talented Bronson, whose stardom was just a couple years away. In the meantime, other casting choices were suggested. In a letter from agent Billy Gordon to Columbia honcho Mike Frankovich, dated June 1, it came to light that the studio was considering Henry Fonda for the role of Fardan, the team leader, after Burt Lancaster was already cast as Dolworth. Copies of this letter were sent to both Brooks and Lancaster, clearly indicating that the star also had casting approval of his co-stars, along with the director. (Brooks guided Lancaster to his Oscar win for Best Actor in *Elmer Gantry*.)[11]

However, Brooks solved the problem of casting five action stars by combining two of the mercenaries from O'Rourke's novel into one and taking the qualities of one and adding them to another man. For instance, Danny Rios now became Jake Sharp, and instead of being a half-breed, he is played by an African-American (Woody Strode), a good acknowledgment of the strides made during the Civil Rights era. Brooks removed Fred Bisley from the story and gave his skill with explosives to the wild, impetuous Bill Dolworth, giving Lancaster more to do than just use his 180-watt smile to charm the ladies. Robert Ryan was not the "short-legged" and "chunky" Ehrengard of the book, but the removal of his violent background fighting for Villa also allowed the real Robert Ryan's compassionate nature to come out on screen, especially when there were scenes concerning the gentle treatment of his horses.

Lee Marvin had evolved into a star at his home studio Columbia, and he had just finished giving fine performances in two of the studio's prestige films, *Ship of Fools* and *Cat Ballou*.

Our story begins when we are introduced to the professionals. We see former military man Rico Fardan (Marvin) train American soldiers in the use of the machine-gun. Then we see foreman Hans Ehrengard (Ryan) ride up to the camera (a wonderful entrance which showed the actor as a good horseman) and punch out a ranch hand for mistreating a horse. It is the violent act of a typical Ryan character and happens mere seconds after his introduction. Yet it's his character's most violent act in the entire film until he shoots dead a wounded horse, and even that was an act of mercy compared to his justifiable rage at the horse-beater. After this, we see African-American tracker and bounty hunter Jake Sharp (Strode), somewhat of a groundbreaking role for a black actor in the genre. In fact, there had actually been far more African-American bounty hunters in the west than Hollywood had acknowledged up to then. The groundbreaking continued when Jim Brown portrayed the Hollywood western's first duly appointed African-American lawman in *100 Rifles* (1970). The irrepressible Bill Dolworth (the irrepressible Lancaster) is introduced to us when he is forced to flee a woman's bedroom.

At the U.S.–Mexican border in 1917, millionaire J.W. Grant (Ralph Bellamy) has invited Fardan to assemble whatever men he needs to rescue his (Grant's) young Mexican wife from the clutches of evil bandit-revolutionary Raza. The boys are to get $10,000 apiece, more money than they would otherwise see in a lifetime, to bring back Marie Grant. Fardan and Dolworth had already fought for Raza and find it hard to believe that the guerrilla would go in for kidnapping.

Down in the Mexican desert, it soon becomes apparent that, under former officer Fardan's command, the four men work like a well-oiled machine, scouting, reconnoitering and planning their every move down to the most minute detail.

When the four get to Raza's stronghold, they realize that there are too many men for them to fight; therefore, they must set up a distraction, meaning Bill's little nitro cocktails shot from arrows specially fashioned by Jake. The distraction works, and Fardan and Dolworth storm the house where Marie (the stunning Claudia Cardinale) is held; soon, Raza (Jack Palance) arrives. Unfortunately, the two mercenaries interrupt a would-be act of lovemaking between "captor" and "kidnap victim," and they both now realize they've been had. Still, 40 grand is 40 grand, so they knock out Raza, grab Mrs. Grant and head back across the desert.

The "rescued" lady is anything but grateful, and even tries to bribe the womanizing Dolworth with her body if she'd then be released, an offer that falls flat when she tries for his gun. Soon, Raza and his men are in pursuit, bringing along with them the charismatic soldera Chiquita (a lively performance by Marie Gomez). Ultimately, the decision is made by Fardan that one man has to stay behind to hold off the guerrillas, in a hit-and-run assault that will whittle Raza's band down to nothing. Dolworth gets the job and, with little effort, picks off Raza's men and wounds the guerrilla chief himself. When Chiquita, who's had a history with the amorous mercenary, rides out as a decoy, Dolworth mortally wounds her, thinking she's just another of Raza's men. Holding her in his arms, Dolworth literally ducks

Yanquis in Mexico: Lee Marvin (left) and Burt Lancaster in *The Professionals*. Frank O'Rourke's novel originally had *five* mercenaries, but director Richard Brooks combined two characters.

the bullet when Chiquita pulls the trigger of an empty pistol at him ("It is not my lucky day," she says weakly). During the siege, both Dolworth and Raza wax philosophically on women and the Revolution, with the guerrilla chief at times sounding surprisingly poetic:

> La Revolución is like a great love affair. In the beginning, she is a goddess. A holy cause. But ... every love affair has a terrible enemy: time. We see her as she is: La Revolución is not a goddess, but a whore. She was never pure, never saintly, never perfect. And we run away, find another lover, another cause. Quick, sordid affairs. Lust, but no love. Passion, but no compassion. Without love, without a cause, we are ... nothing! We stay because we believe. We leave because we are disillusioned. We come back because we are lost. We die because we are committed.

No one in the Mexican Revolution ever talked this way, though one can forgive Brooks for giving the guerrilla chief a sensitive side; it pointed up the fact that, even more than in O'Rourke's novel, nothing was black and white. Still, one finds it hard to dismiss the cynical Dolworth when he says: "The Revolution? When the shooting stops, and the dead are buried, and the politicians take over, it all adds up to one thing: a lost cause."

After knocking off all of Raza's men, Dolworth brings the wounded revolutionary back to the border, where they rendezvous with Fardan and the others. Previously, the cynical, womanizing Dolworth had asked Marie why she was worth $100,000 [sic] to her husband. But after Chiquita dies in his arms, the mercenary has his answer, and he soon sways Fardan and the others to side with the lovers.

When the bullying Grant beats and kicks the wounded Raza, the four men interfere. After releasing the two lovers and giving them a horse and buckboard, the professionals leave the enraged Grant to his misery. However, after the millionaire calls Fardan a bastard, the mercenary responds with the classic line: "Yes, sir. In my case, an accident of birth. But you, sir, you're a self-made man."

Brooks throws in some sharp, amoral dialogue throughout the film. Told by Mrs. Grant to go to hell, Dolworth responds with, "Yes, ma'am. I'm on my way." In his witty exchange with Dolworth during the siege, Raza wryly declares: "Everything is 'as usual.' I need guns and bullets, 'as usual.' The war goes badly, 'as usual.'" Explaining how his explosives will close the pass, Dolworth says, "[Then] dynamite, not faith, will move that mountain into this pass. Peace, brother."

The Professionals was a film focusing on four men who were just that: professionals. After decades of seeing western heroes screw up in one way or another, or men and women whose goodness and honesty usually put them at a disadvantage to the underhanded and ruthless villains, as well as the fates, it was a real pleasure to see good guys who actually *knew* what they were doing.

It was also a pleasure to see four actors who were in their forties and fifties star in a major action film that cleaned up at the box office ($8.8 million in this country alone), something today's youth-oriented Hollywood couldn't possible imagine. Also, the film was directed by an ex–Marine and starred three other ex–Marines and one army veteran (Lancaster), and all had been in the service during World War II, giving a wonderfully real feel to the story of a search-and-rescue mission enacted by four professionals who had previous military experience.

In a letter written by Jack H. Wiener, vice-president in charge of publicity of Columbia's European division, dated December 20, 1966, the executive apprised the Los Angeles home office of the film's popularity in Europe. He enclosed a clipping of a translated article on the film from *Paris Match* which read, in part:

> A sarcastic Lancaster; an impenetrable Marvin; Claudia, taciturn and striking; a fanatic Palance. It's just admirable from beginning to end. But, better still, behind this captivating story, there is an undertone of a far more serious problem (the devotion to a political cause, love, and a Revolution), i.e., an action film that makes one think; that is rare, and it is splendid indeed.[12]

On the heels of this, Richard Brooks picked up the endorsement of a very influential fan, then a young, up-and-coming film critic. In his November 7 letter to the director, Richard Schickel wrote:

> It was really a treat to see that the movie professionals still know how to work the old magic of films and I assure you that such praise of the film that I could convey intellectually in the review was in no way up to the old, below-the-belt, emotional pleasure I took in your movie. So, thanks for having the nerve to go back to first movie principles and the skill to realize them.[13]

The Professionals crystalized the role of the *yanqui* adventurer in Mexico during the Revolution, though with a savage 1960s twist. Seeking money and adventure, the American mercenary usually found honor instead of greenbacks, this motif had been going back to the 1950s when Mitchum and Calhoun were out to get Mexican gold and guns, but instead found *the truth*. But now, by 1966, agendas weren't so clear, and though *The Professionals* showed us that a kidnapping *had* taken place, it's ultimately revealed that the respectable Mr. Grant was the real kidnapper, not the guerrilla chief who still commanded a gang of murdering cutthroats.

Indeed, Dolworth's line still resonates through the years, an incisive comment on the Mexican Revolution, as well as other world conflicts: "Maybe there's been only one revolution since the beginning, the good guys against the bad guys. Question is, who are the good guys?"

With the spaghetti western's continued penchant for locating their stories Down Mexico Way, Hollywood decided to ape this trend and give us films featuring soldiers of fortune shooting down bad guys and looking for the usual stash of hidden gold.

This time, however, Paramount decided to focus on an actual figure from Mexico's history to play opposite that of the all–American mercenary. The studio bought the rights to William Douglas Lansford's 1965 novel *Pancho Villa,* a fictional account of the life of the bandit-revolutionary. Producer Ted Richmond offered the screenplay assignment to Sam Peckinpah. Unofficially blackballed by the studios after his firing from *The Cincinnati Kid* and the failure of *Major Dundee,* Peckinpah was enthusiastic about the chance to write a screenplay about Mexico and, if star Yul Brynner liked the script, Richmond was ready to hire him to direct as well.

Born in 1920 in Russia, the ultimate king of *The King and I* (Brynner) was always cagey about where he was born and gave several stories about his origins, none of which was true. Nevertheless, having Latino roots, especially Mexican ancestry, was emphatically *not* part of the actor's ethnic makeup. Thanks to Hollywood's traditional racism, white actors, even as late as the 1970s, continued to play Latino characters. Grudgingly, the film industry accepted a charismatic actor like Sidney Poitier as their first black star, and gradually let others follow in his wake as the Civil Rights era unfolded, but they stubbornly refused to give the American

Villa Talks!: Robert Mitchum (left) returns to Revolutionary Mexico in *Villa Rides*. Robert Viharo is center as *Villista* Tomás Urbina and, of all people, Yul Brynner is Pancho Villa. Based on William Douglas Lansford's novel *Pancho Villa*, the film was another whitewash of the famed revolutionary.

moviegoing public a *Latino* Poitier. And so, as the American incursion into Vietnam was growing and race riots and student protests continued to spread, Paramount did a Wallace Beery and cast a vain white actor as a mercurial Mexican revolutionary.

But Paramount's bizarre obsession with race didn't stop with the miscasting of the lead role. According to the film's director Buzz Kulik, the studio wanted a "white face"[14] to balance the presence of Pancho Villa. And so, Peckinpah came up with an American soldier of fortune character who first runs guns to Pascual Orozco's anti–Madero Colorados, then aids Villa and his rebels in their fight. Of course, this was a formula as old as MGM's *Viva Villa!* with reporter Stuart Erwin as an American counterbalance to Wallace Beery's badly accented rebel chief. In fact, this formula would continue, in one form or another, down through the decades whenever Hollywood filmed the Revolution. From Van Heflin's *yanqui* mine owner helping the rebels in *Wings of the Hawk* to Rory Calhoun's all–American mercenary helping Gilbert Roland's rebels in *The Treasure of Pancho Villa* (which did *not* have an appearance by the Centaur of the North), Hollywood always felt more comfortable having a "white" character for viewers to identify with since, according to the producers, they couldn't possibly identify with so alien a lead character as a Latino. This not-so-subtle racism even made its way into the European spaghetti westerns of allegedly left-wing filmmakers, such as 1972's *Pancho Villa* (otherwise known as *Vendetta*), by having Villa (played by another bald white actor, Telly Savalas) assisted by a white American merc played by Clint Walker. In reality, though he cheerfully accepted American guns, and sometimes even had American and European mercenaries helping him, Pancho Villa needed no *Anglo* outsiders to win battles. His men were some of the toughest warriors of their day.

Which brings us back to *Villa Rides*. Ted Richmond's dictum that Brynner's approval of the script would green-light Peckinpah's involvement as a director, was about to be enforced. And so, after he read the script, the portrayer of the famous but short-sighted Siamese king said, "No!" Figuring to keep the budget low, Paramount hired TV director Kulik instead of Peckinpah. Apparently Brynner was angry that the Peckinpah script portrayed Villa as "a bad guy." This included Villa's standing order to shoot all prisoners, something that was historically true. (It must also be noted that the opposition, whether they were Huerta's federals, Orozco's Colorados, or the troops of Venustiano Carranza, *also* executed every *Villista* they captured.) It was obvious that Peckinpah wanted a multi-faceted Villa, both hero and mass murderer—which, in essence, he *was*. But at the time, leading men like Brynner didn't like to play heroes who had the capacity to torture and murder their captives.

Predictably, the decision didn't go down well with Peckinpah: "Brynner asked for me to be taken off the film because he said I didn't know anything about Mexico. That surprised me because I was then married to a Mexican and I'd been in and out of Mexico for years."[15]

Especially their cantinas.

Actually, Brynner never accused Peckinpah of not knowing Mexico, and his sometimes using Begoña as a handball as she waited for the divorce to go through didn't necessarily qualify as being "married," as the director had claimed. Still, since the star hated the script, Peckinpah was fired as scenarist as well and replaced by Robert Towne. Typically, in Hollywood, the replacers are never very understanding of the artists they replaced. According to Buzz Kulik: "The Peckinpah script? Three-quarters of it was in Spanish! I think he was married to a Spanish woman he was trying to impress. We threw most of it out, had to start over again. Hired Robert Towne."[16]

Incidentally, Begoña was *Mexican,* not Spanish.

Echoing his director, Robert Towne also claimed that Peckinpah's material was thrown out. Yet despite the repeated claims of Peckinpah, Kulik and Towne as to their immense influence on the script, both the early version and the rewritten one, everyone seemed to have forgotten the *real* author of the material, William Douglas Lansford, who wrote the novel. Peckinpah usually harbored contempt for original material that was not his own and promptly threw out much of Lansford's work, some of which was at least based on actual history.

Lansford was basically a TV writer, with *Pancho Villa* being one of his few novels. His non-artistic life, however, was far more interesting. He was a decorated Marine sergeant during World War II, and later joined the army during the Korean War. He claimed that his ancestors hailed from Mexico and, according to the bio on the back of the Backinprint edition of *Pancho Villa*, "first learned about Villa from his Chihuahua grandmother's memories of the great rebel leader." It also claimed, falsely, that he authored many movies and TV shows; however, according to the IMDb website, his film works seems to have been sporadic, with most of his prolific output coming from TV scripts. For *Villa Rides,* Lansford got credit for adapting his novel for the screen, a little detail Kulik, Towne or Peckinpah have never acknowledged.

Our story begins with a dedication to, of all people, Pancho Villa. In a precursor to *The Wild Bunch* (in fact, this might have been Peckinpah's idea), Kulik includes period photographs behind the title credits. One striking photo shows us the *real* Villa in the forefront of his men, this shot underlining the fact that the actor playing him in the film looks nothing like the real one. Another interesting facet here is that, despite his bitterness, Peckinpah *still* gets a co-screenwriting credit, though his name comes after Towne's.

Soldier of fortune Lee Arnold (an older, wearier-looking Robert Mitchum) flies his plane onto a beach and meets with Colorado General Ramirez (Frank Wolff) to sell guns to the counter-revolutionaries. The filmmakers make a major boo-boo: The Colorados, as run by Pascual Orozco, were guerrillas just like Villa's men; they *didn't* wear federal uniforms. This mistake could easily confuse an audience (at the time period the film was set, Villa was fighting *for* the government, meaning the presidency of Francisco Madero, with the Colorados fighting against the president). Ramirez's men carry a red flag, and the Colorados were also known (basically to the *yanquis*) as "red-flaggers." However, this was not because they carried a red flag, but due to the fact that they had red bands around their hats; some say it was because they wore pants with red stripes down the sides. It seems that Arnold must get his plane repaired, so Ramirez advises him to take it to the local blacksmith. As we know, *all* simple villagers know how to repair airplanes.

Once he's in the village, as a foreigner he's unrealistically welcomed as he rides in on his burro with his plane in tow; needless to say, everyone speaks perfect English. This might be another casualty of sacking Peckinpah's material. Remember that Kulik rather churlishly complained that most of Peckinpah's original script was in Spanish; more Spanish would have made things less unrealistic. Neither the character of Arnold, nor his airplane, nor his visit to a friendly village, were in Lansford's novel. Kulik also claimed that, with time growing short, Towne was forced to write the next day's script *the night before shooting*. This probably explains why the film sometimes borders on the fantastic.

Taken to the friendly blacksmith's home, Arnold is attracted to the blacksmith's lovely daughter Fina (Italian actress Grazia Buccella) and they do the nasty; however, this is 1968, so we don't see very much. The next morning, Ramirez and his men storm the village (the officer had warned Arnold not to linger there too long). Now the mad officer figures to make examples of the blacksmith and others supporting Villa by having nooses tied around their necks; when no one squeals on the guerrilla, Ramirez systematically kicks out the chairs supporting them, and they strangle to death. However, Pancho Villa (Brynner with a toupee) is just over the hill nearby with his men, who include Tomás Urbina (Robert Viharo) and the psychopathic Rodolfo Fierro (the up-and-coming Charles Bronson). When Urbina tells him what's going on in the village, Villa purposely delays the rescue, saying calmly "Not yet" as an almost mocking version of *La Cucaracha* plays on the soundtrack. This alone is amazing in light of Brynner's complaints that Peckinpah portrayed the guerrilla chief as a "bad guy," yet allowed this bit to remain in the film.

Once Ramirez has hanged practically everyone, Villa and his men belatedly ride in to heroic music. After Villa discovers a money belt on his person, Arnold is sentenced to death along with the surviving Colorados, with the sentence to be carried out by the psychotic Fierro. He orders the Colorado prisoners a chance to go over a wall to freedom without his shooting them to death with his two always-loaded pistols (he threatens to shoot the man who's loading them if he's too slow at it). Though claiming to be a bad shot, we quickly see that

Fierro *never* misses. This is one of the few scenes Kulik, Towne and Peckinpah kept from Lansford's novel. Bronson is excellent in this scene. Though he captures a trace of the real Fierro's mania to kill, the star was far too likable an actor to play him. Shorter and fuller in the face than the tall, ugly, hatchet-faced Fierro, the future star of *Death Wish* is clearly playing a villainous character, yet one finds it hard to dislike the man playing him. (Frank Wolff, who plays Ramirez, would have been far easier to hate had *he* played Fierro.) Still, this clinical psychopath is seen as someone positive since he's helping our hero Villa. Realizing that Arnold can use his plane to fly for the *Villistas* and spot opposing troops from the air, Villa orders Fierro to spare him from the "run-for-the-wall-or-die" game.

Arnold learns from a smiling Urbina what we all suspected, that Villa purposely delayed the rescue of the hanged villagers so that the survivors would side with *him* and hate the Colorados. This ruthless and cynical manipulation of people's opinions during a guerrilla war was probably one of the more honest things to come out of this film, and might have been a Peckinpah touch. Perhaps Brynner allowed this into the plot thinking that it made Villa into a clever strategist, but in reality it reveals him (and we see Arnold's look of disgust after Urbina tells him) to be a cold-blooded, unfeeling bastard. Remember, had Villa's men attacked sooner, not only could they have saved the doomed villagers, but they could have prevented the rape of Fina. After accusing Villa of not stopping Ramirez sooner, Arnold is shocked when Villa orders a priest to marry her to the guerrilla chief; this is obviously so no one will dare touch Fina. Still, the episode comments on Villa's neurotic compulsion to marry the girls he plans to seduce. Everyone who's ever made a film on Villa, or written about him (including Lansford), seems to ignore Villa's obvious contempt for women, which included beating or shooting them when they refused his advances.

In a comical scene (played to comical music), Villa is taught how to use Arnold's plane. It goes without saying that, had the *Villistas* had the use of aircraft, for recon or aggressive military intent, they would have beaten the federals and the Colorados a lot sooner than they had. However, Mexico was still very much in the nineteenth century, with poor roads, practically no automobiles, and certainly no air force. Interestingly, though we were far more advanced in tech-

Villa Loves!: Regina de Julian embraces Yul Brynner in *Villa Rides*. Like *Viva Villa!*, the film turned Villa's many marriages and serial womanizing into raucous comedy.

nology during this Industrial Age, the American government did not have the foresight to adequately develop aircraft for military use.

According to historian John S.D. Eisenhower (grandson of the president) in his excellent and highly readable *Intervention: The United States and the Mexican Revolution*:

> Although invented in the United States, the airplane was neglected in this country while it was being developed as a potent weapon of war in Europe. In contrast to the dangerous aircraft the Americans were flying, European commanders on the Western Front in 1916 had planes available that could reconnoiter, photograph and use radio to adjust artillery. Their machine-guns fired through their propellers, and the European aircraft could engage in dogfights with each other and perform in bombardment missions. These aircraft could reach speeds exceeding 110 miles per hour and climb to altitudes of 15,000 feet.[17]

The U.S. government spent less than half a million dollars on aeronautics between 1908 and 1913, while our future enemies in Germany spent a whopping $28 million.[18]

When General Pershing launched his Punitive Expedition against Pancho Villa in 1916, his army only had the use of a few JN-3 airplanes, otherwise known as Jennies. These sometimes rickety aircraft couldn't fly more than fifty miles at a pop, had trouble negotiating the narrow and twisted canyons and mountain ranges around northern Mexico, could barely fly at night, and were hardly useful even for reconnaissance. Out of a squadron of eight Jennies, Pershing lost two of them in one night when they tried to negotiate the windy Mexican mountain passes. Therefore, if American military aircraft like the Jennie–3 was considered a flying death-crate, how did Arnold, as a private citizen, get hold of a plane that could fly low and make sweeping, graceful dives onto Colorado troop trains so he and Fierro could drop Villa's homemade bombs on them with pinpoint accuracy?

Nevertheless, after bombing the train and killing or capturing their enemy, we see Fierro "invent" the peculiar but effective execution method of lining up three enemy soldiers and killing them all with one bullet. In Lansford's novel, it is Villa who thinks this up. At another point, seizing a telegraph outfit, Villa has his men send a message to the garrison at Parral. Pretending to be an anonymous commander, Villa tells the garrison he has been defeated by Villa's men and is using the train to head back to base. Of course, the soldiers are caught by surprise when *Villistas* storm out of the train and take Parral without firing a shot. This was based on fact, and certainly demonstrated Villa's real-life boldness and imagination that won him many battles.

General Victoriano Huerta (a miscast Herbert Lom) addresses his staff, a bottle of cognac at his elbow. Lom was an actor who made much of his fame playing villains and crazed killers. With this in mind, one can see why he was cast as the drunken mass murderer Huerta, the man most responsible for Madero's assassination outside of the officers he hired to actually shoot him. But Lom's Huerta is much too refined, too subtle. The script does not allow the actor to capture the man's insanity, the severe schizophrenia which made him a slobbering drunk one day and a cold-blooded, scary madman the next. Lansford captures this in a scene when he has Villa meet Huerta for the first time: Friendly and happy one day, his Huerta becomes a chilling martinet the next, curtly dressing down Villa for some insignificant departure from military protocol. Villa himself claimed that Huerta could sit in a cantina with a bottle of tequila from dawn and still be seen drinking fourteen hours later. A natural bully and a brute, Huerta's later murder of Madero and his iron-fisted rule of Mexico even turned off the elite who were initially ready to support him.

In the film, during a big victory celebration in Parral, Villa becomes enamored of a senorita dancing for him and quickly marries her, ironically breaking the heart of Fina, the raped girl who was forced to marry him. Consoling her, Arnold does the nasty with her yet again—and her "husband" Villa is aware of all of this. This episode (with Villa claiming all he wants to do is make women "happy") has a comic import which recalls the situation comedy moments of the Pedro Armendáriz Villa films.

Villa has Arnold fly him for a meeting with Madero (played by Canadian actor Alexander Knox) in Mexico City. Their first scene together is revealing in the light of Brynner's idea of the manly Villa; he and Knox *almost* embrace, but it's obvious that the actor playing Villa refuses to complete the hug. The scene is so awkward, it's a surprise Kulik kept it in. Wearing his emotions on his sleeve, the real Villa was a man who happily embraced friends and allies alike, not caring one way or the other how it looked to others. This was *not* Yul Brynner's Villa.

Under orders to make a suicidal charge on a Colorado stronghold, Villa and Fierro see their men slaughtered until Arnold flies overhead and bombs the enemy, thus ensuring a *Villista* victory. It is also the moment when Arnold forgets money and officially joins the rebels. He could have flown away (which is what Villa assumes he's doing), but he stays and helps them, thus foiling Huerta's plan to have Villa's men killed off. He then crash-dives his plane (which is out of gas) into the enemy's barbed wire fortifications. In reality, barbed wire didn't make it to the Mexican Revolution until Álvaro Obregón, studying tactics used in Europe during the World War, initiated its use against Villa himself in 1915.

An angry Huerta finds a pretext to have both Villa and Arnold arrested, with the rebel chief slated for the firing squad. (The squad is commanded by Spanish star Fernando Rey.) Fierro commandeers a telegraph station and has a message sent to Madero to stop the death sentence. In reality, this message (*not* sent personally by Fierro) actually took weeks to get to the president in Mexico City, and there is great suspicion that, in order to not enrage the tender feelings of General Huerta, Madero purposely delayed halting the execution. Indeed, Villa reportedly had sent letter after letter to Madero for months on end, yet they mysteriously either never arrived or the president purposely ignored them. Finally, Madero sends an order to stop the execution. In reality, Villa, confused and actually showing fear for perhaps the first time, broke down in tears. Peckinpah's script has this, and it *is* based on history, yet the scene is also one of the main reasons Brynner wanted Peckinpah out; he did not want *his* manly version of Villa to cry. For his own take, Villa later admitted to shedding tears, but not out of fear, but to play for time, as if he just *knew* that Madero's order to halt the execution would arrive at the last minute. (Since Madero never responded to his letters, Villa never quite explained why the president would respond with such punctuality *this* time.)

Madero's order not only saves Villa, but forces Huerta to deport Arnold over the border to El Paso. Meanwhile, deep in the heart of a Texas barber shop, Arnold runs into an old cowboy friend named Dave (an amusing cameo by John Ireland), where the former gunrunner learns that Madero has been killed by Huerta who promptly took over the country and that Villa has escaped jail. Afterwards, Arnold is dining in a restaurant with a snotty princess (Charles Bronson's future wife, Jill Ireland). Villa, Urbina and the ubiquitous Fierro show up and enlist Arnold's aid in fighting Huerta. Though he turns them down now, after just a few moments with the uppity girl, he decides to return to help Villa and fight for a free Mexico—and presumably return to Fina.

At the fadeout, the titles tell us that Villa was at the head of 50,000 troops when he entered Mexico City; this bit of info neglecting to tell us that, in order to show up Villa, "First Chief" Carranza ordered Alavaro Obregōn to capture Mexico City *first,* and that Villa and his men rode in afterwards.

In a film supposedly based on history but instead bursting with inaccuracies, one can easily lose sight of an actor's poor interpretation of the lead character. Brynner's Pancho Villa may be smarter and more cynical than Wallace Beery's buffoonish version (in fact, the

Villa Saves!: A man (actor unidentified) is about to be rescued by Villa (Yul Brynner) in *Villa Rides*. Brynner had screenwriter Sam Peckinpah replaced by Robert Towne (the move killed Peckinpah's chance to direct the film as well) because the future director of *The Wild Bunch* made Villa look like "a bad guy."

character actually reminds us of his cold yet resourceful, dressed-in-black Chris of *The Magnificent Seven*), but it still falls far short of the real Villa. In fact, Brynner's performance is almost the opposite of Lansford's, in its own way, equally inaccurate depiction of Villa in his novel.

Knowing Spanish, Lansford was able to travel to Mexico and interview surviving revolutionaries for his novel. Besides ripping author Edgecumb Pinchon's version of Villa in his own book, Sergeant Lansford *really* goes on the attack when he writes about Wallace Beery's performance in *Viva Villa!*:

> Everytime [sic] I think of Wallace Beery groaning *car-r-ramba!* and massaging his feet in the *Palacio Nacional* I groan too. Yet Mr. Pinchon's is the only close look *gringo*dom has ever had at Villa, and it was Pinchon (abetted by Ben Hecht's movie script) who almost singlehandedly formed the fat, sweaty Villa we Americans know today. All of this made me wonder if another effort—just one more—shouldn't be made to give Villa back his dignity, and to reweave him back to the texture of humanity.[19]

Lansford endeavored to show us the scholarly research he did for his book. Though claiming to have researched his subject for some fifteen years, the author explains that he had the input of old revolutionaries who were loyal to Villa, as well as Villa's first wife Luz Corral. Already this should have set off alarm bells in even the most jaded author. Seeing their fight as a holy mission to free Mexico and totally ignoring all the wanton murders, rapes and destruction they caused, old *Villistas* certainly were *not* going to be totally honest about their activities while fighting under their bipolar leader. Lansford *does* honestly depict the conniving, greedy Tomás Urbina and the psychopathic Fierro. However, these men were not exactly well-liked by their comrades; in fact, many *Villistas* actually sat by and watched Fierro drown in quicksand while he was attempting to cross a supposedly "shallow" lake. The author also relies on the word of Luz Corral, who is portrayed in his book, not surprisingly, as Villa's one true love, totally ignoring his equally passionate devotion to all his other "true loves" scattered throughout northern Mexico. Outrageously, she also claimed, according to Lansford, that she was bringing in a tray of lunch "for the general" as Fierro shot dead Scottish rancher William Benton (who stormed into Villa's compound to complain about the theft of his cattle), a killing that sparked a near-international incident with Britain. Though no one will know for sure just how Benton was killed, according to historian John S.D. Eisenhower, at least one *Villista's* claims might be the most reliable: Fierro took Benton out into the desert, ordered him to dig his own grave and then bashed his head in when his back was turned—a move that was quite in-character for the homicidal guerrilla.

Despite all his claims to accuracy, Lansford's Villa is only a *little* smarter than Beery's. In reality, Pancho Villa was ruled first and foremost by his emotions; he was an extrovert, an illiterate who might have learned to read and write later in life; he was not a man who connived or calculated. He *was* a liar, thief, murderer, woman-beater and all-around thug, paranoid, sensitive to real or perceived slights, and a borderline schizophrenic whose mood swings went from ecstatic to threatening in microseconds. He was by no means stupid; his vast store of knowledge came from the terrain he rode and the people he knew, not from books. He was a tenacious fighter and a talented military leader, but not a military genius who thought far ahead, as did Obregón who defeated him several times in battle. Unfortunately, Lansford only gives us the "good" Villa, the lover and fighter and misunderstood hero, not the man who shot a woman to death in a hotel because she refused to go with him.

In his review of *Villa Rides* for the *Chicago Sun-Times*, Roger Ebert noted that "the political implications of the Mexican Revolution are never brought to the surface," and that American audiences learn nothing about it "except that Pancho was a romantic fellow who had a moustache and liked to have people lined up three in a row and killed with one bullet."[20] Ebert also reported that that particular scene got a big laugh when he saw it with an audience.

Meanwhile, in Spain, the same nation where *Villa Rides* had been shot, director Damiano Damiani and scenarist Salvatore Laurani were shooting a film that powerfully demonstrated how easily those who fought for the Revolution could have their agendas twisted by a mercenary interloper...

The spaghetti western was born in the 1960s, a subgenre of the western which basically starred Italian actors and had Italian production personnel shooting a film in Spain where most of these Italian actors pretended to be Mexicans. Sometimes, though certainly not always, these films would star either has-been American stars on their way down (Stewart Granger, Rod Cameron) or Hollywood genre veterans who found new stardom in the Euro-western (Clint Eastwood, Lee Van Cleef). Unlike the Hollywood western up to that time, the spaghetti western seemed to be (but decidedly was *not*) a repudiation of the genre, as it supposedly turned conventional elements upside down. These were not the "ranch romances" of Zane Grey or Luke Short; nor were they moral tales in which right triumphs over might. In fact, unlike the Hollywood western of old, the level of violence would be raised. Certainly, depending on which Euro-western one viewed, the level of violence could be different from film to film, much of the time depending on the good taste or mean-spiritedness of the director and/or screenwriters.

On December 7, 1966, audiences in Italy saw a new entrant in the spaghetti western field which added a heavy dose of politics to the usual mayhem.

"A Band of Killers Stalk the Countryside ... LOOTING ... KILLING ... LOVING Everything in Sight!" screamed the film's taglines. Though it is certainly debatable whether this gang of lovable rogues do indeed loot, kill and love everything in sight (in that order!), thanks to the talents of director Damiano Damiani, scenarist Salvatore Laurani and adaptor Franco Solinas, *El Chuncho, Quien Sabe?* (*El Chunco, Who Knows?*), otherwise known as *A Bullet for the General,* still leaves an impression.

Four revolutionaries are shot dead by a federal firing squad (to which women and children are in the enthusiastic audience). Also watching this execution is a well-dressed American named Bill Tate (Lou Castel), an obvious snob: When a boy asks him whether, as an American, he likes Mexico, the cold young man replies, "No, not very much...."

A passenger train that happens to be carrying weapons and federal troops is forced to halt when the engineer spots a kidnapped federal commander on the tracks, chained to a makeshift cross. Atop the surroundings hills, bandits led by the charismatic Chunco Munos aka "El Chucho" (Gian Maria Volonte, who was in *A Fistful of Dollars* and *A Few Dollars More*) and his revolutionary band are firing at the federals aboard the train. Sitting ducks, the federals cannot leave the train to release the poor man without getting shot to pieces. The dying commander insists that the train barrel through his body to save themselves. Though the filmmakers are obviously sympathizing with the rebels, it's awfully hard not to reserve some hatred for Chuncho and his band of assassins comfortably firing from a hill and endangering the civilians, especially women and children, on the train. When the train does indeed run over the officer (we see the wheels grind over what's left of his uniform, as well as his cutlass), a shocked Chuncho says, "They don't even have respect for their own officers!" Apparently he forgot that he and his men were the ones who put the man in danger in the first place.

Taking advantage of the confusion, Tate makes his way to the front and suddenly pulls a gun, killing the engineer. After stopping the train, he grabs a pair of handcuffs off a dead soldier and puts them on. Happily surprised that the train has stopped, Chunco and his men massacre the soldiers. Among the rebels is Chuncho's brother, El Santo (Polish actor Klaus Kinski). Here, not only does the usually temper-prone Kinski *not* look like his brother, but he is rather awkwardly dubbed in with a deep voice that doesn't sound a bit like him. A religious revolutionary, he rides by the cars and announces, "Don't be afraid! We are on the side of God and the people!" Of course, what these thugs have done is murder everyone who got in their way and left a train full of poor women and crying infants stranded in the desert. In fact, the women are witness to their men being shot down in cold blood, with the revolutionaries, like vultures, stripping the corpses of all valuables and then shooting at their bodies to make sure they're dead.

El Chuncho reluctantly accepts Tate's explanation that he stopped the train to help the rebels and that he was handcuffed because he's a wanted outlaw. The bandit chief allows him to ride with them as they raid for the Revolution. However, fighting for the Cause does have its fringe benefits, and their only soldera is a tall, hot brunette named Adelita (played by the tall, hot brunette Martine Beswick). Affectionately called *Niño* (little boy) by Chuncho, the *Americano* is welcomed by the band, with the possible exception of Adelita's boyfriend. That night in camp, though she refuses her boyfriend's advances, her alternately teasing and yet obvious attraction to Tate gets the cold shoulder from the taciturn American, a fact noted by Chuncho. "The boy doesn't drink, doesn't smoke, and doesn't want women," laments the bandit chief. When he asks Tate what he *does* want, his reply is terse, yet to the point: "Money...."

With Tate along, the rebel band sweeps from town to town, killing the federals and grabbing their weapons; this is so they can ultimately sell them to a mysterious rebel warlord named General Elias. Tate insists that Chunco not waste any time and get the guns to the general as soon as possible.

The rebels take over the village of San Miguel. The people there want to hang Don Phillipe, the local *hacendado*. When the rebels are about to rape the man's pretty red-headed wife, Tate shouts at them that they are wasting time and insults one of Chuncho's men. But before the bandit can kill Tate, Chuncho shoots the man dead. The rebel chief himself doesn't believe what he's done, killing an old friend to save the cold, ruthless young *Americano*. In fact, it seems that Tate is purposely starting dissension among the band; eventually most of them are killed off thanks to his machinations.

Attacked in the desert, Chuncho and Tate use their captured machine-gun. ("It is beautiful!" cries Chuncho. "Better than a *woman!*") However, when no one is looking, Tate kills the man holding their money and disposes of it, forcing them to go directly to General Elias for cash. Disillusioned, and with her boyfriend now dead, Adelita leaves them. Now there is only Chuncho and Tate left. Later that night, as Tate is suffering from the cold and Chuncho searches the American's bag for medicine, he finds a little case with a special rifle bullet. Could said bullet be for the *general*? If not, they'd have to change the title.

The Fab Four, Part II: Lou Castel, Klaus Kinski, Martine Beswick and Gian Maria Volonte (left to right) march toward the camera in a publicity shot for *A Bullet for the General*. Directed by spaghetti western icon Damiano Damiani and written by Salvatore Laurani, the film turned Castel's handsome American into a murderous symbol of *yanqui* interventionism.

They arrive at the village and Chuncho is summoned to meet Elias (Jaime Fernandez). After paying the bandit chief, however, the general accuses him of abandoning the people of San Miguel, who were massacred by the federals after the band left. Suddenly, El Santo appears and volunteers to execute his brother. But out in the hills, El Santo is shot dead by Tate shooting from afar with his rifle. However, the enterprising young *yanqui* has also shot dead General Elias with a bullet made of gold—just like the one Chuncho found in Tate's bag.

At the headquarters of the federals, Tate is paid 100,000 pesos in gold for the "hit." Meanwhile, Chuncho, armed with a pistol, has tracked Tate to his swank hotel. Admitting the whole scheme to his rebel comrade, Tate gets the former bandit all dressed up in a suit and plans to take his friend with him to the U.S. He even pays him 50,000 pesos of his money for unwittingly "helping" him. However, when the two plan to take the train up north, Chuncho sees the condescending attitude Tate has with the poor peons also waiting on line at the ticket counter (like at the film's beginning). Realizing that so many people have died, including his brother (even if Tate saved his life by killing him), Chuncho shoots his American "friend" dead before he boards the train. When the dying man asks him why, Chuncho replies, "Who knows?" Escaping the police, the newly reborn rebel chief incites the peons to fight back "with dynamite!"

Certainly, the portrayal of the film's only *yanqui* character as a cold, sexless, clean-cut young psychopath whose only love is the Almighty Dollar might have left American audiences with a sour taste in their collective mouths. However, this didn't stop the film's American release on September 1968, almost two years after its Italian premiere, where spaghetti western–loving fans thrilled to its over-the-top violence and stunning visuals. The film's political stance, euphemistically portraying the American as the fly-in-the-ointment interloper who plays both ends against the middle, spoke volumes to a postwar Europe fed up with American hegemony over world affairs, as well as its deepening involvement in Vietnam. Even self-proclaimed "reformers" like President Woodrow Wilson couldn't keep his hands off Mexico, and worked behind the scenes to have a Mexican president friendly to the U.S. and its interests, though the president hardly strove to attain his goals with the ruthless dispatch used by a killer like Bill Tate. Still, this human automaton *was* allowed to have one tragic flaw that sealed his doom: Now having let down his guard and displayed the only true affection he's shown to any character in the film, even Adelita, the mercenary Tate is gunned down by the man he was hoping to have as his partner. Yet even when he shoots Tate dead, Chuncho doesn't understand why he's done it; he only knows that he *must,* whether to avenge his brother's death, or those of the other victims of Tate's machinations, or to prevent the young American from profiting off of killing anyone else. Indeed, in the complicated dynamics of the Mexican Revolution, where the only difference between the murderers who fought for the government and the murderers who fought for the Revolution was only a change of uniform, *who knows?*

Meanwhile, back in Hollywood, Twentieth Century–Fox was making a film depicting the Revolution as the over-the-top adventure American audiences always wanted to see—and without all that heavy political crap the Europeans were always throwing in. Originally based on a novel by Robert MacLeod and with a screenplay by western author Clair Huffaker, the film would also be a groundbreaker in the portrayal of African-Americans in westerns. It also had an urgent subplot concerning race extermination amidst its risible action scenes.

The Revolution was about to be depicted in an *American* spaghetti western...

> Race was a factor of extreme importance in Mexican society. In 1910 (the year of the Revolution), a third of the population was Indian and half-*mestizo*. As to the extent of racial prejudice, experts differ. On the one hand, many oligarchs were racist, despised the benighted Indian as a drag on the national chain, and embraced a form of social Darwinism whereby Mexico's future lay in transcending its Indian past; for this reason they looked to England and France for their inspiration and sent their children to school there. On the other hand, the national ethos of Mexico took pride in the achievements of the Aztecs and the Mayas, and on a day-to-day basis, overt racial prejudice was rare. Everyone knew, though, that whiteness was the supreme ethic value, and the aim of all aspiring Indians was to be "whitened."[21]

This description of Mexico's attitude towards its Native population, as written by historian Frank McLynn, doesn't scratch the surface of the racial turmoil which engulfed Mexico for centuries—at times, almost overwhelming all its other wars.

Forever in the shadow of the "colossus of the north" and, accompanied by its hatred for "gringos," Mexico always had its own forbidden racist skeletons long buried under its constant declarations of Revolutionary pride and self-determination. Treated as lesser beings by an encroaching Latino majority, the Natives remained stubbornly loyal to their traditions and bravely fought for their lands as the pressure mounted for them to either abandon their culture or be wiped out.

The Yaquis, one of the largest and toughest of Mexico's indigenous population, seem to symbolize the racist oppression that was part and parcel of life under Mexican rule. They fought the Spanish from 1533 until their departure from Mexican soil in the successful War of Independence in 1821. In 1684, Spanish colonists discovered, in what would become the present-day state of Sonora, silver in the Rio Yaqui Valley. With little prompting by the authorities, Spanish people, many of whom happened to be miners and prospectors, started settling on what had previously been Yaqui lands. By 1740, the Yaquis united with other tribes like the Mayos, Opatas and the Pimas (World War II Marine hero and raiser of the flag at Iwo Jima, Ira Hayes, was a full-blooded Pima). By 1742, the tribes were successful in driving out the colonialists, though at the cost of 1,000 Spanish lives and five times as many Natives. The Jesuits, who had always been friendly to the Yaquis, were kicked out by the Spanish authorities in 1767. Then came Mexican independence in 1821, and the landscape would change considerably; however, to the Natives, one Latino oppressor was simply replaced with another. Now having kicked out their occupiers, the new nation would replicate the worst aspects of Spanish rule and use them against their own Native population.

In 1825, a law was passed by Mexico in which the Yaquis were recognized as citizens of the republic. This was not as generous an act as it sounded, for it submitted the tribe to a round of punishing taxes. Since the Yaquis had never paid taxes on land which they rightfully felt was their own, the tribe revolted. The outcome was predictable: In a typical battle between a combined force of Yaquis, Mayas, Opatas and Pimas at Hermosillo in 1827, the tribes with their bows and arrows were handily beaten by Mexicans brandishing captured Spanish firearms. By the 1860s, some tribes, including the Yaquis, sided with the French occupiers in the vain hope that the European invaders would treat them better than their previous Mexican antagonists; this, of course, was not always the case, and many Natives also joined the *Juáristas* in their fight against the colonialists. However, by the time Juárez kicked out the French (with American weaponry and other assistance) and resumed control of the government, and despite his being an Indian as well, Mexican troops had no problem reasserting control over their old antagonists, the Yaquis.

Ignoring the fact that many Yaquis actually *did* fight against the French, the Federals only seemed to remember those Yaquis who fought *for* them; and so, in 1868, Mexican troops massacred 120 Yaqui men, women and children in Vicam. Not stopping there, the soldiers locked the 400 remaining Native prisoners inside a church and then bombarded it with cannon-fire. In 1874, with little provocation, Mexican troops instigated another pogrom and massacred Yaquis in Medano, Sonora, and then pillaged their ranches and farms. Having made their homes in Sonora, the remaining Yaquis would be taken as slaves and deported by Mexican troops to the Yucatán, where the rays of the sun killed them by the thousands. However, it was not as if the Natives were being systematically murdered without *someone* profiting from it. The governor of Sonora and his cronies charged 75 pesos a head for slave labor in the Yucatán plantations, making a tidy profit in a human atrocity just as shocking as the enslavement of African-Americans north of the border. The Natives were also deported to Oaxaca, Veracruz and Guadalajara, where these once-proud warriors were now reduced to cleaning out the stables of Mexican cavalrymen and emptying spittoons.

Despite having Native blood himself, when Porfirio Díaz came to power, he and his thugs lost little time stealing the lands of the Yaquis, as well as other Natives, and forcing them into starvation and finally surrender in 1887. There would be Yaqui uprisings in 1896, '97 and '99, but the results were always the same. In the Mazocoba Massacre of 1900, Mexican troops slaughtered hundreds of Yaquis, not making any distinction between warriors, or women and children. By 1903, President Porfirio Díaz formed a solution to the Yaqui problem; unfortunately, it turned out to be a final solution. Thousands of Yaquis and Mayas, whether rebellious or peaceful, were again deported to the Yucatán. For the next two years, Díaz implemented a policy of search-and-destroy, ordering his chief hatchet-man, General Victoriano Huerta, to lay waste to the Yucatán peninsula, razing their huts, burning their food supplies and driving the survivors into starvation. Between 1904 and 1909, Rafael Izabel, the governor of Sonora, led "organized manhunts" in which 8,000 to 15,000 Yaquis were taken prisoner and enslaved, with a one-way trip to the Yucatán desert in their immediate future. Huerta and Díaz's other generals liquidated the rest.

In 1910, Revolution broke out. Believing Francisco Madero's promise that the Yaquis would get their lands back and their families returned from the Yucatán after the rebels' victory, hundreds of Yaqui warriors died fighting for their new idealistic leader. After Díaz was driven into exile, the Natives then took their grievances to the president; they had shed their blood for the Revolution, and now it was time to call in their notes. The new president had other ideas. As Frank McLynn explains in his scholarly dual biography, *Villa and Zapata, a History of the Mexican Revolution:*

> Madero reluctantly accepted the Yaquis as allies and by June 1911, there were 1,000 Yaqui warriors in the field. Yet Madero had no intention of acceding to Yaqui aspirations. Convinced, like Lampedusa's prince, that things had to change so that everything could remain the same, Madero was about to disappoint every group in Mexico with the exception of the one he had ostensibly overthrown.[22]

After the little president's murder at the hands of Huerta's men, and the later ascension of Venustiano Carranza as president, the arrogant former governor of Chihuahua who spoke so often of land reform, *also* had no intention of giving land back to Mexican *peons,* much less the Yaquis or any other Native tribe. Álvaro Obregón had been brought up among Indians, he knew their traditions and their taboos; but most importantly, he knew that they would be fierce opponents against *Villistas* who remained to threaten his rule. Like so many others, he promised the Yaquis their lands if they would fight under his banner and, like so many others, he quickly forgot his promise once victory was achieved. After his own ascension to president (and after the assassination of President Carranza in 1920), Obregón spent more time consolidating his power than dealing with land reform.

When Obregón's protégé, former Carranza general Plutarco Elías Calles, became president from 1924 to 1928, despite the Revolution having officially ended, there would be no end to the racist genocide of the country's Natives. Still a power behind the throne, Obregón gave Calles his blessing to crush the Yaquis once and for all. And so, for the first time in their already tempestuous history, Yaquis in huts would be bombed into oblivion by President Calles' new air force. Instead of getting their lands back, the tribe who had fought bravely and died honorably for the Revolution would have their homes bombed from the air and their families strafed by machine-gun fire by order of the Revolution's triumphant new leaders. After 1929, a time which marked the last major conflict between the Mexican government and the Yaquis, the Natives who had so much love for their ancestral lands, would now find them occupied by the outposts of the Mexican army. Instead of respect for their proud heritage, they would get rifle barrels pointed in their faces and their homes razed for the construction of new army barracks and even newer *haciendas.*

And the Revolution was *supposed* to have been fought for freedom...

On March 20, 1969, Twentieth Century–Fox released *100 Rifles,* a western adventure starring Jim Brown, Burt Reynolds and the studio's most iconic female sex symbol since Monroe, Raquel Welch. Based on Robert MacLeod's 1960 "coming of age" novel *The Californio, 100 Rifles* focused on a topic rarely explored in films and literature about the Mexican Revolution, basically the oppression of the Native population by the country's rulers. In MacLeod's novel, a young ranch hand named Steve McCall has been adopted and raised by a Mexican family living along the California-Mexico border; he not only knows Spanish, but is an expert at horseflesh. He accompanies his Native friend, Yaqui Joe, to Mexico to purchase horses for his boss–adopted father (Steve is engaged to his cute dark-haired daughter), but the Native wrangler doesn't have the purchase of horses on his mind, but the thought of helping his oppressed people. Instead of haggling over the price of stallions and palominos, the young *Americano* finds himself knee-deep in the killing fields of the Mexican Revolution. The Rurales are under the command of Colonel Emilio Kosterlitzky, a German officer siding with the *Porfirias.* (Kosterlitzky was no creation of MacLeod's, but a real-life officer who fought the Yaquis for Díaz.) Despite this display of Aryan villainy, the book's *real* villain is the brutal Sergeant Verdugo of the Rurales. In a foreshadowing of Nazi persecution, Verdugo lines up Yaqui villagers and shoots dead every third person, be they man, woman or child, who refuses to tell him what he wants. Previously uninterested in Yaqui Joe's passion for helping his people, much less the Revolution itself, Steve becomes a committed fighter after Verdugo shoots dead a Yaqui boy who refuses to tell the sergeant where the young *Americano* is hiding.

MacLeod's novel is brutally realistic, with no romanticizing of the Yaquis or their plight; their food is covered with flies and other insects, their sanitary facilities are, well, let's say *non-existent,* and the proper young Anglo is shocked by the Indians' lack of shame in going around in various stages of undress. Also refreshingly original is the crude language coming out of the mouths of both the *Porfirias* and the Natives. Further crossing the line between good guys and bad, we see that brutality and a cold-blooded lack of mercy are character traits that do *not* belong solely to the oppressors. When the Yaquis take over a hacienda, they brutally shoot down the *hacendados and* their wives and children; when the servants and their families try to flee, they are also ruthlessly cut down without a moment of remorse from any of the supposedly poor-but-noble good guys.

Clair Huffaker's westerns were mostly on the "fun" side, with macho behavior being practiced frequently and often by both hero and villain. Unlike the grim westerns of Marvin H. Albert, Huffaker's work celebrated hell-raising and having a good time while doing it. The screenplay was co-written by him and director Tom Gries, a man who had excelled with a western Charlton Heston called his favorite film, *Will Penny.* An exception to this macho adventure is Huffaker's *Flaming Lance,* which is about Indian-white racial turmoil on the frontier. Filmed by Fox in 1960 with Elvis Presley, it even featured Dolores del Río as the King's sexy mom.

Federals hang the father of the gorgeous Sarita (the gorgeous Raquel Welch), after which the dirty dogs will have their way with her (with said "way" fortunately cut out of the film). Meanwhile in Nogales, General Vargas (promoted from sergeant in the novel, and played by former MGM heartthrob Fernando Lamas) makes his entrance in a Hitler-like touring car aside American railroad agent Grimes (Dan O'Herlihy) and Kosterlitzky clone Lieutenant Von Klemme (Hans Gudegast, before the actor Americanized his name to Eric Braeden). Lamas, an alleged former wife-beater (and beater of former girlfriend Lana Turner), brings a viciousness to his performance as Verdugo. When Yaqui rebels are brought before him, he pulls out his shiny .45 automatic and blows away all three of them with one shot, Pancho Villa–style. In this scene, we see the *Porfiria* general as a thug, and the American railroad man Grimes as a waffling on-the-fence lackey, despairing of violence, but obviously too afraid of Verdugo to take a stand. However, the German officer is a far more complicated individual, and his appearance in Mexico is based on actual history.

Symbolizing German military help to Mexico (or military "advice," meaning training and weaponry), these officers made frequent appearances in the westerns that depicted the Mexican Revolution, particularly *The Wild Bunch*. In reality, German "advisors" would be a common sight among the officer class of Presidents Díaz, Huerta, and even former rebel leader Venustiano Carranza. In fact, the self-appointed First Chief of the Revolution was seriously entertaining German offers to side with Mexico after it promised him the return of all lands captured by the *yanquis* in the Mexican-American War of 1846–49. It was only the revelation of the Zimmermann telegram that stopped the greedy and vindictive "First Chief" from collaborating with the Germans on a purported American invasion. It is even said that Pancho Villa and his band, bitter over President Woodrow Wilson's backing of Carranza over him (and we can see how genuine Carranza's loyalty was!), was prodded to attack Columbus, New Mexico (which was *not* Villa's original target; it was another American border town), to force America to be preoccupied with a war on its southern border and keep her from helping the Allies during World War I.

In the film, Von Klemme is seen as being far wiser than the man he's "advising." Riding his own horse rather than lording it over the town like Verdugo in his touring car, he is intelligent and far more restrained than the volatile general. Reflecting German efficiency, Von Klemme wants Verdugo to successfully put down the Rebels, but without the vindictive, time-wasting savagery that is part and parcel of the Mexican officer's obviously deranged psyche. Von Klemme believes in results, without any obsession with personalities involved. Verdugo keeps ignoring the German's advice and follows his temper instead.

In the film, Yaqui Joe (Burt Reynolds) is half–Yaqui and half–American Southerner, which means that the actor delivers his lines in a good ol' boy accent while looking like an Indian. (The actor actually did have Native American blood.) Off-screen, Reynolds would refer to his role as "third half-breed from the left," but did call *100 Rifles* "a gritty southwestern." We first meet the half-breed revolutionary on the second floor of a hotel where he had just spent a night with a Mexican whore (played by the tragic Soledad Miranda). When he uses the naked *senōrita* as a distraction to Verdugo's troops, the captured Yaquis make a break for it but are ruthlessly gunned down by the general's men. Captured and brought before Verdugo, Yaqui Joe finds that he is also wanted by black lawman Lydecker (Jim Brown) for a bank robbery.

This is Brown's second appearance in a Huffaker screenplay (he was one of the would-be rescuers in Fox's *Rio Conchos* three years before this film). Though *100 Rifles* would be praised many years later as the first major American film showing a sex scene between an

African-American and a Caucasian, the film's *real* groundbreaking distinction is that it is the first time we see a duly appointed African-American lawman in the Old West (even if it's Mexico—which was very much like the American west of the 1880s in 1910). Black lawmen were certainly a far more common sight in the post–Civil War American west than Hollywood would ever show up to that point.

General Verdugo isn't crazy about having his executions interrupted by a black star-toter with an agenda of his own. Alone with Lydecker, Yaqui Joe admits that the thousands of dollars stolen in the bank robbery didn't go for "liquor and whores" as the half-breed outrageously claimed to his captors, but to rifles, one hundred to be exact, to be used to save his people.

After Lydecker and Joe jump out of the window of the railroad car where they're being held, the Big Escape is on. Though these situations would be quite desperate in the real world, they are imbued with humor and the usual macho adventure schtick prized by Huffaker. The two men swipe a horse (one actually loses count of the many, *many* times Federal soldiers are knocked off their horses by our heroes), and head out to the hills to meet Sarita. However, they are recaptured and brought before Verdugo's firing squad. Yet *again,* thanks to Sarita and her rifle-bearing Yaquis, the two men are saved and we see *The Big Escape Part II.* Here, we have a great scene featuring *two* ex-football players-turned-actors running the full length of the Long Yard to freedom (and tripping a soldier's horse in the process). Again, they follow Sarita off into the hills with her tribe.

Off-screen, Brown had admitted that he had two fears, "heights and horses." And so, probably with a wicked grin, Reynolds suggested to director Gries that he and Brown have their rather amiable fight near the edge of a cliff. (In obvious admiration, Reynolds called Gries "my first really good writer-director.") Unlike the life-and-death fight scenes in a Marvin H. Albert pulp western, typical of Huffaker, the fight here is light and full of humor. Yaqui Joe even *thanks* Lydecker for pulling him from the edge of the cliff before slugging him.

Throughout these escapes, Lydecker stubbornly insists that Yaqui Joe has to return to the States with him and stand trial for the robbery. Invited to join the Yaquis in their fight, Lydecker responds with racist sentiments unusual for a black character at the time: "I ain't helpin' no *damn Indians!*" he says bitterly. He isn't the only one who has a problem with inclusion. At one point, Yaqui Joe refers to Lydecker as "this black-ass!" Earlier, Verdugo points out that no one in America will miss "a black cop." In fact, Grimes and, even more surprisingly, the German officer von Klemme, talk to Lydecker man to man and actually treat him with more respect than his erstwhile ally, Yaqui Joe.

Still, Lydecker is not without a heart, and he is touched by the gratitude of the Yaquis, especially one little boy. With Verdugo's men pursuing them, our three heroes leave the Yaqui village to escape off into the hills. Before you can say "harsh reprisal," and against Von Klemme's strenuous protests, Verdugo has the Yaqui village burned to the ground, slaughters many adults and kidnaps the children, including the Yaqui boy Lydecker had befriended. Returning to the village and seeing the aftermath of the federal assault, Lydecker undergoes a change. Previously not wanting to fight for any "damn Indians" (we learn that the lawman had actually been in the cavalry where he fought Apaches), Lydecker now becomes a believer in the Revolution.

Finding their encampment, our Terrific Trio and their Native helpers attack the hacienda compound where the children are held and quietly take over the place, killing all the soldiers

Mexico City Bomber: The lovely Raquel Welch as a Yaqui revolutionary in *100 Rifles*, directed by Tom Gries from a screenplay by western author Clair Huffaker. The oppression of the Yaquis is turned into over-the-top adventure.

in the process and rescuing the kids. As in the novel, the Natives burn down the hacienda, dress in the owners' fancy clothes, loot the place, and then drink up all their booze. However, before the burning, Sarita and Lydecker do the nasty, an event that was radically altered from the book. In the novel, McCall, frustrated beyond belief, is finally won over by the charms of a randy Yaqui girl and does the nasty with *her*.

Now called General Lydecker by all the Yaquis, the black lawman-turned-freedom-fighter comes up with a plan to take over a train loaded with rifles for the Yaquis (100 rifles to be exact). But how does one stop a train loaded with federal troops and a Gatling gun mounted on its roof?

Cut to Sarita taking a shower beneath the cascade of a railroad water tower. Here we see Raquel, her wet blouse and short pants clinging to her supple body (I've personally rerun this scene many times to see if Gries made any goofs in his camera setups), having absolutely no problem stopping a train with randy *Federales*. As soon as they approach Sarita, she brandishes a rifle and she and the others open fire, killing all the soldiers. Using the train as a fast-rolling weapon, our heroes charge into Verdugo's fortress and the battle is on. They kill all the soldiers, but Sarita too is killed (though we don't see how). Verdugo himself is soon surrounded by the Yaquis and killed in true eye-for-an-eye fashion. The last we see of Von Klemme, he is on his horse watching the carnage from afar, as if he had already known the outcome of the battle. Then he rides off, presumably to return to the Fatherland and join his countrymen in the coming World War.

Lydecker decides to return to the States without Yaqui Joe, who now must lead his people to freedom. Though *100 Rifles* takes both MacLeod's serious novel, as well as the real-life persecution of the Yaquis, and turns them into rousing, over-the-top adventure, there might have been some who disagreed with this approach. According to the IMDb website, Clair Huffaker reportedly wanted his name removed from the credits.

In his *New York Times* review of March 27, 1969, Bosley Crowther wrote:

> "This picture has a message: watch out." So proclaim the ads for *100 Rifles*. Wise moviegoers can do even better by ducking it altogether. It is a loud, churning and triumphantly empty exercise.... This project, which has to do with the cruel oppression of the downtrodden Indian peasants in Mexico, was filmed in Spain in color. Most of the time Mr. Brown, as an American sheriff, Miss Welch, as a fiery peasant leader, and Burt Reynolds, as a wily renegade, tensely traipse across the parched, rugged backgrounds pursued by Fernando Lamas, as a cruel military governor.[23]

Roger Ebert also disliked *100 Rifles,* though he did admit that "Brown and Reynolds are good together; Brown has a cool, humorous charm and Reynolds plays it like the other half of a vaudeville team." However, in his April 9, 1969, review in the *Chicago Sun-Times*, Ebert lowered the boom on the film's director:

> ... Gries gives us lots of action. Too much action. He isn't really an action director (as demonstrated when a row of troops is mowed down by a machine-gun and falls forward). He thinks action consists of shots of Brown or Raquel shooting a gun, followed by shots of bad guys clutching their chests and toppling over.
>
> But action has to be directed so we can figure out what's going on. We want to follow the progress of the struggle and get a sense of danger. And we need to know the characters at least well enough to care about them. Without that, we might as well be watching Tom and Jerry.[24]

The critic was right in the film delivering the desired action goods. That is, action without suspense or thinking about it too much. One does wonder what the film would have been like had Fox actually filmed MacLeod's novel, where we would follow its young protagonist's growth from naïve young wrangler to committed fighter for the Revolution. Or had the studio decided to actually depict Mexico's genocide of its Native population, especially the Yaquis.

But if that were the case, why would anyone need to show Raquel Welch showering under a water tower to distract Mexican soldiers?

Soon, another western would debut that was set at the time of the Revolution. However, unlike the Fox film, this one would be regarded as a classic of western cinema. Released four months after *100 Rifles,* the production's maverick director pushed the envelope on depicting violence on American screens, and gave us a story that showed how the Revolution reformed even a group of violent *yanqui* outlaws...

> We all dream of being a child again,
> even the worst of us. Perhaps the worst most of all....

When *The Wild Bunch* was released in the United States on June 16, 1969, it caused a sensation in its unrestrained depiction of violence on-screen. Warner Brothers timidly sheared the film from 151 minutes to 123 minutes. Shot between March 25 and June 30, 1968, it was made at a time when Sam Peckinpah was licking his wounds over his firing from *Villa Rides*.

Justifiably considered a classic, *The Wild Bunch* is Peckinpah's one true masterpiece in a 20-year stop-and-go filmmaking career that gave us a handful of good films and just as many misfires. It was indeed a groundbreaking film, and it's been written about, reviewed, re-reviewed, loved, hated and ruthlessly dissected for its brilliance and attacked for its violence and sleaze (the film's violence has almost made one forget the rather sexist and exploitative treatment of its few female characters, all of whom were Latinas and all of whom have no lines and no function outside of being whores). The film's been critiqued and studied so much that my take on it will reveal nothing that hasn't been written about more fully and insightfully by others far more knowledgeable than I. My main concern is not its overall brilliance, or Peckinpah's indelible stamp on the film, but its plotline and historical background *vis-à-vis* the Mexican Revolution.

It is 1913 on the border with Mexico. Outlaw gang leader Pike Bishop (*fantastic* casting choice; William Holden) leads a gang that consists of close pal Dutch Engstrom (Ernest Borgnine), the Gorch brothers (Ben Johnson and Warren Oates), Mexican revolutionary Angel (Jaime Sanchez) and old man Sykes (Edmond O'Brien), among many others. All but

Yanquis in Mexico, Part II: Bo Hopkins, Jaime Sãnchez, Ernest Borgnine, William Holden, Bill Hart and Ben Johnson (top row, left to right) and Rayford Barnes and Warren Oates (bottom row, left to right) in Sam Peckinpah's classic *The Wild Bunch*. Shot on location in Mexico, the film was set at the time of the Revolution.

Sykes ride into a small Texas town, dressed in stolen army uniforms, and figure to rob the bank of its railroad payroll. On their way in, they pass a group of children who have just dropped a small scorpion on a nest of ants who are devouring the poor creature.

The town is staked out by former Bunch member Deke Thornton (again, perfect casting: Robert Ryan), hired by cold-blooded railroad magnate Harrigan (Albert Dekker, whose strange and mysterious "suicide" after the filming is controversial to this day). Unfortunately, Thornton, every bit a man of integrity as his former friend Bishop, is forced to reluctantly hunt the Bunch or be sent back to Yuma Prison; he is also saddled with cutthroat trash like Coffer (Strother Martin) and T.C. (L.Q. Jones) who are themselves murderers and thieves. After the Bunch robs the bank, a bloody battle ensues that is worth every bit of praise critics have heaped on it. (Peckinpah's son Matthew appears in the scene, hugging a little blonde girl as the chaos goes on around them.) During the shootout, innocent bystanders are tragically killed in the crossfire between the two factions, including temperance league members parading down the main street in front of the bank. Peckinpah allegedly included the temperance league march and a religious sermon delivered by Peckinpah regular Dub Taylor. Typically, anti-alcohol puritans were always good targets for someone like Peckinpah, a man who *never* faced his own drinking problem.

Having lost half their number, the Bunch rides out of town with their swag (which turns out to be bags of washers). They see the same group of children, only now they've dropped dried grass on the ants and the poor scorpion and set fire to the whole thing as the kids smile and laugh sadistically. (Peckinpah's close-up on the face of a cute little girl delighting in the insects' agony is indeed chilling.) I mention this sequence in detail because the inspiration for the scene (which was reportedly not in Walon Green and Peckinpah's original script or Green and Roy Sickner's story) was an idea by the helmsman's new friend, Emilio Fernández. El Indio claimed to him that he used to do that as a kid (which shows what a warped personality he would grow up to become). Reportedly, as Fernandez was telling Peckinpah this idea while both were drinking at the director's beach house, Sam's Mexican fiancée called him up. Angered by the interruption, Peckinpah picked up the phone and screamed at her. In a 1969 interview with Joe Medjuck, he said:

> I was engaged to a Mexican girl at that time and I was to have dinner with her. In Mexico you must have a standby director. Mine was a friend of mine named Emilio Fernández.... He said, "You know, for me the Wild Bunch is like a scorpion on an ant hill." And I said, "*Wait a minute,* what's that?" And my fiancée phoned to see when I was coming for supper, and I told her, "Madam, I am with Emilio Fernández and the pimple on his ass is worth more to me at the moment than our future."[25]

Peckinpah never mentioned who the lady was, but we can assume that the engagement was short-lived.

As far as the casting of El Indio, Peckinpah biographer David Weddle wrote: "Emilio Fernandez, the gun-toting murderer–movie director who lived in his own castle with a harem of fifteen-year-old girls. Fernandez was Mapache incarnate."[26]

Peckinpah and Fernandez were indeed brothers under the skin...

Crossing the Rio Grande, the Bunch takes refuge in Angel's village, the villagers having just gone through a raid by Mapache's federals due to their support of Villa. Feted by the villagers, who respect the outlaws as noble warriors, Angel finds that his girlfriend has gone off willingly with the evil Mapache. In one of many unusually moving scenes in the film that have nothing to do with violence and bloodshed, when the Bunch rides out of the village, the peons serenade them, give them roses and sing their praises, seeing the outlaws as men of integrity who fight back against those who oppress them. Hearing that Mapache is in need of guns, the Bunch rides to his stronghold at Aqua Verde ("Green Water") where Pike will try to make a deal. Also with Mapache and his junta are emissaries of the German government. Historically, it was no surprise that German military "advisors" were aiding the Huerta and Carranza regimes. Here, the Germans are clearly on the side of evil as they aid the psychopathic Mapache in his oppression of the peons. Their interference in the affairs of Mexico is seen as a harbinger to their eventual war with the United States in World War I.

Shortly after the Bunch arrives, Angel sees his treacherous girlfriend in Mapache's arms and shoots her dead. After subduing Angel, the Bunch convince Mapache and his trigger-happy men that they didn't try to kill the general, and a deal is transacted. The Bunch will ride back across the border and steal a shipment of guns for lots of gold. (Mapache wants to maintain good relations with the U.S., and so will not cross the border to raid an American train.) Unbeknownst to the federals, Pike and Dutch plan to let Angel have a crate of guns for his rebel band of Indians. The raid is successful and the Bunch set up a meeting with Mapache officer Herrera (Alfonso Arau) and his men. However, suspecting a double-cross, the Bunch threatens to blow up the guns. Throughout this scene, one is immediately taken with Arau's hilarious but still deadly federal officer. An internationally known actor and comedian on stage, films and TV (and later a noted writer, producer and director), a man who was acclaimed all over Latin America, Arau purposely fashioned his part on the film persona of an actor who had done so much for the portrayal of Mexican banditos and revolutionaries in both Hollywood and his native Mexico. As he said years later:

> Peckinpah told me that with my character he wanted to make an homage to Alfonso Bedoya, the Mexican bandit in *The Treasure of the Sierra Madre,* the one who says, "We don't have to show you no stinking badges!" A fantastic scene. Peckinpah said, "I want to do that." I loved that film, it's one of my favorites, so immediately we had a connection.[27]

There are very few actors who could have played the "negotiation" scene with a wonderful combination of phony charm and homicidal contempt. When one of his men fires on the *Americanos,* thus nearly having the guns blown up, Herrera ruthlessly orders the quick-triggered soldier's execution. It is a standout scene and deservedly belongs to the actor-comedian. In homage to *this* character, *Saturday Night Live*'s Lorne Michaels cast Arau as the bandit chief El Guapo (meaning "the valiant" or "the handsome") in the Mexico-set comedy *¡Three Amigos!*

Soon the Bunch has their gold and Mapache gets his guns. However, finding that one crate is missing, the general's men grab Angel. Returning to Aqua Verde, the Bunch is horrified to see Angel being dragged behind the general's car. After spending an evening with Mapache's prostitutes, Pike makes a decision, telling the Bunch "Let's go!" After one of the most famous walks in screen history, the Bunch demands Angel's release. Instead, Mapache cuts the young rebel's throat, prompting Pike and the others to kill the general. However, what looks like a, pardon the expression, Mexican standoff, quickly turns into a massive shootout when Pike, discovering his patriotism, suddenly guns down one of Mapache's German military advisors. Again, like the shootout that marked the beginning of the film, the famous Battle of Bloody Porch deserves all the accolades heaped on it, especially for Peckinpah's groundbreaking staging as well as Lou Lombardo's razor-sharp editing. As Alfonso

Arau later recalled: "The way Peckinpah staged that massacre, I will never forget it. It was so complicated, and he was so precise and disciplined and methodical. I learned a lot from him."[28]

With the Bunch now dead, along with Mapache and his gang of murderous federals, Thornton arrives and surveys the carnage. After Sikes arrives with the dead Angel's Indian companions, the two ex–Bunch members decide to remain in Mexico and help the people fight the federals.

On a budget of an estimated $6,244,087, *The Wild Bunch* gradually made back its money and grossed $10.5 million by 1970, a year after its initial release.[29] The filming locations were Durango (the train robbery sequence was shot in La Goma) and Parras and Torreón in Coahuila state. Torreón was the location of one of Villa's greatest victories, and Parras happened to be the birthplace of President Francisco Madero. To reaffirm both Mapache's penchant for butchery, as well as the oppressive regime the rebels are fighting, Thornton describes the general as "a killer for Huerta." Indeed, Mapache seems like a more local version of the brutal and frequently drunken general-dictator.

Though the film has a refreshing feel of history, unfortunately Green, Sickner and Peckinpah made some bad mistakes. Though set in 1913, the sight of Mapache's car prompts Sykes and Bishop to mention airplanes. "They're using 'em now in the war," says Bishop, despite the fact that World War I hadn't started yet. At a campsite with Dutch, Bishop brings up the fact that Pershing's men "are all along the border," even though the Punitive Expedition didn't start for another three years (only *Cannon for Cardoba,* released the following year, would top this inaccuracy *vis-à-vis* Pershing's Punitive Expedition). The accuracy of period weaponry usually takes a hit in these films, with the stolen machine-gun used at the film's climactic battle actually a Browning 1917 model which was, to say the least, unusual to find in 1913.

Shooting in Mexico, Peckinpah and Warners had to deal with the thin-skinned bureaucrats of the Mexican government. Trying for a Mexican release,

Holden Onto Trouble: William Holden brandishes a .45 automatic and a Winchester in *The Wild Bunch*. The film broke ground in its presentation of violence on screen, and darkened the image of the All-American western hero forever.

Peckinpah had to journey back to Mexico with editor Lou Lombardo to assuage the feelings of government officials. On March 9, 1970, several months after the film's U.S. release, in a memo to Warner executive Richard Lederer, Peckinpah wrote: "I am making preliminary changes in *The Wild Bunch* according to my discussion with Mexican officials and as per our discussion this day. I am intending to return next week with a print which I think will be more acceptable to them."[30]

One wonders just *what* would end up being "acceptable" to the Mexican government. Nevertheless, for one reason or another, Peckinpah's fabled charm (when he was sober, that is) failed. According to the Internet Movie Database, the film wouldn't be released in Mexico until June 15, 2002, long after the deaths of the director and the various Mexican officials who blocked its release over thirty years before.[31]

In Vincent Canby's *New York Times* review of June 26, 1969 (he and other critics across the nation were allowed to see the uncut 145-minute version), he describes the film's time as "1913, when Pancho Villa was tormenting a corrupt Mexican Government while the United States watched cautiously from across the border." The critic continued:

> Although the movie's conventional and poetic action sequences are extraordinarily good and its landscapes beautifully photographed (lots of dark foregrounds and brilliant backgrounds) by Lucien Ballard, who did *Nevada Smith,* it is most interesting in its almost jolly account of

Final Confrontation: Ben Johnson, Warren Oates, William Holden and Ernest Borgnine (left to right) on their way to the climactic "Battle of Bloody Porch" in *The Wild Bunch*.

chaos, corruption and defeat. All personal relationships in the movie seem somehow perverted in odd mixtures of noble sentimentality, greed and lust.

Canby ends his review with an unsubtle swipe at critics who attacked the film's violence:

> In *The Wild Bunch,* which is about men who walk together, but in desperation, [Peckinpah] turns the genre inside out. It's a fascinating movie and, I think I should add, when I came out of it, I didn't feel like shooting, knifing, or otherwise maiming any of Broadway's often hostile pedestrians.[32]

In 1995, when the uncut version of *The Wild Bunch* premiered at San Francisco's Castro Theater, Peter Stack of the *San Francisco Chronicle,* in his review of March 3, wrote:

> It's an exciting thing, an event, to see director Sam Peckinpah's 1969 classic again, to be worn down by it, yet to feel the pulse of it, forebodingly calm one minute, pumping like shotgun blasts the next. The film is in your face with a leathery, sun-belt and guilt-crippled bravado.
>
> To some, of course, *The Wild Bunch* is a bunch of overdone macho posturing, a "guy thing," a tedious, self-absorbed gang film that elevates violence for its own sake, glorifying men killing men for the sheer thrill of it. But even people who hate the film can't dismiss its visceral impact, its twisted ethos, its balletic imagery. It must be art.[33]

Despite its various controversies, it certainly is that.

Somehow, it was quite natural that in the wake of the bloody and controversial *The Wild Bunch,* the next western actioner set in Revolutionary Mexico would be an almost defiant answer to the mean-spiritedness and violence of the Peckinpah film. And whose work could possibly be the antithesis of the blood-spurting, sleazy and gratuitously violent world of Sam Peckinpah than the simple good-vs.-evil, pro-family and amiable westerns of Big John Wayne?

It was fairly obvious that the Duke detested the new trend towards violence and sleaze that the western was taking and, as the years progressed, answered this trend by stubbornly sticking with a formula from his days with John Ford. Traditionalists *loved* the Duke's films and he would still remain in the top ten box office stars (though by the mid-seventies, he would fall off the list for the first time in decades).

On October 4, 1969, Twentieth Century–Fox released *The Undefeated,* an action-packed commentary on the different factions operating as the Civil War came to a close and the revolution against the French in Mexico had already started. With a screenplay by veteran Wayne scenarist James Lee Barrett, from a screen story by Stanley Hough (and possibly an original novel or treatment by western veteran Lewis B. Patten, but this is not verified), and directed by western helmsman Andrew McLaglen (son of Wayne's pal Victor), *The Undefeated* steadfastly refuses to cast blame on anyone, neither Union, Confederacy, French or *Juáristas.* In this film, war is the enemy, as well as a few crooked individuals hoping to profit from it.

It's the end of the Civil War. Sick of the killing fields, Colonel John Henry Thomas (Wayne) leaves the army and recruits his men to go with him in the horse-selling business. Soon we see a rousing scene of these newborn wranglers roping and capturing beautiful wild stallions out on the Plains. Set to sell them to the army, Thomas at first rejects their sale to two emissaries from Maximilian's puppet government. However, he finds that the two buyers for the army are taking some of the profits for themselves (one of the traders is western veteran Gregg Palmer, now part of the Duke's repertory company). Predictably, Thomas punches out the two crooks (the conservative actor's traditional distrust of the federal bureaucracy is on full display here). Thomas and his sidekicks, Short Grubb (Ben Johnson) and Webster (Harry Carey, Jr.), call back the French representatives and sell the horses to *them*. Of course, to Thomas and his men, being on the wrong side of history and selling much-needed horse-flesh to colonial occupiers is *not* the issue, they're doing it to make a profit, period. Yet screenwriter Barrett doesn't duck the issue that our heroes are dealing with the enemy (French designs on America were hardly a secret), and he has Thomas bluntly address the issue in a few wry bits of dialogue to his men: "Trouble? Well, let's see.... We've got Maximilian on one hand and Juárez on the other, and bandits in between. And on top of that, we're Americans in Mexico taking a cavvy of horses to a very unpopular government. Why should we expect trouble?"

As the film progresses, these Americans will soon find out that saving lives will take precedence over profit.

Confederate Colonel James Langdon (Rock Hudson taking over for originally cast James Arness) is a proud officer who physically tosses a Northern carpetbagger back into his own buggy rather than sell his Southern mansion at a loss. After burning down the house, he takes his brood, which includes his wife Margaret (Lee Meriwether), widowed sister Ann (Marian McCargo), teen daughter Charlotte (Melissa Newman), and former rebel Captain Anderson (Edward Faulkner), to Mexico. Langdon is hoping to hook up with other former Confederates in Mexico and, backed by Maximilian's French army, "liberate" the South from Union troops. Thomas has also brought with him his adopted Native American son Blue Boy (played by football player Roman Gabriel in a long black wig). When Thomas and Blue Boy happen upon the Southern group (rather foolishly pitching camp out in the open in bandit country), the former enemies are friendly towards one another; meanwhile, the teenage Charlotte and Blue Boy begin falling in love. No slouch in the romance department himself, and without one kiss between them, Thomas is hitting it off with the widowed Ann. "Windage and elevation, Mrs. Langdon," Thomas advises her in how to aim her rifle. Predictably, in the western genre, when a man teaches a woman the proper use of a firearm, it can only lead to romance.

When a bandit chief named Escalante (Pedro Armendáriz, Jr., the son of Wayne's frequent co-star in John Ford films) shows up and demands gold, guns and the women, Thomas shoots him dead. This triggers a shootout and, despite their valiant efforts to fight the bandits, it look like the marauders will win until Blue Boy arrives with Thomas' men. Soon the Northerners and Southerners bond at, ironically, a Fourth of July celebration. Of course, as in practically all John Ford-John Wayne westerns, the two groups also bond with plenty of alcohol and even more "harmless" fisticuffs.

After they all part, Langdon's party rides into a fortress commanded by General Rojas (third-billed "special guest star" Antonio Aguilar, ridiculously billed as *Tony* Aguilar). Soon the Southerners are held at gunpoint and it is revealed that Rojas is really a *Juárista* general. The officer threatens Langdon and his people with the firing squad unless the Southerner can convince his friend Thomas to turn all his horse-flesh (slated for delivery to the French) over to the *Juáristas*. At first rejecting the offer, Langdon bends when his men are physically threatened and soon rides out to find the Yankees. In an incredibly short time, the men vote with Thomas to give the horses to Rojas and just shrug off the hard work it took to capture them. When the two French reps overhear this, they ride off to warn their troops to stop Thomas' men from delivering the horses to their enemies.

The Duke in Mexico: Big John Wayne as the ex–Union colonel-turned horse trader, with Rock Hudson (right, with ridiculous feather in hat) as the Confederate officer hoping to have Maximilian's French troops aid the South, in *The Undefeated*. Both protagonists start the film agreeing with French colonialist aims *vis-a-vis* Mexico, but they'll be toasting the *Juáristas* by the end.

When they get to a certain pass, Thomas, Langdon and the Northerners are met by a skirmish line of French soldiers. With little ado, the Americans make soufflé out of the Frenchmen and ride on through. Their cantankerous cook McCartney (ironically, Peckinpah veteran Dub Taylor) is killed in the fight. In a film that promotes co-existence between former enemies, as almost a reminder of Peckinpah's own mean-spiritedness, and with the exception of the evil Escalante, Taylor plays the only *truly* ornery son of a bitch in the whole film.

With less than five minutes to spare, they arrive with the horses, much to the relief of Rojas and the captives. In Rojas' quarters, the three military veterans, Thomas, Langdon and *el generala,* have a toast to the success of the Revolution, meaning the triumph of Mexican patriots against their French occupiers. In fact, though it looked like the film was going to swing towards the French, both Barrett and McLaglen change the direction of the plot, having the heroes militarily beat the obstinate colonialists and ultimately side with the *Juáristas.* Though no fan of revolutions, the Duke was also pro–Mexico, his own production company having made films in Durango many times (every one of the Duke's wives were also Latinas), and he was a follower of Mexican history. Though one does see the controversy of a good guy fighting for a just cause using hostages to attain horses for their army, screenwriter Barrett steadfastly refuses to pass judgment; the horses were to be used to fight against an invader of North America who had no qualms in supplying the beaten Confederacy and eventually conquering the Union.

Certainly, *The Undefeated* is a film that rejects prejudice and preconceptions (with the possible exception of having an African-American as one of the sleazy carpetbaggers early in the film). Even though the Northerners and the Rebs had seen each other as enemies, both factions bond rather quickly; Charlotte rejects her dull Southern boyfriend (Jan-Michael Vincent) for a Native American hunk; the French horse-buyers are seen as the lesser of two evils compared to the American army buyers, but it is they who alert the French soldiers to attack the Americans; with the *Juáristas* originally seen as the bad guys, by the end, they are accepted by the Americans, despite the hostage-taking, as the future inheritors of Mexico.

There are the usual glitches. Though it is set in the mid–1860s, everyone's firearms, whether rifle or handgun, are from a later period, with the 1873 Springfield "Trapdoor" carbine being a particularly common weapon in the film. "Windage and elevation" indeed! The Duke also got injured in a couple of horse falls, fracturing three ribs and a bone in his shoulder. With Wayne's arm useless, McLaglen had to shoot around him for a while, but the Duke, not wanting to disappoint his fans, rushed back to the set and continued to film while in deep pain.

Wayne's basic decency on- and off-screen didn't escape the always insightful Roger Ebert. In his December 2, 1969, review in the *Chicago Sun-Times*, the critic wrote:

> He shelves his broken-down Rooster Cogburn image from *True Grit* (1969) and rides high in the saddle again. He courteously courts a lady, from a distance, and he shows the usual Wayne distaste for violence. What's strange is that Wayne should have a reputation for violent screen portrayals, when in fact a Wayne character is nearly always more civilized and chivalrous than anything out of Italy these days.[34]

Ebert was more accurate than he thought. In the years ahead, Hollywood, Europe and Mexico would collectively show us a Mexican Revolution whose idealism would be long forgotten, yet its violence would remain forever...

VI

Violencia, 1970–1989

Censorship Disappears as Depictions of Revolutionary Mexico Get Even Bloodier

The year 1970 was an especially brutal year. As young people took to the streets and protested the Vietnam War on American campuses, Hollywood balanced its counter-culture products like *Easy Rider, Medium Cool* and *Getting Straight* with escapist adventures set during certain periods of history. Thanks to Europe's spaghetti westerns, Hollywood would now make westerns set during the Mexican Revolution that emphasized action scenes over any discussion of the social issues for which the Revolution was fought. And so, as America was suffering its way through a sometimes violent counter-culture revolution, Hollywood made escapist adventures set in a nation crying out for change and featuring characters who used violence to effect that change.

Produced by, of all people, MGM, *The Five Man Army* was an American-Italian co-production. In this way, Hollywood could collaborate with the spaghetti western's main producers, use the subgenre's usual actors, and yet retain the elements of both the Hollywood caper film and its own home-grown westerns—but without the bitter left-wing indictments prevalent in many European products.

Even the production personnel were equally divided between the two nations backing the project. The film's American version was directed by Don Taylor and the screenplay was co-written by Marc Richman. Taylor was a veteran TV director since the 1950s and would be constantly employed in the medium well into the 1980s, with *The Five Man Army* being one of his few theatrical works. Richman was also a TV veteran, but his contributions as a writer was basically from family-oriented or children's shows; he even wrote episodes of *The Soupy Sales Show*.

The Italian halves of the directing-writing partnership couldn't have been more different. Director Italo Zingarelli was an old hand at writing, directing and producing the most successful genres produced by the Italian film industry that found favor with international audiences: the western, the war film and the gladiator movie. Yet it was Richman's writing partner on *The Five Man Army* who not only became more famous than any of his collaborators, but effectively helped create a subgenre within the horror film that continues to entertain generations to this day. Dario Argento was one of the few postwar directors to redefine the horror film, taking up the *giallo* where Mario Bava left off, adding new elements of violence and increasing the mystery, with audacious directorial flourishes that propelled the action and also added to the suspense.

In the mid–1960s, Argento was a scenarist who wrote spaghetti westerns. And so, just

The Fab Five: Nino Castelnuevo, James Daly, Bud Spencer, Tetsurō Tanba and Peter Graves (left to right) in *The Five Man Army*. Screenwriters Marc Richman and future horror master Dario Argento turned the Mexican Revolution into a violent but black-humored romp.

before making his successful directorial debut with *The Bird with the Crystal Plumage*, Argento took on the writing assignment of *The Five Man Army*. Here, the future *giallo* maven used his particular talent for conveying both violence and black humor in a story where opposing factions will do *anything* to win. Opposite kiddie-show writer Richman, Argento's work stands out like a knife-wielding slasher at a five-year-old's birthday party.

Over the title credits, we see authentic pictures of the violence committed during the Mexican Revolution as a familiar kind of music thunders off the screen. Yes, like an old friend, it's an Ennio Morricone score greeting us with the promise of violent action and underhanded dealings during times of revolutionary chaos. However, *this* time, the music is heard in a production principally financed by *Hollywood*.

Robber and gunman Luiz Dominguez (Nino Castelnuevo) rounds up three men for a shadowy mercenary called "The Dutchman." They are the super-strong Mesito (frequent spaghetti western star Bud Spencer); former war veteran Captain Nicolas Augustus (James Daly), an explosives expert; and knife-throwing expert Samurai (the only Asian member of the cast, Tetsurō Tanba). All these men immediately give up their degrading occupations and answer the Dutchman's summons. Now, to Morricone's thundering score, we see the four men ride on to their appointed meeting with the Dutchman in a nearby village.

Apparently, the federals are about to execute Manuel Estaban (Claudio Gora), a rebel chief—that is, until our heroes, including the Dutchman (Peter Graves), interfere. As the five men plug the federals, the action inspires the downtrodden villagers to attack their oppressors. Estaban has alerted the Dutchman to the existence of a gold shipment of half a million dollars to be transported to Mexico City by train—a train guarded by dozens of federal troops. On their way to another village, they are joined by the entire village that they just saved. When Mesito asks where everyone's going, Dominguez replies bitterly that they cannot stay after killing all those soldiers, an implication of hideous federal reprisals typical of the Mexican government. Indeed, Morricone's music, so lively and perfectly attuned to the action onscreen, now takes on a tragic import; the composer's score becoming mournful as we witness the exodus of a persecuted people seen far too often down through history.

As explained by the Dutchman, the gold is to be sent to General Huerta as a payment by the European nations to protect their interests. Unfortunately, this was far too true, with both Europeans (especially Britain) and many American industrialists backing the Huerta regime over the rebels, whose agenda practically promised the nationalizing of vital industries, especially Mexico's rich oil and mining operations.

However, before you can say "snagged," the group is snagged and imprisoned in a federal stockade. They are put in a cell with their hands tied behind their backs, but a young Mexican woman who's taken a shine to Samurai sneaks a knife to him, an action akin to smuggling a Colt .45 to Annie Oakley. Easily freeing himself and his friends, Samurai and Dominguez break into the federal commander's office. Using his sword, the Asian slices the federals and even splits the skull of the brutal commander. In the shootout that follows, the five-man army once again triumphs and massacres the federals.

In three days' time, the group stops a truck filled with federal troops and kills them, then puts on their uniforms (which, of course, fit our heroes *perfectly*). During a respite, Augustus laments to the Dutchman how old he's gotten and that the two are has-beens. Seeing their caper as a suicide mission, he sadly predicts that all of them will get killed. Daly's monologue is touching, as he speaks of his hand shaking when setting a charge, or how his nerves are just not the same. However, there may have been more than a bit of sad truth behind the veteran actor's performance; Daly was 51 years at the time he performed in *The Five Man Army,* but he actually looks twenty years older. Though certainly no has-been (the actor was constantly busy on TV, especially in the series *Medical Center*), his health would take a turn for the worse by the end of the decade and he would die of a heart attack at age 59 in 1978.

With Mesito posted at the railroad house to switch the gold train from the Mexico City line, the other four, dressed in their federal uniforms, are held by harnesses under the moving train until it is out in the countryside. Using knives and slingshots (gunfire would alert the garrison riding in the cars), Samurai and Dominguez kill all the soldiers riding on top of the train. Then Dutchman holds one of the engineers at gunpoint (the younger engineer is pro–Revolution). Using their disguises, the group even smiles and wave at federal troops in the surrounding hills all along the train's route.

After successfully uncoupling cars, locking the federals in their car, re-routing the gold car off the Mexico City track and ditching their uniforms, the men are ready to get their one thousand dollars each and then turn the balance over to the rebels. However, double-crosses are in the air, and when Dominguez and the others want *all* the gold, the Dutchman, looking like he's double-crossing the rest, actually plans to turn the gold over to Estaban's revolutionaries as originally agreed.

The Dutchman tells the group about the murder of his wife by federals and that he plans to turn the gold over to the rebels to free Mexico's people. When soldiers suddenly ride into the village looking for the gold, they are massacred by the seasoned mercenaries. After their victory, the predicted Mexican standoff between the Dutchman and the rest is broken by the rifle-wielding Dominguez, who proclaims that he's joining the Revolution. As if on cue, Estaban and his men, as well as hundreds of villagers displaced earlier in the movie, arrive and proclaim the five-man army heroes.

Well-acted by the principals (especially Graves who was doing this kind of thing every week on *Mission Impossible*), *The Five Man Army* delivered the requisite action goods. It also reinforced the image of the Revolutionaries as noble fighters for the people and the federals (in this case, under Huerta's regime) as uncompromisingly evil; and as such, these murderous soldiers become cathartic stick figures to be stabbed, sliced, shot, blown up, gutted like fish and thrown from roofs—kind of like the horror films featuring zombies that would be prevalent in movies and TV forty years later. Predictably, Argento used the character of Samurai to raise the film's kill factor, as he writes in scenes showing the swordsman slicing soldiers and throwing knives into their chests with stunning skill. At one point, even Mesito gets into the gore act, throwing a bayonetted rifle like a spear into the chest of a soldier.

One can easily see Argento's black humor contributions all through the film. Hanging under the train, the Dutchman is plagued by a little boy innocently waving at him as a platoon of soldiers stands nearby. After slaughtering the soldiers guarding the top of the train, Samurai and Dominguez are forced to physically prop up the dead men to look as if they were alive; in one truly grisly moment that is pure Argento, Samurai waves the arm of one dead soldier as, hidden from the troops' view, a knife is still protruding from the corpse's back. The film was good action double-bill fodder, and had a long life playing for appreciative action fans in some Times Square theaters as well as nationwide.

To both European and Hollywood filmmakers, Revolutionary Mexico was box office gold. The next American-made western detailing the hero's endless quest for stolen gold would return to the Revolutionary Mexico of Benito Juárez—and it would feature a former spaghetti western star on his way to becoming an American film icon.

It also had Shirley MacLaine...

> Clint Eastwood ... the deadliest man alive ... takes on a
> whole army with 2 guns and a fistful of dynamite![1]

So begins one of the taglines for Universal's big western release of 1970. The ad blurb (and the studio's p.r. guys) shamelessly allude to Clint's legendary performances in Sergio Leone's successful Man with No Name trilogy. In fact, despite the property originating as a script by Budd Boetticher, as directed by frequent Eastwood collaborator Don Siegel, the new film owes more to Leone than the man who directed *Ride Lonesome* and *The Tall T*.

The film's backstory begins in Salzburg, Austria, in 1968. Eastwood was busy wrapping up location shooting for MGM's *Where Eagles Dare,* co-starring Richard Burton and set during World War II. He became friends with Burton and his superstar wife Elizabeth Taylor; and it was during their get-togethers in Europe that Liz gave Eastwood a treatment for a script (sent to her by her agent) written by Boetticher. It told the story of an American gunfighter hooking up with the *Juáristas,* and hoping to make a killing (financially as well as literally) against the French occupiers. Along the way, he saves a Mexican nun from rape and discovers that she is also a fighter (though a non-violent one) against the French. There is, of course, a huge comedy of manners between the rough, violent ways of the gunfighter and the peaceful, religious ways of the starchy but attractive nun—that is, until the shocking denouement when we see that she is not exactly everything she claims to be.

Eastwood was interested in the script, and with the actor's new box office clout in the late 1960s, the studios took his ideas for projects seriously (this is *before* his groundbreaking *Dirty Harry* in 1971). Signed to a non-exclusive contract with Universal Pictures, Eastwood was able to get the studio to bankroll the project and hire a man who was fast becoming the actor's favorite director: Don Siegel. Unfortunately, this decision to hire Siegel instead of original writer Boetticher left the former helmsman out in the proverbial cold. In a 1969 interview with Eric Sherman and Martin Rubin, Boetticher made these revealing statements as the film was being prepped for shooting:

> I really want to get back to making westerns. They have a fine screenplay of mine that Clint Eastwood and Shirley MacLaine are doing at Universal. It's called *Two Mules for Sister Sara*. Originally, I was signed to direct. Now they've hired Don Siegel, and they want to pay me off. It's awfully tough to write a script and fall in love with the characters, and then have somebody else direct it. No matter how good Don is, he'd be the first to admit that I should've made it.[2]

He then went on to mention that he was suing Universal for $4,000,000.

Yet now we see that *Shirley MacLaine*, not Taylor, was set to play the nun. In his own memoirs, Siegel explains why Taylor ultimately didn't do the film: "Richard Burton was set to do the picture entirely in Spain. Liz insisted that *Two Mules for Sister Sara* be shot there too. Her reason was unshakable. She wanted, at all times, to be near her husband, whom she loved dearly."[3]

However, to budget-conscious Universal and screenwriter-producer Rackin (whom Siegel mercilessly roasts over the coals as a glorified hack), shooting in Spain (and paying Liz' salary) was far more expensive than shooting in just-over-the-border Mexico. However, shooting "just over the border" turned out to be Zapata's former home base of Morelos, standing in for Chihuahua way up north.

Now with Taylor gone, the geniuses at Universal (and possibly Rackin himself) quickly came up with Shirley MacLaine as Sister Sara. Siegel wrote that, despite her being a fine actress with a sense of humor, "her skin was fair, her face—the map of Ireland. She most likely would look ridiculous if she played a Mexican nun."[4]

Further changes were made to correct this ridiculous miscasting. Boetticher's material was rewritten by formerly blacklisted writer Albert Maltz. So it was conservative actor Clint Eastwood we can thank for giving the Communist screenwriter his first on-screen credit in over two decades. (Eastwood and Siegel hired Maltz again for their production of *The Beguiled* two years later.) However, a quick rewrite allowed Sister Sara to now become an American expatriate who supports the *Juáristas*. Besides, as shooting commenced on *Two Mules for Sister Sara*, Universal was releasing *Sweet Charity* starring MacLaine, a big-budgeted musical based on the Neil Simon play that the studio was certain would be a surefire hit (it *wasn't*).

Our story begins in northern Mexico in the 1860s at the time of the French occupation in Mexico. With Ennio Morricone's spaghetti western–like music playfully coming over the soundtrack, *Americano* gunfighter Hogan (Eastwood) rides the desert. In a closeup, we see

Hogan's horse step on and crush a tarantula. This bit may have been conceived to show the cruelty of the border lands; however, it is more likely Siegel's in-joke *vis-à-vis* his iconic star. In his days as a contract player for Universal in the mid–50s, Eastwood played the bit part of the Air Force pilot who dropped the napalm on the title monster of the studio's *Tarantula* way back in 1955. (Though you briefly heard Eastwood's voice, his face is hidden behind a pilot's helmet and oxygen mask.) Here, Eastwood again triumphs over the tarantula; however, Siegel invests the scene with Peckinpah-like cruelty to animals. Slow down the DVD player and you'll see that the tarantula has been *nailed to the ground* before the horse crushes it and puts the poor thing out of its misery.

Hogan interrupts three drunken Mexicans about to rape a naked woman. Though promising to share both the booze and the woman with him, two of the men pull guns, only to be shot down by the quick-draw gunfighter. When the third pulls a gun and uses the woman as a hostage, Hogan uses a boulder as a little fort and tosses back (with pinpoint accuracy) a lit stick of dynamite. Fleeing in terror (as Hogan knew he would), the would-be rapist is shot in the back several times and then the gunfighter calmly walks down and extinguishes the fuse before it can ignite the dynamite. According to Siegel, the director wanted Eastwood to run over and extinguish the fuse; however, the actor improvised a slow walk, a bit Siegel himself approved of and later admitted created more suspense. Eastwood knew his screen persona every which way but loose, and he stayed inside the Man with No Name's essential aura of cool—especially when danger was present. Invited to the Hollywood premiere of the film in June of 1970, Boetticher was seated behind Eastwood and Siegel and later claimed (apparently not to their faces) that he was infuriated by the scene, especially the slow, *slow* walk Hogan does before finally putting out the burning fuse. Despite Boetticher's complaints about the scene, it was the right acting choice, with bits like this adding to Eastwood's growing mystique.

After the rescue, Hogan is shocked to discover that the grateful woman is actually a nun named Sister Sara (the pale-

A Nun's Gotta Know Her Limitations: A totally miscast Shirley MacLaine as a "nun" and Clint Eastwood in his Man with No Name persona (though he *does* have a name in this picture) in *Two Mules for Sister Sara*. Set at the time of the French occupation of Mexico, Budd Boetticher's screen story was turned into an American spaghetti western (with Ennio Morricone music) by director Don Siegel.

faced MacLaine). When a French column passes, Hogan hopes to unload Sister Sara, but she quickly explains that she is on their death list for aiding the *Juáristas*. Throughout the film, there is an interesting byplay between the starchy but cute young nun and the laconic, cut-to the-chase gunfighter. When Sara uses precious canteen water to bless the three dead banditos, Hogan stops her with the classic admonition: "Bless 'em dry!" Hogan wants to hook up with *Juáristas* so they can attack the French garrison at Chihuahua and he'll get paid with gold; Sara criticizes his doing it for money. However, Hogan had fought for the Cause (the Confederacy) during the Civil War, and now only works for the coin—lots of it. During this journey, Hogan is open about his lust for Sara, but the gunman is also a gentleman and, unlike the three drunken louts, he turns away from her, swigs some booze and goes to his blankets alone.

Thanks to an attack by Yaquis in which Hogan got an arrow in the shoulder (dutifully removed by Sister Sara), the two are now late to blow up a trestle bridge and destroy a French military supply train in Chihuahua. This is an interesting little plot point, especially since Chihuahua had no railroad going through it in the 1860s. Though wounded, the weak Hogan is able to fire his rifle at the planted explosives and wreck the train.

During all this mishegas and clash of ideologies, we already see that Sara isn't as pious and devout as she claims. When Hogan's back is turned, she puffs on one of his cigars (the patented Clint Eastwood cigarillos yours truly used to smoke in high school in loving imitation), guzzles his whiskey and, after knocking him down with a rather un-nunly right cross, calls him a bastard. After Sara is coerced into blessing a dying French colonel, the officer at once recognizes her from somewhere and oddly calls her a "filthy bitch," an outburst dismissed as delirium by the colonel's men.

The two mismatched travelers meet up with the *Juáristas* led by Colonel Beltran (Manuel Fábregas). The patriotic Mexican colonel and Hogan argue over the gunfighter's lack of fire for the cause and his obvious desire for money, but with Sara's encouragement they form a plan to get into the tightly guarded French fortress. During the group's visit to a whorehouse (where the whores unrealistically are siding with the guerrillas), Hogan learns that Sara was—well, a *whore,* a revelation which angers the gunfighter. Using female peons and their children as a ruse (they use piñatas filled with gunpowder), the guerrillas prepare to storm the place.

Now the battle is on and Siegel doesn't spare the gore. At one point, an old *Juárista* throws a machete into a French soldier's face; then, another French soldier's arm is sliced off with a cutlass. These two bits were removed from British prints of the film. Having done this sort of thing many times in his other movies, Eastwood easily guns down his opponents or tosses lit sticks of TNT at them; he even commandeers a captured Gatling gun and turns it against the French troops below. After the battle, Sara is in the whorehouse smoking a cigar while taking a bath as Hogan suddenly bursts in with a wheelbarrow of French treasure. The two then kiss in the tub, with true love now equated with the spaghetti western's usual MacGuffin of captured gold.

Released on June 16, 1970, the film was considered one of the best of the year, making $5,048,812 in the U.S. alone,[5] but Boetticher condemned the production as having turned his wonderful script into a spaghetti western. Unaware of Boetticher's gripes, the moviegoing public was also ignorant of the many, *many* historical inaccuracies in the film. Primarily, all the firearms in the film, especially the handguns, belong to the *post*–French occupation period. When Hogan shoots dead the three banditos at the beginning of the film, and later when he guns down a French officer and his adjutants, he fires his gun by either pulling the trigger or fanning the hammer, both times *without* cocking the hammer first. This is a virtual impossibility during the immediate post–Civil War period, yet Hogan is definitely using an 1870s Colt Peacemaker. Samuel Colt did not come up with double-action revolvers until 1867. (Similarly, in *The Outlaw Josie Wales,* Eastwood uses Civil War–era Navy Colts which amazingly fired without cocking the hammers.) Another little glitch is the fact that *no one* had sticks of dynamite immediately after the Civil War; they were invented by Alfred Nobel in Europe in 1867. Not until Quentin Tarantino's absurdly cartoonish *Django Unchained* would historical accuracy, especially *vis-à-vis* weaponry, be so blatantly ignored. Also, with a *Juárista* attack on the fortress set for Bastille Day, none of the filmmakers noticed that France didn't have a Bastille Day in 1866 (it started on July 14, 1880).

With Siegel and Eastwood's approval, Rankin hired the great Gabriel Figueroa as photographer. However, both star and director had to deal with that bundle of tempestuous bitchiness and firm believer in reincarnation, the redoubtable Shirley MacLaine. Though later admitting she "loved Clint," MacLaine also had to backhandedly say "even though he was a Republican." And though admitting that "Shirley was great fun," Clint didn't think so when MacLaine had a screaming match with Siegel on how to dismount from the back of a burro and stormed off the set, an act which prompted Eastwood to call her "unprofessional," probably among many other names. In an interview conducted by Stuart M. Kaminsky in 1971, Eastwood admitted that casting Shirley as a nun "stretched the imagination a bit." Indeed, all through the film it looked like Sara had been helping the *Juáristas* by just staying indoors; even for an *Americano,* her nun-turned-whore is unrealistically pale after years in Mexico. To add to MacLaine's obvious miscasting is her annoying habit of wearing false eyelashes and eyeliner throughout the film, something you'd think the canny Hogan would notice early on.

However, as far as a certain European audience was concerned, the voiceover accompanying the coming attraction trailer was revealing in what was *not* said: "Clint Eastwood declares war and the Foreign Legion in Mexico never knew what hit them."

Notice there is absolutely no mention of an occupying *French army*. Instead, we are told of a mysterious "Foreign Legion," without mentioning it as belonging to any country, a "foreign legion" which, of course, was never in Mexico. This was done with the French box office in mind (the film was released in France two weeks after its American release, on July 1). Also notice that the trailer concentrates on Eastwood and his new amoral screen persona, and totally ignores MacLaine, perhaps another reason she barely mentions the film in the autobiography of her Hollywood years, *My Lucky Stars.*

In his *New York Times* review of June 25, Roger Greenspan wrote: "Intelligence is the operative word, for although the film is also charming, funny, cruel, sad and occasionally quite terrifying, it is the richness and complex vigor with which it combines events, ideas, images and people that it chiefly lives."[6] Greenspan praised Figueroa's photography as well as the "collaboration" between Siegel and Boetticher, obviously unaware that the latter had already been squeezed out of the production. Roger Ebert wrote in a January 1, 1970, review that the movie was:

> a step or two above the usual Clint Eastwood Western. To be sure, it has plenty of the obligatory Eastwood violence, and the conventional scene of Eastwood lighting dynamite with his cigar. But that's okay. One of the pleasures of movies is seeing stars doing their thing.

This time, though, there's more to the movie than Eastwood's schtick. Siegel is a first-rate action director, with a knack for directing violence so that it's more exhilarating than disturbing. And his writer, Albert Maltz, has laid a human and funny story on top of the obligatory Eastwood scenes so *Two Mules* is successful on a couple of levels.[7]

By and large, the *Juáristas* triumph over their French occupiers at the end of the film. The French occupation and the Mexico's fight against them would rarely be put on film again until the Mexican-shot *Cinco de Mayo: La Batalia* of 2013.

In the meantime, American audiences would return to the Mexican Revolution of the 1910s in a low-budget effort from United Artists. As historically inaccurate as the Eastwood-MacLaine film, its background was that of a famous American incursion into Mexico...

On January 19, 1916, seventy *Villistas* under the command of General Pablo López halted a passenger train traveling between Chihuahua City and the American-owned Cusihuiriáchic mine at the Santa Isabel River. Among the passengers were eighteen American executives of the mining company, as well as some engineers. In a chilling forerunner of the process later used in Nazi-occupied Europe known as *selectia* (the separation of Jews from the general population slated for immediate extermination), the newly reborn anti–American *Villistas* separated the *yanqui* mining employees from the rest of the passengers, pulled them off the train and marched them towards the river. Armed with Mausers, the *Villistas* acted promptly upon Lopez's angry shouted order and shot dead seventeen of the Americans. Not merely shot, but *riddled,* as if the act were fueled by some kind of fanatical, insane hatred for a people of a certain nationality. One man, feigning death, lay under a pile of his comrades; he lived to report the deed to American authorities afterwards.

Already outraged by German militarism overseas, the American public demanded action. President Wilson was under great pressure to act against Villa, but with a war in Europe on the horizon, he tried to tamp down any jingoistic rhetoric from his fellow countrymen, especially the Hearst newspapers. For his part, Villa would always claim that Lopez exceeded his authority and promised a severe punishment for the deed. Lopez claimed that his men panicked when their captives tried to run away—though it was extremely doubtful that the men would have ran unless they absolutely *knew* that they were going to be killed. Also, if the lone survivor was found feigning death beneath bodies in one spot, then the men *couldn't* have run very far, if indeed they ever did. Soon, Villa's example of "punishment" came when he had two of his officers, including one Juan Rodriguez, murdered and had their bodies publicly displayed in Ciudad Juárez. However, besides the unknown Rodriguez (who could have easily been some innocent resident of the town), the venal Lopez was *not* the other dead man.

Within two months of this massacre, Villa and his killers would top even this outrage.

At 4:20 a.m. on the morning of March 9, 1916, about 400 of Villa's men (without Villa himself) rode into Columbus, New Mexico, and shot up the place. They set fire to buildings, stole horses and property and murdered eighteen Americans, most of them harmless civilians. However, Villa found, to his growing horror, that his spies who were supposed to apprise him of the town's defenses, seriously misinformed him. Instead of the fifty soldiers defending the town, he found out that Camp Furlong contained *600* soldiers. Despite the fact that the attackers tried to set fire to most of the town's businesses, including the thriving Commercial Hotel, soldiers and citizens rallied to the town's defense. Breaking into Camp Furlong's mess hall, *Villistas* were literally sliced to pieces by angry cooks who attacked them with knives, axes, pots of scalding water and baseball bats.

One of the reasons for the attack (that is, besides Villa's now-fanatical anti–American hatred) was that gunrunner Sam Ravel's office was in the Commercial Hotel and the raiders hoped to murder Ravel and rob his safe. However, the merchant disappointed them since he was visiting kin in El Paso at the time. His brother Louis saw the raiders and quickly hid under a pile of hides within Sam's emporium. Louis was not aware that the *Villistas* angrily got hold of his younger brother Arthur and beat him to try to make him reveal the store's safe combination, but the youngster knew nothing. Taking Arthur across the street to the Commercial Hotel (possibly for more beatings), the *Villistas* "escorting" him were shot down by American army snipers, and the young man escaped. Unfortunately for the *Villistas,* when they set fire to the town's hotels and retail stores, the advantage of their early morning attack, namely darkness, was gone as the fires illuminated the street and made the raiders perfect targets for army machine-gunners. By the time Villa's men rode out ninety minutes later, they had lost roughly a quarter of their number, over 100 *Villistas* killed in the town's streets and alleyways (some say 70; still, not a casualty list that Villa could shrug off).

The result of the attack was Brigadier General John J. Pershing's famous Punitive Expedition which followed two weeks later.

In 1970, United Artists released a film about a small detachment of Pershing's men infiltrating the fortress of a powerful and thuggish Villa-like general. It questioned the wisdom of American incursions into foreign lands...

> They aimed him at Cordoba's fortress and pulled the trigger!
> The army followed—to pick up the pieces![8]

With *yanquis* down in Mexico now seen as surefire box office, thanks in large part to the spaghetti western, United Artists released *Cannon for Cordoba* in October 1970. To hedge their low-budget bets, the studio went to fast-shooting TV people to get the film made in a hurry. They hired TV writer (later producer and director) Stephen Kandel to do the screenplay and Paul Wendkos (whose work was now mostly TV-movies) to direct. Keeping with the "TV" approach, they starred George Peppard, a handsome actor whose film career began with promise in the Oscar-winning *Breakfast at Tiffany's,* but by the end of the decade, it was already foundering. In a few years, he would make a comeback thanks to TV with the hit show *The A-Team,* doing essentially the same thing he'd be doing in *Cannon for Cordoba.*

> In 1912, the border between Texas and Mexico was aflame with the raids of Mexican bandit hordes who called themselves Revolutionaries. To combat them, the American government dispatched General John J. (Blackjack) Pershing to deal with the bandit raiders, one of the most dangerous of whom was General Hector Cordoba!

It was pretty obvious at this time that Kandel, Wendkos and UA were banking on the theory that Americans in the audience of 1970 would still remember Pershing, whose reputation as a heroic commander of World War I was well-known, yet *not* remember any great details about his Punitive Expedition which did *not* begin in 1912 but in mid–March 1916, two weeks after Pancho Villa's sneak attack on Columbus, New Mexico (*not* Texas). In fact, in 1912, Villa was still very pro–American, and wouldn't have dreamed of attacking people he saw at the time as friends. (Besides a pro–Villa image of him in the press, individual Americans shipped weapons to *Villistas.*)

As the titles come on, so does Elmer Bernstein's horrid, circus-like comedy music, totally inappropriate to this film. We see rancher Warner (John Larch) address Pershing (John Russell) about the bandit problem. Pershing replies that he doesn't have muscle, but makes up for it in speed, meaning his frequent use of trains. Certainly, during the actual expedition, the anti–American President Venustiano Carranza rather spitefully cut off the use of rolling stock to the Americans, forcing Pershing and his men to slog across a merciless desert, mostly by horse.

When an arrogant captain tries to get one group of men to salute, he is told by Captain Rod Douglas (Peppard) that they don't have to "salute, drill, work or anything else but fight." These men include Jackson Harkness (Don Gordon), Peter (Nino Minardos) and Andy Rice (the tragic Pete Duel). Douglas' men are his and Pershing's own personal A-Team, the bad boys who don't play by the rules that have been created by filmmakers in the wake of the Bay of Pigs fiasco and other examples of American Black Ops, though *these* spooks wear uniforms. Watching the transport from afar, especially taking note of the army's six cannons, is rebel general Hector Cordoba (Raf Vallone) and his Swedish (that's right; *Swedish*) military "advisor," Colonel Swedborg (Hans Meyer). "I want those guns!" declares the general.

Off in the hills, now dressed in civvies, Douglas and Harkness meet up with Jackson's little brother Adam, (Richard Pendrey), a new member of the team who's itching for action. As soon as Douglas tells Adam that he won't have his older brother looking after him, we *know* beyond a shadow of a doubt that Adam is toast. Sure enough, no sooner are Douglas and Harkness accepted into Cordoba's band that we see poor Adam hung upside down and lowered into a raging fire so he will tell the rebels where Pershing's men are going to attack. To stop an anguished Jackson from interfering and blowing their cover, Douglas punches him out. Adam is shot dead as soon as he cooperates, but Jackson will harbor bitterness against his commander for failing to save his brother.

In the same town where Pershing's train (with the cannons) is settled, Cordoba and his slugs arrive along with our heroes. During an attack by Cordoba and his men which replicates the *Villista* raid on Columbus, the train is stolen. As the firefight rages, Pershing is portrayed as courageous enough to return fire with his army .45 but then Douglas prompts him to jump off the train before it takes off down the rails. This act of bravery one completely expects, not only from "Blackjack" Pershing, but from *any* character played by ex–Marine (and ex–*Lawman*) John Russell. During the battle, both soldiers and *Cordobiristas* are killed, but the cannons are gone.

"With those six cannons," laments a grim Captain Douglas, "he's the hero of every peon in Northern Mexico!" This is an interesting statement which goes into the pedigree of the character of General Cordoba. He doesn't dress like a rebel general, but a hated *federale*. However, the mention of the peons of Northern Mexico certainly suggests Pancho Villa; though Cordoba has Villa's thuggishness, he lacks his talent for military operations. Also, rebels like Villa were *already* in possession of artillery pieces they had stolen from Mexican garrisons in their raids. Six American cannons were nice to have, but they would not be enough to match the firepower that *Villistas* and other rebels already possessed. Villa was a master at ordering cavalry charges backed by artillery support. He also had the good fortune of having the aid of former Carranza officer Felipe Ángeles, who used his knowledge of artillery pieces to train Villa's men in how to operate them for maximum effect.

Abandoning the idea of recapturing the weapons, Pershing wants them destroyed.

VI—Violencia, 1970–1989

A "Cannon" for Cordoba: George Peppard points his big .45 as he's about to kidnap evil revolutionary general Raf Vallone in *A Cannon for Cordoba*. The 1970 film euphemistically compared General John J. Pershing's Punitive Expedition into Mexico to America's involvement in the Vietnam War.

Dressed down for losing the cannons, Douglas has to argue against the military's plan for a "gringo invasion" into Mexico. When a colonel arrogantly claims that the Mexicans "should be taught a lesson," Douglas replies that lessons should be learned in a classroom; and adds, "You are talking about killing people to prove a point. Those people will *fight* to prove a point!" Here, the filmmakers were not only repeating the general consensus that the Punitive Expedition was a mistake, but also a certain other military action then being taken in Vietnam.

The orders are plain: Douglas and his hand-picked team are to destroy the cannons, and a Mexican lieutenant is reluctantly brought along to bring Cordoba to trial in Mexico City. This American-Mexican cooperation in the film was an imaginative myth, for at no time had Mexican and American military personnel cooperated on a mission since the days of the Apache raids into both nations during the 19th century. Nevertheless, in the film Pershing's orders make it clear that, if caught, the men will be shot as spies and their American superiors will categorically deny ever having seen them; an example of plausible deniability then making headway as a plot device as more and more anti-government films started to come out of Hollywood.

As he's gathering his men, two of them, Peter and Andy, are breaking out of military jail, the comedy and/or anarchy of this situation not exactly approaching the level of the recently released *MASH*. In their barracks, in one chilling moment, especially considering what happened to him in just a few years, Pete Duel puts a gun to his head and pulls the trigger (though we hear a click). Meanwhile, Douglas has been having an affair with Warner's wife, who spitefully reveals to the captain that the rancher is a traitor and spy in the employ of Cordoba. When the Fab Four hit the trail to Cordoba's fortress (in late 1960s hippie mode, the long-haired Andy brings along his guitar), they kidnap Warner as well. During their ride they are attacked by Cordoba's men, and Warner is killed in the shootout.

Douglas meets a Mexican lieutenant and his agent, gorgeous Mexican babe Leonora (second-billed Giavanna Ralli). Douglas' first line to her is *not* a good beginning to their partnership: "You're volunteering for a job a whore might turn down." It seems that Cordoba has murdered the *senorita's* family and raped her; therefore she wants to get close enough to the general to exact revenge.

At Cordoba's fortress, Douglas is found out and he and the lieutenant are put in the compound's jail. That night, the other three return and free Douglas. During the wild gunfight that follows, the cannons are blown up, but Andy, Peter and the Mexican lieutenant are killed. Taking a measure of revenge, Douglas slices the charging Swedborg with a saber.

Apparently abandoning her personal vengeance, Leonora joins Douglas and Harkness in grabbing the unarmed Cordoba and smuggling him out of the fortress for that trial in Mexico City. Afterwards, the revolutionaries are all killed in the massive shootout and cataclysmic explosion that completely destroys the fortress. Alone out on the desert the next morning, Harkness challenges Douglas to shoot it out to avenge his brother, but when the captain refuses, Jackson merely knocks him down. Having seen too much killing already, Harkness grudgingly abandons his ideas of revenge. Ironically, when they check on the prone General Cordoba, they find that he's been accidentally shot dead by one of his own men during their getaway. When Leonora tells Douglas he'll be considered a hero, he delivers the film's final line: "The trouble with being a hero is the morning after...."

Released in that heady counter-culture year of 1970, *Cannon for Cordoba* almost, though not quite, compared General Pershing's Punitive Expedition to the then-current Vietnam War. But this was no counter-culture Jane Fonda vehicle which indicted all Americans, yet gave our enemies a free pass. The Mexican enemies the film depicted were emphatically *not* poverty-stricken peons (whom we never see in the entire film anyway). These "revolutionaries" are totally devoid of any ideology, and it is certainly inferred that the power-mad Cordoba wants the cannons so his men can loot, pillage and destroy at will, as if other factions in the Mexican Revolution didn't have any artillery pieces of their own.

Meanwhile, Down Mexico Way, one of the nation's major stars was returning to the world of Revolutionary Mexico for the final time...

La Generala was shot by Churubusco-Azteca Studios in the fall of 1970 and released in Mexico on January 14 the following year. As directed and co-written by Juan Ibañez, it was set during the Revolution; however, unlike the traditionally government-sanctioned versions of the Revolution coming out of the country in earlier years, the film took the Great Struggle for Mexico's Freedom and turned it into an insane bloodbath. What Ibañez and co-writer Arturo Rosenblueth did was give us a microcosm of the Revolution in the persona of an embittered woman who thirsts for revenge against the ruthless federal officer who murdered her husband. Besides its virtually unrestrained violence (proof positive that Mexico had followed Hollywood's lead on abandoning screen censorship), *La Generala* was also the screen swan song for one of Mexico's iconic leading ladies.

María Félix was one of the Mexican cinema's more striking beauties. A stunning presence who almost literally towered over her co-stars, she was the empowered woman against the *macho* men of a long-entrenched sexist Latino culture. Men who crossed her could only pray for mercy once her ire was roused—and it would be roused in many a film. She always carried herself well, but she rarely conveyed the same kind of refinement and elegance that her main rival in Mexican cinema, Dolores del Río, had. Poised and beautiful, del Río had always exhibited an aristocratic upbringing. A pious Catholic, loyal to family and friends, and keeping her films clearly along clean, family-oriented lines, the former Hollywood star turned Mexican icon would never do half the things in her own films that Félix got away with. More of a victim of men on screen than victimizer, del Río exposed sexism in her own quiet way. In many ways, the two women epitomized both the Light and the Dark side of Mexican cinema's portrayal of women on-screen. Whereas Félix was always ready to brandish a whip or a gun on her male enemies, del Río had more subtle means at her disposal. Having seen the wild side of fame up close during her Hollywood years (when she almost died from too much of that fast living in the early 1930s), the classy actress made sure that her films were dramas or comedies that rejected violence and raunchy sex; it was a sure thing that a vehicle like *La Generala* was not going to be *her* last film. As it turned out, Dolores ended her film career in 1978 in the powerful family drama *The Children of Sanchez,* a Mexican-American co-production shot in Mexico and co-starring Anthony Quinn.

By the 1970s, Mexican films were beginning to show us a Revolution Gone Wrong. Not since the controversial *Let's Go with Pancho Villa* had the heroes of the Revolution been portrayed as such bastards. *Zapata!*, with Antonio Aguilar in the title role, depicted monsters on both sides of the battlefield, with the star's portrayal of the iconic freedom fighter showing us that, despite all the idealistic platitudes, revolutions were indeed *not* fought by gentlemen.

La Generala is set in Revolutionary Mexico where Colonel López (Eric del Castillo) a psychopathic federal officer, even bullies around the old man who is his general. Taking over a village, he offers the residents a chance to live if they give up their weapons. The aristocratic Manuel Sampedero (Carlos Bracho), who has been aiding the rebels, decides to accept the colonel's offer and turns in his weapons; however, revolutionary Rosauro (the ubiquitous Ignacio López Tarso, who played Trinidad in *La Cucaracha* and Piquinto in *Juana Gallo*) thinks Don Sampedro is a fool and literally walks away from the colonel along with his dwarf sidekick Ismael (Santanón).

Manuel's wife is the striking beauty Mariana Sampedro (played by the striking beauty Maria Felix), a woman who commands great loyalty from Rosauro and Ismael. Though she loves her husband, she is also disgusted with his quick surrender to Colonel López, a man she clearly doesn't trust. As we'll soon see, Mariana's instincts are right. When Manuel and his followers (Rosauro and Ismael are not among them) swim naked in the local lake, they are met at the shoreline by the colonel and a platoon of his men, who open up with their rifles and the wet former rebels are soon drowning in their own blood. Mariana witnesses this atrocity, but she is saved by Ismael, who literally pulls her to the ground out of harm's way.

Soon she meets a rich blonde-haired American, referred to by the jealous Rosauro as El Rubio (the blonde one; and played by Argentinian actor Sergio Kleiner). El Rubio sympathizes with the rebels, but advises restraint against López, a man who can literally wipe out the town. When Mariana and El Rubio attend mass to pray for her late husband, a federal soldier chases a suspected rebel into the church. In a scene that could have been a harbinger for the Obregón-Calles years, the soldier opens fire in the church and kills the rebel. Horrified, the worshippers, including Mariana and El Rubio, flee the church only to be fired upon by López's troops, who are looking for more rebels. Adding to the bloodbath, several revolutionaries return fire and soon both sides are indiscriminately murdering helpless bystanders caught between them. Mariana and El Rubio throw themselves to the ground to avoid the bullets. The carnage apparently turns on the blood-stained woman and she kisses her companion passionately during the shooting.

The die is now cast: Mariana wants Colonel López dead. As she and El Rubio are attending a performance of Shakespeare's *Measure for Measure,* López arrives with his deb Raquel (Evangelina Elizondo) and they interrupt the performance with their raucous laughter. Mariana boldly gets up from her box and publicly calls out the colonel for his rudeness. Intrigued instead of outraged, López arranges a four-way dinner with Raquel, Mariana and El Rubio. The officer is clearly fascinated by his dark-haired antagonist.

Mariana gets López up to her room and gets him to strip naked and then, at her signal, he is suddenly attacked by Rosauro and Ismael. After tying him to the bed, Rosauro hands Mariana a curved knife. There's a judicious cut-away (in more ways than one) and we hear the colonel's blood-curdling scream. Mariana comes into camera frame with the bloody knife. Disgusted by his girlfriend's vengeance-crazed act of castration, El Rubio allows the colonel to recuperate in his home.

Now, the definitely tormented Mariana, dressed in sloppy clothes and slouch hat, rides into villages with her rebels, supposedly to liberate them from the federals. In reality, however, her men are as bloodthirsty as the men they profess to hate, and they plunder wherever they attack. Only Mariana's orders *not* to molest women and young girls stop these lunatics from committing even more atrocities. Many of her men see Mariana as an impediment to their fun, and want to be rid of her. Indeed, her rebel band is one in name only, with exercising power over helpless people being the main goal rather than helping them.

When she is about to hang one of the men helping López (they had already hanged the old man who was his general), El Rubio insists on showing him mercy. Mariana hesitates, so Rosauro draws his gun and shoots the man while he still has the unused noose around his neck. Angrily, he then goes off with the band and leaves the disillusioned Mariana with El Rubio.

Soon, López and his men capture Rosauro, Ismael and the village that Mariana and her goons had just left. After shooting the dwarf, and torturing Rosauro to death, López threatens to murder the villagers one by one if Mariana does not appear before him. Interrupted in her romantic idyll with El Rubio, Mariana knows that she must go back to López and an almost certain death. After forcing El Rubio to stay behind, she rides on horseback to the colonel, the murderer of her husband. After they stare at each other for what seems like an eternity, Mariana draws her pistol and riddles the colonel with bullets. As he falls dead, his troops open fire and kill Mariana.

At the end of *Juano Gallo,* the film flashes ahead to present-day Mexico and the voice of Captain Verlarde is heard repeating his speech about Mexico's future: modern cities, prosperous industries and contented citizens living in a land of freedom and equality, all thanks to the fighters of the Revolution. At the end of *El Generala,* there are no stirring speeches extolling the glories of the Revolution as depicted in *this* film. Populated by psychopaths and dysfunctional losers, *El Generala* takes a battle of the sexes between a driven woman and a ruthless man and turns it into a larger comment on a Revolution that was not as glorious as previously thought. Personal hatred and vengeance between two sick people is now put on a national landscape. With atrocities committed by both sides, and the innocent in between, this particular version of the Revolution shows us not the glory, but the macabre (as demonstrated in the nightmare sequence where Mariana dreams of herself as a frizzy-haired Medusa and her friends as white-faced corpses dancing around a fire). There is even the character of a madwoman screeching and laughing and following Mariana around throughout the film; she closely resembles Ellen Degeneres wearing Coke bottle–lensed glasses and dressed in rags. Cackling maniacally, she eventually strangles the cat she had been carrying throughout the film; and in a truly gross scene, she actually waves around the feline's bloody corpse before a shocked Mariana and El Rubio. We can only see her as a microcosm of the insanity committed during the film for the sake of victory.

With this, her final death scene, the great María Félix had her last moments on film. She seems to have left just in time, before film content would get even more gross than the violence displayed here. Certainly, every massacre in the film is powerfully captured by veteran director of photography Gabriel Figueroa, and somehow it seems poetic that María would have her final moments before the camera of a man who had done so much for her career during *Época Dorada*.

Meanwhile, in Italy, where both the western and the Mexican Revolutionary film were making a comeback, a master of both genres would have his own take on revolutions and the kind of people that make them...

It is said that Sergio Leone invented the spaghetti western. In reality, the Italian western had been around years before Leone popularized this subgenre for an international audience. In the famous *Dollars* trilogy, he gave new life to the tired genre by focusing on the amoral rather than the virtuous. In one of his favorite films, *Once Upon a Time in the West,* his violent parodies of the genre became decidedly more bitter. Added to his usual sendup of western clichés was a larger indictment of American expansion into the frontier, a place where the establishment of towns and the building of railroads were started by the most unscrupulous of men, as well as the trenchant observation that America was a land built upon the bodies of others.

Leone the man was also a confounding soul for those who knew and worked with him. Apparently, he enjoyed having, or rather couldn't help getting into, bitter feuds with his former collaborators. He angered Sergio Donati and Luciano Vincenzoni by not crediting them with co-writing *The Good, the Bad and the Ugly;* upset Tonino Valeril by strong-arming his way into the director's chair for *My Name Is Nobody*; as producer of *Duck, You Sucker,* he pretended to hire Peter Bogdanovich to direct, then fired him so he could direct it himself; and he was famously sued by Japanese helmsman Akira Kurosawa for stealing his *Yojimbo* and turning it into *A Fistful of Dollars*. He even jealously attacked Clint Eastwood whose career was far outpacing his own.

This brings us to a western Leone shot between April and July 1970 in Almeria, Spain, while the Vietnam War was raging and the excesses of the counter-culture movement rose to a fever pitch. *Duck, You Sucker,* aka *A Fistful of Dynamite,* tried to cover all the bases with

Leone's victimized collaborators. He credited Luciano Vincenzoni and Sergio Donati for co-writing (with himself) the screenplay, gave Claudio Mancini billing as associate producer, as well as his usual production manager chores; and even insisted that Ginacarlo Santi, his assistant director on *The Good, the Bad and the Ugly* and *Once Upon a Time in the West*, be given a chance to direct the film. However, his stars, Rod Steiger and James Coburn, had different ideas. Originally told that Leone was to direct, the two Americans balked at Leone's sudden whim to have the unknown and untried Santi helm the production and threatened to quit if the A.D. took the assignment.

Starting the film off with a bang—or actually a tinkle—Leone first gives us a quote from, of all people, Communist dictator Mao Tse-Tung. As the quote informs us that the Revolution is not a social dinner and cannot be done with elegance and courtesy but is an act of violence, informed members of the audience might have thought of the Chinese leader's own genocidal purges of those who, paraphrasing his own imagery, weren't good enough to be seated at his table. Then, as Leone cuts in for a close-up of some flies and ants milling around on a log, a steady stream of urine drowns most of them. Perhaps Leone was trying to shock us with this tasteless way to begin a film, but in reality the director came up with a brutally accurate commentary on those who fought for, as well as against, the Revolution.

Juan Miranda (that great Latino actor, Rod Steiger) buttons up his fly and, barefoot and sloppy, tries to hitch a ride on a passing stagecoach. Once aboard, he is forced to sit far

Explosive Personality: James Coburn as the Irish revolutionary transferring his talents to the Mexican Revolution in Sergio Leone's *Duck, You Sucker!* Though the federal army is compared to genocidal Nazis throughout the story, Leone's film also takes aim at the hypocrisy behind revolutionary movements.

away from several wealthy representatives of the *Porfiriato*: a racist American Southerner, a snobby woman and a priest. All of them make merciless fun of Juan's parentage, his clothes, etc., and then segue into calling the rebels "brutes" and "animals." We even have a bitter comment that Madero was giving the peasants "their" land, something the filmmakers never bothered to research since the murdered president rarely confiscated the *hacendados'* land, despite his many promises to do so. Then, in one of the truly gross-out sequences in film history, Leone gives us some of his fabled close-ups, though they're of these wealthy people eating ravenously as their hate-filled comments on the lower classes is repeated endlessly on the soundtrack. And so, against our collective will, we are forced to see ruby-red tongues, busy tonsils, teeth with food particles wedged between them and lips dripping chewed morsels all over the camera lens. If Leone wanted us to hate these characters, he failed miserably, since, by calling attention to his own direction with these microscopic close-ups, audience rage is instead focused on *him*. At this point, Juan's rambunctious sons show up and it turns out that the poor soul is actually a robber. Again, Leone invites us to cheer as the wealthy are stripped naked and abused. Then, chasing the fleeing rich woman, Juan eventually catches up and rapes her; in typical sexist, macho filmmaker mode, Leone has the woman enjoy her rape. Were we supposed to applaud this too?

As the family enjoys their spoils, a man on a motorcycle comes along and, after Juan puts a bullet in one of the tires, they all laugh at him. This man is Irish revolutionary Sean Malory (James Coburn, whose accent is less than convincing). Their laughter disappears when he almost blows them up with bombs. Uneasily, Juan proposes an alliance, seeing that Sean's explosives can help him crack the nearest bank. However, the former enemy of British rule has his own agenda, using the rancid-looking bandito to strike a blow for the Mexican Revolution and at the same time elevate his social conscience. Thinking he's using Sean, Juan is actually being used in turn to blow up federal outposts and trains. Going into town to supposedly rob a bank, Juan is shocked to find that the bank has no money and that the place is actually used as a stockade for imprisoned revolutionaries. Now, against his will, the movement regards the mercenary Juan as a hero for freeing the rebel prisoners, and they promptly take back the town from the federals. "I don't want to be a hero! All I want is *the money!*" cries Juan as he's carried off by the grateful men he reluctantly liberated (and he gives Sean the finger).

Unfortunately for the rebels, they are being hunted by the cruel German officer Colonel Gunther Raza (Domingo Antoine), another allusion to the Mexican government's close alliance with a belligerent Germany. Taking a cue from the slimy German officers in *The Wild Bunch,* films about the Revolution now showed Teutonic autocrats providing military assistance to their villainous Mexican clients, whether they were federals *or* revolutionaries. It is a German colonel who stands by as brutal federals institute a "final solution" on the Yaqui population in the otherwise escapist *100 Rifles;* and a German officer even appears in the Revolution-set comedy, *¡Three Amigos!*

At camp, when John tells Juan that the Revolution is being fought against "Huerta, the government, the landowners, Gunther and his locusts," Juan explodes, declaring that the people who read the books tell the people who don't read (meaning the poor) that they have to make a change, and while the people who read sit around and talk, the poor fight and, predictably, get killed. He ends his tirade with, "Then the same fucking thing happens all over again!" This is certainly far more honest dialogue about revolutions that one ordinarily heard in the Euro-western; in this telling scene, it is Juan, the illiterate bandit, who is far more knowledgeable than the professional revolutionary Sean. Leone's ironic use of the men as two halves of the same revolutionary coin is aided by their having, despite different nationalities, the same first name (Ennio Morricone's soundtrack even chimes in every once in a while with "John-John," a play on their names).

When rebel leader Dr. Villega (Romolo Valli) sets up an ambush for Gunther and his federals in the mountains, the danger is considered too great, so Juan sends his sons away with the rest of the band while he remains behind with Sean. After the band leaves, Juan reluctantly decides to stay just to show up Sean. Firing at the bridge with mounted machine-guns and using the Irishman's planted caches of TNT, the two massacre most of Gunther's men, but merely wound the German commander. However, when the two men arrive at the purported meeting place in a cave, they find the whole band murdered, including all of Juan's sons. The irony of Juan spitefully staying behind with John has actually saved his life. Scouting the vicinity in the rain, Sean discovers the remainder of the band shot dead by federals, with Dr. Villega standing nearby; obviously, it was *he* who had betrayed his comrades.

Gathering more rebels, the group hopes to destroy a federal troop train with Gunther and his men. However, when Sean and the traitorous Dr. Villega take over a freight train going in the opposite direction and send it down the tracks towards their target, while Sean jumps off just in time, the guilt-ridden doctor remains and is killed when the two masses of rolling stock collide. In a firefight, all the federals are killed, and the ubiquitous Gunther shoots and mortally wounds Sean, but Juan angrily riddles the German with his machine-gun. Then the dying Irish rebel warns Juan with the phrase he always used before setting off his bombs: "Duck, you sucker," and blows himself up. Now without Sean, his social conscience, Juan asks himself, "What about me?"

Released by UA as *A Fistful of Dynamite* on June 30, 1972, the "Americanized" version of the film was now minus some of the more violent scenes and many uses of the "F" word (still considered a no-no in American films at the time). Extended scenes that more graphically show the bodies of Juan's family and the rebels were cut, as were multiple subplots and double-crosses between the two leads. The U.S. cut was 121 minutes; Leone's cut (shown in London's National Theater upon its original release in September 1971) runs 157 minutes. Then nineteen minutes were cut and it premiered in Italy on October 20, 1971. Throughout the film, Sean has flashbacks of an idyllic life with his best pal and his girlfriend in Ireland. Before the trains collide and Dr. Villega passionately defends his treachery to Sean, the Irishman flashes back for a last time, and we see that his friend had informed to the British, causing Sean to shoot him dead in a pub. In the uncut 157-minute version of the film, Sean shows jealousy when the friend is getting *too* friendly with his girl, giving extra meaning to Mallory's execution of his friend that isn't clear in the trimmed versions.

Three days before its re-release in the U.S. on November 21, 2003, the film was reviewed by *The Village Voice*. Titling the article *"The Revolution Will Be Westernized: Leone's Nutty Lefty Epic,"* J. Hoberman examined the restored 138-version before it made its way to DVD, declaring that the film "belongs with the crazy left-wing westerns that mark the post '60s wreck of revolutionary dreams...." After referring to the controversial scene on the coach as "a relentless exercise in class vengeance," Hoberman writes:

> The cynicism meter oscillates between outrageously callous and merely irresponsible. Every "up against the wall" is countered with a "duck, you sucker!" (According to Peter Bog-

Rebels Fall Out: James Coburn stands up to a gun-toting Rod Steiger in *Duck, You Sucker!* Coburn's professional revolutionary seeks to teach petty thief Steiger about fighting for a cause, but by the end of the film, it is the illiterate peon who teaches a thing or two to the revolutionary.

danovich, who was briefly attached to the project, Leone insisted that this lame phrase was common American slang.) Long before the apocalyptic closer, lumpen metaphors are crashing down like boulders—a bank turns out to be a political prison, Juan finds himself an inadvertent hero of the revolution, Sean tosses away his Bakunin to take an individualist stand against the Mexican army. History is swept away by the avalanche of allegory. The genocidal *federales* are modeled on Nazi storm troopers and the revolutionaries on Italian partisans.[9]

Unlike the fanatically reverent depictions of the Revolution by Mexican filmmakers, *Duck, You Sucker,* though praising those who forment revolution, is certainly not as violently "left-wing" as Hoberman claims. Justifiably showing the barbarities of the *Huertistas,* Leone and his writers have shown far more ambiguities with the Revolution and those who fought it than most Euro-western filmmakers did at the time, despite its opening Maoist quote.

However, there were certainly other Euro-western filmmakers who had no qualms about embracing the Revolution and portraying all who opposed it as capitalist oppressors, particularly Mexico's large and wealthy neighbor to the north.

In 1972, some American communists made a film supposedly depicting the life of a Revolutionary icon and used his story as an indictment of the nation that had almost literally kicked them out...

A major trait of the spaghetti western was the politics of the folks behind the camera. As it embodied an anti–Hollywood western attitude, the Euro-western attracted filmmakers who had their own ax to grind *vis-à-vis* America in general and Hollywood in particular. Given this, it's no surprise that the subgenre employed screenwriters and directors whom were blacklisted by Hollywood in the 1950s. Deemed unemployable in the States, these people found favor in a Europe perhaps dismayed by America's success and resentful of its having "rescued" the continent during World War II.

But many of the plots of these films concerned the Mexican Revolution. With left-wing scenarists and directors (who apparently ignored the racist casting of Italian actors as Latinos), one didn't have long to ponder just how they would portray the most cataclysmic event in Mexican history. However, depicting the revolutionaries as heroes, and the Díaz regime as inherently corrupt, any complications or depth within the personalities involved would never be shown. In this respect, the films written by these blacklisted scenarists lacked the subtlety of their Hollywood work and gave us cartoonish yet noble revolutionary heroes and dastardly and sometimes buffoonish villains who wore Mexican army uniforms, routinely barked out orders like "Silencio!" and hanged villagers at the drop of a sombrero.

The life of Pancho Villa wasn't what you'd call uproarious slapstick, but apparently the leftist screenwriters who filmed 1972's *Pancho Villa* (original title, *Vendetta*) saw something amusing about the bandit-revolutionary's fight against the Díaz regime. Communist producer-screenwriter Bernard Gordon and his frequent writing partner Julian Zimet (also known as Julian Halevy) had been blacklisted in the 1950s. Collaborating with European spaghetti western and horror film director Eugenio Martin (real name Eugenio Martin Marquez, whose name Gordon Anglicized in the credits as "Gene Martin"), the former Hollywood Reds also turned Pancho Villa's fight to free Mexico as an attack on the *yanqui* imperialists to the north.

In *Pancho Villa,* this violence against capitalist pillars of society would be tempered with outrageous scenes of black humor and a constant tweaking of American sensibilities, especially its military prestige. The federals are transporting an imprisoned Pancho Villa (Greek-American Telly Savalas) to be hanged. In his jail cell, he is getting his head shaved; this haircut obviously gives the bald actor playing Villa a chance to appear more or less as himself through the entire film. Fortunately for Villa, he's rescued by American gunman Scotty (no last name; and played by the former Cheyenne Bodie himself, Clint Walker).

As the film progresses, Villa is a bandit-revolutionary whose mercurial temper rises and falls every other minute. In this regard, Gordon, along with Zimet and Martin (the screenwriters) are right on the money. Villa's personality was full of violent mood swings; in this film, the scenarists turn this quite serious schizophrenic behavior into comedy. It was a good performance by Savalas, going full-tilt as he swaggers throughout the film, bestowing favors on his friends and followers one moment and then shooting someone else moments later. Savalas' Villa is not only a megalomaniac but a ham, and despite some terrible inaccuracies, a likable one. He is an underdog who clearly enjoys his status as an icon for revolutionary change, and delights in leading the pack. Walker's character is given scenes where he tries to get back his saloon gal ex-wife (a waste of time for the still-gorgeous Anne Francis), but Savalas' Villa steals our attention and never lets it go.

As Villa alternately shoots down enemies or pushes them through windows, we are reminded of the film's politics, particularly its anti–Americanism. Martin and Zimet, obviously backed by an enthusiastic Gordon, give us the character of an American officer, the martinet Colonel Wilcox (played in an extremely stiff-necked manner by the Rifleman himself, Chuck Connors). At one point, he orders his men to kill an annoying fly that found its way into the fort's mess hall. It is a scene that is so cartoonish, it's doubtful anyone but the filmmakers would actually find it funny; again, it is the work of embittered ex-blacklistees ripping the American military by turning them into knockabout buffoons.

Seeking to punish a double-crossing gunrunner across the border, Villa and his band simply march over to the American checkpoint in broad daylight, along with their women and their families apparently, and order the guards to surrender. Of course, Villa had his men attack Columbus, New Mexico, in the pre-dawn hours of March 9, 1916. Not only was this sneak attack performed in total darkness, but the hundreds of *Villistas* who took part in it emphatically did *not* bring along their families. Still, the scene of Villa, Scotty and their people naively marching up to the American outpost is played to goofy-sounding comedy music, and one forgets the real-life tragedy that took the lives of many Columbus citizens as well as over a hundred *Villistas*. However, when the American garrison fires on the rebels and kills several of them, Villa returns fire and kills them, suddenly (and uncomfortably) jarring the audience.

The climax to this cartoonish farce has Villa and his men commandeering a speeding train, and Wilcox and his men on another train, both on the same track, hurtling down the tracks towards each other. Despite the fact that the men on both sides are jumping off their respective trains, Villa and Wilcox refuse to budge, both insisting that the *other* train be pushed off the tracks. Needless to say, a horrible collision is in the offing. Here, though played for comedy, the filmmakers actually show Villa as stubborn and crazed as Wilcox— a comedic tableau showing two military leaders from opposing camps leading their men on a suicidal collision, a not-so-subtle indictment of militarism on both sides of the conflict. The upshot of the collision is predictable: Villa survives uninjured while Wilcox is comically bandaged from head to toe.

In one the final scenes, the colonel is visited by General Pershing (veteran character villain Walter Coy). With Pershing, hardly a comic figure, trying to ignore the colonel's appearance as he praises him, we see the filmmakers cynically poking fun at another American hero. However, in the next scene, Martin and Zimet suddenly switch gears again: Villa pretends to be a mere survivor of the crash who claimed that the bandit leader (him) has escaped. There is a strong implication that the formerly comical Pershing *knows* that the man he's interrogating is Villa. This is confirmed when, after he releases Villa, he says to him, "If you ever run into Villa, tell him that every great man began as a bandit." Villa nods knowingly and rejoins Scotty and his band. Ironically, after all the misfired parody and over-the-top action, this unusual understanding by an American general for his implacable enemy is undoubtedly the best moment in the film (though after the raid, Pershing would have had him arrested, not released him).

In the years to come, the western genre would again return to the complicated, iconic figure of Pancho Villa, as did one low-budget production released at the end of the decade by a future producer of schlock...

This new project was based on an enduring novel written in 1943 by a South Texas author and psychologist named Cleo Dawson. Born in Oklahoma City in 1902, Dawson traveled with her family across the Texas plains to help build the small hamlet of Mission, close to the Mexican border (the state of Nuevo Leon) as well as the town of McAllen,

Texas. The journey was rough, and the little girl's memories of the trip remained with her always. She went to school in Mission and grew up there, then attended Baylor College in Waco, Southern Methodist University and the University of Kentucky, graduating with a Ph.D. She was the first educator to teach Spanish at the Mission High School, and in 1926, she got married to a soldier named George Smith and moved to Lexington, Kentucky. She had written extensively of her parents' journey to Mission in the local paper, the *Mission Times*. Those writings were expanded into a sprawling novel which she wrote at the tender age of 21, *She Came to the Valley, a Novel of the Lower Rio Grande Valley*. Cleo Dawson had written extensively about the Revolution through the years, and was a popular lecturer in the region on the Rotary Club circuit. She had also written an unpublished novel called *The Jeweled Crown: A Legend of Mexico*.

As a psychologist, Dawson appeared on *The Merv Griffin Show* in the 1960s and '70s and one particular show in the 1970s was watched by producer Albert Band (real name, Alfredo Antonini). Dawson was talking about her family's pioneer experiences, and her novel about the trek looked like something that quickie producer Band could bring to the screen on a low budget. With a career that went back into the early 1950s (he adapted *The Red Badge of Courage,* starring Audie Murphy, for John Huston's 1951 production), Band produced and scripted cheap productions both in America and Europe, including the continent's usually over-the-top spaghetti westerns. His productions were sometimes badly edited patchworks, with grimy photography, amateurish acting and rushed direction. One does wonder how the producer of films with titles like *The Tramplers, Hellbenders* and *Little Cigars* would end up as the mover and shaker of a film based on a novel that went through some nineteen printings and three translations.

With a script co-written by Band and co-producer Frank Ray Perilli, the film reduces Dawson's sprawling novel to a little over ninety minutes. The story deals with the Westall family of Oklahoma (Dawson's thinly veiled version of her own family), headed by husband and father Pat (standing in for her father Ed) and his wife Willy (standing in for her mother Helen). They have two little girls named Amara and Srita (standing in for Cleo and her sister Connie). Seeking a better life, Pat puts his family and their belongings in their covered wagon and brings them to Texas. An accident practically cripples Pat and he limps for the rest of his life. With her husband physically infirm, Willy essentially becomes the "man" of the household, building things, handling the carpentry, unloading supplies off the buckboard and doing the bulk of the farm work. Soon they welcome into their home handsome young drifter Bill Lester, whom Willy is definitely attracted to. However, it seems that Bill is more than just a fellow who stopped by to help out the family and play with the girls. He has also been running guns for Pancho Villa.

The production was set to start filming on location in Mission in the summer of 1977 (with the enthusiastic cooperation of the locals who were always fond of their local celebrity Dawson). According to the author of the Cleo Dawson website, Daniel Garcia Ordaz, Sissy Spacek was set to star as Willy Westall (Spacek's mother Virginia was supposedly born in Mission). The actress and Cleo Dawson had been grand marshals of the town's Texas Citrus Fiesta Parade. Hosting the Mission premiere of her film *Carrie,* enthusiastic Spacek got carried away and announced that she would star in the film version of Dawson's book. It seems that the actress spoke too soon, and without consulting her handlers. Band was notified by Spacek's managers that the actress' status in the industry has changed; now that she was nominated for a Best Actress Oscar for *Carrie,* it wouldn't be a good idea for her to appear in a low-budget production like *She Came to the Valley.* Working fast, Band and his crew chose Idaho-born country singer-actress Ronee Blakley, who had already made an impact in *Nashville* (she was nominated for Best Supporting Actress for the film). Band hired another country singer, Texas-born Freddy Fender, to portray Pancho Villa. The production received the full backing of Dawson, who appears briefly as a party guest.

The film opens in 1913, when Willy Westall (Blakley) and her daughters are in their store with their friends when Mexican bandits attack their town and set fire to their store as well as the other buildings. After this attack, the film flashes back several years. Willy and her husband Pat (Dean Stockwell) trek across the plains on their journey to Texas; born along the way are two little girls named Amara and Srita (played by adorable real-life sisters Anna and Jennifer Jones). After establishing their home in Texas, Pat's legs are hurt by a falling crate and he has to hobble around on crutches while Willy handles all the chores. Drifter Bill Lester (Scott Glenn) shows up and immediately hits it off with the family; however, one day when Mexicans with guns show up close to the homestead, Bill is able to ride over to them and amazingly convince them to ride off peacefully. Willy and Pat wonder what Bill could have said to these dangerous-looking men to make them Vamoose.

Once the Westalls move to the growing community of Mission, they quickly make friends and soon open their store. They also run into Bill. The moody and frustrated Pat soon notices the growing attraction between Willy and Bill and, angry at the drifter, complains loudly about Pancho Villa's recent border raids which have resulted in the deaths of many townspeople and the burning of property. Bill defends Villa, claiming that Venustiano Carranza's men have been dressing up as *Villistas* and committing the raids so that the guerrilla chief will be blamed and the American government will send men after him. He also admits that he's been running guns to Villa.

Wanting to see the proof for himself, Pat decides to join Bill and go to the "bandits'" camp. Here they discover German military advisors named Klaus and Zimmer working with the *Carrancistas* (otherwise known as "Constitutionalists"). With German help, the *Carrancistas* have been attacking American border towns so that the U.S. will be preoccupied with Villa and not send their armies to help the Allies defend themselves against a belligerent Germany just before the start of World War I. When Bill and Pat open fire on them, the Germans and their Mexican helpers are killed. Pat is accidentally run over and killed by the Germans' car.

Instead of being distraught, Willy insists on being brought to Pancho Villa (Freddy Fender), who turns out to be pro–American. After the violent attack on Mission that begins the film, Villa and his men retaliate, killing all of Carranza's men. At the end, Bill says goodbye to Willy, at least for the time being, in order to inform the American garrison in San Antonio what's been happening. But there is an implication that he'll soon return to Willy and the girls.

The most fascinating part of the film is its take on the international politics behind the Mexican Revolution. Unfortunately, this is still buried beneath Cleo Dawson's bedtime-story version of Pancho Villa, a false depiction of the guerrilla chief that Hollywood had promoted for the past half century and beyond. Not an actor ordinarily, Fender wisely underplays, and though the depiction of the revolutionary by Dawson is clearly misleading, the singer is at least tolerable in the role, rejecting the usual shouting and comic set-pieces so prized by Ben Hecht, Howard Hawks and the Calles government in the Wallace Beery version.

Despite pointing out Venustiano Carranza's very real collaboration with the Kaiser's government (much as the Zimmermann telegram would reveal Carranza's desire for Germany to conquer America and return its southern border lands to Mexico), Dawson and screenwriters Band and Perilli also promote the fantasy that Villa was a victim of their machinations (his being framed for the attacks). Dawson was certainly around when Villa's men, on his direct orders, attacked Columbus, New Mexico, on March 9, 1916. The raiders who murdered nineteen American soldiers and civilians weren't sent by Carranza. Dawson also seemed to have forgotten the murders of American executives and workers by *Villistas* at Santa Isabel in 1915, as well as other atrocities ordered by the Centaur of the North. In fact, there is probable cause that Villa himself, still angry at Woodrow Wilson for choosing to support Carranza over him, might have himself actively collaborated with German officials in attacking America's border towns so that we'd be too distracted by Mexico to help the victims of German aggression in Europe. So far, there is no absolute proof of this; and it was not in Villa's usually xenophobic makeup to collaborate with the hated gringos, much less *German* gringos. Still, it could be possible.

She Came to the Valley (which really should have been called *They Came to the Valley*) premiered in several Texas border towns, including nearby McAllen where the showing would feature special quest Luz Corral, the first Mrs. Villa (and, obviously, not the *only* one). Confined to a wheelchair, she arrived at the premiere with an orderly and a nurse's aide. With an amazing amount of gall, she peddled her "book" about the life of her famous husband to the audience. According to Daniel Garcia Ordaz:

> Due to the exclusive presence of the famous widow, [*She Came to the Valley* producer-actor Sol] Marroquin said the actors and the movie were almost forgotten—practically ignored by both the public and the media alike. Mrs. Villa's orderly sold copies of a book called *Mi Vida con Pancho Villa* (*My Life with Pancho Villa*), which was more of a pamphlet than a book and included many photos and scant writing. No one, including the producers, had a problem with her orderly selling the booklets or with her autograph-granting.[10]

Luz Corral, still in denial over her husband's many, *many* loves besides her, ended her tacky appearance with an insult, though Freddy Fender certainly didn't take it that way. After seeing the film, someone from the media asked her what she thought of Fender's portrayal of her husband. Standing next to the singer-actor, she took a long look at him and, already forgetting the tactless attempt to sell her pamphlets at someone else's event, acidly replied, "Mi esposo era mas guapo": "My husband was better-looking."

She Came to the Valley was not a box office smash, perhaps verifying the belief of Sissy Spacek's handlers that it would be a failure not worthy of their client's participation. Now public domain, it's been retitled *She Came from the Valley* as well as *Texas in Flames* and *Texas Is Burning*, though a few buildings in Mission set on fire at the beginning of the film hardly qualifies as all of Texas being engulfed in flames.

A decade later, after a glut of films about the war in Vietnam, a major opponent of that war starred in a film that returned American audiences to the world of Revolutionary Mexico. Based on a novel by one of Mexico's greatest authors, it theorized about the disappearance of a famous American author down in Mexico and how he thought he could find his soul while aiding the fighters of the Revolution...

If Panama-born Mexican author Carlos Fuentes was anti–American and pro–Marxist, even *his* politics would be considered tame and subtle compared with the actress in charge of the film version of his novel *Old Gringo*.

In Fuentes' book, the story begins in Revolutionary Mexico. Seventy-one-year-old American author Ambrose Bierce crosses the border from El Paso and into Mexico, finds young rebel general Tomás Arroyo headquartered in a captured train and proclaims his desire to fight for the Revolution, a statement that provokes derisive laughter from Arroyo and his men. After challenging Arroyo to a shooting contest in which the old man's accuracy with his pistol is proven, the band takes "the gringo" more seriously and he is allowed to remain with them. At the same time, an American spinster is in Mexico where she had been recently hired to tutor the children of a *hacendado*. However, the wealthy man has just been overthrown by Arroyo and the young woman stubbornly refuses to leave the scene. Ultimately she also joins up with Arroyo's party of soldiers and their solderas and children. Meanwhile, Arroyo, a former peon whose mother had been raped and murdered by the *hacendado*, finds himself liking being head of the manor, all while claiming that he was really returning the land to the oppressed Indians.

The film *Old Gringo* for the most part remains loyal to Fuentes' book. But Jane Fonda (the star and producer) had *another* scene written into the film before the two American protagonists even get to Mexico. In the screenplay by credited scenarists Aida Bortnik and Luis Puenzo (both born in Buenos Aires), there is a scene set in Washington D.C. in 1913. In a speech before a writers' think tank, Ambrose Bierce (the aging Gregory Peck) indicts the group as "selling their pens to the highest bidder!" Watching this scene from high above the room, the spinsterish Harriet Winslow (the *rapidly* aging Fonda) is impressed with the author's righteous stand, though saner individuals might have called it rude and boorish behavior. Back in the home of her stodgy mother, Harriet brutally reveals to her mom that she knows that her father didn't die in the Spanish-American War, but actually fell in love with a Cuban woman he met; it seems that all the time they were mourning the old man's death, his grave was empty. Fed up with her ignorant and materialistic mom, she travels to Mexico to tutor the children of a *hacendado* named Miranda, with the spinster obviously ignorant of the dynamics behind the Revolution.

Both Americans meet rebel chieftain General Arroyo (TV's Jimmy Smits), a young hotshot follower of Villa whose swaggering persona hides psychic turmoil; he wants to take over Miranda's spread and return it to the Indians whose lands the government had always taken away (and whose lands would *continue* to be taken away by the Revolution's triumphant leaders—though you'd never know it from this film). Attacking the federals guarding the Miranda estate, the rebels triumph. Luis Puenzo's direction is superb during this sequence, and the action reminds one of Gries' filming of the slam-bang action in *100 Rifles*. One is sorry that Jim Brown, Burt Reynolds and Raquel Welch are not in this ponderous film.

Unfortunately, it's downhill from there, with the gringos getting to know their Mexican hosts, and with the locals (even their soldera-whores) judgmentally indicting Americans as judgmental. Through the film's dragging pace, some incredibly uninteresting events occur: Arroyo makes love to the virginal 50-year-old—I mean 31-year-old Harriet, the 71-year-old Bierce (played by the 73-year-old Peck) kisses Harriet on the mouth (yuck!), and peons have a dance party in the former owners' mansion, a truly boring scene that seems to go on forever.

Arroyo refuses to leave the Miranda spread. Waving around old Indian deeds locked away by the former owner, the former peon will not give orders for his men to decamp and join up with Villa. Meanwhile, Bierce gets crabbier and crabbier, indicting William Randolph

Hearst in a way the real Bierce never did, sampling one of the band's whores, and generally hoping to use the Mexicans' struggle to find an honorable way to die. After Harriet robs the cradle with the younger revolutionary, Bierce tries to provoke Arroyo's anger by riding around on the rebel chief's precious stallion. Instead of shooting the writer, the revolutionary actually kills his own horse. When Bierce sets fire to the precious deeds, telling Arroyo that they are

Anarchist Chic: Jimmy Smits (left), Gregory Peck and Jane Fonda in a publicity still for the film version of Carlos Fuentes' *Old Gringo*. The 50-year-old Fonda cast herself as Fuentes' 31-year-old heroine, desired by both a young revolutionary and an aging Ambrose Bierce. A poor screenplay and Fonda's miscasting caused the film to bomb at the box office.

just an excuse to stay at the hacienda, the rebel shoots the author three times in the back. During this scene, one almost applauds Peck's death; so stiff and cranky does he make Bierce that it is a relief when he's killed off so we don't have to see his horrible performance. Indeed, one is truly sorry Columbia dumped Burt Lancaster in the role and used Peck instead (with Lancaster filing a lawsuit against Fonda's company and Columbia shortly afterwards). If the audience has any rage for Arroyo, it's not for killing Bierce but for shooting that beautiful horse.

Pancho Villa takes charge and demotes Arroyo. Here, we see the best casting in the film, if not the most ironic, with Pedro Armendáriz Jr. cast as Villa. He's not as over-the-top as his old man when he played Villa, but it's an interesting portrayal of the guerrilla chief as a far more calculating man than he probably was in real life. In fact, acknowledging political realities, Armendáriz Jr.'s Villa knows that he must order Arroyo's death by firing squad in order to keep up revolutionary discipline. By remaining at the hacienda, Arroyo disobeyed orders to link up with Villa's band, and so must now pay the penalty.

Ironically, Arroyo now finds himself standing next to Bierce, the dead man propped up against the wall so that the firing squad's bullets will show that he was shot in the front; the back-shooting of a famous American author might cause an international incident. In real life, Villa clumsily handled the murder of Scottish rancher William Benton by first claiming that he didn't know what happened to the rancher, then claiming that the rancher was shot when he pulled a gun and tried to attack Villa, and then claiming that Benton was shot by a *Villista* firing squad without Villa's approval. In reality, none of the above happened. Benton had his head smashed in by a shovel-wielding Rudolfo Fierro and his body was dumped in an unmarked grave, never to be returned to his family. *Old Gringo* corrects the real-life Villa's blatant stupidity by showing us a canny Villa who realizes how bad things would look if the real story of Bierce's death was discovered. At times, Armendáriz Jr.'s Villa almost reminds one of de Fuentes' depiction of the guerrilla chief in *Let's Go with Pancho Villa*.

At the end, Harriet claims Bierce's body as her own father's, thus showing us why the author "disappeared" during his time in Mexico. Her reasoning is that no one will mourn him, though we assume the death of a famous author would actually bring out quite a crowd. With both her "lovers" dead, a now-grown Harriet takes an ox cart over a bridge back into the United States. She will never forget her time in Mexico—though audiences the world over will certainly try to...

Most, if not all, of the film's failure might be laid at the feet of its producer-star. In the novel, Harriet is described by Bierce as "young and beautiful," and Fuentes clearly puts her age at 31. When Fonda saw herself as this "young and beautiful" but cloistered spinster, the actress was 50. No makeup artist in the world was going to make her wrinkles and stretch marks magically disappear. A mannered and whining actress despite her two Oscars, Fonda's performance in *Old Gringo* devolves into a mass of wide-eyed reaction shots befitting a potential victim in a slasher movie rather than a cloistered woman dealing with the twisted politics of the Mexican Revolution. Why Fonda decided not to cast a younger actress (even her own niece Bridget!) remains a mystery, though we can only conclude that the old radical's vanity might have had something to do with it. While Fonda was enacting her role as a young woman who is desired by two men, off-screen her marriage to antiwar activist husband Tom Hayden was crumbling. Ultimately, he told Fonda that he was leaving her for a woman twenty years her junior on her 51st birthday.

According to the Internet Movie Database, *Old Gringo* returned a measly $3,574,256 in the United States. The TCM website claims it was actually less than even that, $2,335,652. The *Rolling Stone* magazine review (October 9, 1989) included the comment, "Instead of opening your eyes, it bores you blind."[11]

According to Roger Ebert in his October 6 review in the *Chicago Sun-Times*:

> *Old Gringo* makes a stab at social commentary, as when Arroyo, occupying the mansion as his headquarters, begins to act more like a landowner than like a revolutionary. But the film has a very thin story, and the director, Luis Puenzo, fills out the running time with expensively-staged crowd scenes that run on far too long. There is an endless battle, followed by another endless battle, followed by an endless dance, and so on, with hundreds of extras running through dust and dodging explosions while nothing much is actually happening.[12]

Unfortunately, films about revolutions in Mexico, a sub-genre of the western, were disappearing as the Revolution itself was reaching the hundred-year mark.

However, in the 21st century, a few Mexican-American co-productions (as well as American productions shot in Mexico) would keep the memory of the Revolution and its heroes alive for new generations…

VII

Centenario, 1990–2014

A Brief Look at the Films of Revolutionary Mexico as the Revolution Hits the 100-Year Mark

As the twentieth century started to fade away and a new century dawned, a new Hollywood returned to the subject of the Mexican Revolution, though with a satiric twist. Again focusing on Pancho Villa, a new cable TV film showed the absurdity of celebrity and myth-making while a war was going on. *And Starring Pancho Villa as himself* (2003) was both comedy and drama, and even a little biography, though farce seems to be the best fit for this TV-movie originally broadcast on HBO, as befits a teleplay by comedy writer Larry Gelbart.

The film dealt with the Mutual Film Company's collaboration with Pancho Villa to film the battle of Ojinaga. Though Antonio Banderas gave a good performance, it was still hard to accept him as Villa. He lacks the guerrilla chief's jowly face and slatternly appearance, as well as Villa's lightning-quick mood swings. One finds more character shadings in Domingo Soler's Villa in de Fuentes' *Let's Go with Pancho Villa*. Predictably, the film scores less in its recitation of history than in its satire, with Mutual's people (especially Eion Bailey as co-producer Frank N. Thayer) insisting that Villa confine his battles to daylight hours, with the exigencies of war taking a backseat to good cinematography. Unfortunately, Gelbart also makes B director Christy Cabanne into a pompous ass. As played by comic actor Michael McKean, the future director of low-budget westerns is depicted as a smarmy and, at times, cowardly individual who faints before Villa's mock firing squad and accepts the *Villistas'* whores as actresses (they have better on-camera reactions than the ordinary peons the company tried to enlist for the shoot). The depiction of him as a shallow Hollywood hack is amazing since Cabanne was a navy veteran and prolific novelist as well as filmmaker. The film also contrives a romance between the handsome Thayer and actress Teddy Sampson (Alexa Davalos). A definite asset to the production is Alan Arkin as Villa's Jewish mercenary Sam Drebben, the aging actor doing a superb job of giving appropriately acidic Jewish wisecracks and cynical observations (one of which called attention to William Randolph Hearst's territorial ambitions in Mexico). At the climax, Villa is assassinated driving his car in Parral, though the details are about as accurate as Pedro Armendáriz's death in the final film of his Pancho Villa trilogy; meaning, not very.

For the Greater Glory: The True Story of the Cristiada was released in the U.S. on June 1, 2012. Its box office failure was in the cards and the film was put on DVD a little over two months later, on September 11. The film starred Cuban actor Andy Garcia as Mexican Cristero leader General Enrique Gorostieta. With the production backed by the

Knights of Columbus, the film openly mentions the heroic general's service under dictator Victoriano Huerta, while avoiding the brutal implications of the association. (The film also avoids the fact that the atheist Gorostieta accepted the leadership of the Cristeros for the high salary they were paying him, as well as his ambition to take over the country from Calles.) In this situation, however, revolutionary roles are switched, with the leftist President Plutarco Elías Calles, a former general in the Revolution (a cold-blooded performance by Ruben Blades), now in power and Gorostieta, a former *Huertista* general, as the rebel chief.

Indeed, by the mid–1920s, Mexico had a new rebellion brewing, that of its Catholic population against the anti-clerical Calles regime. Carranza and Obregón fired the first shots when the two leftist leaders targeted Mexico's churches—and anyone who happened to be in them—for extermination.

In an ironic sidenote to the Cristero War, after the Knights of Columbus offered the Cristeros financial support, the Ku Klux Klan in the United States offered President Calles $10,000 to help fight the Catholic Church in Mexico. Certainly, the KKK didn't have to give Calles financial inducements to increase his hatred of Christianity. According to a telegram sent to Mexico's ambassador to France, Alberto Jose Pani Arteaga, Calles wrote that the Catholic Church in Mexico "is a political movement, and must be eliminated in order to proceed with a Socialist government free of religious hypnotism which fools the people.... Within one year without the sacraments, the people will forget the faith...."[1]

The Cristero Rebellion had brought back memories of the guerrilla warfare of the *Villistas*, though without a mercurial icon with a magnetic personality at the head of it. Yet there was no doubt that the Cristeros were essentially fighting for the same things the revolutionaries of the 1910s were fighting for, freedom; only this time the enemies of freedom were the very same revolutionary heroes who had triumphed over home-grown tyranny just a few years ago.

In 2013, Mexico gave us *Cinco de Mayo, La Batalla* (*The Fifth of May, the Battle*). Written and directed by Rafael Lara, it is a fast-paced historical drama with a documentary feel (including titles depicting timelines leading up to the day of the battle). *Cinco de Mayo* is a well-made and powerful film, both tribute to Mexican heroism and an insightful historical document. Unlike *Mexican War Cry*, this is no wartime propaganda piece; in the climactic battle, there is no Pedro Infante to inspire Mexican troops at Puebla with a patriotic song. The actual figures of history are all there: General Zaragoza (Kuno Becker), General Mejia (Pablo Abitia), Benito Juárez (Noe Hernández) and Porfirio Díaz (Pascacio López). A standout is Daniel Martinez's performance as Mexican Quizling General Leonardo Márquez. An arrogant and bigoted officer, he sees the Mexican campaign as spreading France's natural right to rule into North America, with a few well-placed bits of dialogue predicting the northern march of French troops onto American soil itself—that is, until the Mexican army taught them otherwise.

Much of the action is centered on a cowardly soldier named Juan (Christian Vazquez) and cute, dark-haired señorita, Citlali (the cute, dark-haired Liz Gallardo), who had lost her mom to a French bombardment. Juan wishes to desert, with a firing squad in his future if caught. He and Citlali witness a brutal French officer torture and murder his friend by hanging the poor young man on ropes between two horses. Later, Juan finds his courage and fights bravely during the *batalla*. Running into the murderer of his friend, he uses his own lariat to pull the officer's leg off. Dying, the torturer is verbally indicted by another French officer for his previous sadism: "You are *not* France!" he cries. In a film made about the French incursion from a Mexican filmmaker, this is a sharp turn from past portrayals of Napoleon's soldiers. Breaking with his colleagues' previous depictions of French soldiers as purely evil, writer-director Lara gives us a compassionate French officer who despises his superior's penchant for torturing Mexican prisoners. *Finally,* a Mexican director is saying that not all Frenchmen were racists or mass murderers; since he has the quality of mercy within him, the righteous Frenchman is merely arrested rather than killed outright.

The battle itself, with its non-stop, frenzied camera movement and loud, whizzing pyrotechnics of shot and shell (and tracer bullets, which weren't around during the early 1860s), is well-staged. Still, the film doesn't lessen the human story of how Juan finds his courage, of how a weaker nation beat a more powerful one (with the patient Zaragoza constantly having to restrain the eager Porfirio Díaz from launching a full frontal assault that the general knows will wipe the Mexicans out) and how the reluctant Citlali finally falls for the brave private.

Unfortunately, this fine film, despite its rousing patriotic feeling for Mexico and its unusually painstaking historical accuracy, lost money. It was released on DVD less than five months after its initial release...

Did the Revolution really end in 1920? Did the struggle for freedom in Mexico end as soon as the man who became president proclaimed its end? Or were the presidents who followed Venustiano Carranza and Álvaro Obregón only *slightly* less murderous, only *slightly* less corrupt? It would be hard to believe that the need for Revolution ever disappeared. In the years following 1920, the new federal army, now commanded by the former leaders of *La Revolución,* continued to murder enemies of the regime on a massive scale, especially Mexico's Native and Catholic populations.

Mexico, Hollywood and Europe depicted the Revolution in hundreds of films, all with their own particular slant on the conflict. The cliché has always been that there are heroes and villains on both sides of a conflict. Yet during the Mexican Revolution of the 1910s, even this cliché would be turned on its head. There were damn few heroes on the side of the *Porfirias* and *Huertistas,* and far less villains on the side of the *Revolutionistas*. In short, the Revolution *had* to be fought, if only to pull Mexico, kicking and screaming, into the glare of the twentieth century; if only that the children of Mexico should grow up in a nation devoid of all forms of inequality; if only that the poor had every opportunity to compete fairly with the rich and the affluent; if only that the men they elected benefitted the people they served, not their political cronies. The sad fact that the goal of the Revolution is still, to a certain extent, but a dream is beside the point. The Revolution may not have always fulfilled the dream, but it made the dream *far* more attainable.

The real heroes of Revolutionary Mexico then were not the Villas and Zapatas, the Carranzas and Obregóns and Calleses, and the thousands of politicos and guerrillas who claimed to have fought the good fight for the people, but the People themselves; those who lived in the land called Mexico, who fought and endured as much as any people in world history have for far too many years. It is these people and their heroism which rarely appeared on the screens of any nation, including Mexico itself. Their film industry lionized their revolutionary heroes who commanded armies, but never gave tribute to the citizen who *didn't* command an army, or carry a gun, or write manifestos; the citizens who triumphed by surviving and making a future for themselves and their children. They were indeed the *real* heroes of the Revolution.

As we watch the next classic of the Revolution from *Epoco Dorada* or watch our *yanqui* hero change from opportunist to fighter for justice, remember the people they fought for. There wouldn't have been any Revolution without them...

Chapter Notes

Chapter I

1. Marilyn Ann Moss, *Raoul Walsh: The True Adventures of Hollywood's Legendary Director* (Lexington: University Press of Kentucky, 2011), p. 109.
2. Ibid., p. 37.
3. Eugene O'Neill, *Ten "Lost" Plays* (New York: Dover, 1995), p. 190.
4. Ibid., p. 196.
5. Ibid., p. 201.
6. Harry M. Geduld and Ronald Gottesman, editors, *Sergei Eisentstein and Upton Sinclair: The Making & Unmaking of Que Viva Mexico!* (Bloomington: Indiana University Press, 1970), p. 417.
7. Mandy Merck, *Hollywood's American Tragedies: Dreiser, Eisenstein, Sternberg, Stevens* (Oxford: Berg, 2007), p. 40.
8. Bob Herzberg, *The Left Side of the Screen: Communist and Left-Wing Ideology in Hollywood, 1929–2009* (Jefferson, NC: McFarland, 2011), p. 16.
9. Geduld and Gottesman, p. 4.
10. Ibid., p. 4.
11. Merck, p. 16.
12. Geduld and Gottesman, p. 14.
13. Ibid., Letter from Hunter Kimbrough to Upton Sinclair, Dec. 22, 1930, p. 36
14. Ibid., p. 36
15. Ibid., p. 41.
16. Ibid., May 1931, p. 77.
17. Ibid., Letter from Upton Sinclair to L.I. Monosson, June 18, 1931, p. 86.
18. Ibid., Letter from Sergei Eisenstein to Upton Sinclair, p. 107.
19. Ibid., Letter from Upton Sinclair to Sergei Eisenstein, October 5, 1931, p. 152.
20. Ibid., Letter from Hunter Kimbrough to Upton Sinclair, October 9, 1931, p. 163.
21. Ibid., Letter from Upton Sinclair to L.I. Monosson, October 25, 1931, p. 167.
22. Ibid., Page 269.
23. Ibid., Telegram from Josef Stalin to Upton Sinclair, November 21, 1931, p. 212.
24. Joyce Milton, *Tramp: The Life of Charlie Chaplin* (New York: Da Capo Press, 1998), p. 304.
25. Frank McLynn, *Villa and Zapata: A History of the Mexican Revolution* (Philadelphia: Basic Books, 2009), p. 59.
26. Ibid., p. 60.
27. "Pancho Villa," Wikipedia.
28. Todd McCarthy, *Howard Hawks, the Grey Fox of Hollywood* (New York: Grove Press, 1997), p. 190.
29. McLynn, p. 128.
30. Ibid., p. 190.
31. Ibid., p. 190–191.
32. William MacAdams, *Ben Hecht: A Biography* (New York: Barricade Books, 1990), p. 157.
33. Ibid., p. 157.
34. E.J. Fleming, *The Fixers: Eddie Mannix, Howard Strickling and the MGM Publicity Machine* (Jefferson, NC: McFarland, 2005), pp. 175, 177.
35. "Viva Villa," taglines, Internet Movie Database.
36. Mordaunt Hall, *New York Times*, April 11, 1934.
37. Studio memo, February 24, 1934, Margaret Herrick Library, Special Collections.
38. Ibid.
39. Ibid.
40. McCarthy, p. 193–194.
41. Ibid., p. 194–195.
42. "Viva Villa," articles, Turner Classic Movies Database,
43. "Viva Villa," taglines, Internet Movie Database.
44. Mordaunt Hall, *New York Times*, April 11, 1934.
45. *Variety*, December 3, 1933.
46. Zuzana M. Pick, *Constructing the Image of the Mexican Revolution* (Austin: University of Texas Press), p. 86.
47. Ibid., p. 86.
48. "Interview with Domingo Soler," *Ilustrado*, February 13, 1936."
49. O'Malley quoted in Pick, p. 89.
50. Pick, p. 89.

Chapter II

1. Bernard F. Dick, *Hal Wallis, Producer to the Stars* (Lextington: University Press of Kentucky, 2004), p. 53.
2. Aeneas MacKenzie, Production Notes, September 30, 1937, USC–Warner Brothers (hereafter USC–WB) file on *Juarez*.
3. Ibid.
4. William Dieterle, Memo to Wolfgang Reinhardt, February 15, 1938, *Juarez*, USC-WB.
5. Paul J. Vanderwood, "Introduction," *Juarez*, Warner Brothers Screenplay Series (Madison, University of Wisconsin Press, 1983), p. 31–32.
6. Paul Muni, comment, *Juarez* pressbook, USC–WB.

7. Carl J. Mora, *Mexican Cinema: Reflections of a Society, 1896-1980* (Berkeley: University of California Press, 1982), p. 51.
8. Robert Emmet Long, editor, *Conversations with John Huston* (Jackson: University Press of Mississippi, 2001), p. 98.
9. Ibid., p. 98.
10. Paul Muni, Memo to Hal Wallis, March 1939, *Juarez*, USC-WB.
11. Ibid.
12. Paul J. Vanderberg, "Introduction," *Juarez*, p. 37–38.
13. Ibid.
14. Dick, p. 54.
15. Bosley Crowther, *New York Times*, February 15, 1940.

Chapter III

1. Dolores Tierney, *Emilio Fernández: Pictures in the Margins* (Manchester: Manchester University Press, 2007), p. 70–71.
2. "Dolores del Río," trivia, IMDB,
3. "Dolores del Río," Wikipedia.
4. *Hollywood Reporter*, undated; "Dolores del Río," Wikipedia.
5. Barbara Leaming, *Orson Welles: A Biography* (New York: Viking, 1985), p. 281.
6. Pick, notes on p. 228, Chapter 6, paragraph 2.
7. "The Torch," taglines, IMDB.
8. Norman Freeman, Letter to Joseph I, Breen, August 18, 1949, *Enamorada* file, Margaret Herrick Library.
9. Ibid.
10. "T.M.P.," *New York Times*, August 21, 1950.

Chapter IV

1. Steve Sekely, Letter to Joseph Breen, March 6, 1950, *The Torch* file, Margaret Herrick Library.
2. Ronald L. Davis, *Zachary Scott: Hollywood's Sophisticated Cad* (Jackson: University Press of Mississippi, 2006), p. 148.
3. Ibid., p. 149.
4. Ibid., p. 148.
5. John Steinbeck, Robert E. Morsberger, editor, *Zapata: A Newly Discovered Narrative by John Steinbeck with His Screenplay of* Viva Zapata! (New York: Penguin, 1993), p. 53.
6. Zanuck to Elia Kazan and John Steinbeck, May 3, 1950," in Rudy Behlmer, editor, *Memos from Darryl F. Zanuck: The Golden Years at Twentieth Century–Fox* (New York: Grove Press, 1993), p. 171.
7. Ibid., p. 174.
8. Ibid., Memo to Kazan, May 2, 1951, p. 178.
9. Richard Schickel, *Elia Kazan: A Biography* (New York: Harper-Collins, 2005), p. 238.
10. Ibid., p. 239.
11. Ibid., p. 247.
12. Joseph Breen, Letter to Alex Gottlieb, August 21, 1952, *The Fighter* file, Margaret Herrick Library.
13. Joseph Breen, Letter to Universal-International producer William Gordon, February 19, 1953, *Wings of the Hawk* file, Margaret Herrick Library.
14. Ibid.
15. Gene Blottner, *Universal-International Westerns, 1947–1963* (Jefferson, NC: McFarland, 2000), p. 306.
16. C. Courtney Joyner, *The Westerners: Interviews with Actors, Directors, Writers and Producers* (Jefferson, NC: McFarland, 2009), p. 106.
17. Joseph Breen, Letter to William Gordon, May 29, 1953, *Border River* file, Margaret Herrick Library.
18. "Brog" from *Variety*, January 4, 1954.
19. Joseph Breen, Letter to Flora Productions official Cheri Redmonds, February 22, 1954, *Vera Cruz* file, Margaret Herrick Library.
20. Kate Buford, *Burt Lancaster: An American Life* (New York: Da Capo Press, 2000), p. 140.
21. Shelley Winters, *Shelley II: The Middle of My Century* (New York: Simon & Schuster, 1989), p. 7–8.
22. "Earl Felton," trivia, IMDB.
23. Earl Felton, cable to Robert Mitchum, undated, *Bandido* file, Margaret Herrick Library.
24. Geoffrey Shurlock, Letter to Frank McFadden, October 18, 1955.
25. "Bandido," taglines, IMBD.
26. "Brog" of *Variety*, August 14, 1956.
27. Unknown reviewer, *Hollywood Reporter*, August 14, 1956.
28. Geoffrey Shurlock, Letter to Frank McFadden, October 18, 1955.
29. Shurlock, Letter to McFadden, November 8, 1955.
30. Lee Server, *Robert Mitchum: "Baby, I Don't Care"* (New York: St. Martin's Press, 2001), p. 301.
31. "Margia Dean Interview," *Western Clippings*, no date, www.westernclippings.com.
32. Ibid.
33. Linda Hall, *Dolores del Río: Beauty in Light and Shadow* (Stanford, CA: Stanford University Press, 2013), p. 255.
34. Ibid., p. 256.
35. Ibid., p. 256.
36. Howard Thompson, *New York Times*, November 1, 1961

Chapter V

1. Alberto J. Misrachi, Letter to John Huston, June 25, 1963, file on Pedro Armendáriz, Margaret Herrick Library.
2. Michael Atkinson, "Back in the Saddle," *Village Voice*, March 29, 2005.
3. David Weddle, *"If They Move, Kill 'Em!": The Life and Times of Sam Peckinpah* (New York: Grove Press, 1995), p. 301.
4. Atkinson.
5. Weddle, p. 231.
6. Marshal Fine, *Bloody Sam: The Life and Times of Sam Peckinpah* (New York: Donald I. Fine, 1991), p. 100.
7. James L. Fields, Letter to Hal Fisher, January 26, 1965, *The Professionals* file, Margaret Herrick Library.
8. Ibid.

9. Ibid.
10. Frank O'Rourke, Letter to Richard Brooks, April 15, 1965, *The Professionals* file, Margaret Herrick Library.
11. Billy Gordon, Letter to Mike Frankovich, June 1, 1965, Margaret Herrick Library.
12. Jack H. Wiener, Letter to R. Ferguson, December 20, 1966, Margaret Herrick Library.
13. Richard Schickel, Letter to Richard Brooks, November 7, 1966, Margaret Herrick Library.
14. Server, p. 418.
15. Fine, p. 111.
16. Server, p. 218.
17. John S.D. Eisenhower, *Intervention! The United States and the Mexican Revolution, 1913–1917* (New York: W.W. Norton & Co., 1993), p. 254–255.
18. Ibid., p. 255.
19. William Douglas Lansford, *Pancho Villa* (Los Angeles: Sherbourne Press, 1965), Appendix A, p. 271.
20. Roger Ebert, *Chicago-Sun Times*, June 25, 1968.
21. McLynn, p. 33.
22. Ibid., p. 104.
23. Bosley Crowther, *New York Times*, March 27, 1969.
24. Roger Ebert, *Chicago Sun-Times*, April 9, 1969.
25. Joe Medjuck, "Interview," in Kevin J. Hayes, editor, *Sam Peckinpah: Interviews* (Jackson: University Press of Mississippi, 1008), p. 26.
26. Weddle, p. 322.
27. Ibid., p. 322.
28. Ibid.
29. "The Wild Bunch," budget, IMDB.
30. Sam Peckinpah, Letter to Richard Lederer, March 9, 1970.
31. "The Wild Bunch," release dates, IMDB.
32. Vincent Canby, *New York Times*, June 26, 1969.
33. Peter Stack, *San Francisco Chronicle*, March 3, 1995.
34. Roger Ebert, *Chicago Sun-Times*, December 2, 1969.

Chapter VI

1. "Two Mules for Sister Sara," taglines, IMDB.
2. Eric Sherman and Martin Rubin, editors, *The Director's Event* (New York: Atheneum, 1969), p. 73.
3. Don Siegel, *A Siegel Film: An Autobiography* (London: Faber & Faber, 1993), p. 323.
4. Ibid., p. 323.
5. "Two Mules for Sister Sara," box office, IMDB.
6. Roger Greenspan, *New York Times*, June 25, 1970.
7. Roger Ebert, *Chicago Sun-Times*, June 1, 1970.
8. "Cannon for Cordoba," taglines, IMDB.
9. J. Hoberman, "The Revolution Will Be Westernized: Leone's Nutty Leftist Epic," *Village Voice*, November 21, 2003.
10. Cleo Dawson: An Inventory of Her Papers, 1972–1979, www.utexas.edu.
11. Unknown reviewer, *Rolling Stone*, October 9, 1989.
12. Roger Ebert, *Chicago Sun-Times*, October 6, 1989.

Chapter VII

1. "The Cristero War," Wikipedia.

Bibliography

Atkinson, Michael. "Back in the Saddle," *Village Voice*, March 29, 2005. www.villagevoice.com.

Behlmer, Rudy, editor. *Inside Warner Brothers, 1935–1951*. New York: Simon & Schuster, 1985.

———. *Memos from Darryl F. Zanuck: The Golden Years of Twentieth Cenutry Fox*. New York: Grove Press, 1993.

———. *Memos from David O. Selznick*. New York: Modern Library, 2000.

Billingsley, Kenneth Lloyd. *Hollywood Party: How Communism Seduced the American Film Industry in the 1930s and 1940s*. Rocklin, CA: Prima Publishing, 1998.

Blancke, W. Wendell. *Juárez of Mexico*. New York: Praeger, 1971.

Blottner, Gene. *Universal-International Westerns, 1947–1963*. Jefferson, NC: McFarland, 2000.

Buford, Kate. *Burt Lancaster: An American Life*. New York: Da Capo Press, 2000.

Canby, Vincent. Film Reviews, *New York Times*, multiple dates.

Cleo Dawson: An Inventory of Her Papers, 1972–1979, Texas Archival Resources Dateline, at the Southwest Collection/Special Collections Library. www.utexas.edu.

Clinch, Minty. *Burt Lancaster*. Briarcliff Manor, NY: Stein & Day, 1984

Crowther, Bosley. Film Reviews, *New York Times*, multiple dates.

Daniel, Douglass K. *Tough as Nails: The Life and Films of Richard Brooks*. Madison: University of Wisconsin Press, 2011.

Dashiell, Chris. "Eisenstein's Mexican Dream," *CineScene*, 1998. www.cinescene.com.

Davis, Ronald L. *Zachary Scott: Hollywood's Sophisticated Cad*. Jackson: University Press of Mississippi, 2006.

De Orellana, Margarita. *Filming Pancho: How Hollywood Filmed the Mexican Revolution*. London: Verso Publishing, 2009.

Dick, Bernard F. *Hal Wallis: Producer to the Stars*. Lexington: University Press of Kentucky, 2004.

Doherty, Thomas. *Hollywood's Censor: Joseph I. Breen and the Production Code Administration*. New York: Columbia University Press, 2007.

Ebert, Roger. Film Reviews, *Chicago Sun-Times*, mulitple dates.

Eisenhower, John S.D. *Intervention! The United States and the Mexican Revolution, 1913–1917*. New York: W.W. Norton & Co., 1993.

Eisenstein, Sergei, and Richard Taylor, editor. *The Eisenstein Reader*. London: Palgrave-Macmillan, 1998.

Eyman, Scott. *Print the Legend*. Baltimore, MD: Johns Hopkins University Press, 1999.

Fine, Marshall. *Bloody Sam: The Life and Times of Sam Peckinpah*. New York: Donald I. Fine, 1991.

Fleming, E.J. *The Fixers: Eddie Mannix, Howard Strickling and the MGM Publicity Machine*. Jefferson, NC: McFarland, 2005.

Frayling, Christopher. *Sergio Leone: Something to Do with Death*. Minneapolis: University of Minnesota Press, 200, 2012.

Fuentes, Carlos. *Old Gringo*. New York: Harper & Row, 1985.

García Ordaz, Daniel. "Cleo Dawson: The Making of the Film, *She Came to the Valley*." http://www.angelfire.com/folk/artes/artists/artist/cleo.html.

Geduld, Harry M., and Ronald Gottesman. *Sergei Eisenstein and Upton Sinclair: The Making & The Unmaking of* Qué Viva México! Bloomington: Indiana University Press, 1970.

Greene, Graham. *The Power and the Glory*. New York: Viking Press, 1940.

Grieb, Kenneth J. *The United States and Huerta*. Lincoln: University of Nebraska Press, 1969.

Hall, Linda. *Dolores del Río: Beauty in Light and Shadow*. Stanford, CA: Stanford University Press, 2013.

Hall, Mordaunt. Film Reviews, *New York Times*, multiple dates.

Hayes, Kevin J., editor. *Sam Peckinpah: Interviews*. Jackson: University Press of Mississippi, 2008.

"Herbert Kline, Obituary." *The Independent*, February 18, 1999, www.independent.co.uk.

Hershfield, Joanne, and David R. Maciel. *Mexico's Cinema: A Century of Film and Filmmakers*. Wilmington, DE: Scholarly Resources, 1999.

Herzberg, Bob. *Hang 'Em High: Law and Disorder in Western Films and Literature.* Jefferson, NC: McFarland, 2013.

_____. *The Left Side of the Screen: Communist and Left-Wing Ideology in Hollywood, 1929–2009.* Jefferson, NC: McFarland, 2011.

_____. *Shooting Scripts: From Pulp Western to Film.* Jefferson, NC, McFarland, 2005.

Hoberman, J. "The Revolution Will Be Westernized: Leone's Nutty Leftist Epic," *Village Voice*, November 18, 2003. www.villagevoice.com.

Holden, Stephen. "Meet Eisenstein: Punker, Misfit and Gay Renegade," *New York Times*, January 2, 2001.

Jarlett, Franklin. *Robert Ryan: A Biography and Critical Filmography.* Jefferson, NC: McFarland, 1990.

Joyner, C. Courtney. *The Westerners: Interviews with Actors, Directors, Writers and Producers.* Jefferson, NC: McFarland, 2009.

Kapsis, Robert E., and Cathie Coblentz, editors. *Clint Eastwood: Interviews.* Jackson: University Press of Mississippi, 1999.

Kitses, Jim. *Horizons West.* Bloomington: Indiana University Press, 1969.

Lansford, William Douglas. *Pancho Villa.* Los Angeles: Sherbourne Press, 1965.

Lawrence, Jerome. *Actor: The Life and Times of Paul Muni.* New York: Samuel French, 1974.

Leaming, Barbara. *Orson Welles: A Biography.* New York: Viking, 1985.

Long, Robert Emmet. *Conversations with John Huston.* Jackson: University Press of Mississippi, 2001.

MacAdams, William. *Ben Hecht: A Biography.* New York: Barricade Books, 1990.

Manso, Peter. *Brando: The Biography.* New York: Hyperion Books, 1994.

"Margia Dean Interview." *Western Clippings*, no date. www.westernclippings.com.

Marriot, Barbara. *Outlaw Tales of New Mexico.* Guilford, CT: Globe Pequot Press, 2007.

McCarthy, Todd. *Howard Hawks, the Grey Fox of Hollywood.* New York: Grove Press, 1997.

McLynn, Frank. *Villa and Zapata: A History of the Mexican Revolution.* Philadelphia: Basic Books, 2000.

Merck, Mandy. *Hollywood's American Tragedies: Dreiser, Eisenstein, Sternberg, Stevens.* Oxford: Berg, 2007.

Meyers, Jeffrey. *Gary Cooper: American Hero.* London, Aurum Press, 1998.

Milton, Joyce. *Tramp: The Life of Charlie Chaplin.* New York: Da Capo Press, 1998.

Mora, Carl J. *Mexican Cinema: Reflections of a Society, 1896–1980.* Berkeley: University of California Press, 1982.

Moss, Marilyn Ann. *Raoul Walsh: The True Adventures of Hollywood's Legendary Director.* Lexington: University Press of Kentucky, 2011.

Mulcahey, Martin. "The First Latina to Conquer Hollywood," *Film International*, December 29, 2011. www.filmint.com.

O'Neill, Eugene. *Ten "Lost" Plays.* New York: Dover, 1995.

O'Rourke, Frank. *The Professionals.* New York: New American Library, 1964.

Pick, Zuzana M. *Constructing the Image of the Mexican Revolution.* Austin: University of Texas Press, 2010.

Robert, Randy and, James S. Olson. *John Wayne: American.* New York: Simon & Schuster, 1995.

Sarf, Wayne Michael. *God Bless You, Buffalo Bill: A Layman's Guide to History and the Western Film.* East Brunswick, NJ: Cornwall Books, 1983.

Scheina, Robert L. *Santa Anna: A Curse Upon Mexico.* Washington, D.C.: Potomac Books, Inc, 2002.

_____. *Villa: Soldier of the Mexican Revolution.* Washington, D.C.: Potomac Books, Inc., 2004.

Schickel, Richard. *Clint Eastwood: A Biography.* New York: Alfred A. Knopf, 1996.

_____. *Elia Kazan: A Biography.* New York: HarperCollins, 2005.

Server, Lee. *Robert Mitchum: "Baby, I Don't Care."* New York: St. Martin's Press, 2001.

Sherman, Eric, and Martin Rubin. *The Director's Event.* New York: Atheneum, 1969.

Siegel, Don. *A Siegel Film: An Autobiography.* London: Faber & Faber, 1993.

Simmons, Garner. *Peckinpah: A Portrait in Montage.* New York: Limelight Editions, 1976, 1998.

Smith, Wendy. *Real Life: The Group Theater and American Drama, 1931–1940.* New York: Alfred A. Knopf, 1990.

Stack, Peter. "'Wild Bunch' Rides Again/Director's Cut of '69 Classic," *San Francisco Chronicle*, March 3, 1995. www.sfgate.com.

Steinbeck, John, and Robert E. Morsberger, editor. *Zapata: A Newly Disovered Narrative By John Steinbeck, with His Screenplay of* Viva Zapata. New York: Penguin, 1993.

Stout, Joseph A., Jr. *Border Conflict: Villistas, Carrancistas and the Punitive Expedition 1915–1920.* Fort Worth: Texas Christian University Press, 1999.

Thompson, Howard. Film Reviews, *New York Times*, multiple dates.

Tierney, Dolores. *Emilio Fernández: Pictures in the Margins.* Manchester: Manchester University Press, 2007.

Travers, Peter. "The Old Gringo," *Rolling Stone*, October 6, 1989. www.rollingstone.com.

Tuchman, Barbara W. *The Zimmermann Telegram.* New York: Balantine Books, 1958, 1966.

Vanderwood, Paul J. *Disorder and Progress: Bandits, Police and Mexican Development.* Lincoln: University of Nebraska Press, 1981.

____, editor, and Tino Balio, series editor. *Juarez*. Warner Brothers Screenplay Series. Madison: University of Wisconsin Press, 1983.

Warner Brothers Files. Margaret Herrick Library, Special Collections Desk. University of Southern California, School of Cinema Arts.

Weddle, David. *"If They Move, Kill 'Em!": The Life and Times of Sam Peckinpah*. New York: Grove Press, 1995.

Werfel, Franz, and Ruth Langer. *Juarez and Maximilian: A Dramatic History in Three Phases and Thirteen Pictures*. New York: Published for the Theatre Guild by Simon & Schuster, 1926.

Winters, Shelley. *Shelley II: The Middle of My Century*. New York: Simon & Schuster, 1989.

Index

Las Abandonadas 78, 151
Acosta, Rudolfo 121, 143
Adams, Gerald Grayson 120
Adams, Julie 120, 121, 123
Aguillar, Antonio 154, 155, 213
Aguillar, Luis 158
Ahearn, Brian 61, 66, 73
Albert, Marvin H. 186, 188
Aldrich, Robert 129, 131
Alexander Nevsky 21
All Through the Night 76
And Pancho Villa Starring as Himself 229
Angelitos Negros 90
Ankrum, Morris 129
Apache 129
Arau, Alfonso 193
Argento, Dario 200–201, 203
Arkin, Alan 229
Armendáriz, Pedro 75–78, 92–94, 98–99, 105, 125–126, 128, 137, 147, 151–152, 159–160
Armendáriz, Pedro, Jr. 197, 227
Armstrong, R.G. 161
Arness, James 197
Asi era Pancho Villa 145–147
Atwill, Lionel 71, 72, 73–74

Band, Albert 222, 223
Banderas, Antonio 229
Bandido 141–145
Barrymore, John 37
Bart, Jean 70, 71
Bedoya, Alfonso 78, 93, 101–102, 126, 128
Beery, Noah, Jr. 121–122, 123
Beery, Wallace 27, 28–29, 34, 35, 106, 150, 179
Bellamy, Ralph 168
Benton, William 179, 227
Berger, Santa 161
Beswick, Martine 181
Black, Maurice 47, 48
Blades, Ruben 230
Blakely, Ronee 223
Blood and Sand (novel) 18
Boetticher, Budd 119–120, 121, 123–125, 133, 203–204, 205, 206–207
Bogart, Humphrey 38, 76
Border River 4, 125–128, 160, 163

Borgnine, Ernest 129, 191, 194
Braeden, Eric 187
Brando, Marlon 106, 109, 111, 113
Brandon, Henry 129–130, 142
Breen, Joseph I. 2–3, 49, 98, 100, 117, 121, 126, 131, 142
Brent, Evelyn 71, 72
Bresler, Jerry 162, 163
Broccoli, Albert "Cubby" 29, 159
Broken Lance (film) 153
Bronson, Charles 129, 174, 175, 177, 179
Brooks, Richard 166, 167–168, 170, 171
Brown, Jim 186, 187–188, 190
Brown, Vanessa 116, 119
Brynner, Yul 171–173, 174–175, 178
A Bullet for the General 148, 180–183

Cabanne, William "Christy" 7–9, 229
Café Colon 156
Calhoun, Rory 133–135, 136
The Californio 186, 189, 190
Calleia, Joseph 62, 134
Calles, Plutarco Elias 2, 14, 25–28, 34, 39, 69, 185, 230
Camacho, Manuel Avila 79, 87
Cameron, Rod 180
Capone, Al 79
Cárdenas, Lázaro 26, 27–28, 50, 56–57, 68–69
Cardinale, Claudia 169
Carey, Harry, Jr. 197
Carlota (Empress) 52–53, 61–62, 65, 66, 67–68, 86, 102, 153
Carranza, Venustiano 2, 3, 25, 111, 112, 158, 173, 178, 185, 210, 223–224
Carrillo, Leo 30, 50, 82, 148
Castel, Lou 181, 182
Chaplin, Charles 11, 12, 95
Chodorov, Joseph 71
Cinco de Mayo, La Batalla 208, 230–231
Citizen Kane 82–83
Cobb, Lee J. 117
Coburn, James 216, 217
Comanche 133

Connors, Chuck 220
The Conqueror 99
Conte, Richard 117, 118, 119
Conway, Jack 24, 34, 35, 39
Cook, Donald 31
Cooper, Gary 95, 129, 130–132
Corral, Luz 24, 179, 224
Coy, Walter 221
Crisp, Donald 61, 72, 73
Cuando ¡Viva Villa!...es la Muerte 157
La Cucaracha 150–151, 153–155

Daly, James 201, 202
Damiano, Damiani 180
Darcel, Denise 130, 132
Davis, Bette 53, 58–59, 72, 73–74, 83, 151
Dawson, Cleo 221–222, 223
Dead Ringer 151
Dean, Margia 148, 149–150
DeCarlo, Yvonne 126, 128
De Cordova, Arturo 102, 103
de Fuentes, Fernando 41, 45, 46, 85, 227, 229
Dekker, Albert 192
De Kova, Frank 112
del Rio, Dolores 39, 80–83, 91–92, 95, 151, 152, 213
de Novara, Medea 69, 70, 71, 73–74
De Toth, André 104–105
Díaz, Porfirio 1, 2, 122, 167, 184–185
Dieterle, William 56, 58, 65
Digges, Dudley 54–55
Django Unchained 207
La Doña Barbara 85, 151
La Doña Diabla 85
La Doña Perfecta 151, 153
Douglas, Kirk 131
Dreiser, Theodore 11
Duck, You Sucker! (*A Fistful of Dynamite*) 215–219
Duel, Peter 210, 211–212

Eastwood, Clint 180, 203–204
Eisenstein, Sergei M. 10–21
Enamorada 85, 93–95, 96, 151
Erwin, Stuart 30, 35, 39
La Escondida 137–140

239

Index

Fairbanks, Douglas 11, 12
Farrow, John 141
Felix, Maria 84–85, 93, 94, 97, 98, 137, 151, 157, 159, 213, 215
Felton, Earl 141–142, 144
Fender, Freddy 223, 224
Fernandez, Emilio 76–77, 78–80, 91–92, 93, 94, 96, 151–152, 153, 155, 192
Fierro, Rudolfo 30, 40, 148, 150, 167, 174, 175, 227
The Fighter 116–119
Figueroa, Gabriel 46, 92, 96, 107–108, 151, 152, 179, 207, 215
Finkel, Abem 66
The Five-Man Army 200–203
Fleischer, Richard 141, 142, 144, 145
Fleming, Ian 159–160
Flor Silvestre 78, 91–93
Fonda, Henry 152, 168
Fonda, Jane 212, 225, 226, 227
For the Greater Glory 229–230
Ford, Glenn 124
Ford, John 106, 151, 152–153
Fowley, Douglas 142
Franz Joseph (Emperor) 61
From Russia with Love 75, 159–160
Fuentes, Carlos 224, 225, 227
The Fugitive (1947) 106, 159–160

Garcia, Andy 229
Garfield, John 59, 60, 64–65
Gavaldon, Roberto 137, 138, 140
La Generala 212–215
Girl of the Rio 39, 82
Glenn, Scott 223
Goddard, Paulette 95–96, 97, 98–99
Goebbels, Dr. Joseph 10
Gomez, Marie 169
Gonzalez, Gen. Pablo 112
Gordon, Bernard 220
Gordon, Don 210
Gottlieb, Alex 116, 117
Granger, Stewart 182
Grant, Gen. Ulysses S. 127
Graves, Peter 201, 203
Greene, Graham 151, 152
Gries, Tom 186
Griffith, D.W. 7–8, 9
Guajardo, Col. Jesus 112

Harris, Julie 106
Harris, Richard 161
Hawks, Howard 24–25, 29, 36–37, 38–39
Hayden, Tom 227
Hayes, Ira 184
Hearst, William Randolph 82
Hecht, Ben 24, 30, 32, 25, 105, 179
Heflin, Van 120, 121, 124
Hemingway, Ernest 159, 160

Henry, Will 46
Herzberg, Harry 136
Heston, Charlton 161, 163, 186
Himmler, Heinrich 50
Hitler, Adolf 66, 74, 86, 116
Holden, William 191, 194
Hoyos, Rudolfo, Jr. 117, 147–148, 149
Hudson, Rock 197, 198
Huerta, Gen. Victoriano 2, 3, 33, 122, 176, 177, 194, 230
Huffaker, Clair 183, 186, 187, 190
Huston, John 57, 60, 66–67, 71, 160

El Indio 76
Infante, Pedro 88, 90–91
Ireland, Jill 177
Ireland, John 177
La Isla de la Pasion 76, 77
Ivan the Terrible, Parts I & II 17

James, Rian 151
Johnson, Pres. Andrew 127
Johnson, Ben 161, 191, 195, 197
Jones, L.Q. 167, 192
Journey to Shiloh (film) 46
Journey to Shiloh (novel) 46
Juana Gallo 157–159, 214
Juarez 3, 4, 49, 53, 56–61, 62–67, 68–69, 70, 72, 73
Juárez, Benito 1, 3–4, 51–53, 63–64, 68–69, 86–87, 128, 161
Juarez and Maximilian (play) 53–56
Juárez y Maximiliano 53, 69, 70
The Jungle (the novel) 12
Jurado, Katy 153

Kandel, Aben 116
Kazan, Elia 24, 33, 105, 106–107, 108, 110, 111, 112–113, 119
Keene, Tom 46–47
Keith, Brian 148, 149, 150
Kimbrough, Hunter 13–18
Kinski, Klaus 181
Kline, Herbert 116, 117, 118, 119
Knox, Alexander 177
Korngold, Erich Wolfgang 61, 65–66, 71, 72
Kulik, Buzz 172, 173, 174

Lake, Veronica 95, 96, 101, 103, 104–105
Lamas, Fernando 187
Lancaster, Burt 129, 131, 132, 165, 167, 168, 169, 227
Lane, Abbe 121
Lansford, William Douglas 171, 173, 175, 176, 178–179
Leone, Sergio 215–216, 217, 218–219
Let's Go with Pancho Villa! 41–44, 46, 85, 137, 213, 227, 229
Lewis, George J. 110, 126

The Life of General Villa 5, 8–9
Lincoln, Abraham 60, 62–63, 126, 127
Lom, Herbert 110–111, 176
London, Jack 113–114, 115, 118
Love, Montague 61, 64
Lunt, Alfred 54

MacArthur, Charles 25
Mackenzie, Aeneas 57–58, 60, 66, 71
Mackenzie, Col. Ranold S. "Bad Hand" 160–161
MacLaine, Shirley 203, 204, 205–206, 207
MacLeod, Robert 183, 186, 190
Macready, George 130
The Mad Empress 70–74
Madero, Francisco, Jr. 2, 21, 106–107, 146, 174, 177, 185, 194
The Magnificent Seven 132
Major Dundee 4, 160–164
Maltz, Albert 204
The Man from the Alamo 123
Mann, Anthony 129
Maria Candelaria 78
The Mark of Zorro (1920) 12
Martin, Strother 192
Marvin, Lee 165, 168, 169
Maximilian (Emperor) 52–53, 61–62, 65, 66, 67–68, 86, 102
Mayer, Louis B. 15, 27, 38–39
McCrea, Joel 82, 125, 126, 128, 160
McGlaglen, Andrew 196, 198
The Mexican (short story) 11, 113–114, 118
Mexicanos el Grito de Guerra 87–90
Milland, Ray 96
Miller, Marvin 96
Miranda, Carmen 51
Mitchum, Robert 141, 142, 143, 145, 172
Moctezuma, Carlos Lopez 146, 157
Montalban, Ricardo 105–106
Montiel, Sara (Sarita) 129, 131
Morricone, Ennio 201, 202, 204–205, 218
The Movie Man 9–10
La Mujer Que Yo Perdí 90
Las Mujeres de Mi General 91
A Mule for the Marquesa 165–166
Muni, Paul 53, 56–57, 58, 59, 61, 62–63, 66–67
Muñoz, Rafael F. 41, 45
Murphy, Audie 222

Nagel, Conrad 71, 73
Napoleon III (Emperor) 61, 65, 72–73, 86, 128
Negrete, Jorge 85, 137
Nelson, Baby-face 79

Index

Oates, Warren 161, 191, 195
Obregon, Alvaro 2, 25–26, 3536, 146, 157, 177, 178, 179, 185
O'Brien, Edmond 191
Old Gringo (film) 225–228
Old Gringo (novel) 224–225, 227
100 Rifles 168, 186–190, 217
O'Neill, Eugene 9, 10
O'Neill, Henry 63
O'Rourke, Frank 164–165, 166–167, 168
Orozco, Pascual, Jr. 122–123, 167, 174
La Otra 94, 151

Paiva, Nestor 112
Palacios, Begoñia 161, 162–163, 173
Palance, Jack 169
Pancho Villa (film) 220–221
Pancho Villa (novel) 171, 173
Pancho Villa y Valentina 157
Peck, Gregory 225, 226
Peckinpah, Sam 4, 67, 160, 161, 162–163, 164, 171, 173, 174, 175, 178, 191, 192
Peppard, George 209, 211
La Perla 105
Pershing, Gen. John J. ("Blackjack") 142, 176, 209, 210, 212
Peters, Jean 106, 110
The Phantom Crown 53–54, 70
Piana, Maria Teresa 72, 102
Pinchon, Edgecumb 23–24, 105, 179
Powell, Dick 159
Power, Tyrone 106
The Professionals 166–171

Que Viva Mexico! 10–21
Quinn, Anthony 106, 109, 110, 213

Rains, Claude 60, 71, 88
The Red Badge of Courage (film) 222
Reed, Alan 111, 148
Reed, Walter 96
Reinhardt, Max 54
Reinhardt, Wolfgang 57, 60, 66, 71
Reynolds, Burt 186, 187, 188, 190
Rio Escondido 85
Robinson, Edward G. 54, 55
Rodriguez, Ismael 46, 87–88, 90–91, 145, 146, 147, 155, 157
Roland, Gilbert 61, 133, 135, 136, 137, 143
Romero, Cesar 129, 148, 149

Roosevelt, Pres. Franklin D. 49–50, 69
Russell, John 210
Ryan, Robert 165, 168, 192

Sanchez, Jaime 191
Sanders, Hugh 117
Savalas, Telly 148, 172, 220
Schildkraut, Joseph 32, 39
Scott, Randolph 160
Scott, Zachary 102, 103–104, 142
Sekely, Steve 100, 104–105
Selznick, David O. 23, 24, 25
She Came to the Valley (film) 222
She Came to the Valley (novel) 222
Sherman, George 125, 127
Shurlock, Geoffrey 144–145
Siegel, Don 204, 205, 206, 207–208
Silva, Henry 111
Silvera, Frank 110–111, 116, 119
Sinclair, Mary Craig 13, 14, 20
Sinclair, Upton 12–20
Sitting Bull 145
Smits, Jimmy 225, 226
Soler, Domingo 41, 45–46, 137
Sondergard, Gale 60, 72
Soy Puro Mexicano! 76–78
Spacek, Sissy 222–223
Spencer, Budd 201
Stalin, Joseph 11, 14, 20, 108, 111, 116
Stanwyck, Barbara 84, 85
Steiger, Rod 216
Steinbeck, John 24, 105, 106–107, 108, 111, 113
Steiner, Max 142
Stockwell, Dean 223
Strode, Woody 165, 168
Stronghold 100–105, 125, 163

Talbot, Lyle 123
Taylor, Dub 192, 198
Taylor, Elizabeth 203–204
Taylor, Robert 29, 142, 166
Thayer, Frank 8
Theiss, Ursula 142, 143, 144
¡Three Amigos! 193, 217
Toland, Gregg 107
The Torch 95–99
Torres, Manuel Contreras 69, 70
Towne, Robert 173
Tracy, Lee 29, 37–39
The Treasure of Pancho Villa 133–136
Turner, Lana 187
Two Mules for Sister Sara 204–207

The Undefeated 163, 196–199
Under Strange Flags 4, 46–48
Urbina, Tomás 42, 148, 179

Valdez Is Coming 119
Valentino, Rudolph 79, 81
Vallone, Raf 210, 211
Van Cleef, Lee 180
Vega, Isela 163
Vera Cruz 129–133, 163
Villa!! 147–150
Villa, Pancho 2, 3, 7–8, 21–23, 35–36, 111, 122, 149, 158, 167, 176, 208, 223–224, 227
Villa Rides! 173–175, 179–180, 191
Viva Villa! 3, 7, 8, 23–25, 29–41, 82, 106
Viva Zapata! 33, 105–113, 119
Volonte, Gian Maria 181, 182
Von Sternberg, Josef 11

Walker, Clint 172, 220
Wallach, Eli 132
Wallis, Hal 56, 66, 70
Walsh, Raoul 8–10
Warner, Jack L. 56–57, 59, 82, 103–104, 151
Wayne, John 159, 160, 163, 196, 197, 198, 199
Wayne, Pilar 159
Welch, Raquel 186, 189
Welles, Orson 80, 82–83
Wendkos, Paul 209
Werfel, Franz 53–54, 55, 56, 59
The Wet Parade (film) 15
The Wet Parade (novel) 15
The Wild Bunch 163, 174, 190–196, 217
Wilson, Pres. Woodrow 2, 21, 183, 208, 224
Wings of the Hawk 120–121, 123–125, 133, 143
Winters, Shelley 134, 136–137
Wiseman, Joseph 109–110
Wolff, Frank 174
Wray, Fay 31, 33–34, 39

Young, Terence 159, 160

Zacharias, Miguel 75–76
Zanuck, Darryl F. 105–106, 107, 109, 111, 112–113
Zapata! (film made in Mexico) 213
Zapata, Emiliano 2, 108, 111, 112, 144
Zaragoza, Gen. Ignacio 53, 86–87
El Zorro de Jalisco 76

www.ingramcontent.com/pod-product-compliance
Lightning Source LLC
Chambersburg PA
CBHW081550300426
44116CB00015B/2832